Pearson Education
Test Prep Series

for

AP® CHEMISTRY

Pearson Education
Test Prep Series

for

AP® CHEMISTRY

EDWARD L. WATERMAN

To accompany:

CHEMISTRY: THE CENTRAL SCIENCE
THIRTEENTH EDITION
AP® EDITION

BROWN   LEMAY
BURSTEN   MURPHY
WOODWARD   STOLTZFUS

PEARSON

Boston   Columbus   Indianapolis   New York   San Francisco   Upper Saddle River
Amsterdam   Cape Town   Dubai   London   Madrid   Milan   Munich   Paris   Montréal   Toronto
Delhi   Mexico City   São Paulo   Sydney   Hong Kong   Seoul   Singapore   Taipei   Tokyo

Editor in Chief: Adam Jaworski

Senior Acquisitions Editor: Terry Haugen

Acquisitions Editor: Chris Hess, Ph.D.

Executive Marketing Manager: Jonathan Cottrell

Associate Team Lead, Program Management, Chemistry and Geosciences: Jessica Moro

Team Lead, Project Management, Chemistry and Geosciences: Gina M. Cheselka

Project Manager: Erin Kneuer

Full-Service Project Management/Composition: PreMediaGlobal

Operations Specialist: Christy Hall

Supplement Cover Designer: Seventeenth Street Studios

Cover Image Credit: "Metal-Organic Frameworks" by Omar M. Yaghi, University of California, Berkeley

Credits and acknowledgments borrowed from other sources and reproduced, with permission, in this textbook appear on the appropriate page within the text.

PEARSON

www.PearsonSchool.com/Advanced   ISBN-10: 0-13-359802-0; ISBN-13: 978-0-13-359802-5

About the Author

Ed Waterman is a writer, a public speaker, and a retired high school chemistry teacher. He taught chemistry and Advanced Placement Chemistry from 1976 to 2007 at Rocky Mountain High School in Fort Collins, Colorado. From 1971 to 1976, he taught general, organic, and analytical chemistry at Colorado State University.

Mr. Waterman is the author or coauthor of five high school chemistry textbooks. His publications include *Pearson Chemistry*, a popular text for first-year high school chemistry, and *Small-Scale Chemistry Laboratory*, also published by Pearson. In addition, he has published numerous professional papers in peer-reviewed journals including the *Journal of the American Chemical Society*, the *Journal of Organic Chemistry*, and the *Journal of Chemical Education*.

Mr. Waterman holds a Bachelor of Science degree in chemistry from Montana State University and a Master of Science degree in synthetic organic chemistry from Colorado State University. In his free time, he enjoys exploring wild places by hiking, kayaking, and cross-country skiing in the Rocky Mountains and on the Colorado Plateau. He also presents photo-essay lectures about the natural history of molecules, engaging the general public in an appreciation for and an understanding of chemistry.

This book is dedicated to all the hard-working teachers of Advanced Placement Chemistry across the United States and Canada. Your important contributions to chemical education, your dedication to your students, and the significant and beneficial effects you continue to build into the fabric of our society can never be measured, only acknowledged. The students who take up the challenge of Advanced Placement Chemistry are indeed fortunate to have you as a teacher, a coach, and a mentor. I hope that you will continue to find only the greatest satisfaction in helping young people reach for their dreams. Please accept my heartfelt thanks for your efforts and my best wishes for your continued success.

Ed Waterman
Rocky Mountain High School (retired)
Fort Collins, Colorado

Table of Contents

To the Teacher

The *Pearson Education Test Prep Workbook for AP® Chemistry* is designed especially for student success on the Advanced Placement® Chemistry examination. Thoroughly revised and redesigned, this *Test Prep Workbook for AP® Chemistry* correlates to the new *AP® Chemistry Curriculum Framework* (CF) launched in the 2013–2014 school year.

The new *Pearson Education AP® Test Prep Series: Chemistry*:

- Is designed to accompany the 13th edition of Pearson's *Chemistry: The Central Science* by Brown & LeMay

- Concisely summarizes all the important content in the 6 Big Ideas and the 117 Learning Objectives of the new CF

- Clearly explains and provides questions and problems for new content including photoelectron spectroscopy (PES), mass spectrometry, chromatography, UV–VIS spectrophotometry, and Coulomb's law

- Outlines the structure and content of the new AP® Chemistry Exam

- Offers many useful test-taking strategies for students to practice while they study AP chemistry throughout the year

- Includes hundreds of revised multiple choice and free response practice questions, formatted for the new curriculum and aligned to the 117 Learning Objectives, with complete answers and explanations

- Contains many new and revised Your Turn conceptual questions designed to allow students to connect to content, analyze data, and write clear, concise, focused answers in the way that the new AP® Exam requires

- Identifies many common misconceptions and corrects them with clear and concise explanations

- Includes two complete practice tests with thorough answers and explanations, and a unique scoring guide

- Gives students control of the required content and provides them with ample practice to master the material

- Is suitable for use with any AP chemistry text

Many AP chemistry teachers use this book as the primary source to guide them through the new Curriculum Framework and direct them to the important course topics. Teachers find that students command a significant competitive advantage when taking the AP® Chemistry Exam. When teaching AP chemistry, I found that if each of my students used a personal copy to review, their scores increased significantly. With this book, my role changed from chemistry teacher to chemistry coach. It made a challenging job much easier.

To order, use ISBN: 0-13-359802-0 / 978-0-13-359802-5 at Pearsonschool. com or call 1-800-848-9500.

For more information, please contact your Pearson General Account Manager at Pearsonschool.com.

Best wishes for continued success teaching Advanced Placement® Chemistry and good luck to your students on the upcoming exam.

Ed Waterman
Rocky Mountain High School (Retired)
Fort Collins, Colorado

Introduction

Advanced Placement® Chemistry is more than just a course in first-year college general chemistry. Whether or not your AP® Exam score qualifies you for college credit, there are many advantages of taking Advanced Placement® Chemistry. It is an opportunity to prepare for college by challenging yourself with rigorous college-level work while you are still in high school. Your classmates will be some of the best and brightest students at your school and the peer group you study with will enhance your own abilities as a student. Likely your teacher will be among the best at your school and he or she will have invaluable knowledge and insight. Besides acquiring advanced knowledge of chemistry, the science central to all other scientific disciplines, you will develop your skills in analytical thinking, abstract reasoning, problem solving, and effective communication. You will enhance your study skills, both as an individual and within a group, and you will increase your own ability to learn how to learn. A second year of chemistry in high school will give you a decided competitive advantage over your future college classmates who have not taken Advanced Placement® classes in high school. Advanced Placement® Chemistry can serve as a measure of "survival insurance" for that upcoming pivotal year in life: the first year of college.

Advanced Placement® Chemistry and College Credit

By taking the Advanced Placement® Exam, you could qualify for college chemistry credit. Many public colleges and universities grant credit for scores of 3 or higher. More competitive public institutions and many private colleges have higher standards. Generally, the higher your score, the more potential credit you receive. Because all colleges set their own standards, be sure to check the website of any college you are considering attending or call or write the office of admissions for details about how that institution grants credit for Advanced Placement® scores. To expedite the process, go to the College Board website at http://collegesearch .collegeboard.com/apcreditpolicy/index.jsp/, type in the name of the college or university you are interested in, and the site will take you directly to that institution's credit policy for Advanced Placement®.

How to Use This Book?

This book is designed to help you score well on the Advanced Placement® Examination in Chemistry. Each numbered topic is a chapter summary and correlates directly with the chapter of the same number in *Chemistry: The Central Science* published by Pearson. Because many other college chemistry texts are suitable for Advanced Placement® Chemistry, you can use this book even if you do not have access to *Chemistry: The Central Science*.

During the first half of your Advanced Placement® course, focus on the course work your teacher emphasizes and what is in your text. Especially focus on solving the challenging quantitative problems and writing short, concise, directed answers to qualitative questions based on chemical principles. **Be sure you are able to interpret data tables, graphs, charts and atomic and molecular representations of matter.**

Halfway through the course, in about December or January, as you continue with your class work, begin reviewing about two topics a week using this book. Read each topic summary and answer each Your Turn question as you come across it. The Your Turn questions, while not always at the AP level, are designed to focus your attention on one specific point and provide you with practice in writing clear, concise, directed responses, much as the AP® Exam requires. At the end of each topic summary, you will find multiple choice and free response questions. Answer these questions and check your answers with the detailed answers at the end of each topic. If you do not know how to do a problem or if you get a question wrong, go back and review the topic summary and/or the corresponding chapter in *Chemistry: The Central Science*. Be sure to read the explanation for each question, even if you answered it correctly the first time.

In February, ask your teacher about the procedure for ordering and paying for the Advanced Placement® Exam. This needs to be done well before the exam and different high schools have different procedures.

In February and March, continue working through your review, two topics per week.

Finally, about a month before the exam, work through Practice Test 1 within the suggested time limits, check your answers, and calculate your score. This will give you a measure of your progress in mastering the twenty topics. Go back and review the material you have not yet mastered. Be sure to read the explanations for each question. When you are ready to try again, work Practice Test 2. These two practice tests are designed to simulate the Advanced Placement® Exam, each emphasizing different topics. Be sure to download and work some of the past Advanced Placement® Exams posted on the College Board website at http://www.collegeboard.com/student/testing/ap/chemistry/samp.html?chem.

A week before the exam, read through the equations list that you will use on exam day. Do not memorize what is on the equation sheet because you will have it to refer to during the exam. The point is to know what is on the equation sheet and where to find specific information as you work the exam. Look at each item and ask yourself, "What would I use this for?"

Also, skim through the answers you wrote for the Your Turn questions and the multiple choice and free response questions at the end of each topic. Gather your thoughts and prepare to go into the Advanced Placement® Exam, recognizing that you will not know everything, but confident that you will score high because you have worked hard and prepared well.

What to Do on Exam Day?

*   Be sure to get a couple of good nights' sleep before the exam.

*   Eat a healthy breakfast the day of the exam.

*   Bring a calculator with fresh batteries and a spare calculator, just in case. Know how to use the spare calculator!

*   Bring at least six sharpened number two pencils with good erasers.

*   Bring a water bottle and a nutritious energy snack to consume during the short break.

*   Bring a photo ID and an admission ticket, if required.

*   Bring a watch to keep track of the time. Be sure to turn off the alarm, if it has one.

*   Arrive at the examination site at least 20 minutes early. If the door closes before you arrive, you will not be allowed to take the exam.

*   Be prepared for poor working conditions—some rooms provide only arm-chair desks with little room to work. Sometimes right-handed students will be assigned left-handed desks and vice versa!

*   Dress in layers. Some rooms are unnecessarily air-conditioned; others are not air-conditioned at all.

*   Leave backpacks and personal belongings at home. All you need is a photo ID, two reliable calculators, a sharp pencil, and a mind to match.

Calculator Use

You can use a calculator only for Section II, the free response section. Most silent types of scientific, programmable, and graphing calculators are permitted, if they do not have typewriter-style (QWERTY) keyboards. You need not clear your calculator memory. You may not share a calculator with another student during the exam. You may not use a calculator on Section I, the multiple choice section of the exam.

The Content and Nature of the AP® Exam in Chemistry

The Advanced Placement® Examination in Chemistry is a comprehensive evaluation of knowledge of all areas of general chemistry at the first-year college level. It consists of two sessions of 90 and 105 minutes. Section I contains 60 multiple choice questions worth 50% of the total score. Three long and four short free response questions, counting for another 50%, compose Section II. Use of calculators is allowed only on the free response section. A periodic table and a list of pertinent equations and constants are available for the entire exam. Please refer to the end of this section for a periodic table and a list of equations and constants similar to what will be provided for use on the exam.

For more information and published examples of recent exams, please refer to the College Board's Advanced Placement website at http://apcentral.collegeboard .com/. Also two complete practice exams, similar to the Advanced Placement® Examination in Chemistry, are included at the end of this book. You will also find a scoring guide and complete answers and explanations. *Be cautious about studying older exams or guidebooks because the format and content of the exam changed in 2014.*

Tips for Writing the Multiple Choice Section

- Make a note of the start time at the top of the question page. Add 90 minutes to define the stop time. Remember, you have 90 minutes to answer 60 questions. Pace yourself accordingly.

- Read each question carefully. Do not assume you know what it asks without a careful reading.

- Pay close attention to words such as EXCEPT and DOES NOT and look for the response that does not belong.

- When simple math is involved (remember, no calculators!), pay attention to factors of 2 and 3.

- Eliminate answers you know are wrong. There is no penalty for guessing, so it is to your advantage to answer every question.

- Never assume a question has two valid answers unless there is an "all of these" response. Closely analyze the two responses you think might be correct. How do they differ? Does the question include words such as EXCEPT or DOES NOT?

- Keep track of answers by marking the correct answer on both the test questions and the answer sheet to expedite a self-check later.

- Periodically check that you are marking the answer sheet correctly and check your watch to monitor your progress.

- Give yourself time to answer all the questions you know how to answer. The last question is worth the same number of points as the first question. Do not spend too much time on the harder or more time-consuming questions at the expense of not having enough time to answer the ones you can.

- As you read through and answer the questions, consider using the "answer/plus/minus" method. It works like this:

Answer: Answer any question you immediately know the answer to.

Plus: Mark a "+" (on the exam, not on the answer, sheet!) next to any question you know how to answer but feel will take too much time to work. Be sure to skip the corresponding number on the answer sheet. You can come back to the questions marked "+" when you have finished reading all the questions and answering as many as you know.

Minus: Mark a "−" next to any question you really do not understand. After you have finished the other questions, including the ones you have marked with a "+," use the time remaining to reconsider the "−" questions. Often a second reading will give you fresh insights.

- Be sure to answer every question. There is no penalty for guessing. The more difficult questions tend to be toward the end of the exam, so do not panic if, after your best effort, you do not finish.

- Finally, if there is still time, skim through all the questions, comparing the answers you have marked on the exam with those you have marked on the answer sheet. Correct any obvious errors, both in accurately marking the answer sheet and in choosing the best answer. Be sure to make any changes to the answer sheet by first erasing cleanly and leaving no stray marks.

- When your watch shows that there are 10 minutes left, make a decision about how you can finish the question(s) that will score the most points. Be sure to stop when time is called.

Tips for Writing the Free Response Section

- Make a note of the start time at the top of the question page. Add 105 minutes to define the stop time. Remember, you have 105 minutes to answer all seven free response questions. Pace yourself accordingly.

- Be sure to read each question carefully.

- Read all the questions once before you decide which question to answer first.

- You need not answer the questions in order, but be sure to clearly label your answers in the answer booklet with the number and letter of each part.

- Fight off fear and apprehension. It is not likely that you are going to know everything! Remember, scoring well is a numbers game. You can make up for not knowing how to do one question by scoring well on another.

- Reread the question that seems easiest to you. Determine what is asked and answer the question directly and specifically.

- With numerical problems, show your work clearly and logically. You need not show any arithmetic, but the grader is looking for a logical progression of your ideas. Circle any numerical final answer.

- In written responses, be clear and concise.

- Write in complete sentences or bulleted phrases. Do not assume the reader knows what you are trying to say. Avoid one-word answers.

- Do not be afraid to state the obvious. What is obvious to you might be exactly what the grader is looking for.

- Avoid pronouns, especially the word, "it," even if your writing seems redundant.

- Underline and define key terms to make them stand out, if appropriate, but do not overdo it.

- Write what you know and stop. Two sentences often fully express an answer to any one part of a question. These are not essay questions. They are more like short answer questions, requiring clear and concise answers with justifications. The grader does not want to see any more than what is specifically asked for.

- Do not hesitate to use a picture, a diagram, or an equation to illustrate your answer, if appropriate.

- Review your writing. Does it make sense to you? Will it make sense to the grader? Does it specifically answer the question that is asked? Have you used chemical terminology correctly?

- Keep in mind that partial credit is often given, so make sure you put something down for every part.

- If you are not clear about an answer, rewrite the question in your own words. Often this practice will jump-start your thinking and allow you to arrive at the answer. What you write, even if it only partially answers the question, might score partial credit.

- When your watch shows that there are 10 minutes left, make a decision about how you can finish the question(s) that will score the most points. Be sure to stop when time is called.

Equations and Constants

The following pages contain a list of equations and constants and a periodic table similar to those provided by the Advanced Placement® Chemistry Exam, which you can use during the entire test. Do not memorize this information. Rather, know that it will be available to you as you take the test and refer to it often as you study Advance Placement® Chemistry.

Common units

L, mL = liter, milliliter atm = atmosphere

g = gram $mm\ Hg$ = millimeter of mercury

nm = nanometer J, kJ = joule, kilojoule

mol = mole V = volt

Light and Atomic Structure

$E = h\nu$ E = energy of a photon or quantum state

$\nu = c/\lambda$ ν = frequency of light

                     λ = wavelength of light

c = speed of light = 3.00×10^8 m/s = 3.00×10^{17} nm/s

h = Planck's constant = 6.63×10^{-34} J-s

N = Avogadro's number = 6.02×10^{23} molecules/mol

e = electric charge = -1.60×10^{-19} coul/electron

Equilibrium

Law of mass action for $aA + bB \rightleftharpoons cC + dD$,

$K_{eq} = ([C]^c[D]^d)/([A]^a[B]^b)$ K_{eq} = equilibrium constant

$Q = ([C]^c[D]^d)/([A]^a[B]^b)$ Q = reaction quotient

$K_a = [H^+][A^-]/[HA]$ K_a = weak acid ionization constant

$K_b = [OH^-][HB^+]/[B]$ K_b = weak base ionization constant

$K_w = [H^+][OH^-] = 1.0 \times 10^{-14}$ at 25 °C K_w = autoionization constant for water

$K_w = K_a \times K_b$ K_p = gas pressure equilibrium constant

$pH = -\log[H^+]$ K_c = molar concentration constant

$pOH = -\log[OH^-]$ K_{sp} = solubility product constant

$pH = pK_a + \log([A^-]/[HA])$ R = gas constant = 8.31 J/mol-K

$pK_a = -\log K_a$

$pK_b = -\log K_b$

$K_p = K_c(RT)^{\Delta n}$

Δn = mol gaseous products − mol gaseous reactants

Thermodynamics

$$\Delta H^{\circ}_{rxn} = \sum \Delta H^{\circ}_{f\,products} - \sum \Delta H^{\circ}_{f\,reactants}$$

$$\Delta G^{\circ}_{rxn} = \sum \Delta G^{\circ}_{f\,products} - \sum \Delta G^{\circ}_{f\,reactants}$$

$$\Delta S^{\circ}_{rxn} = \sum S^{\circ}_{products} - \sum S^{\circ}_{reactants}$$

$$\Delta G^{\circ} = \Delta H^{\circ} - T\Delta S^{\circ}$$

$$\Delta G^{\circ} = -RT \ln K$$

$$\Delta G^{\circ} = -nFE^{\circ}$$

$$\Delta G = \Delta G^{\circ} + RT \ln Q$$

$$C_p = \Delta H / \Delta T$$

$$q = mc\Delta T$$

c = specific heat capacity in J/g K

F = Faraday's constant, the charge on a mole of electrons = 96,500 C/mol e^-

1 amp = 1 coul/sec   1 volt = 1 joul/coul

H° = standard enthalpy

G° = standard free energy

S° = standard entropy

T = Kelvin temperature

K = equilibrium constant

E° = standard cell potential

Q = reaction quotient

C_p = molar heat capacity in J/K

q = heat in J, m = mass in g

n = moles of electrons

Gases

$$PV = nRT$$

P = pressure, V = volume

R = gas constant = 0.0821 L-atm/mol-K

= 8.31 J/mol-K = 62.4 L torr/mol-K

$$P_a = P_t \times X_a$$

$$P_t = P_a + P_b + P_c + \ldots$$

$$K = {}^{\circ}C + 273$$

$$KE_{molecule} = \tfrac{1}{2}mv^2$$

1 atm = 760 mmHg = 760 torr

P_a = partial pressure of gas a

P_t = total pressure

X_a = mole fraction of gas = mol a/total moles

T = Kelvin temperature

KE = kinetic energy

Solutions

M = moles solute/liters of solution M = molarity

$A = abc$ A = absorbance, a = molar absorptivity, b = path length, c = concentration

Electrochemistry

Amperes = coulombs per second $E^{\circ}_{cell} = E^{\circ}_{red} + E^{\circ}_{ox}$

n = moles of electrons

$\Delta G^{\circ} = -nFE^{\circ} = -RT \ln K$ K = equilibrium constant

F = Faraday's constant = 96,500 C per mole of electrons

E° is the standard cell potential in volts

Kinetics

$\ln[A]_t - \ln[A]_o = -kt$ k = rate constant

$1/[A]_t - 1/[A]_o = kt$ t = time

$t_{1/2} = 0.693/k$ $t_{1/2}$ = half life

Main groups

Main groups

| 1Aᵃ 1 | | | | | | | | | | | | | | | | | | 8A 18 |

The periodic table:

Period	1Aᵃ / 1	2A / 2	3B / 3	4B / 4	5B / 5	6B / 6	7B / 7	8B / 8	8B / 9	8B / 10	1B / 11	2B / 12	3A / 13	4A / 14	5A / 15	6A / 16	7A / 17	8A / 18
1	1 **H** 1.00794																	2 **He** 4.002602
2	3 **Li** 6.941	4 **Be** 9.012182					Transition metals						5 **B** 10.811	6 **C** 12.0107	7 **N** 14.0067	8 **O** 15.9994	9 **F** 18.998403	10 **Ne** 20.1797
3	11 **Na** 22.989770	12 **Mg** 24.3050											13 **Al** 26.981538	14 **Si** 28.0855	15 **P** 30.973761	16 **S** 32.065	17 **Cl** 35.453	18 **Ar** 39.948
4	19 **K** 39.0983	20 **Ca** 40.078	21 **Sc** 44.955910	22 **Ti** 47.867	23 **V** 50.9415	24 **Cr** 51.9961	25 **Mn** 54.938049	26 **Fe** 55.845	27 **Co** 58.933200	28 **Ni** 58.6934	29 **Cu** 63.546	30 **Zn** 65.39	31 **Ga** 69.723	32 **Ge** 72.64	33 **As** 74.92160	34 **Se** 78.96	35 **Br** 79.904	36 **Kr** 83.80
5	37 **Rb** 85.4678	38 **Sr** 87.62	39 **Y** 88.90585	40 **Zr** 91.224	41 **Nb** 92.90638	42 **Mo** 95.94	43 **Tc** [98]	44 **Ru** 101.07	45 **Rh** 102.90550	46 **Pd** 106.42	47 **Ag** 107.8682	48 **Cd** 112.411	49 **In** 114.818	50 **Sn** 118.710	51 **Sb** 121.760	52 **Te** 127.60	53 **I** 126.90447	54 **Xe** 131.293
6	55 **Cs** 132.90545	56 **Ba** 137.327	71 **Lu** 174.967	72 **Hf** 178.49	73 **Ta** 180.9479	74 **W** 183.84	75 **Re** 186.207	76 **Os** 190.23	77 **Ir** 192.217	78 **Pt** 195.078	79 **Au** 196.96655	80 **Hg** 200.59	81 **Tl** 204.3833	82 **Pb** 207.2	83 **Bi** 208.98038	84 **Po** [208.98]	85 **At** [209.99]	86 **Rn** [222.02]
7	87 **Fr** [223.02]	88 **Ra** [226.03]	103 **Lr** [262.11]	104 **Rf** [261.11]	105 **Db** [262.11]	106 **Sg** [266.12]	107 **Bh** [264.12]	108 **Hs** [269.13]	109 **Mt** [268.14]	110 **Ds** [281.15]	111 **Rg** [272.15]	112 **Cn** [285]	113 [284]	114 **Fl** [289]	115 [288]	116 **Lv** [292]	117 [294]	118 [294]

*Lanthanide series	57 *La 138.9055	58 Ce 140.116	59 Pr 140.90765	60 Nd 144.24	61 Pm [145]	62 Sm 150.36	63 Eu 151.964	64 Gd 157.25	65 Tb 158.92534	66 Dy 162.50	67 Ho 164.93032	68 Er 167.259	69 Tm 168.93421	70 Yb 173.04
†Actinide series	89 †Ac [227.03]	90 Th 232.0381	91 Pa 231.03588	92 U 238.02891	93 Np [237.05]	94 Pu [244.06]	95 Am [243.06]	96 Cm [247.07]	97 Bk [247.07]	98 Cf [251.08]	99 Es [252.08]	100 Fm [257.10]	101 Md [258.10]	102 No [259.10]

ᵃThe labels on top (1A, 2A, etc.) are common American usage. The labels below these (1, 2, etc.) are those recommended by the International Union of Pure and Applied Chemistry.
Except for elements 114 and 116, the names and symbols for elements above 113 have not yet been decided.
Atomic weights in brackets are the masses of the longest-lived or most important isotope of radioactive elements.
Further information is available at http://www.webelements.com
The production of element 116 was reported in May 1999 by scientists at Lawrence Berkeley National Laboratory.

The 6 Big Ideas and 117 Learning Objectives of the AP® Chemistry Curriculum Framework

Big Idea 1. All matter is composed of atoms.

Learning Objectives

1.1 Justify that the elemental mass ratio in any pure compound is always identical using atomic molecular theory.

1.2 Identify or infer from mass data the quantitative compositions of pure substances and mixtures.

1.3 Use calculations of mass data to determine the identity or purity of a substance.

1.4 Interconvert quantities of substances: number of particles, moles, masses, and volumes.

1.5 Use data to explain electron distributions in atoms or ions.

1.6 Analyze data of electron energies for patterns and relationships.

1.7 Describe atomic electronic structure using Coulomb's law, ionization energy, and data from photoelectron spectroscopy.

1.8 Analyze measured energies to explain electron configurations using Coulomb's law.

1.9 Predict atomic properties and explain their trends using the shell model and atomic placement on the periodic table.

1.10 Use experimental evidence to explain the arrangement of the periodic table and apply periodic properties to chemical reactivity.

1.11 Analyze and identify patterns in data for binary compounds to predict properties of related compounds.

1.12 Explain how data sets support the classical shell atomic model or the quantum mechanical model.

1.13 Justify that an atomic model is consistent with a given set of data.

1.14 Use mass spectral data to identify elements and the masses of isotopes.

1.15 Explain why different types of spectroscopy are used to measure vibration and electronic motions of molecules.

1.16 Design and interpret an experiment that uses spectrophotometry to determine the concentration of a substance in solution.

1.17 Use both symbols and particle drawings in balanced chemical equations to quantitatively and qualitatively express the law of conservation of mass.

1.18 Apply conservation of atoms to particle views of balanced chemical reactions and physical changes.

1.19 Design and interpret data from a gravimetric analysis experiment to determine the concentration of a substance in solution.

1.20 Design and interpret data from a titration experiment to determine the concentration of a substance in solution.

Big Idea 2. Chemical bonding and intermolecular forces explain the chemical and physical properties of matter.

Learning Objectives

2.1 Predict properties based on chemical formulas and explain properties using particle views.

2.2 Explain the relative strengths of acids and bases using molecular structure, intermolecular forces, and solution equilibrium.

2.3 Use particulate models and energy considerations to explain the differences between solids and liquids.

2.4 Use kinetic molecular theory and intermolecular forces to predict and explain the macroscopic properties of real and ideal gases.

2.5 Use particle representations, mathematical models, and macroscopic observations to explain the effect of changes in the macroscopic properties of gases.

2.6 Use data to calculate temperature, pressure, volume, and moles for an ideal gas.

2.7 Use intermolecular forces to explain how solutes separate by chromatography.

2.8 Draw and interpret particle representations of solutions showing interactions between the solute and solvent particles.

2.9 Create and use particle views to interpret molar concentrations of solutions.

2.10 Design an experiment to separate substances using filtration, paper chromatography, column chromatography, or distillation and explain how substances separate citing intermolecular interactions.

2.11 Use London dispersion forces to predict properties and explain trends for nonpolar substances.

2.12 Analyze data for real gases to identify deviations from ideal behavior and explain using molecular interactions.

2.13 Explain how the structural features of polar molecules affect the forces of attraction between them.

2.14 Using particle views, qualitatively apply Coulomb's law to explain how the solubility of ionic compounds is affected by interactions between ions, and attractions between ions and solvents.

2.15 Explain the solubility of ionic solids and molecules in water and other solvents using entropy and particle views to show intermolecular forces.

2.16 Use the strengths and types of intermolecular forces to explain the properties of molecules such as phase, vapor pressure, viscosity, melting point, and boiling point.

2.17 Predict the type of bonding in a binary compound based on electronegativity of the elements and their locations on the periodic table.

2.18 Rank and justify bond polarity using location of atoms on the periodic table.

2.19 Use particle views of ionic compounds to explain the effect of microscopic structure on macroscopic properties such as boiling point, solubility, hardness, brittleness, low volatility, and the lack of malleability, ductility, and conductivity.

2.20 Explain how the electron-sea model of delocalized electrons affects the macroscopic properties of metals such as electrical and thermal conductivity, malleability, ductility, and low volatility.

2.21 Use Lewis diagrams and VSEPR to predict geometry and polarity of molecules and identify hybridization.

2.22 Design and evaluate an experimental plan to collect and interpret data to deduce the types of bonding in solids.

2.23 Create a visual representation of an ionic solid showing its structure and particle interactions.

2.24 Use a visual representation of an ionic solid to explain its structure and particle interactions.

2.25 Compare properties of alloys and metals, identify alloy types, and explain properties at the atomic level.

2.26 Use the electron-sea model to explain the macroscopic properties of metals and alloys.

2.27 Create a visual representation of a metallic solid showing its structure and particle interactions.

2.28 Use a visual representation of a metallic solid to explain its structure and particle interactions.

2.29 Create a visual representation of a covalent solid showing its structure and particle interactions.

2.30 Use a visual representation of a covalent solid to explain its structure and particle interactions.

2.31 Create a visual representation of a molecular solid showing its structure and particle interactions.

2.32 Use a visual representation of a molecular solid to explain its structure and particle interactions.

Big Idea 3. Chemical reactions involve the rearrangement of atoms and describe how matter changes.

Learning Objectives

3.1 Interpret macroscopic observations of change using symbols, chemical equations, and particle views.

3.2 Interpret an observed chemical change using a balanced molecular (complete), ionic, or net ionic equation and justify why each is used in a given situation.

3.3 Use stoichiometry calculations to model laboratory chemical reactions and analyze deviations from the expected results.

3.4 Apply stoichiometry calculations to convert measured quantities such as masses, solution volumes, or volumes and pressures of gases to other quantities in chemical reactions, including reactions with limiting reactants or unreacted products.

3.5 Design an experiment and analyze its data for the synthesis or decomposition of a compound to confirm the conservation of mass and the law of definite proportions.

3.6 Use data from synthesis or decomposition of a compound to confirm the conservation of mass and the law of definite proportions.

3.7 Use proton-transfer reactions to identify compounds such as Brønsted–Lowry acids and bases and conjugate acid–base pairs.

3.8 Use electron transfer to identify redox reactions.

3.9 Design or interpret the results of a redox titration experiment.

3.10 Classify a process as a physical change, a chemical change, or an ambiguous change using macroscopic observations and the formation or breaking of chemical bonds or intermolecular forces.

3.11 Create symbolic and graphical representations to describe energy changes associated with a chemical or physical change.

3.12 Use half-cell reactions, potentials, and Faraday's laws to make quantitative predictions about voltaic (galvanic) or electrolytic reactions.

3.13 Analyze voltaic (galvanic) or electrolytic cell data to identify properties of redox reactions.

Big Idea 4. Molecular collisions determine the rates of chemical reactions.

Learning Objectives

4.1 Design and interpret an experiment to determine the factors that affect reaction rate such as temperature, concentration, and surface area.

4.2 Analyze concentration versus time data to determine the rate law for a zeroth-, first-, and second-order reaction.

4.3 Determine half-life from the rate constant of a first-order reaction and explain the relationship between half-life and reaction order.

4.4 Explain how rate law, order, and rate constant for an elementary reaction relate to the frequency and success of molecular collisions.

4.5 Explain effective and ineffective reactant collisions using energy distributions and molecular orientation.

4.6 Make qualitative predictions about the temperature dependence of reaction rate using an energy profile for an elementary reaction showing reactants, transition state, and products.

4.7 Evaluate alternative reaction mechanisms to determine which are consistent with rate data, and infer the presence of intermediates.

4.8 Use various representations including energy profiles, particle views, and chemical equations to describe chemical reactions that occur with and without catalysts.

4.9 Explain rate changes due to acid–base, surface, and enzyme catalysts, and select appropriate mechanisms with or without catalysts.

Big Idea 5. Thermodynamics describes the role energy plays in physical and chemical changes.

Learning Objectives

5.1 Create and interpret graphical representations that show the dependence of potential energy on the distance between atoms to explain bond order, bond length, bond strength, and the relative magnitudes of intermolecular forces between polar molecules.

5.2 Explain how temperature relates to molecular motion using particle views of moving molecules and plots of Maxwell–Boltzmann distributions.

5.3 Use molecular collisions to explain or predict the transfer of heat between systems.

5.4 Use conservation of energy to explain energy transfer between systems including the quantity of energy transferred, the direction of energy flow, and the type of energy (heat or work).

5.5 Use conservation of energy to calculate and explain the quantity of energy change that occurs when two substances of different temperatures interact.

5.6 Calculate or estimate energy changes associated with a chemical reaction (heat of reaction), a temperature change (heat capacity), or a phase change (heat of fusion or vaporization), and relate energy changes to $P\Delta V$ work.

5.7 Design and interpret a constant pressure calorimetry experiment to determine change in enthalpy of a chemical or physical process.

5.8 Use bond energies to calculate or estimate enthalpies of reaction.

5.9 Explain and predict the relative strengths and types of intermolecular forces acting between molecules using molecular electron density distributions.

5.10 Classify and justify physical and chemical changes using intermolecular forces and changes in chemical bonds.

5.11 Identify the intermolecular forces, such as hydrogen bonds and London dispersions, to explain the shapes and functions of large molecules.

5.12 Use particle views and models to predict the signs and relative magnitudes of the entropy changes associated with chemical or physical processes.

5.13 Use the signs of both $\Delta H°$ and $\Delta S°$ for calculation or estimation of $\Delta G°$, to predict the thermodynamic favorability of a physical or chemical change.

5.14 Calculate the change in standard Gibbs free energy to determine the thermodynamic favorability of a chemical or physical change.

5.15 Explain how nonthermodynamically favored processes can be made favorable by coupling them with thermodynamically favored reactions.

5.16 Use Le Châtelier's principle to predict direction of reaction for a system in which coupled reactions share a common intermediate.

5.17 Use the equilibrium constant for combined reactions to make predictions for a system involving coupled reactions sharing a common intermediate.

5.18 Explain how initial conditions can greatly affect product formation for both thermodynamically favored and unfavored reactions using thermodynamic and kinetic arguments.

Big Idea 6. Equilibrium represents a balance between enthalpy and entropy for reversible physical and chemical changes.

Learning Objectives

6.1 Given a set of experimental observations, explain on the molecular level, the reversibility of a chemical, biological, or environmental process.

6.2 Predict how manipulating a chemical equation by reversing it, doubling its coefficients, or adding it to another equation affects the value of Q or K.

6.3 Predict the change in relative rates of forward and reverse reactions using Le Châtelier's principle and principles of kinetics.

6.4 Given initial conditions, use the relative values of Q and K to predict the direction a reaction will progress toward equilibrium.

6.5 Calculate the equilibrium constant, K, given the appropriate tabular or graphical data for a system at equilibrium.

6.6 Given initial conditions and the equilibrium constant, K, use stoichiometry and the law of mass action to determine equilibrium concentrations or partial pressures.

6.7 Determine which chemical species will have relatively large and small concentrations given an equilibrium system with a large or small K.

6.8 Use Le Châtelier's principle to predict the direction a reaction at equilibrium will progress when a change is applied such as concentration, pressure, or temperature.

6.9 Design a set of conditions that will optimize a desired result using Le Chatelier's principle.

6.10 Use Le Châtelier's principle to explain the effect a change will have on Q or K for a reversible reaction.

6.11 Construct a particle representation for a strong or weak acid or base to illustrate which species will have large and small concentrations at equilibrium.

6.12 Compare and contrast pH, percentage ionization, concentrations, and the amount of titrant required to reach an equivalence point for solutions of strong and weak acids.

6.13 Interpret titration data to determine concentration of a weak acid or base and its pK_a or pK_b.

6.14 Explain why a neutral solution requires $[H^+] = [OH^-]$ rather than pH $= 7$, using the dependence of K_w on temperature.

6.15 Calculate or estimate the pH and the concentrations of all species in a mixture of strong acid or base.

6.16 Identify a solution as a weak acid or base, calculate its pH and the concentrations of all species in the solution, and infer its relative strength.

6.17 Given a mixture of weak and strong acids and bases, identify the chemical reaction and tell which species are present in large concentrations at equilibrium.

6.18 Select an appropriate conjugate acid–base pair to design a buffer solution with a target pH and estimate the concentrations needed to achieve a desired buffer capacity.

6.19 Given the pK_a, predict the predominant form of a weak acid in a solution of a given pH.

6.20 Identify a buffer solution and explain how it behaves upon addition of acid or base.

6.21 Predict and rank the solubilities of various salts, given their K_{sp} values.

6.22 Interpret solubility data for various salts to determine or rank K_{sp} values.

6.23 Use data to predict the influence of pH and common ions on the relative solubilities of salts.

6.24 Use particle representations to explain changes in enthalpy and entropy associated with the dissolution of a salt.

6.25 Use the relationship between $\Delta G°$ and $K(\Delta G° = -RT \ln K)$ to estimate the magnitude of K and the thermodynamic favorability of a process.

Introduction: **MATTER AND MEASUREMENT**

You probably learned most of this material in first-year chemistry. When you finish reviewing this topic, be sure you are able to

- Know the differences between elements, compounds, and mixtures
- Explain that separation of mixtures is based on their physical properties
- Use SI units for measurement
- Apply dimensional analysis and significant figures to calculations

Classifications of Matter Section 1.2

Matter is classified as pure substances or mixtures.

Pure substances are either elements or compounds.

An **element** is a substance all of whose atoms contain the same number of protons.

A **compound** is a relatively stable combination of two or more chemically bonded elements in a specific ratio.

Mixtures consist of two or more substances.

Homogeneous mixtures are uniform throughout. Air, seawater, and a nickel coin (a mixture of copper and nickel metals called an alloy) are examples.

Heterogeneous mixtures vary in texture and appearance throughout the sample. Rocks, wood, polluted air, and muddy water are examples.

Properties of Matter Section 1.3

Physical properties can be measured without changing the identity or composition of the substance. Physical properties include color, density, melting point, and hardness.

Chemical properties describe the way a substance changes (reacts) to form other substances. The flammability of gasoline is a chemical property because the gasoline reacts with oxygen to form carbon dioxide and water.

Intensive properties do not depend on the amount of substance in a sample. Temperature, density, and boiling point are intensive properties.

Extensive properties depend on the quantity of the sample. Energy content, mass, and volume are examples of extensive properties.

A **physical change** changes the appearance of a substance but does not change its composition. Changes of physical state, from solid to liquid or from liquid to gas, are examples.

A **chemical change** (also called a chemical reaction) transforms a substance into a different substance or substances. When the chief component of natural gas, methane, burns in air, the methane and the oxygen from the air are transformed into carbon dioxide and water.

Differences in physical properties, as determined by intermolecular forces (see Topic 11), are used to separate the components of mixtures.

Filtration separates a solid from a liquid.

Distillation separates substances based on their differences in boiling points.

Chromatography is a technique that separates substances based on their differences in intermolecular forces and their abilities to dissolve in various solvents. Chromatography is discussed in more detail in Topic 13.

Section 1.4   # Units of Measurement

Chemists often use preferred units called SI units after the French *Système International d'Unités*. Table 1.1 lists the base SI units and their symbols.

Table 1.1   SI base units.

Physical Quantity	Name of Unit	Abbreviation
Mass	Kilogram	kg
Length	Meter	m
Time	Second	s or sec
Temperature	Kelvin	K
Amount of substance	Mole	mol
Electric current	Ampere	A or amp
Luminous intensity	Candela	cd

Table 1.2 lists metric prefixes that indicate decimal fractions or multiples of various units.

Table 1.2   Selected prefixes used in the metric system.

Prefix	Abbreviation	Meaning	Example
Giga	G	10^9	1 gigameter (Gm) $= 1 \times 10^9$ m
Mega	M	10^6	1 megameter (Mm) $= 1 \times 10^6$ m
Kilo	k	10^3	1 kilometer (km) $= 1 \times 10^3$ m
Deci	d	10^{-1}	1 decimeter (dm) $= 0.1$ m
Centi	c	10^{-2}	1 centimeter (cm) $= 0.01$ m
Milli	m	10^{-3}	1 millimeter (mm) $= 0.001$ m
Micro	μ*	10^{-6}	1 micrometer (μm) $= 1 \times 10^{-6}$ m
Nano	n	10^{-9}	1 nanometer (nm) $= 1 \times 10^{-9}$ m
Pico	p	10^{-12}	1 picometer (pm) $= 1 \times 10^{-12}$ m
Femto	f	10^{-15}	1 femtometer (fm) $= 1 \times 10^{-15}$ m

*This is the Greek letter mu (pronounced "mew").

Temperature is commonly measured using either the Celsius scale or the Kelvin scale.

$$K = {}^{\circ}C + 273$$

Derived units are units derived from SI base units.

Volume, the space occupied by a substance, is commonly measured in cubic meters, m^3, or cubic centimeters, cm^3. A non–SI unit commonly used by chemists is the liter, L. One liter is the volume of a cube measuring exactly 10 cm on a side.

$$1 \text{ L} = 1000 \text{ cm}^3 = 1000 \text{ mL}$$
$$1 \text{ cm}^3 = 1 \text{ mL}$$

Density, the amount of matter packed into a given space, is often measured in g/cm^3 for liquids and solids and g/L for gases.

$$\text{Density} = \text{mass}/\text{volume}$$

Uncertainty in Measurement   Section 1.5

Exact numbers are known exactly and are usually defined or counted. One liter equals 1000 cm^3 describes a defined number. There are 32 students in this class describes a counted number.

Inexact numbers have some degree of error or uncertainty associated with them. All measured numbers are inexact.

Measured numbers are generally reported in such a way that only the last digit is uncertain. **Significant figures** are all digits of a measured number including the uncertain one.

Zeros in measured numbers are either significant or merely there to locate the decimal place. The following guidelines describe when zeros are significant:

1. Zeros between nonzero digits are always significant.

2. Zeros at the beginning of a number are never significant.

3. Zeros at the end of a number are significant only when the number contains a decimal point.

In calculations involving measured quantities, the least certain measurement limits the certainty of the calculated quantity and determines the number of significant figures in the final answer. Exact numbers do not limit the certainty.

For multiplication and division, the number of significant figures in the answer is determined by the measurement with the fewest number of significant figures.

For addition and subtraction, the result has the same number of decimal places as the measurement with the fewest number of decimal places.

Common misconception: The guidelines for determining the number of significant figures in a result obtained by carrying measured quantities through calculations do not always give the correct number of significant figures. This is principally why the AP test usually allows full credit for answers reported to plus or minus one significant figure. In this book, numerical answers are usually rounded to three significant figures.

Section 1.6   Dimensional Analysis

Dimensional analysis is a way of converting a written question into an algebraic equation, followed by manipulating factors until the unit of the known quantity is converted into the unit of the unknown quantity.

Example:

How many microseconds are there in one year?

Solution:

The algebraic equivalent to the given question is:

$x\,\mu s = 1$ yr.

Now multiply the right side of the equation by what is known about a year in such a way that the unit of years cancels giving another unit. Continue to do this until the result has the unit of microseconds, μs.

$x\,\mu s = 1$ yr (365 days/yr) (24 h/day) (60 min/h) (60 s/min)

$(10^6\,\mu s/s) = 3.15 \times 10^{13}\,\mu s$

ATOMS, MOLECULES, AND IONS

The content in this topic is the basis for mastering Learning Objectives 1.1, 1.13, and 1.14 as found in the Curriculum Framework.

Except for the information on mass spectrometry, you may have learned much of this material in first-year chemistry. Although nomenclature is not specifically tested on the AP exam, it is helpful to review the names and formulas of ionic and molecular compounds. When you finish reviewing this topic, be sure you are able to:

- Describe the basic structure of the atom using the terms protons, neutrons, electrons, nucleus, electron cloud, atomic number, mass number, isotope, atomic mass

- Describe the key experimental evidence that led scientists to understand the modern atom

- Cite specific experimental evidence that supports various atomic models and evidence that is contradictory

- Use data from mass spectra to identify elements and individual isotopes

- Justify that, in a pure sample of a compound, the ratio of the masses of its constituent elements is always the same

- Distinguish between a molecular and an ionic compound and a molecular and an empirical formula

- Name common ions and ionic and molecular compounds and write their formulas

- Know the structures and names of alkanes, alcohols, and carboxylic acids

The Atomic Theory of Matter   Section 2.1

Scientists formulate models based on experimental observations. They then use these scientific models to make predictions and test the predictions with experiments. When new data are inconsistent with a model's predictions, that model must be revised or replaced. The development and refinement of the atomic theory of matter illustrates this fundamental process of science.

Dalton's Atomic Theory

Nineteenth-century English chemist John Dalton proposed that matter is composed of tiny indivisible particles called atoms. Figure 2.1 summarizes Dalton's basic ideas.

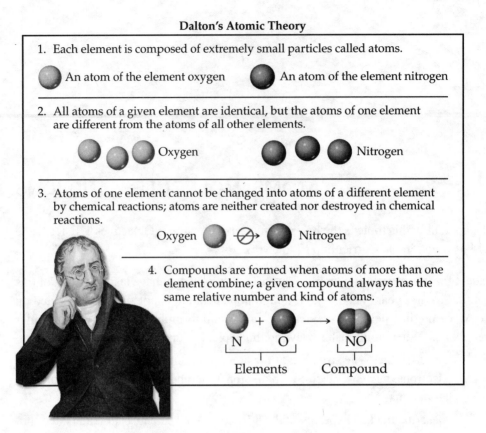

Dalton's Atomic Theory

1. Each element is composed of extremely small particles called atoms.

   An atom of the element oxygen   An atom of the element nitrogen

2. All atoms of a given element are identical, but the atoms of one element are different from the atoms of all other elements.

   Oxygen   Nitrogen

3. Atoms of one element cannot be changed into atoms of a different element by chemical reactions; atoms are neither created nor destroyed in chemical reactions.

   Oxygen ⊘→ Nitrogen

4. Compounds are formed when atoms of more than one element combine; a given compound always has the same relative number and kind of atoms.

   N + O → NO
   Elements   Compound

Figure 2.1 Summary of Dalton's atomic theory.

Dalton's theory explains three fundamental laws:

The **law of constant composition** states that in a given compound, the relative numbers and kinds of atoms are constant.

The **law of conservation of mass** states that the mass of materials does not change in a chemical reaction.

The **law of multiple proportions** states that when two elements combine to form a compound, their masses always exist in a ratio of small whole numbers.

Today we accept three of Dalton's four ideas expressed in Figure 2.1. Only the second idea is incorrect. We now know that atoms of a given element are not identical. Evidence from mass spectra (described later in this topic) clearly demonstrates that atoms of the same element can be composed of different isotopes, each having different masses and different numbers of neutrons.

The Thomson Model

J. J. Thomson showed that cathode rays are streams of negative particles and he is credited with discovering the electron. Thomson postulated that all atoms contain electrons, contradicting Dalton's assumption that atoms are indivisible. Thomson proposed that an atom consisted of a uniform positive sphere in which electrons were embedded like plums in a pudding (Figure 2.2).

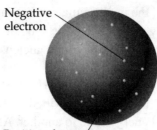

Figure 2.2 J. J. Thomson's plum-pudding model of the atom. Ernest Rutherford proved this model wrong.

The Rutherford Experiment

Ernest Rutherford's gold-foil experiment, illustrated in Figure 2.3, showed that atoms are mostly empty space having a tiny dense nucleus. Rutherford's evidence is inconsistent with Thomson's assumption that atoms are solid particles. Rutherford

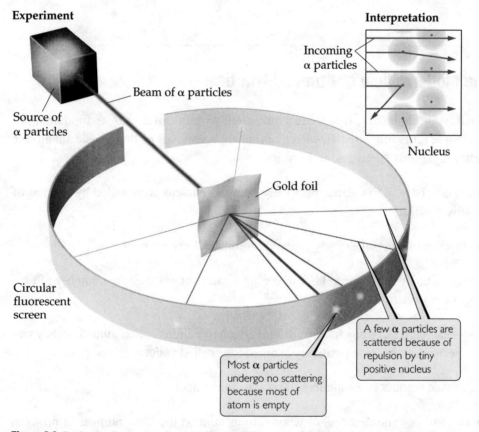

Figure 2.3 Rutherford's α-scattering experiment. When α particles pass through a gold foil, most pass through undeflected but some are scattered, a few at very large angles. According to the plum-pudding model of the atom, the particles should experience only very minor deflections. The nuclear model of the atom explains why a few α particles are deflected at large angles. For clarity, the nuclear atom is shown here as a sphere, but remember that most of the space around the nucleus is empty except for the tiny electrons moving around.

proposed that electrons circle the nucleus much like planets orbit the sun. However, he offered no explanation why an atom is stable. Classical physics predicts that orbiting electrons would lose energy and fall into the nucleus and this does not happen.

Niels Bohr explained why atoms are stable. He postulated that the lines of the atomic emission spectrum of hydrogen (described in Topic 6) represent transitions of electrons from one allowed energy state to another. Atoms are stable because their electrons occupy fixed energy states preventing orbital decay.

Your Turn 2.1

For each atomic model proposed by Dalton, Thomson, and Rutherford, cite at least one piece of experimental evidence that is inconsistent with that model. Write your answer in the space provided.

Section 2.3

The Modern View of Atomic Structure

In studying chemistry, it is often convenient to think of atoms as fundamental, indivisible units of matter. However, atoms are composed of three basic subatomic particles: protons, electrons, and neutrons.

Atoms consist of a tiny dense positively charged nucleus surrounded by a cloud of negative electrons.

The **nucleus** contains positively charged protons and neutral neutrons.

Atoms are electrically neutral because each atom contains the same number of protons as electrons.

Atoms can gain electrons to form negatively charged ions called **anions** or they can lose electrons to become positively charged ions called **cations**.

The **atomic number** is the number of protons in the nucleus.

An **element** is a substance all of whose atoms contain the same number of protons. Each element is defined by its atomic number.

The **mass number** is the number of protons and neutrons in the nucleus of an atom.

Isotopes are atoms containing the same number of protons but different mass numbers.

Symbols are often used to denote various elements and to distinguish isotopes. For example, the isotope of carbon containing six protons and six neutrons is designated like this:

^{12} = mass number = number of protons plus neutrons

C

^{6} = atomic number = number of protons

Because carbon is the element that always contains six protons, often the atomic number designation is omitted and the following symbols all designate the same isotope of carbon:

$$^{12}_{6}C = {}^{12}C = carbon-12 = C-12$$

Carbon has several isotopes and each is distinguished by its mass number. Their respective number of neutrons is calculated by subtracting the atomic number from the mass number. Here are symbols for various isotopes of carbon with the number of neutrons each isotope possesses.

$^{11}_{6}C$	$^{12}_{6}C$	$^{13}_{6}C$	$^{14}_{6}C$
5 neutrons	6 neutrons	7 neutrons	8 neutrons

The **atomic mass unit**, **amu**, is a convenient way to express the relative masses of tiny atoms. One amu equals 1.66054×10^{-24} g. However, it is more useful to compare the masses of atoms to the mass of one carbon-12 isotope. One carbon-12 atom has a defined mass of exactly 12 amu.

Atomic mass is the weighted average mass of all the isotopes of an element based on the abundance of each isotope found on the earth. Atomic masses are expressed in amu. All atomic masses reported on the periodic table are based on the carbon-12 standard. For example, the atomic mass of magnesium is 24.3040 amu. This means that the average mass of all the magnesium isotopes is a little more than twice the mass of a carbon-12 atom.

Mass Spectrometry

Mass spectrometry is a method that measures precise masses of atoms and molecules.

A **mass spectrometer** is an instrument that bombards a sample with high-energy electrons. It converts the sample to charged particles which are accelerated and deflected in a magnetic field. The extent of deflection depends on the mass of the particle, thereby separating different particles according to their masses. The spectrometer detects the masses and relative abundances of the charged particles.

A **mass spectrum** is a graph of intensity of the detector signal versus particle atomic mass.

Figure 2.4a shows a schematic diagram of a mass spectrometer. Figure 2.4b shows a typical mass spectrum.

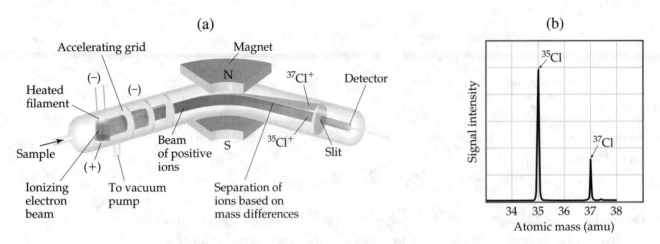

Figure 2.4 (a) A mass spectrometer. Cl atoms are introduced at *A* and are ionized to form Cl$^+$ ions, which are then directed through a magnetic field. The paths of the ions of the two Cl isotopes diverge as they pass through the field. (b) Mass spectrum of atomic chlorine. The fractional abundances of the isotopes ^{35}Cl and ^{37}Cl are indicated by the relative signal intensities of the beams reaching the detector of the mass spectrometer.

Mass spectrometers dramatically demonstrate the existence of isotopes and they accurately measure the individual masses of each isotope and their relative abundances.

Mass spectrometry is the most accurate way to determine atomic masses.

Example:

Detailed analysis of data from the mass spectrum of chlorine shown in Figure 2.5 reveals that there are two different isotopes of chlorine. Cl-35 has a mass of 34.969 amu and a relative abundance of 75.77%. Cl-37 has a mass of 36.966 amu and a relative abundance of 24.23%. Calculate the atomic mass of chlorine.

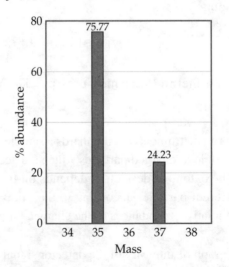

Figure 2.5 Mass spectrum of atomic chlorine.

Solution:

The atomic mass of an element is the weighted average of the masses of the isotopes. Multiply each individual mass by its relative abundance.

Average atomic mass =
(mass of Cl-35)(abundance of Cl-35) + (mass of Cl-37)
(abundance of Cl-37) =
(34.969 amu)(0.7577) + (36.966 amu)(0.2423) = 26.496 +
8.957 = 35.453 = 35.45 amu

(This result compares favorably, within significant figures, with 35.453, the atomic mass of chlorine found on the periodic table.)

The method of radio carbon dating of ancient artifacts uses a technique called accelerator mass spectrometry, AMS. The mass spectrometer measures the ratio of C-12 to C-14. Because C-14 is radioactive, it decays to N-14 at a known rate. The less carbon-14 an object contains, the older it is. The age of a sample is calculated from the measured C-12:C-14 ratio.

Besides measuring the masses of isotopes, mass spectrometry accurately measures the masses of molecules and provides a powerful method to identify them. The high-energy beam of electrons striking a molecule produces a "parent ion," which breaks into a collection of smaller pieces that are characteristic of the molecule. The resulting mass spectrum shows the molecular mass (mass of the parent ion) of the sample and a pattern of fragmented masses that is a characteristic "fingerprint" of the molecule.

Your Turn 2.2

Figure 2.6 shows the mass spectrum of lead. How many different isotopes of lead are represented in the figure? Justify your answer. Identify each isotope. Tell how many electrons, protons, and neutrons are contained in the atoms of each isotope of lead. Write your answer in the space provided.

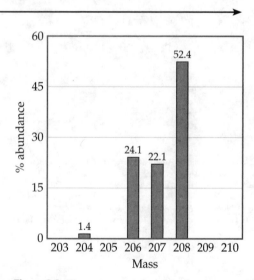

Figure 2.6 The mass spectrum of lead.

Section 2.5   The Periodic Table

The **periodic table** is an arrangement of elements in order of increasing atomic number with elements having similar properties placed in vertical columns. The vertical columns are called **groups** or families and the horizontal rows are called **periods**. Figure 2.7 shows the periodic table with the symbol, atomic number, and atomic mass of each element. It also shows two commonly used numbering systems for the groups. Elements are classified as metals, nonmetals, and metalloids.

1Aᵃ 1																	**8A** 18
1 **H** 1.00794	**2A** 2											**3A** 13	**4A** 14	**5A** 15	**6A** 16	**7A** 17	2 **He** 4.002602
3 **Li** 6.941	4 **Be** 9.012182											5 **B** 10.811	6 **C** 12.0107	7 **N** 14.0067	8 **O** 15.9994	9 **F** 18.998403	10 **Ne** 20.1797
11 **Na** 22.989770	12 **Mg** 24.3050	**3B** 3	**4B** 4	**5B** 5	**6B** 6	**7B** 7	8	**8B** 9	10	**1B** 11	**2B** 12	13 **Al** 26.981538	14 **Si** 28.0855	15 **P** 30.973761	16 **S** 32.065	17 **Cl** 35.453	18 **Ar** 39.948
19 **K** 39.0983	20 **Ca** 40.078	21 **Sc** 44.955910	22 **Ti** 47.867	23 **V** 50.9415	24 **Cr** 51.9961	25 **Mn** 54.938049	26 **Fe** 55.845	27 **Co** 58.933200	28 **Ni** 58.6934	29 **Cu** 63.546	30 **Zn** 65.39	31 **Ga** 69.723	32 **Ge** 72.64	33 **As** 74.92160	34 **Se** 78.96	35 **Br** 79.904	36 **Kr** 83.80
37 **Rb** 85.4678	38 **Sr** 87.62	39 **Y** 88.90585	40 **Zr** 91.224	41 **Nb** 92.90638	42 **Mo** 95.94	43 **Tc** [98]	44 **Ru** 101.07	45 **Rh** 102.90550	46 **Pd** 106.42	47 **Ag** 107.8682	48 **Cd** 112.411	49 **In** 114.818	50 **Sn** 118.710	51 **Sb** 121.760	52 **Te** 127.60	53 **I** 126.90447	54 **Xe** 131.293
55 **Cs** 132.90545	56 **Ba** 137.327	71 **Lu** 174.967	72 **Hf** 178.49	73 **Ta** 180.9479	74 **W** 183.84	75 **Re** 186.207	76 **Os** 190.23	77 **Ir** 192.217	78 **Pt** 195.078	79 **Au** 196.96655	80 **Hg** 200.59	81 **Tl** 204.3833	82 **Pb** 207.2	83 **Bi** 208.98038	84 **Po** [208.98]	85 **At** [209.99]	86 **Rn** [222.02]
87 **Fr** [223.02]	88 **Ra** [226.03]	103 **Lr** [262.11]	104 **Rf** [261.11]	105 **Db** [262.11]	106 **Sg** [266.12]	107 **Bh** [264.12]	108 **Hs** [269.13]	109 **Mt** [268.14]	110 **Ds** [281.15]	111 **Rg** [272.15]	112 **Cn** [285]	113 [284]	114 **Fl** [289]	115 [288]	116 **Lv** [292]	117 [294]	118 [294]

Main groups — Transition metals — Main groups

*Lanthanide series	57 *****La** 138.9055	58 **Ce** 140.116	59 **Pr** 140.90765	60 **Nd** 144.24	61 **Pm** [145]	62 **Sm** 150.36	63 **Eu** 151.964	64 **Gd** 157.25	65 **Tb** 158.92534	66 **Dy** 162.50	67 **Ho** 164.93032	68 **Er** 167.259	69 **Tm** 168.93421	70 **Yb** 173.04
†Actinide series	89 †**Ac** [227.03]	90 **Th** 232.0381	91 **Pa** 231.03588	92 **U** 238.02891	93 **Np** [237.05]	94 **Pu** [244.06]	95 **Am** [243.06]	96 **Cm** [247.07]	97 **Bk** [247.07]	98 **Cf** [251.08]	99 **Es** [252.08]	100 **Fm** [257.10]	101 **Md** [258.10]	102 **No** [259.10]

ᵃThe labels on top (1A, 2A, etc.) are common American usage. The labels below these (1, 2, etc.) are those recommended by the International Union of Pure and Applied Chemistry.
The names and symbols for elements 110 and above have not yet been decided.
Atomic weights in brackets are the masses of the longest-lived or most important isotope of radioactive elements.
Further information is available at http://www.webelements.com
The production of element 116 was reported in May 1999 by scientists at Lawrence Berkeley National Laboratory.

Figure 2.7 The periodic table of the elements.

Table 2.1 shows the special names given to four element groups.

Table 2.1 Names given to four groups of elements on the periodic table.

Group Number	Name of Group
1 or 1A	alkali metals
2 or 2A	alkaline earth metals
17 or 7A	halogens
18 or 8A	noble gases

Molecules and Molecular Compounds   Section 2.6

Although the atom is the smallest representative particle of an element, most matter is composed of molecules or ions, which are combinations of atoms.

A **molecule** is an assembly of two or more atoms tightly bonded together. For example, a molecule that is made up of two atoms is called a diatomic molecule. Figure 2.8 shows the names, formulas, and pictorial representations of some simple molecules.

Hydrogen, H_2 Oxygen, O_2

Water, H_2O Hydrogen peroxide, H_2O_2

Carbon monoxide, CO   Carbon dioxide, CO_2

Methane, CH_4 Ethylene, C_2H_4

Figure 2.8 Molecular models. Notice how the chemical formulas of these simple molecules correspond to their compositions.

Seven elements normally occur as **diatomic molecules**. They are hydrogen, oxygen, nitrogen, fluorine, chlorine, bromine, and iodine. The formulas for these diatomic molecules are written like this:

$$H_2, O_2, N_2, F_2, Cl_2, Br_2, I_2$$

The subscript displayed in each formula indicates that two atoms are present in each molecule.

Common misconception: Chemists often use the name oxygen to refer to both O and O_2, even though the latter's official name is dioxygen to distinguish it from monatomic oxygen. For chemists, the correct species can easily be inferred by the context of the sentence. For example, the oxygen we breathe is O_2, and the oxygen in the water molecule is O. Most texts use the monatomic names for the diatomic elements. Pay close attention to the context in which these names are used to determine the exact meaning.

Your Turn 2.3

Tell which chemical form of chlorine is implied in these two sentences: (a) Chlorine is a toxic gas. (b) Common table salt contains the element chlorine. Write your answer in the space provided.

Compounds are substances consisting of two or more different elements. Generally, there are two types of compounds: molecular compounds and ionic compounds.

Molecular compounds are composed of molecules and usually contain only nonmetals. A **molecular formula** indicates the actual number and type of atoms in the molecule and is the most often used formula for molecular compounds.

Figure 2.9 shows various ways chemists represent molecular compounds.

CH$_4$

Molecular formula

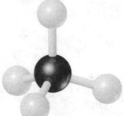

Structural formula

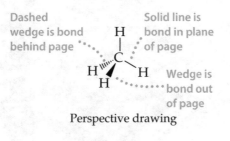

Dashed
wedge is bond
behind page

Solid line is
bond in plane
of page

Wedge is
bond out
of page

Perspective drawing

Ball-and-stick model

Space-filling model

Figure 2.9 Different representations of the methane (CH$_4$) molecule. Structural formulas, perspective drawings, ball-and-stick models, and space-filling models correspond to the molecular formula, and each helps us visualize the three-dimensional arrangement of atoms.

Ions and Ionic Compounds   Section 2.7

Ions are charged particles composed of single atoms (called **monatomic ions**) or aggregates of atoms (called **polyatomic ions**). A **cation** is a positive ion, and an **anion** is a negative ion.

Ionic compounds are composed of ions and usually contain both metals and nonmetals.

An **empirical formula** gives only the relative number of atoms of each type in the compound. Empirical formulas are usually used for ionic compounds and sometimes used for molecular compounds.

Unlike molecular compounds, ionic compounds do not consist of discrete molecules. Ionic compounds are a collection of many ions arranged in a regular pattern as shown in Figure 2.10. Rather than draw the ionic arrangement of sodium chloride, chemists use the much simpler empirical formula, NaCl, to represent the compound.

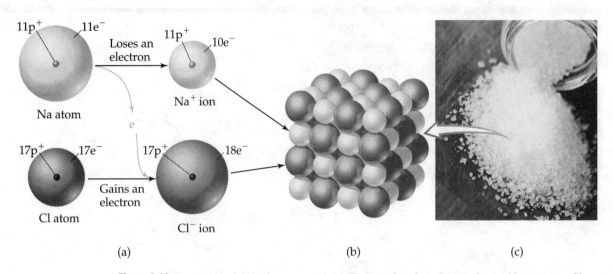

Figure 2.10 Formation of an ionic compound. (a) The transfer of an electron from a Na atom to a Cl atom leads to the formation of a Na^+ ion and a Cl^- ion. (b) Arrangement of these ions in solid sodium chloride, NaCl. (c) A sample of NaCl crystals.

Metal atoms can lose electrons to become monatomic cations.

Nonmetal atoms gain electrons to become monatomic anions.

The periodic table is useful in remembering the charges of monatomic cations and anions. Figure 2.11 shows the common charges of ions derived from elements on the left and right sides of the periodic table. Notice that the cations of the A groups carry a positive charge equal to the group number, and the anions carry a negative charge equal to the group number minus 8. Transition metals tend to form cations of more than one charge value.

1A	2A	3B	4B	5B	6B	7B	8B			9B	10B	3A	4A	5A	6A	7A	8A
H^+																H^-	
Li^+														N^{3-}	O^{2-}	F^-	
Na^+	Mg^{2+}											Al^{3+}			S^{2-}	Cl^-	
K^+	Ca^{2+}	Sc^{3+}	Ti^{2+} Ti^{4+}	V^{2+} V^{4+}	Cr^{2+} Cr^{3+}	Mn^{2+} Mn^{4+}	Fe^{2+} Fe^{3+}	Co^{2+} Co^{3+}	Ni^{2+} Ni^{3+}	Cu^{2+} Cu^+	Zn^{2+}				Se^{2-}	Br^-	
Rb^+	Sr^{2+}									Ag^+	Cd^{2+}		Sn^{2+} Sn^{4+}		Te^{2-}	I^-	
Cs^+	Ba^{2+}									Au^+ Au^{3+}	Hg^{2+} Hg_2^{2+}		Pb^{2+} Pb^{4+}				

Figure 2.11 Charges of some monatomic cations and anions are consistent within groups on the periodic table. Notice that some transition metals form ions having more than one charge.

Naming Inorganic Compounds   Section 2.8

Names of Monatomic Cations

Monatomic cations have the same name as the metal. If the metal forms cations of different charges, a Roman numeral in the name indicates the charge.

$$K^+ = \text{potassium ion} \qquad Ca^{2+} = \text{calcium ion}$$
$$Co^{2+} = \text{cobalt(II) ion} \qquad Co^{3+} = \text{cobalt(III) ion}$$

Notice that most transition metals form cations with more than one charge. However there are four common exceptions.

$$Sc^{3+} = \text{scandium ion} \qquad Ag^+ = \text{silver ion}$$
$$Zn^{2+} = \text{zinc ion} \qquad Cd^{2+} = \text{cadmium ion}$$

Most non–transition metals form cations having only a single charge. Note the two common exceptions.

$$Sn^{2+} = \text{tin(II) ion} \qquad Sn^{4+} = \text{tin(IV) ion}$$
$$Pb^{2+} = \text{lead(II) ion} \qquad Pb^{4+} = \text{lead(IV) ion}$$

Names of Monatomic Anions

Monatomic anions replace the end of the element name with -ide as shown in Table 2.2.

Table 2.2 Names and formulas of common monatomic ions.

Group 1A	Group 5A	Group 6A	Group 7A
H^- hydride			
	N^{3-} nitride	O^{2-} oxide	F^- fluoride
		S^{2-} sulfide	Cl^- chloride
		Se^{2-} selenide	Br^- bromide
		Te^{2-} telluride	I^- iodide

Common misconception: The names and formulas of monatomic anions need not be memorized. Simply locate the atom on the periodic table, assign the charge based on the group number, and change the ending to -ide.

A few common diatomic anions also end in -ide.

$$OH^- \text{ hydroxide} \quad CN^- \text{ cyanide} \quad O_2^{2-} \text{ peroxide}$$

Names of Polyatomic Cations

Polyatomic (containing more than one atom) cations formed from nonmetals end in -ium.

$$NH_4^+ = \text{ammonium} \quad CH_3NH_3^+ = \text{methylammonium}$$
$$(CH_3)_2NH_2^+ = \text{dimethylammonium}$$

Polyatomic Oxyanions (Anions-Containing Oxygen)

Some polyatomic anions end in -ate or -ite. These are called oxyanions because they contain oxygen. Because there is no logical way to predict their formulas or charges these must be memorized.

Table 2.3 lists the names and formulas of some common oxyanions (polyatomic anions containing oxygen).

Some polyatomic oxyanions have a hydrogen ion attached. The word hydrogen or dihydrogen is used to indicate anions derived by adding H^+ to an oxyanion. An added hydrogen ion changes the charge by $1+$.

Table 2.3 Names and formulas of some common oxyanions listed by charge.

Charge	3–	2–	1–
Name and formula	phosphate PO_4^{3-}	hydrogen phosphate HPO_4^{2-}	dihydrogen phosphate $H_2PO_4^-$
		sulfate SO_4^{2-}	hydrogen sulfate HSO_4^-
		carbonate CO_3^{2-}	hydrogen carbonate HCO_3^-
			nitrate NO_3^-
			acetate (also ethanoate) CH_3COO^-

Oxyanions are polyatomic anions that usually end in -ate or -ite. The ending -ate denotes the most common oxyanion of an element. The ending -ite refers to an oxyanion having the same charge but one fewer oxygen.

The halogens form a series of four oxyanions and use prefixes to distinguish them.

ClO^- hypochlorite; hypo- denotes one fewer oxygen
ClO_2^- chlorite
ClO_3^- chlorate
ClO_4^- perchlorate; per- denotes one more oxygen

Names of Ionic Compounds

Names of ionic compounds consist of the cation name followed by the anion name.

$MgBr_2$ = magnesium bromide
$Ca_3(PO_4)_2$ = calcium phosphate
Fe_2O_3 = iron(III) oxide
FeO = iron(II) oxide

(Remember that the Roman numerals III and II refer to the 3+ and 2+ charges of the iron cations, respectively. Notice that the charge on the iron atom in each case is inferred by the ratio in which iron combines with the 2− charged oxide ion.)

Your Turn 2.4

Name the following ionic compounds: KI, MgSO$_4$, FeS, Al$_2$O$_3$, Pb$_3$(PO$_4$)$_2$. Write your answers in the space provided.

Names and Formulas of Acids

The names and formulas of some common acids, an important class of hydrogen-containing compounds, are listed in Table 2.4. In all cases, the formulas of acids are composed of one or more hydrogen ions added to a common monatomic anion or oxyanion. Acids of monatomic ions are called binary acids and acids of oxyanions are called oxyacids.

Table 2.4 Names and formulas of some common acids.

Binary Acids		Oxyacids	
HF	hydrofluoric acid	HNO$_3$	nitric acid
HCl	hydrochloric acid	H$_2$SO$_4$	sulfuric acid
HBr	hydrobromic acid	H$_3$PO$_4$	phosphoric acid
HI	hydroiodic acid	CH$_3$COOH	acetic acid
H$_2$S	hydrosulfuric acid	H$_2$CO$_3$	carbonic acid
H$_2$Se	hydroselenic acid	HNO$_2$	nitrous acid
		H$_2$SO$_3$	sulfurous acid
		HClO$_4$	perchloric acid
		HClO$_3$	chloric acid
		HClO$_2$	chlorous acid
		HClO	hypochlorous acid

To name binary acids, replace the -ide ending of the anion with -ic acid and add the prefix hydro-.

_____ide becomes hydro_____ic acid.

Bromide, Br$^-$, becomes hydrobromic acid, HBr.

To name oxyacids, replace the -ate ending of the oxyanion with -ic acid or the -ite ending of the oxyanion with -ous acid.

_____ate becomes _____ic acid.

Nitrate, NO_3^-, becomes nitric acid, HNO_3.

_____ite becomes _____ous acid.

Hypochlorite, ClO^-, becomes hypochlorous acid, $HClO$.

Some common exceptions:

Phosphate, PO_4^{3-}, becomes phosPHORic acid, H_3PO_4.

Sulfate, SO_4^{2-}, becomes sulfURic acid, H_2SO_4.

Names of Binary Molecular Compounds

A binary molecular compound contains two nonmetals. The rules for naming binary molecular compounds are the following:

1. Name the first element.

2. Name the second element giving it an -ide ending.

3. Use prefixes to denote how many of each element are present in the formula. The prefixes are shown in Table 2.5.

Table 2.5 Prefixes used in naming binary compounds formed between nonmetals.

Prefix	Meaning
mono-	1
di-	2
tri-	3
tetra-	4
penta-	5
hexa-	6
hepta-	7
octa-	8
nona-	9
deca-	10

CO_2 = carbon dioxide

SO_3 = sulfur trioxide

N_2O_5 = dinitrogen pentoxide

P_4O_{10} = tetraphosphorus decoxide

Name the following compounds: SCl_2, CF_4, BrI_3, PBr_5, SF_6. Write your answers in the space provided.

Some Simple Organic Compounds   Section 2.9

Organic chemistry is the study of carbon compounds.

Hydrocarbons are compounds containing only carbon and hydrogen.

Alkanes are hydrocarbons containing only C—C single bonds.

Table 2.6 shows the names and formulas of some common alkanes. Notice that in each name a prefix indicates the number of carbon atoms in the formula. The prefix is followed by the suffix -ane to indicate that the formula is an alkane.

Table 2.6 Names and formulas of some simple alkanes. The prefix of the name tells how many carbon atoms are in the formula.

Number of Carbon Atoms	Prefix	Name	Formula
1	meth-	methane	CH_4
2	eth-	ethane	CH_3CH_3
3	prop-	propane	$CH_3CH_2CH_3$
4	but-	butane	$CH_3CH_2CH_2CH_3$
5	pent-	pentane	$CH_3CH_2CH_2CH_2CH_3$
6	hex	hexane	$CH_3CH_2CH_2CH_2CH_2CH_3$
7	hept-	heptane	$CH_3CH_2CH_2CH_2CH_2CH_2CH_3$
8	oct-	octane	$CH_3CH_2CH_2CH_2CH_2CH_2CH_2CH_3$
9	non-	nonane	$CH_3CH_2CH_2CH_2CH_2CH_2CH_2CH_2CH_3$
10	dec-	decane	$CH_3CH_2CH_2CH_2CH_2CH_2CH_2CH_2CH_2CH_3$

The same prefixes are used to name organic compounds having **functional groups**, groups of atoms that give rise to the structure and properties of an organic compound. For example, the functional group of a class of organic compounds classified as **alcohols** is —OH. The functional group of a **carboxylic acid** is —COOH. Table 2.7 lists the names and formulas of simple alcohols and carboxylic acids. In Chapter 25 of *Chemistry: The Central Science*, you will study organic compounds in more detail.

Table 2.7 Names and formulas of some simple alcohols and carboxylic acids. The prefix tells how many carbon atoms are in the formulas.

Alcohols		Carboxylic Acids	
Name	Formula	Name	Formula
methanol	CH_3OH	methanoic acid	H_2COOH
ethanol	CH_3CH_2OH	ethanoic acid	CH_3COOH
1-propanol	$CH_3CH_2CH_2OH$	propanoic acid	CH_3CH_2COOH
2-propanol	$CH_3CHOHCH_3$		
1-butanol	$CH_3CH_2CH_2CH_2OH$	butanoic acid	$CH_3CH_2CH_2COOH$
2-butanol	$CH_3CH_2CHOHCH_3$		

Your Turn 2.6

Predict which element or mixture of elements the mass spectrum below represents. Justify your answer with evidence.

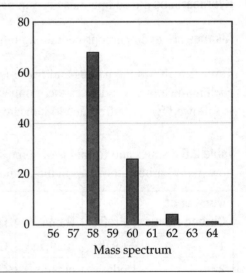

Multiple Choice Questions

1. *Fluorine gas is bubbled through an aqueous solution of calcium bromate.*
   Besides water, this statement refers to which chemical formulas?

   A) F_2 and $CaBr_2$

   B) F and $CaBr_2$

   C) F_2 and $Ca(BrO_3)_2$

   D) F_2 and $CaBrO_3$

2. *Magnesium nitride reacts with water to form ammonia and magnesium*
   hydroxide. Besides water, this statement refers to which chemical formulas?

   A) Mg_3N_2, NH_3, and $Mg(OH)_2$

   B) $Mg(NO_3)_2$, NH_4^+, and MgH_2

   C) $Mg(NO_3)_2$, NH_3, and MgH_2

   D) Mg_3N_2, NH_3, and $MgOH$

3. *The mineral spinel is an ionic compound containing only the elements*
   magnesium, aluminum, and oxygen. Its simplest formula is probably

   A) $MgAlO_3$

   B) Mg_2AlO_4

   C) $MgAl_2O_4$

   D) $Mg_2Al_2O_3$

4. *The mineral chromite, $FeCr_2O_4$, consists of a mixture of iron(II) oxide*
   and chromium(III) oxide. What is the most likely ratio of iron(II) oxide to
   chromium(III) oxide in chromite?

   A) 1:1

   B) 1:2

   C) 2:3

   D) 3:2

5. Which formula represents a peroxide?

   A) K_2O

   B) K_2O_2

   C) KO_2

   D) CaO

6. What is the general formula for an alkaline earth metal hydride?

   A) MH

   B) M_2H

   C) MH_2

   D) $M(OH)_2$

7. Which of the following compounds contains only four carbon atoms?

   A) propane

   B) butanoic acid

   C) ethylmethyl ether

   D) 2-pentanol

8. Bromine has just two major isotopes giving it an atomic mass of 79.904 amu. Based on this information, which of the following statements can explain the atomic mass value?

   A) The isotope, Br-81, is more common than Br-79.

   B) Br-79 and Br-81 exist in about equal proportions.

   C) Br-78 is about twice as abundant as Br-81.

   D) The two major isotopes of Br have 45 and 46 neutrons.

9. Which is a collection of only molecular compounds?

   A) NO, CS_2, PCl_3, HBr

   B) $NaNO_3, CCl_4, CuS$

   C) Ar, NH_3, SF_4, PCl_5

   D) Cl_2, CCl_4, NO_2, SF_6

10. Which is true of the $^{243}Am^{3+}$ ion?

	Protons	Electrons	Neutrons
A)	148	148	243
B)	95	98	243
C)	95	95	148
D)	95	92	148

Refer to the following information to answer Questions 11–16.

The mass spectrum of a natural abundance of chlorine atoms is shown in the figure:

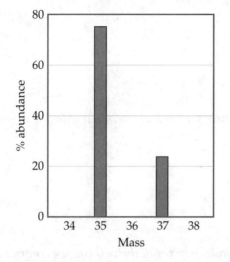

Detailed analysis shows that the two stable isotopes of chlorine have masses of 34.969 amu and 36.966 amu.

11. *What are the mass numbers of the two isotopes of chlorine?*

    A) *34.969 and 36.966*

    B) *34 and 36*

    C) *35 and 37*

    D) *17 and 17*

12. *What is the approximate % abundance of the lighter isotope?*

    A) *20*

    B) *25*

    C) *50*

    D) *75*

13. *How many types of molecules with different masses exist in a sample of chlorine gas if the sample exists entirely as diatomic molecules?*

    A) *1*

    B) *2*

    C) *3*

    D) *4*

14. What is the approximate mass of the most abundant naturally occurring Cl_2 molecule?

   A) 70

   B) 71

   C) 72

   D) 74

15. How many neutrons does the less abundant chlorine atom have?

   A) 17

   B) 18

   C) 19

   D) 20

16. Why are the individual masses of the two isotopes, not integers?

   A) Atomic mass of an element is the average mass of all isotopes.

   B) The masses of a proton and a neutron are not integers.

   C) Atomic mass of an element is the sum of the number of protons and neutrons in an atom.

   D) Mass number of an element is the average mass of all isotopes.

17. A compound whose empirical formula is C_2H_4O has a molar mass that lies between 100 and 150 g/mol. What is the molecular formula of the compound?

   A) C_2H_4O

   B) $C_4H_8O_2$

   C) $C_6H_{12}O_3$

   D) $C_6H_{12}O_2$

18. Find the empirical formula for a compound only one element of which is a metal. The compound's percentage composition by mass is 40.0% metal, 12.0% C, and 48.0% O.

   A) $CaCO_3$

   B) Na_2CO_3

   C) $NaHCO_3$

   D) $Al_2(CO_3)_3$

Free Response Questions

1. Use the data provided for Multiple Choice Questions 11–16 to perform the following mathematical operations:

   a. Calculate the mass of the chlorine molecule having the largest molecular mass.

   b. Calculate the % abundance of the more abundant chlorine isotope.

2. Like chlorine, iodine is a halogen and forms similar compounds. Write the names and formulas of the four oxyanions and the four oxyacids of iodine.

3. Consider the four systems in the figure:

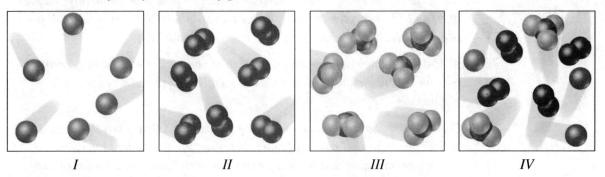

I II III IV

a. Identify each system as a pure substance or mixture. Explain your answer.

b. Identify each pure substance as an element or a compound. Justify your answer.

c. When physically divided, which system, III or IV, will always contain particles that have identical ratios of masses? Explain using atomic molecular theory.

Multiple Choice Answers and Explanations

1. C. Fluorine is one of the seven diatomic elements and its formula is written F_2. Calcium, in Group 2A, forms a Ca^{2+} ion. Bromate is an oxyanion having the formula, BrO_3^-.

2. A. Magnesium, from Group 2A, forms Mg^{2+} ions. Nitrogen, from Group 5A, forms nitride ions, N^{3-}. Ammonia is the name given to NH_3. Hydroxide ion is OH^-. The correct formulas of magnesium nitride, ammonia, and magnesium hydroxide, respectively, are, Mg_3N_2, NH_3, and $Mg(OH)_2$.

3. C. Ions of magnesium, aluminum, and oxygen carry charges of 2+, 3+, and 2−, respectively. Mg^{2+}, Al^{3+}, and O^{2-} will combine in a way that the sum of the charges is zero. Of the choices given, only $MgAl_2O_4$ fits the criterion.

4. A. Iron(II) oxide is FeO and chromium(III) oxide is Cr_2O_3. Combining one formula unit of FeO with one formula unit of Cr_2O_3 yields $FeCr_2O_4$.

5. B. Peroxide is O_2^{2-}. Potassium is in Group 1A, so it loses one electron to form a K^+ ion. K^+ and O_2^{2-} combine to form potassium peroxide, K_2O_2.

6. C. Hydride is H^-. Alkaline earth metals are metals of Group 2A, all of which lose two electrons to form ions with a 2+ charge. M^{2+} and H^- combine as MH_2.

7. B. The prefix but- signifies four carbon atoms. (Note: Ethylmethyl ether has three carbon atoms because the prefix ethyl- means two carbon atoms and the prefix methyl- implies one carbon atom.)

8. B. The atomic mass of an element is the weighted average of the mass of all the isotopes. If Br-79 and Br-81 are in about equal proportions, the atomic mass of bromine will be about 80 amu. If Br-81 is the most abundant, the

mass would be greater than 80. If Br-78 is twice as abundant as Br-81, then the atomic mass would be about 79. (78 + 78 + 81)/3 = 79. If Br-82 is more abundant than Br-79, then the atomic mass would be greater than 80.5. (82 + 79)/2 = 80.5. Isotopes having 45 and 46 neutrons would have masses of 80 and 81, respectively. The average mass of those isotopes would fall between 80 and 81, depending on their relative abundances.

9. A. *Molecular compounds contain more than one type of atom and generally contain only nonmetals. Na and Ca are metals and Ar and Cl_2 are not compounds.*

10. D. *Americium has an atomic number of 95, meaning that it has 95 protons and 95 electrons in the neutral atom. However, the americium ion carries a 3+ charge, meaning that there are three fewer electrons than protons giving it 92 electrons. The number of neutrons is the mass number minus the atomic number, 243 − 95 = 148 neutrons.*

11. C. *The mass spectrum shows that the two isotopes have masses of approximately 35 and 37.*

12. D. *Reading the spectrum, the lighter isotope having a mass of approximately 35 is about 75% abundant.*

13. C. *Because there are two isotopes of chlorine atoms, there are three different ways they can combine to form diatomic molecules: Cl-35 with Cl-35, Cl-35 with Cl-37, and Cl-37 with Cl-37.*

14. A. *Because Cl-35 is the more abundant isotope, the most abundant molecule is $^{35}Cl - {}^{35}Cl$.*

    Its mass is 2 × 34.969 = 69.938 amu.

15. D. *The less abundant isotope is Cl-37. Number of neutrons equals the mass number minus the atomic number: n^0 = 37 − 17 = 20.*

16. B. *The mass is not a whole number because the masses of protons and neutrons are not integers. Also nuclear binding energies have tiny mass equivalents. While Answers A and E are accurate statements, they do not answer the question. Mass number is the total number of protons and neutrons in the nucleus.*

17. C. *The molecular formula of a compound is an integer multiple of the empirical formula. The molecular formula $C_6H_{12}O_3$ is three times the given empirical formula and has a molar mass of 132 g/mol.*

18. A. *Calcium carbonate has a molar mass of 100 g/mol. The molar masses of Ca, C, and O are 40.0, 12.0, and 16.0, respectively. When considering three moles of oxygen which total 48.0, the given percentages are consistent.*

Free Response Answers

1. a. *The chlorine molecule having the largest molecular mass is $^{37}Cl - {}^{37}Cl$. Its mass is 2 × 36.966 = 73.932 amu.*

b. To solve this problem, you need the atomic mass of chlorine listed on the periodic table: 35.4527 amu. Let y = % abundance of Cl-37. Let x = % abundance of Cl-35.

$x + y = 1$

$35.4527 = 36.966y + 34.969x$

$35.4527 = 36.966(1 - x) + 34.969x$

$x = 0.7578 = 75.78\%$ Cl-35

2. Chlorine and iodine are in the same family so they will be expected to form analogous oxyions and oxyacids.

IO^- hypoiodite	HIO hypoiodous acid
IO_2^- iodite	HIO_2 iodous acid
IO_3^- iodate	HIO_3 iodic acid
IO_4^- periodate	HIO_4 periodic acid (pronounced "per-iodic")

3. a. Systems I, II, and III are pure substances because they each contain only one kind of particle. System IV is a mixture because it contains more than one kind of particle.

b. Systems I and II are elements because the particles of each consist of only one kind of atom. System III is a compound because each particle is of the same shape and consists of exactly the same number and type of atoms.

c. When physically divided, the ratio of masses of the constituent elements of System III will always be identical because each molecule contains the same number and kind of atoms.

Your Turn Answers

2.1. The Dalton model assumed that all atoms are indivisible yet Thomson showed that they all contain electrons.

The Thomson model proposed that electrons are embedded in a uniform positive sphere, yet Rutherford showed that the atom is mostly empty space having a tiny dense nucleus surrounded by electrons.

Classical physics predicts that Rutherford's planetary model would not be stable, yet atoms are stable. Bohr proposed that electrons do not fall into the nucleus because they are held in stable, fixed (quantized) energy levels.

2.2. The mass spectrum shows four signals, corresponding to four isotopes of lead: Pb-204, Pb-206, Pb-207, and Pb-208. Because the atomic number of lead is 82, all neutral lead atoms contain 82 protons and 82 electrons. The number of neutrons in any isotope is the mass number minus the atomic number. From lowest to highest mass number, the nucleus of each lead isotope contains 122, 124, 125, and 126 neutrons, respectively.

2.3. a. Chlorine is a toxic gas that refers to the free element dichlorine, Cl_2.

b. Common table salt contains the element chlorine, which refers to monatomic Cl.

2.4. *KI = potassium iodide. MgSO$_4$ = magnesium sulfate. FeS = iron(II) sulfide.*
     Al$_2$O$_3$ = aluminum oxide. Pb$_3$(PO$_4$)$_2$ = lead(II) phosphate.

2.5. *SCl$_2$ = sulfur dichloride. CF$_4$ = carbon tetrafluoride. BrI$_3$ = bromine triiodide.*
     PBr$_5$ = phosphorus pentabromide. SF$_6$ = sulfur hexafluoride.

2.6. *The mass spectrum is of nickel because the masses and abundances of the*
     isotopes are consistent with the atomic mass of nickel (58.6934 amu). The major
     isotopes have masses (approximate abundances) of 58(0.70) + 60(0.25) +
     62(0.05) = 58.7. This data is consistent with an atomic mass significantly
     greater than 58 but significantly less than 59. Cobalt's mass is too high at al-
     most 59 so nickel is the only element that meets these criteria.

Stoichiometry: CALCULATIONS WITH CHEMICAL FORMULAS AND EQUATIONS

The content in this topic is the basis for mastering Learning Objectives 1.2, 1.3, 1.4, 1.17, 1.18, 3.1, and 3.4 as found in the Curriculum Framework.

You may have learned some of this material in first-year chemistry. When you finish reviewing this topic, be sure you are able to:

- Apply the law of conservation of mass to balance a chemical equation using symbols for atoms and molecules and particle drawings
- Use the mole as a quantitative model for chemical composition
- Interconvert moles, mass, number of particles, and volume of a gas
- Use calculations of mass data to determine the identity or purity of various substances
- Calculate the percentage composition of a compound
- Calculate the empirical and molecular formulas of a compound and of a hydrate from combustion and decomposition data
- Apply mathematical calculations to mass data to infer the identity of a substance and/or its purity
- Calculate the masses and moles of reactants and products using stoichiometry
- Determine limiting reactants and percent yields from experimental data

Chemical Equations   Section 3.1

Stoichiometry is the area of study that examines the quantities of substances involved in chemical reactions.

A **chemical reaction** is a process by which one or more substances are converted to other substances.

Chemical equations use chemical formulas to symbolically represent chemical reactions. For example, the chemical sentence, "Hydrogen burns in air to produce water," can be expressed as chemical symbols or as a molecular picture of the particles as shown in Figure 3.1.

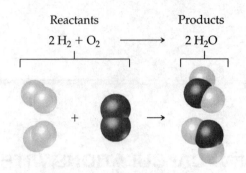

Figure 3.1 A balanced chemical equation.

When the reaction is more complex, chemists prefer to write the equation using only chemical symbols to represent the particle pictures. For example, the following chemical equation describes how butane, C_4H_{10}, burns in air:

$$2C_4H_{10}(g) + 13O_2(g) \rightarrow 8CO_2(g) + 10H_2O(l)$$

$$\text{reactants} \rightarrow \text{products}$$

The equation is a "chemical sentence" written in the symbolic "words" of chemical formulas and symbols. The formulas on the left are reactants, and the formulas on the right are products. The equation reads:

"Two molecules of gaseous butane react with thirteen molecules of oxygen gas to produce eight molecules of carbon dioxide gas and ten molecules of liquid water."

A **balanced chemical equation** has an equal number of atoms of each element on each side of the arrow. The coefficients preceding each formula "balance" the equation. Notice that, because of the coefficients, on each side of the arrow there are eight carbon atoms, twenty hydrogen atoms, and twenty-six oxygen atoms.

The symbols (g), (l), (s), and (aq) are used to designate the physical state of each reactant and product: gas, liquid, solid, and aqueous (dissolved in water).

Your Turn 3.1

Write a chemical sentence to illustrate how to "read" the following chemical equation:

$$CO_2(g) + 2NH_3(g) + H_2O(l) \rightarrow 2NH_4^+(aq) + CO_3^{2-}(aq)$$

Convert each formula of the equation to a particle representation. Write your answer in the space provided.

To balance simple equations, start by balancing atoms other than hydrogen or oxygen. Balance hydrogen atoms next to last and balance oxygen atoms last.

Example:

Balance the following equation:

$$H_2SO_4(aq) + NaHCO_3(s) \rightarrow CO_2(g) + H_2O(l) + Na_2SO_4(aq)$$

Solution:

1. S and C are already balanced so start with Na.

$$H_2SO_4(aq) + 2NaHCO_3(s) \rightarrow CO_2(g) + H_2O(l) + Na_2SO_4(aq)$$

2. Now balance carbon.

$$H_2SO_4(aq) + 2NaHCO_3(s) \rightarrow 2CO_2(g) + H_2O(l) + Na_2SO_4(aq)$$

3. Next balance H.

$$H_2SO_4(aq) + 2NaHCO_3(s) \rightarrow 2CO_2(g) + 2H_2O(l) + Na_2SO_4(aq)$$

4. Check to see that oxygen is balanced and double-check all other atoms. (As in algebraic equations, the numeral 1 is usually not written.)

Some Simple Patterns of Chemical Reactivity   Section 3.2

Predicting the products of chemical reactions is an essential skill to acquire in the study of chemistry. Sometimes reactions fall into simple patterns and recognizing these patterns can be helpful in predicting which products will be produced from given reactants. Topic 4 addresses predicting products of chemical reactions in more depth. For now, here are a few patterns to learn to recognize.

1. In a combination reaction, two elements combine to form one compound. (Other combinations are possible and Topic 4 describes better ways to predict what will happen.)

Example:

A metal reacts with a nonmetal to produce an ionic compound. Write an equation to describe what happens when solid sodium is exposed to chlorine gas.

Solution:

$$2Na(s) + Cl_2(g) \rightarrow 2NaCl(s)$$

Your Turn 3.2

Write an equation to describe what happens when solid magnesium metal reacts at high temperature with nitrogen gas. Write your answer in the space provided.

---

2. In a decomposition reaction, one reactant changes to two or more products.

Example:

Upon heating, metal carbonates decompose to yield metal oxides and carbon dioxide. Write an equation to describe what happens when solid magnesium carbonate is heated.

Solution:

$$MgCO_3(s) \rightarrow MgO(s) + CO_2(g)$$

Your Turn 3.3

Write an equation to describe what happens when liquid water is decomposed to its elements by an electrical current. Write your answer in the space provided.

3. A combustion reaction usually involves oxygen, often from air, reacting with hydrocarbons or other organic molecules containing carbon, hydrogen, and oxygen to produce carbon dioxide and water.

Example:

Write an equation to describe what happens when liquid ethanol burns in air.

Solution:

$$CH_3CH_2OH(l) + 3O_2(g) \rightarrow 2CO_2(g) + 3H_2O(g)$$

(Recall that encoded in the name "ethanol" is a two-carbon alcohol having the –OH functional group.)

Your Turn 3.4

Write an equation to describe what happens when liquid hexane is burned in air. Write your answer in the space provided.

Avogadro's Number and the Mole   Section 3.4

Avogadro's number is 6.02×10^{23}. It represents the number of atoms in exactly 12 g of isotopically pure ^{12}C. Because all atomic masses are based on ^{12}C, the atomic mass of any element expressed in grams represents Avogadro's number (6.02×10^{23}) of atoms of that element.

A **mole** is the amount of matter that contains 6.02×10^{23} atoms, ions, molecules, or formula units.

The **molar mass** of a substance is the mass in grams of one mole of that substance. To calculate a molar mass of any substance, add the atomic masses of all the atoms in its formula. (For convenience, atomic masses are often rounded to three significant figures.) Table 3.1 shows the molar masses of various substances.

Common misconception: "Molar mass" is a universal term that is often used to replace the terms atomic mass, molecular mass, and formula mass. Molar mass is used to express the mass of one mole of any substance, whether it is an atom (atomic mass), a molecule (molecular mass), an ion (formula mass), or an ionic compound (formula mass).

Table 3.1 The molar mass of any substance is the mass in grams of 6.02×10^{23} particles or one mole of that substance.

Formula	Number of Particles	Representative Particles	Molar Mass	Alternate Term
Ar	6.02×10^{23}	Atoms	39.9 g/mol	Atomic mass
CO_2	6.02×10^{23}	Molecules	44.0 g/mol	Molecular mass
NaBr	6.02×10^{23}	Formula units	103 g/mol	Formula mass
CO_3^{2-}	6.02×10^{23}	Ions	60.0 g/mol	Formula mass

Grams, moles, and representative particles (atoms, molecules, ions, or formula units) are converted from one to another using the "Mole Road" described in Figure 3.2.

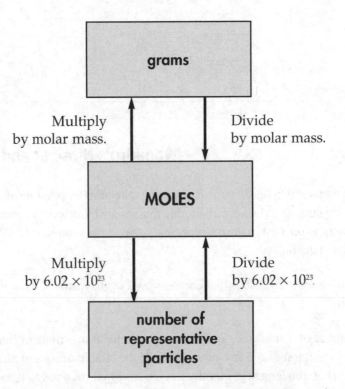

Figure 3.2 The "Mole Road." Divide to convert to moles. Multiply to convert from moles.

Calculating Percentage Composition of a Compound

The percentage composition of a compound is the percentage by mass contributed by each element in the compound. To calculate the percentage composition of an element in any formula, divide the molar mass of the element multiplied by the number of times it appears in the formula, by the molar mass of the formula, and multiply by 100.

% composition = 100 × (molar mass of element × subscript for element)/(molar mass of substance)

Example:

What is the percentage composition of Na_2CO_3?

Solution:

$\% \, Na = 100 \times 2(23.0) \, g \, Na/[2(23.0) + 12.0 + 3(16.0) \, g] = 43.4\% \, Na$

$\% \, C = 100 \times 12.0 \, g \, C/[2(23.0) + 12.0 + 3(16.0) \, g] = 11.3\% \, C$

$\% \, O = 100 \times 3(16.0) \, g/[2(23.0) + 12.0 + 3(16.0) \, g] = 45.3\% \, O$

Empirical Formulas from Analyses   Section 3.5

The **empirical formula** for a compound expresses the simplest ratio of atoms in the formula. The percentage composition of a compound can be determined experimentally by chemical analysis and the empirical formula can be calculated from the percentage composition.

Example:

What is the empirical formula of a compound containing 68.4% chromium and 31.6% oxygen?

Solution:

In chemistry, percentage always means mass percentage, unless specified otherwise. The data mean that for every 100 g of compound, there are 68.4 g of Cr and 31.6 g of O.

1. Write the formula using number of grams.

$Cr_{68.4} \, O_{31.6}$

2. Convert grams to moles by dividing by the molar mass of each element.

$Cr_{68.4/52.0} \, O_{31.6/16.0} = Cr_{1.315} \, O_{1.975}$

3. Convert to small numbers by dividing each mole quantity by the smaller mole quantity.

$Cr_{1.315/1.315} \, O_{1.975/1.315} = Cr_1 \, O_{1.5}$

4. *If necessary, multiply each mole quantity by a small whole number that converts all quantities to whole numbers.*

$$Cr_{1 \times 2} O_{1.5 \times 2} = Cr_2 O_3$$

Molecular Formulas from Empirical Formulas

A **molecular formula** tells exactly how many atoms are in one molecule of the compound. The subscripts in a molecular formula are always whole number multiples of the subscripts in the empirical formula. Molecular formulas can be determined from empirical formulas if the molar mass of the compound is known.

Example:

A compound containing only carbon, hydrogen, and oxygen is 63.16% C and 8.77% H. Mass spectrometry shows that the compound has a molar mass of 114 g/mol. What is its empirical formula and its molecular formula?

Solution:

1. *Write the formula using number of grams.*

$$C_{63.16} H_{8.77} O_{28.07}$$

(Calculate the grams of oxygen by subtracting the grams of carbon and grams of hydrogen from 100 g.

$$x \, g \, O = 100 \, g - 63.16 \, g \, C - 8.77 \, g \, H = 28.07 \, g \, O.)$$

2. *Convert grams to moles by dividing by the molar mass of each element.*

$$C_{63.16/12.0} H_{8.77/1.00} O_{28.07/16.0} = C_{5.263} H_{8.77} O_{1.754}$$

3. *Convert to small numbers by dividing each mole quantity by the smallest mole quantity.*

$$C_{5.263/1.754} H_{8.77/1.754} O_{1.754/1.754} = C_3 H_5 O_1$$

empirical formula

4. *All quantities are whole numbers.*

5. *Divide the known molar mass by the mass of one mole of the empirical formula. The result produces the integer by which you multiply the empirical formula to obtain the molecular formula.*

$$(114 \, g/mol)/(57.0 \, g/mol) = 2$$

$$C_{3 \times 2} H_{5 \times 2} O_{1 \times 2} = C_6 H_{10} O_2$$

molecular formula

Empirical Formulas from Combustion Analysis

When a compound containing carbon, hydrogen, and oxygen is completely combusted, all the carbon is converted to carbon dioxide, and all the hydrogen becomes water. The empirical formula of the compound can be calculated from the measured masses of the products.

Example:

A 3.489 g sample of a compound containing C, H, and O yields 7.832 g of CO_2 and 1.922 g of water upon combustion. What is the simplest formula of the compound?

The unbalanced chemical equation is:

$$C_xH_yO_z + O_2 \rightarrow CO_2 + H_2O$$

X is the number of moles of carbon in the compound because all the carbon in the compound is converted to CO_2. X equals the number of moles of CO_2 because there is one mole of carbon in one mole of CO_2.

$$X = mol\ C = 7.832\ g\ CO_2/44.0\ g/mol = 0.178\ mol\ C$$

Y is the number of moles of hydrogen in the compound because all the hydrogen becomes water. Y equals twice the number of moles of water because there are two moles of hydrogen in one mole of water.

$$Y = mol\ H = (1.922\ g\ H_2O/18.0\ g/mol) \times 2 = 0.2136\ mol\ H$$

Z is the number of moles of O. To obtain the number of grams of O in the compound, subtract the number of grams of C (X mol × 12.0 g/mol) and the number of grams of H (Y mol × 1.00 g/mol) from the total grams of the compound. Convert the result to moles of O by dividing by 16.0 g/mol.

$$Z = mol\ O = [3.489 - (12.0)(0.178) - (1.00)(0.2136)]/16.0$$
$$= 0.0712\ mol\ O$$

Convert to small numbers by dividing each mole quantity by the smallest mole quantity.

$$C_{0.178}\ H_{0.2136}\ O_{0.0712} =$$
$$C_{0.178/0.0712}\ H_{0.2136/0.0712}\ O_{0.0712/0.0712} = C_{2.5}H_3O_1$$

Finally, multiply each mole quantity by a small whole number that converts all quantities to whole numbers.

$$C_{2.5 \times 2}\ H_{3 \times 2}\ O_{1 \times 2} = C_5H_6O_2$$

Formulas of Hydrates

Ionic compounds often form crystal structures called hydrates by acquiring one or more water molecules per formula unit. For example, solid sodium thiosulfate decahydrate, $Na_2S_2O_3 \cdot 10H_2O$, has ten water molecules per formula unit of sodium thiosulfate. Heating a sample of hydrate causes it to lose water. The number of water molecules per formula unit can be calculated from the mass difference before and after heating.

Example:

When 21.91 g of a hydrate of copper(II) sulfate is heated to drive off the water, 14.00 g of anhydrous copper(II) sulfate remain. What is the formula of the hydrate?

Solution:

This is a variation of an empirical formula problem. The solution lies in calculating the ratio of H_2O moles to the moles of $CuSO_4$. The chemical equation is:

$$CuSO_4 \cdot X\,H_2O(s) \rightarrow CuSO_4(s) + X\,H_2O(g)$$
$$\quad\quad 21.91\,g \quad\quad\quad\quad 14.00\,g$$

Calculate the grams of water by subtracting the grams of copper(II) sulfate from the grams of the hydrate.

$x\,g\,H_2O = 21.91\,g - 14.00\,g = 7.91\,g\,H_2O$

$mol\,H_2O = 7.91\,g\,H_2O/18.0\,g/mol = 0.439\,mol\,H_2O$

$mol\,CuSO_4 = 14.00\,g/159.5\,g/mol = 0.08777\,mol\,CuSO_4$

$mol\,H_2O/mol\,CuSO_4 = 0.439\,mol/0.08777\,mol = 5.00$
The formula has five moles of water per mole of copper(II) sulfate:
$CuSO_4 \cdot 5H_2O$.

Section 3.6

Quantitative Information from Balanced Equations

Stoichiometry refers to the quantities of substances involved in chemical reactions. The coefficients in a balanced chemical equation indicate both the relative number of molecules (or formula units) involved in the reaction, and the relative number of moles. For example, the equation for the combustion of octane, C_8H_{18}, a component of gasoline is:

$$2C_8H_{18}(l) + 25O_2(g) \rightarrow 16CO_2(g) + 18H_2O(g)$$

The four coefficients that balance the equation are proportional to one another and can be used to relate mole quantities of reactants and/or products.

Example:

How many moles of octane will burn in the presence of 37.0 moles of oxygen gas?

Solution:

The balanced equation tells us that two moles of octane will burn in 25 moles of oxygen gas, so the answer to the question involves the ratio 2 mol C_8H_{18} per 25 mol O_2.

$x\,mol\,C_8H_{18} = 37.0\,mol\,O_2\,(2\,mol\,C_8H_{18}/25\,mol\,O_2) = 37.0 \times 2/25$
$= 2.96\,mol\,C_8H_{18}$.

Alternatively, we can use the mole road:

To convert mol O_2 to mol C_8H_{18}, multiply by 2/25.

x mol C_8H_{18} = 37.0 mol(2/25) = 2.96 mol C_8H_{18}

(Always multiply by the coefficient at the head of the arrow and divide by the coefficient at the tail of the arrow.)

$$mol\ C_8H_{18} \underset{\times 25/2}{\overset{\times 2/25}{\rightleftarrows}} mol\ O_2$$

To convert mol C_8H_{18} to mol O_2, multiply by 25/2.

Figure 3.3 shows an expanded mole road to include the relationship between the moles of any reactant or product in a balanced chemical equation.

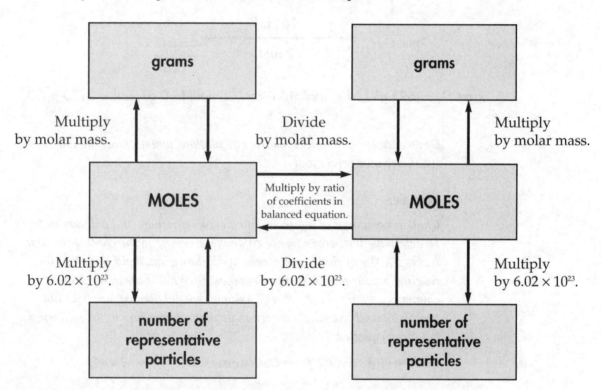

Figure 3.3 The stoichiometry "Mole Road." Divide to convert to moles. Multiply to convert from moles. Multiply by the ratio of coefficients in a balanced equation to convert moles of one substance to moles of another substance.

This stoichiometry mole road allows us to relate any quantity in a balanced equation to any other quantity in the same equation.

Example:

How many grams of carbon dioxide are obtained when 695 g (about 1 gallon) of octane are burned in oxygen?

Solution:

Follow the road map:

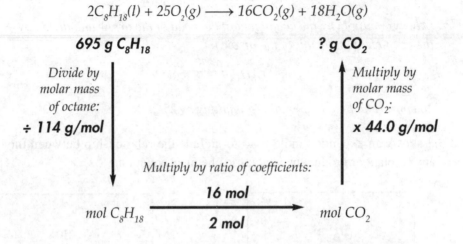

$$2C_8H_{18}(l) + 25O_2(g) \longrightarrow 16CO_2(g) + 18H_2O(g)$$

695 g C₈H₁₈   **? g CO₂**

Divide by molar mass of octane:
÷ 114 g/mol

Multiply by molar mass of CO₂:
x 44.0 g/mol

Multiply by ratio of coefficients:

16 mol

mol C₈H₁₈ ⟶ *mol CO₂*

2 mol

x g CO₂ = (695 g)(114 g/mol)(16.0 mol/2 mol)(44.0 g/mol) = 2150 g CO₂

Often chemists use stoichiometric calculations to determine the purity of a substance as a percentage.

Example:

Chalk is composed of a mixture of calcium carbonate and calcium sulfate. To determine the percentage of calcium carbonate in the chalk, a student reacts 100.0 g of chalk with excess hydrochloric acid and finds that the reaction produces 33.0 g of carbon dioxide. What is the percentage of calcium carbonate in the chalk? Assume that calcium sulfate does not react with acid and calcium carbonate reacts according to the following balanced equation:

$$CaCO_3(s) + 2HCl(aq) \rightarrow CaCl_2(aq) + CO_2(g) + H_2O(l)$$

Solution:

The amount of carbon dioxide generated by reaction with the calcium carbonate in the chalk is directly proportional to the amount of calcium carbonate in the mixture.

$x\ g\ CaCO_3 = 33.0\ g\ CO_2(1\ mol\ CO_2/44.0\ g\ CO_2)$

$(1\ mol\ CaCO_3/1\ mol\ CO_2)(100.0\ g\ CaCO_3)/1\ mol\ CaCO_3)$

$= 75.0\ g\ CaCO_3$

$\%\ CaCO_3 = (g\ CaCO_3/g\ chalk)(100) = 75.0\ g/100.0\ g = 75\%$

Limiting Reactants   Section 3.7

The **limiting reactant** is the reactant that is completely consumed in a chemical reaction. The limiting reactant limits the amount of products formed.

The **excess reactant** is usually the other reactant. Some of the excess reactant is left unreacted when the limiting reactant is completely consumed.

A stoichiometric mixture means that both reactants are limiting and both are completely consumed by the reaction. There is an excess of neither. Because of their subtle nature, quantitative limiting reactant problems are among the most difficult. The mole road is a useful tool in solving limiting reactant problems.

Common misconception: Stoichiometry calculations can calculate only how much reactants react or how much products are formed. Stoichiometry cannot calculate how much excess reactant is left unreacted. To calculate how much excess reactant remains after the reaction is complete, first calculate how much is consumed and then subtract that amount from how much total reactant was initially present.

Example:

255 g of octane and 1510 g of oxygen gas are present at the beginning of a reaction that goes to completion and forms carbon dioxide and water according to the following equation.

$$2C_8H_{18}(l) + 25O_2(g) \rightarrow 16CO_2(g) + 18H_2O\ (g)$$

a. What is the limiting reactant?
b. How many grams of water are formed when the limiting reactant is completely consumed?
c. How many grams are consumed of the reactant in excess?
d. How many grams of excess reactant are left unreacted?

Solution:

a. To find the limiting reactant, first compare the number of moles of reactants relative to the ratio in which they react. To do this, divide the number of moles of each reactant by its corresponding coefficient that balances the equation. The resulting lower number always identifies the limiting reactant. Then use the mole road to solve the problem based on the identified limiting reactant.

$$2C_8H_{18}(l) \; + \; 25O_2(g) \; \longrightarrow \; 16CO_2(g) \; + \; 18H_2O(g)$$

255 g   1510 g   ? g

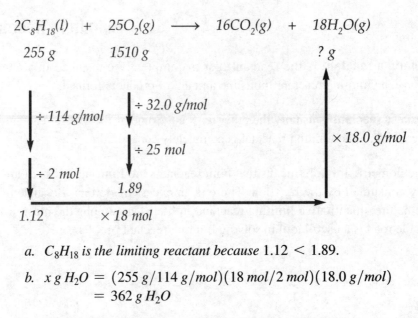

a. C_8H_{18} is the limiting reactant because $1.12 < 1.89$.

b. $x \, g \, H_2O = (255 \, g/114 \, g/mol)(18 \, mol/2 \, mol)(18.0 \, g/mol)$
    $= 362 \, g \, H_2O$

c. $2C_8H_{18}(l) \; + \; 25O_2(g) \; \longrightarrow \; 16CO_2(g) \; + \; 18H_2O(g)$

    255 g   1510 g   ? g

    $? \, g \, O_2 \, react$

    $\div 114 \, g/mol$

    $\times 32.0 \, g/mol$

    $\times 25 \, mol/2 \, mol$

$$x \, g \, O_2 = (255 \, g/114 \, g/mol)(25 \, mol/2 \, mol)(32.0 \, g/mol)$$
$$= 895 \, g \, O_2 \, react$$

d. $g \, O_2 \, left \, unreacted = 1510 \, g - 895 \, g = 615 \, g \, O_2 \, unreacted$

Theoretical, Actual, and Percent Yields

The **theoretical yield** of a reaction is the quantity of product that is calculated to form.

The **actual yield** is the amount of product actually obtained and is usually less than the theoretical yield.

The **percent theoretical yield** relates the actual yield to the theoretical yield:

Percent theoretical yield = (actual yield)/(theoretical yield) × 100

Example:

In the previous example, the theoretical yield of water is calculated to be 362 g. What is the percent yield if the actual yield of water is only 312 g?

Solution:

Percent theoretical yield = 312 g/362 g × 100 = 86.2%

Multiple Choice Questions

1. Ammonia forms when hydrogen gas reacts with nitrogen gas. If equal number of moles of nitrogen and hydrogen are combined, the maximum number of moles of ammonia that could be formed will be equal to

    A) the number of moles of hydrogen

    B) the number of moles of nitrogen

    C) two-thirds the number of moles of hydrogen

    D) twice the number of moles of nitrogen

2. If $C_4H_{10}O$ undergoes complete combustion, what is the sum of the coefficients when the equation is completed and balanced using smallest whole numbers?

    A) 8

    B) 16

    C) 22

    D) 25

3. What are the products when lithium carbonate is heated?

    A) $LiOH + CO_2$

    B) $Li_2O + CO_2$

    C) $LiO + CO_2$

    D) $LiC + O_2$

4. Beginning with 48 moles of H_2, how many moles of $Cu(NH_3)_4Cl_2(aq)$ can be obtained if the synthesis of $Cu(NH_3)_4Cl_2(aq)$ is carried out through the following sequential reactions? Assume that a 50% yield of product(s) is (are) obtained in each reaction.

    1. $3H_2(g) + N_2(g) \rightarrow 2NH_3(g)$

    2. $4NH_3(g) + CuSO_4(aq) \rightarrow Cu(NH_3)_4SO_4(aq)$

    3. $Cu(NH_3)_4SO_4 + 2NaCl \rightarrow Cu(NH_3)_4Cl_2(aq) + Na_2SO_4(aq)$

    A) 1

    B) 2

    C) 4

    D) 8

5. *What mass of water can be obtained from 4.0 g of H_2 and 16 g of O_2?*

$$2H_2(g) + O_2(g) \rightarrow 2H_2O$$

A) 9.0 g

B) 18 g

C) 36 g

D) 54 g

6. *The empirical formula of pyrogallol is C_2H_2O and its molar mass is 126. Its molecular formula is*

A) C_2H_2O

B) $C_4H_4O_2$

C) $C_2H_6O_3$

D) $C_6H_6O_3$

7. *What is the maximum amount of water that can be prepared from the reaction of 20.0 g of HBr with 20.0 g of $Ca(OH)_2$?*

$$2HBr + Ca(OH)_2 \rightarrow CaBr_2 + 2H_2O$$

A) $(20/81)(2/2)(18)$ g

B) $(20/74)(2/2)(18)$ g

C) $(20/81)(2/1)(18)$ g

D) $(20/74)(2/1)(18)$ g

8. *How many moles of ozone, O_3, could be formed from 96.0 g of oxygen gas, O_2?*

A) 0.500

B) 1.00

C) 2.00

D) 3.00

9. *The percentage of oxygen in $C_8H_{12}O_2$ is*

A) $(16/140)(100)$

B) $(32/140)(100)$

C) $(16/124)(100)$

D) $(140/32)(100)$

10. A compound contains 48.0% O, 40.0% Ca, and the remainder is C. What is its empirical formula?

    A) $O_3C_2Ca_2$

    B) O_3CCa_2

    C) O_3CCa

    D) O_3CCa_2

11. Calculate the maximum number of grams of $MgCl_2$ that can be prepared from the reaction of 20.0 g of HCl with 20.0 g of $Mg(OH)_2$.

    A) $(20.0/36.5)(1/2)(58.3)$

    B) $(20.0/36.5)(95.3)$

    C) $(20.0/36.5)(1/2)(95.3)$

    D) $(20.0/58.3)(1/2)(95.3)$

12. Calculate the maximum number of grams of CO_2 that can be produced from 50.0 g each of sulfuric acid and sodium hydrogen carbonate. The unbalanced equation is:
    $$NaHCO_3 + H_2SO_4 \rightarrow CO_2 + H_2O + Na_2SO_4$$

    A) $(50.0/98.0)(1/2)(44.0)$

    B) $(50.0/98.0)(44.0)$

    C) $(50.0/84.0)(2)(44.0)$

    D) $(50.0/84.0)(44.0)$

13. Heating Br_2O_7 causes it to decompose to its gaseous elements. What is the ratio of bromine to oxygen molecules in the product?

    A) 1 to 7

    B) 2 to 7

    C) 7 to 2

    D) 7 to 1

14. A sample of hydrated copper(II) sulfate, $CuSO_4 \cdot X\ H_2O$ weighs 24.95 g. When the water is driven off, the anhydrous form weighs 15.95 g. What is the value of x in the formula of the hydrated salt?

    A) 2

    B) 3

    C) 4

    D) 5

15. *The mass spectrum shown is most likely that of*

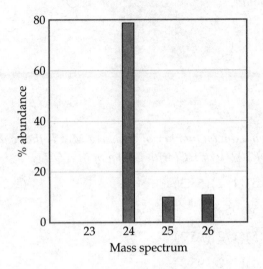

Mass spectrum

A) *magnesium*

B) *sodium*

C) *a mixture of magnesium and sodium*

D) *a mixture of Cr, Mn, and Fe*

Free Response Questions

1. *Combustion of 8.652 g of a compound containing C, H, O, and N yields 11.088 g of CO_2, 3.780 g of H_2O, and 3.864 g of NO_2.*

   a. *How many moles of C, H, and N are contained in the sample?*

   b. *How many grams of oxygen are contained in the sample?*

   c. *What is the simplest formula of the compound?*

   d. *If the molar mass of the compound lies between 200 and 300, what is its molecular formula?*

   e. *Write and balance a chemical equation for the combustion of the compound.*

2. *A student finds that 344.0 g of a pure sample of the mineral gypsum contains 80.00 g of calcium.*

   a. *Show a mathematical calculation to demonstrate that the pure mineral sample does not contain pure calcium sulfate.*

   b. *If gypsum is hydrated calcium sulfate, use the data from the experiment to derive the chemical formula for gypsum. (How many waters of hydration does the formula contain?)*

3. *Decomposition of 36.54 g of a pure solid compound produces 4.06 g of nitrogen gas, 10.44 g of water, and a solid metal oxide. The metal oxide is found to contain 68.42% chromium.*

   a. *What is the simplest formula for the metal oxide?*

   b. *What is the oxidation number of chromium in the oxide?*

   c. *How many moles of each element are present in the unknown compound?*

   d. *What is the simplest formula for the unknown compound?*

   e. *Express the formula of the compound with a common cation–anion pair and name the compound.*

   f. *Write and balance a chemical equation for the decomposition reaction.*

Multiple Choice Answers and Explanations

1. *C. The equation is $3H_2(g) + N_2(g) \rightarrow 2NH_3(g)$. If equal number of moles of reactants are mixed, the limiting reactant is H_2 because the reaction requires three times as much H_2 as it does N_2. The number of moles of ammonia depends on the limiting reactant, H_2, and is two-thirds the amount of H_2 present.*

2. *B. The products of a complete combustion of $C_4H_{10}O$ are carbon dioxide and water. The correctly completed and balanced equation is:*

   $$C_4H_{10}O + 6O_2 \rightarrow 4CO_2 + 5H_2O$$

   The sum of the coefficients is $1 + 6 + 4 + 5 = 16$.

3. *B. Upon heating, a metal carbonate decomposes to a metal oxide and carbon dioxide gas. $Li_2CO_3(s) \rightarrow Li_2O(s) + CO_2(g)$.*

4. *A. Reaction 1 will yield $48(2/3) \times 0.50 = 16$ mol of NH_3. Reaction 2 will yield $16(1/4) \times 0.50 = 2$ mol of $Cu(NH_3)_4SO_4(aq)$. Reaction 3 will yield $2(1/1) \times 0.50 = 1$ mol of $Cu(NH_3)_4Cl_2(aq)$.*

5. *B. 4.0 g H_2 is 2 mol. 16 g O_2 is 0.5 mol. O_2 is the limiting reactant. 0.5 mol of O_2 will produce 1.0 mol H_2O, which is 18 g.*

6. *D. The ratio of the molar mass to the mass of the empirical formula is $126/42 = 3$. This means that the molecular formula has there three times as many atoms as the empirical formula.*

7. *A. The limiting reactant is HBr.*

   $(20.0\ g)/(81g/mol)/2 < (20.0\ g)/(74g/mol)/1.$

   The 20.0 g of HBr will limit how much water will be formed.

   $x\ g\ H_2O = 20.0\ g\ HBr(1\ mol/81g)(2\ mol\ H_2O/2\ mol\ HBr)$

   $(18g/mol)$

8. *C. The balanced equation is: $3O_2(g) \rightarrow 2O_3(g)$*

   $x\ mol\ O_3 = 96.0\ g\ O_2(1\ mol/32.0\ g)(2\ mol\ O_3/3\ mol\ O_2)$

   $= 2.00\ mol$

9. B. $\% O = [(2 \times atomic\ mass\ of\ O)/(molar\ mass\ of\ C_8H_{12}O_2)] \times 100$

$$= (2 \times 16)/(140) \times 100 = (32/140)(100)$$

10. C. The percentage composition is the number of grams of each element contained in 100 g of compound. The percentage of carbon is $100 - 48.0 - 40.0 = 12.0\%$. Convert grams of each atom to moles by dividing by the respective atomic mass.

$O_{48.0/16.0}C_{12.0/12.0}Ca_{40.0/40.0} = O_3C_1Ca_1$

This is calcium carbonate, $CaCO_3$.

11. C. The reaction is: $2HCl + Mg(OH)_2 \rightarrow MgCl_2 + 2H_2O$. The limiting reactant is HCl so the maximum number of grams of magnesium chloride is dependent on the 20.0 grams of HCl.

$x\ g\ MgCl_2 = (20.0\ g\ HCl)(1\ mol/36.5\ g)(1\ mol\ MgCl_2/2\ mol\ HCl)(95.3\ g/mol)$

12. D. The balanced equation is: $2NaHCO_3 + H_2SO_4 \rightarrow 2CO_2 + 2H_2O + Na_2SO_4$
Sodium hydrogen carbonate is the limiting reactant.

$x\ g\ CO_2 = 50.0\ g\ NaHCO_3(1\ mol/84.0\ g)(2\ mol\ CO_2/2\ mol\ NaHCO_3)(44.0\ g/mol)$

13. B. The balanced equation is: $2Br_2O_7(g) \rightarrow 2Br_2(g) + 7O_2(g)$.

14. D. The molar mass of anhydrous $CuSO_4$ is 159.5 g/mol. 15.95 g is 0.100 mol $CuSO_4$. 9.00 grams of water is 0.5 mol water or five times as many moles of water as copper(II) sulfate. The formula of the hydrate is $CuSO_4 \cdot 5H_2O$.

15. A. The mass spectrum shows three isotopes, the weighted average of which would be consistent with the atomic mass of magnesium (24.305 amu). The atomic mass of sodium (22.98977 amu) is lighter than the lightest isotope in the spectrum.

Free Response Answers

1. a. The moles of carbon are equal to the moles of carbon dioxide because there is one mole of C in every mole of CO_2. Divide the grams of CO_2 produced by the molar mass of CO_2 to obtain the moles of carbon. Divide the mass of water by the molar mass of water, and multiply by two, to obtain the moles of hydrogen. Repeat for the moles of N.

$mol\ C = 11.088\ g\ CO_2/44.0\ g/mol = 0.252\ mol\ CO_2$

$= 0.252\ mol\ C$

$mol\ H = 3.780\ g\ H_2O/18.0\ g/mol = 0.210\ mol\ H_2O \times 2$

$= 0.420\ mol\ H$

$mol\ N = 3.864\ g\ NO_2/46.0\ g/mol = 0.0840\ mol\ NO_2$

$= 0.0840\ mol\ N$

b. *To obtain the number of grams of oxygen in the formula, subtract from the given sample mass the number of grams of each of the other elements, C, H, and N. To obtain their masses, multiply the number of moles calculated in Part a by the atomic masses of the respective elements.*

$x \, g \, O = 8.652 \, g \, compound - g \, C - g \, H - g \, N$

$x \, g \, O = 8.652 \, g - (0.252 \, mol \, C \times 12.0 \, g/mol) - (0.420 \, mol \, H$
$\qquad \times \, 1.00 \, g/mol) - (0.0840 \, mol \, N \times 14.0 \, g/mol) = 4.032 \, g \, O$

c. *To obtain the empirical formula, convert the mass of O calculated in Part b to moles by dividing by the atomic mass of oxygen. Then convert each mole quantity to small whole numbers by dividing each by the lowest of the mole quantities.*

$Mol \, O = 4.032 \, g/16.0 \, g/mol = 0.252 \, mol \, O$

$C_{0.252}H_{0.420}N_{0.0840}O_{0.252}$

$C_{0.252/0.0840}H_{0.420/0.0840}N_{0.0840/0.0840}O_{0.252/0.0840}$

$C_3H_5N_1O_3$

d. *To obtain the molecular formula, calculate the molar mass of the empirical formula determined in Part c. Multiply the result by small integers until an integer multiple of the molar mass is a number between 200 and 300. Multiply each subscript in the empirical formula by this integer. Check your work by calculating the molar mass of the resulting molecular formula to see that it lies between 200 and 300 g/mol.*

$Molar \, mass \, of \, C_3 \, H_5 \, N_1 \, O_3 = 3(12.0) + 5(1.00) + 1(14.0)$
$\qquad\qquad + 3(16.0) = 103 \, g/mol$

$2 \times 103 \, g/mol = 206 \, g/mol.$

$C_{3\times2}H_{5\times2}N_{1\times2}O_{3\times2} = C_6 \, H_{10} \, N_2 \, O_6$

e. *Balance in order, C, N, H, and O:*

$2C_6H_{10}N_2O_6 + 15O_2(g) \rightarrow 12CO_2(g) + 10H_2O(g) + 4NO_2(g)$

2. a. *The percentage of calcium in pure $CaSO_4$ is:*

$\% \, Ca = (g \, Ca/g \, CaSO_4)(100) = 40.0 \, g/136.0 \, g = 29.4 \, \%$

The percentage of calcium in the mineral is:
$\% \, Ca = (g \, Ca/g \, mineral)(100) = 80.00 \, g/344.0 \, g = 23.26 \, \%$

The mineral is not pure calcium sulfate because its percentage of calcium is too low.

b. *Hydrated calcium sulfate would have the formula $CaSO_4 \cdot XH_2O$ where X equals the number of water molecules per formula unit. Use the equation for the percentage of calcium in the hydrate to find the molar mass of the hydrate:*

$\% \, Ca = (g \, Ca/g \, mineral)(100)$

$23.26 = (40.0 \, g \, Ca/molar \, mass \, of \, CaSO_4 \cdot XH_2O)(100)$

Molar mass of $CaSO_4 \cdot XH_2O = (40.0)(100)/23.26$
   $= 172.0$ g/mol

Mass of H_2O in 172.0 g of $CaSO_4 \cdot XH_2O = 172.0$
   $- 136.0$ g $CaSO_4 = 36.0$ g H_2O

36.0 g H_2O represents exactly 2 mol H_2O so each formula unit of
$CaSO_4 \cdot XH_2O$ contains two moles of water: $CaSO_4 \cdot 2H_2O$

3.   a. $\%O = 100 - 68.42 = 31.58\%$ O

$Cr_{68.42/52.0} O_{31.58/16.0} = Cr_{1.316} O_{1.974}$

$Cr_{1.316/1.316} O_{1.974/1.316} = Cr_1 O_{1.5} = Cr_2O_3$

b. $2(3 +) + 3(2 -) = 0$ $Cr = 3+$

c.   g metal oxide $= 36.54$ g $- 10.44$ g $- 4.06$ g $= 22.04$ g

   mol Cr $= (22.04$ g$)(0.6842$ g Cr/g oxide$)(1$ mol/52.0 g$) = 0.290$ mol Cr
   mol O $=$ mol O from oxide $+$ mol O from water
   mol O $= (22.04$ g$)(0.3158$ g O/g oxide$)(1$ mol/16.0 g$) + (10.44$ g/18.0 g/mol$)$
     $= 0.435 + 0.580 = 1.02$ mol O
   mol H $= (10.44$ g H_2O/18.0 g/mol$) \times (2$ mol H/mol $H_2O) = 1.16$ mol H
   mol N $= (4.06$ g N$)(1$ mol/14.0 g$) = 0.290$ mol N

d. $Cr_{0.290/0.290} O_{1.02/0.290} H_{1.16/0.290} N_{0.290/0.290} = Cr_1 O_{3.52} H_4 N_1 = Cr_2O_7H_8N_2$

e. Cr_2O_7 suggests the dichromate ion, $Cr_2O_7^{2-}$.

   H_8N_2 comprises two ammonium ions, NH_4^+.

   $(NH_4)_2 Cr_2O_7$, Ammonium dichromate.

f. $(NH_4)_2 Cr_2O_7 \rightarrow N_2 + 4H_2O + Cr_2O_3$

Your Turn Answers

3.1. One molecule of gaseous carbon dioxide reacts with two molecules of ammonia gas and one molecule of liquid water to produce two aqueous ammonium ions and one aqueous carbonate ion.

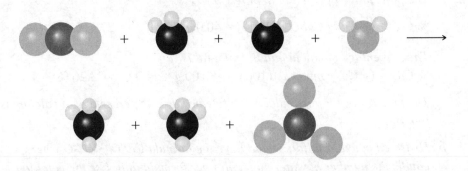

3.2. $3Mg(s) + N_2(g) \rightarrow Mg_3N_2(s)$

3.3. $2H_2O(l) \rightarrow 2H_2(g) + O_2(g)$

3.4. $2C_6H_{14}(l) + 19O_2(g) \rightarrow 12CO_2(g) + 14H_2O(l)$

Alternatively: $C_6H_{14}(l) + 19/2\, O_2(g) \rightarrow 6CO_2(g) + 7H_2O(l)$

AQUEOUS REACTIONS AND SOLUTION STOICHIOMETRY

The content in this topic is the basis for mastering Learning Objectives 3.2, 3.3, 3.4, 3.8, and 3.9 as found in the Curriculum Framework.

You may have learned some of this material in first-year chemistry. When you finish reviewing this topic, be sure you are able to:

- Distinguish chemical formulas as strong, weak, and nonelectrolytes
- Identify the formulas of strong and weak acids
- Write chemical equations for the ionization of strong and weak acids and bases
- Write balanced net ionic equations for precipitation reactions, neutralization reactions, and reactions between acids and bases
- Identify redox reactions and the electron transfer in redox reactions
- Use an activity series to write balanced net ionic equations for redox reactions between metals and metal ions
- Assign oxidation numbers to elements in a chemical formula
- Perform limiting reactant and solution stoichiometry calculations
- Interpret the results of a redox titration

General Properties of Aqueous Solutions
Section 4.1

A **solution** is a homogeneous mixture of two or more substances.

A **solvent** is the dissolving medium, usually the substance present in the greatest quantity in a solution.

Aqueous solutions are solutions in which water is the solvent.

Solutes are other substances in the solution.

An **electrolyte** is a substance whose aqueous solution contains ions. The solution conducts electricity because the ions are free to migrate throughout the solution.

Strong electrolytes are substances that exist in solution, completely ionized. Ionic compounds and some molecular compounds called strong acids are strong electrolytes. For example, when solid sodium chloride dissolves in water, the ions dissociate completely:

$$NaCl(s) \rightarrow Na^+(aq) + Cl^-(aq)$$

Similarly, the **strong acid**, sulfuric acid, H_2SO_4, ionizes completely in aqueous solution:

$$H_2SO_4(l) \rightarrow H^+(aq) + HSO_4^-(aq)$$

Strong bases, such as potassium hydroxide, also dissociate completely:

$$KOH(s) \rightarrow K^+(aq) + OH^-(aq)$$

Your Turn 4.1 ←————————————————————————————

Write an equation for the ionization of gaseous hydrogen chloride in water. Write your answer in the space provided.

Table 4.1 lists the names and formulas of common strong acids and strong bases.

Table 4.1 The names and formulas of common strong acids and strong bases.

Strong Acids		Strong Bases	
sulfuric acid*	H_2SO_4	lithium hydroxide	LiOH
nitric acid	HNO_3	sodium hydroxide	NaOH
perchloric acid	$HClO_4$	potassium hydroxide	KOH
chloric acid	$HClO_3$	rubidium hydroxide	RbOH
hydrochloric acid	HCl	cesium hydroxide	CsOH
hydrobromic acid	HBr	calcium hydroxide**	$Ca(OH)_2$
hydroiodic acid	HI	strontium hydroxide**	$Sr(OH)_2$
		barium hydroxide**	$Ba(OH)_2$

*Sulfuric acid is a diprotic acid (it has two H^+ ions), and only the first H^+ ion ionizes completely.

**$Ca(OH)_2$, $Sr(OH)_2$, and $Ba(OH)_2$ are dibasic (they each have two OH^- ions).

Common misconception: The terms "ionize" and "dissociate" are often used interchangeably by many texts, even though their meanings differ in a subtle way. Both imply that ions exist in solution when a solute dissolves. When an ionic compound dissolves, dissociation of ions already present occurs. An electrolyte that is a covalent compound ionizes in solution because the ions are not present in the pure compound.

Weak electrolytes exist mostly as molecules in solution, with a small fraction in the form of ions. Molecular compounds called weak acids and weak bases are weak electrolytes. For example, acetic acid, CH_3COOH, and ammonia, NH_3, are weak electrolytes. Only about 1% or less of each molecular compound's molecules ionize in aqueous solution. The percent dissociation is concentration dependent.

$$CH_3COOH(l) \rightarrow H^+(aq) + CH_3COO^-(aq)$$
$$NH_3(g) + H_2O(l) \rightarrow NH_4^+(aq) + OH^-(aq)$$

A **nonelectrolyte** is a substance that does not form ions in solution and its solution does not conduct electricity. A nonelectrolyte usually consists of a molecular compound, which when dissolved in water, usually consists of intact, un-ionized molecules. For example, when ethanol dissolves in water, its molecules remain intact:

$$CH_3CH_2OH(l) \rightarrow CH_3CH_2OH(aq)$$

Your Turn 4.2

Classify each of these compounds as strong, weak, or nonelectrolytes: calcium chloride; ammonium sulfate; hydrocyanic acid, HCN; glucose, $C_6H_{12}O_6$. Explain your reasoning. Write your answer in the space provided.

Precipitation Reactions

Section 4.2

A **precipitate** is an insoluble solid formed by a reaction in solution. For example, aqueous lead(II) nitrate reacts with aqueous sodium bromide to form solid lead(II) bromide and sodium nitrate. The **complete equation** for the reaction is:

$$Pb(NO_3)_2(aq) + 2NaBr(aq) \rightarrow PbBr_2(s) + 2NaNO_3(aq)$$

If the soluble strong electrolytes are shown as ions, a more accurate representation of the reaction is a **complete ionic equation**:

$$Pb^{2+}(aq) + 2NO_3^-(aq) + 2Na^+(aq) + 2Br^-(aq) \rightarrow$$
$$PbBr_2(s) + 2Na^+(aq) + 2NO_3^-(aq)$$

Spectator ions are ions that appear in identical form among both reactants and products of a complete ionic equation.

A **net ionic equation** omits spectator ions because they do not change from reactants to products:

$$Pb^{2+}(aq) + 2Br^-(aq) \rightarrow PbBr_2(s)$$

Predicting Products of Precipitation Reactions

To predict the products of precipitation reactions and to write their net ionic equations, use the following simplified guidelines:

The cations and anions that generally do not form precipitates are:

ammonium	sodium	potassium	and	nitrate
NH_4^+	Na^+	K^+		NO_3^-

Therefore, the formulas of precipitates will not contain these four ions. There are no common exceptions. Ammonium, sodium, potassium, and nitrate ions are usually spectator ions in aqueous solution.

When predicting the products of precipitation reactions and writing their net ionic equations, apply the rules in Table 4.2. Make sure that the formulas for any precipitates never contain the above ions.

Table 4.2 General rules for writing net ionic equations.

1.	Write all the reactants that are indicated to be solids (s), liquids (l), or gases (g).
2.	Rewrite the formulas of the aqueous reactants, omitting the spectator ions (NH_4^+, Na^+, K^+, and NO_3^-).
3.	Predict and write the product(s).
4.	If necessary, use ions to balance the mass and charge. Then balance using coefficients. Check to see if the charges are balanced.

Examples:

Write a net ionic equation for each of the following laboratory situations. Assume a reaction occurs in all cases. (Note: Although the Advanced Placement Exam does not require students to show the phases of reactants or products [g, l, s, aq], the phases are indicated in these examples for clarity.)

a. *Aqueous solutions of silver nitrate and sodium phosphate are mixed.*

> **Solution:**
>
> *1. No solids, liquids, or gases are indicated as reactants.*
>
> *2. Nitrate and sodium ions are spectator ions, so omit them.*
>
> $$Ag^+(aq) + PO_4^{3-}(aq)$$
>
> *3. To predict the product, combine the ions to make a correct formula.*
>
> $$Ag^+(aq) + PO_4^{3-}(aq) \rightarrow Ag_3PO_4(s)$$
>
> *4. The Ag^+ ion requires a coefficient of 3 to balance the mass and charge:*
>
> $$3Ag^+(aq) + PO_4^{3-}(aq) \rightarrow Ag_3PO_4(s)$$

b. *Aqueous copper(II) nitrate is added to solid sodium carbonate.*

> **Solution:**
>
> *1. Sodium carbonate is the only solid indicated.*
>
> $$Na_2CO_3(s)$$
>
> *2. Omit nitrate, a spectator ion.*
>
> $$Na_2CO_3(s) + Cu^{2+}(aq)$$
>
> *3. Because sodium compounds are soluble, copper(II) ion replaces sodium ion.*
>
> $$Na_2CO_3(s) + Cu^{2+}(aq) \rightarrow CuCO_3(s)$$
>
> *4. Two sodium ions added to the right side of the equation balances the mass and charge. Notice that, in this case, Na^+ is not a spectator ion because it changes form from solid to aqueous during the reaction.*
>
> $$Na_2CO_3(s) + Cu^{2+}(aq) \rightarrow CuCO_3(s) + 2Na^+(aq)$$

c. *Hydrogen chloride gas is bubbled through an aqueous solution of lead(II) nitrate.*

> **Solution:**
>
> *1. The statement identifies HCl as a gas.*
>
> $$HCl(g)$$
>
> *2. Nitrate is a spectator ion.*
>
> $$HCl(g) + Pb^{2+}(aq)$$
>
> *3. Combine lead(II) and chloride ions to form a precipitate.*
>
> $$HCl(g) + Pb^{2+}(aq) \rightarrow PbCl_2(s)$$
>
> *4. Place two H^+ ions on the right side of the equation to balance the mass and charge.*
>
> $$2HCl(g) + Pb^{2+}(aq) \rightarrow PbCl_2(s) + 2H^+(aq)$$

Your Turn 4.3

← ─────────────────────────────────

Write a net ionic equation for the reaction of aqueous sodium carbonate with solid nickel(II) nitrate. Write your answer in the space provided.

Section 4.3

Acids, Bases, and Neutralization Reactions

Acids are substances that ionize in aqueous solution to form H^+ ions.

Bases are substances that react with H^+ ions.

Strong acids and strong bases are strong electrolytes. They completely ionize in solution. Table 4.1 lists the names and formulas of common strong acids and bases.

Weak acids and bases are weak electrolytes. They ionize only slightly in water solution. For example, a neutralization reaction between an acid and a metal hydroxide produces water and a salt:

Complete equation:

$$Ca(OH)_2(s) + 2HNO_3(aq) \rightarrow 2H_2O(l) + Ca(NO_3)_2(aq)$$

Net ionic equation:

$$Ca(OH)_2(s) + 2H^+(aq) \rightarrow 2H_2O(l) + Ca^{2+}(aq)$$

To predict the products of acid–base reactions and to write their net ionic equations, keep in mind that water is usually a product of neutralization reactions and apply the rules in Table 4.2 for writing net ionic equations. Because strong acids and bases are strong electrolytes, their ions are usually spectator ions in acid–base reactions.

Examples:

Write a net ionic equation for each of the following laboratory situations. Assume a reaction occurs in all cases.

a. Aqueous hydrochloric acid is mixed with a solution of sodium hydroxide.

Solution:

1. *Neither reactant is indicated as a solid, liquid, or gas.*

2. *Both chloride (hydrochloric acid is a strong electrolyte) and sodium ions are spectator ions.*

$$H^+(aq) + OH^-(aq)$$

3. Water is a product of a neutralization reaction.

$$H^+(aq) + OH^-(aq) \rightarrow H_2O(l)$$

b. Gaseous hydrogen chloride is bubbled through a solution of sodium hydroxide.

Solution:

1. HCl is indicated as a gas.

$$HCl(g)$$

2. Sodium ion is a spectator ion.

$$HCl(g) + OH^-(aq)$$

3. Water is a product of a neutralization reaction.

$$HCl(g) + OH^-(aq) \rightarrow H_2O(l)$$

4. One chloride ion on the right side of the equation balances the mass and charge.

$$HCl(g) + OH^-(aq) \rightarrow H_2O(l) + Cl^-(aq)$$

Notice that the reactants in Questions a and b are the same but, because of the difference in phase of hydrochloric acid, the net ionic equations are different.

c. Solid potassium hydroxide is mixed with aqueous sulfurous acid.

Solution:

1. KOH is identified as a solid.

$$KOH(s)$$

2. Sulfurous acid is a weak acid (it does not appear on the list of strong acids in Table 4.1), so it is shown in its molecular form.

$$KOH(s) + H_2SO_3(aq)$$

3. Water is a product of a neutralization reaction.

$$KOH(s) + H_2SO_3 \rightarrow H_2O(l)$$

4. When the H^+ ion of the acid reacts with the base, free sulfite ion is a product and $2K^+$ are needed to balance the mass and charge.

$$2KOH(s) + H_2SO_3 \rightarrow 2H_2O(l) + 2K^+(aq) + SO_3^{2-}(aq)$$

(Note: Because this problem does not specify the relative amounts of acid and base added, it is also correct to assume a one-to-one mole ratio. The following equation is also acceptable:

$$KOH(s) + H_2SO_3 \rightarrow H_2O(l) + K^+(aq) + HSO_3^-(aq))$$

Your Turn 4.4

Write a net ionic equation for the reaction of aqueous potassium hydroxide with aqueous acetic acid. Write your answer in the space provided.

Acid–Base Reactions and Gas Formation

Ionic compounds containing carbonate, sulfite, or sulfide ions produce gases when they react with acids.

Metal carbonates and metal hydrogen carbonates react with acids to produce carbon dioxide gas and water.

Complete equation: $NaHCO_3(aq) + HBr(aq) \rightarrow CO_2(g) + H_2O(l) + NaBr(aq)$

Net ionic equation: $HCO_3^-(aq) + H^+(aq) \rightarrow CO_2(g) + H_2O(l)$

Complete equation: $Na_2CO_3(s) + 2HCl(aq) \rightarrow CO_2(g) + H_2O(l) + 2NaCl(aq)$

Net ionic equation: $Na_2CO_3(s) + 2H^+(aq) \rightarrow CO_2(g) + H_2O(l) + 2Na^+(aq)$

Examples:

Write a net ionic equation for each of the following laboratory situations. Assume a reaction occurs in all cases.
a. Calcium hydrogen carbonate solid is added to an aqueous solution of acetic acid.

Solution:

1. Calcium hydrogen carbonate is identified as a solid.

$Ca(HCO_3)_2(s)$

2. Acetic acid is a weak acid because it is not listed among the strong acids in Table 4.1. So it is written in molecular form.

$Ca(HCO_3)_2(s) + CH_3COOH(aq)$

3. The products are carbon dioxide and water.

$Ca(HCO_3)_2(s) + CH_3COOH(aq) \rightarrow CO_2(g) + H_2O(l)$

4. *Calcium ions and acetate ions are needed to balance the mass and charge.*

$$Ca(HCO_3)_2(s) + 2CH_3COOH(aq) \rightarrow 2CO_2(g) + 2H_2O(l) +$$

$$Ca^{2+}(aq) + 2CH_3COO^-(aq)$$

b. *Gaseous hydrogen chloride is bubbled through an aqueous solution of potassium carbonate.*

Solution:

1. *HCl is identified as a gas.*

$$HCl(g)$$

2. *Potassium ion is a spectator ion.*

$$HCl(g) + CO_3^{2-}(aq)$$

3. *The products are carbon dioxide gas and water.*

$$HCl(g) + CO_3^{2-}(aq) \rightarrow CO_2(g) + H_2O(l)$$

4. *Balance the mass and charge using two molecules of HCl and two chloride ions.*

$$2HCl(g) + CO_3^{2-}(aq) \rightarrow CO_2(g) + H_2O(l) + 2Cl^-(aq)$$

Your Turn 4.5

Write a net ionic equation for the reaction of aqueous nitric acid with solid lithium carbonate. Write your answer in the space provided.

Oxidation–Reduction Reactions

Section 4.4

Oxidation–reduction reactions (also called **redox reactions**) are reactions that transfer electrons between reactants.

For example, acids react with active metals to produce hydrogen gas.

An acid reacts with a metal to produce hydrogen gas:

Complete equation:

$$2HNO_3(aq) + 2Na(s) \rightarrow H_2(g) + 2NaNO_3(aq)$$

Net ionic equation:

$$2H^+(aq) + 2Na(s) \rightarrow H_2(g) + 2Na^+(aq)$$

In the reaction, electrons are transferred from sodium atoms to hydrogen ions. The sodium atoms lose one electron each to become sodium ions. The hydrogen ions gain one electron each to become a diatomic hydrogen molecule.

Oxidation is the loss of electrons. In this case, sodium atoms lose electrons and are oxidized.

Reduction is the gain of electrons. In this case, hydrogen ions gain electrons and are reduced.

Metals also react with metal ions to exchange electrons:

Complete equation:

$$Mg(s) + Zn(NO_3)_2(aq) \rightarrow Mg(NO_3)_2(aq) + Zn(s)$$

Net ionic equation:

$$Mg(s) + Zn^{2+}(aq) \rightarrow Mg^{2+}(aq) + Zn(s)$$

The metal is oxidized and the metal ion is reduced.

An **activity series** is a list of metals arranged in order of decreasing ease of oxidation. Any metal on the list can be oxidized by ions below it. Table 4.3 shows an activity series for metals in aqueous solution. Notice that the metals copper, silver, and gold are below the $H_2 \rightarrow 2H^+$ reaction. This means that Cu, Ag, and Au will not dissolve in acid solution, whereas other metals listed will react with acids.

Table 4.3 An activity series. Metals at the top of the list are most likely to be oxidized (lose electrons).

Li(s)	$\rightarrow$	Li$^+$	(aq)	+	1 e$^-$
K(s)	$\rightarrow$	K$^+$	(aq)	+	1 e$^-$
Ca(s)	$\rightarrow$	Ca^{2+}	(aq)	+	2 e$^-$
Na(s)	$\rightarrow$	Na$^+$	(aq)	+	1 e$^-$
Mg(s)	$\rightarrow$	Mg^{2+}	(aq)	+	2 e$^-$
Al(s)	$\rightarrow$	Al^{3+}	(aq)	+	3 e$^-$
Zn(s)	$\rightarrow$	Zn^{2+}	(aq)	+	2 e$^-$
Fe(s)	$\rightarrow$	Fe^{2+}	(aq)	+	2 e$^-$
Ni(s)	$\rightarrow$	Ni^{2+}	(aq)	+	2 e$^-$
Pb(s)	$\rightarrow$	Pb^{2+}	(aq)	+	2 e$^-$
H$_2$(g)	$\rightarrow$	2H$^+$	(aq)	+	2 e$^-$
Cu(s)	$\rightarrow$	Cu^{2+}	(aq)	+	2 e$^-$
Ag(s)	$\rightarrow$	Ag$^+$	(aq)	+	1 e$^-$
Au(s)	$\rightarrow$	Au^{3+}	(aq)	+	3 e$^-$

$\longrightarrow$ *Your Turn 4.6*

Aluminum metal and nickel metal are placed in a solution containing 1.0 M
$Ni(NO_3)_2$ *and 1.0 M* $Al(NO_3)_3$. *Write a net ionic equation for the reaction that will*
ensue. Tell which reactant loses electrons and which gains electrons. Write your
answer in the space provided.

Oxidation state, also called **oxidation number**, is a positive or negative whole number
assigned to an element in a chemical formula based on a set of formal rules. The
oxidation state is used to track electron transfer in redox reactions. Table 4.4 lists the
rules for assigning oxidation numbers to elements in chemical formulas.

Table 4.4 Simplified rules for determining oxidation numbers.

1.	The oxidation number of combined oxygen is usually $2-$, except in the peroxide ion, O_2^{2-}, where the oxidation number of oxygen is $1-$.
	Examples: In H_2O and H_2SO_4, the oxidation state of oxygen is $2-$. In H_2O_2 and BaO_2, O is $1-$.
2.	The oxidation number of combined hydrogen is usually $1+$, except in the hydride ion, H^-, where it is $1-$.
	Examples: In H_2O and H_2SO_4, the oxidation state of hydrogen is $1+$. In NaH and CaH_2, H is $1-$.
3.	The oxidation numbers of all individual atoms of a formula add to the charge on that formula. When in doubt, separate ionic compounds into common cation–anion pairs.
	Examples:

$$O_2 \quad Na \quad K^+ \quad Cl_2 \quad Ca^{2+} \quad H_2SO_4 \quad NO_3^- \quad Mg_3(PO_4)_2 = Mg^{2+} \quad PO_4^{3-}$$
$$0 \quad\ 0 \quad 1+ \quad\ 0 \quad\ 2+ \quad 1+6+2- \quad 5+2- \quad\ 2+5+2- \quad\ 2+ \quad\ 5+2-$$

Your Turn 4.7

What is the oxidation number of each atom in potassium aluminum sulfate,
$KAl(SO_4)_2$? Write your answer in the space provided.

Section 4.5

Concentrations of Solutions

A **solution** is a homogeneous mixture consisting of a solvent and one or more solutes.

Concentration is the amount solute dissolved in a given amount of solvent or solution.

Molar concentration, also called **molarity** (abbreviated M), is the number of moles of solute dissolved in a liter of solution.

Molarity = moles of solute/volume of solution in liters

For example, 1.5 M $Na_3PO_4(aq)$ means that every liter of solution contains 1.5 moles of sodium phosphate.

Because Na_3PO_4 is a strong electrolyte, its ions dissociate completely in aqueous solution:

$$Na_3PO_4(s) \rightarrow 3Na^+(aq) + PO_4^{3-}(aq)$$

A 1.00 M solution of Na_3PO_4 contains 3.00 M Na^+ ions and 1.00 M PO_4^{3-} ions.

Dilution, adding water to a solution, decreases the molar concentration of each substance in the solution by a factor called the dilution factor. The dilution factor is the ratio of the original volume to the new volume.

> **Example:**
> Enough water is added to 500 mL of 1.00 M Na_3PO_4 to make the final volume 800 mL. What are the molar concentrations of each ion upon dilution?

> **Solution:**
> 1.00 M Na_3PO_4 = 3.00 M Na^+ ions and 1.00 M PO_4^{3-} ions.
> $(3.00 \, M \, Na^+ \, ions)(500 \, mL/800 \, mL) = 1.88 \, M \, Na^+$.
> $(1.00 \, M \, PO_4^{3-} \, ions)(500 \, mL/800 \, mL) = 0.625 \, M \, PO_4^{3-}$.

Figure 4.1 illstrates a laboratory procedure for diluting a copper(II) sulfate solution.

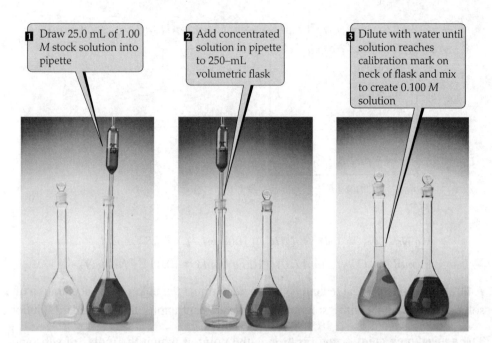

Figure 4.1 Preparing 250.0 mL of 0.100 M $CuSO_4$ by dilution of 1.00 M $CuSO_4$

Solution Stoichiometry and Chemical Analysis   Section 4.6

Solution stoichiometry involves calculations that relate moles of reactants and products to the volumes of solutions and their molar concentrations. Figure 4.2 illustrates the mole road for converting grams, moles, molarity, and liters.

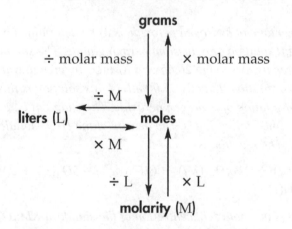

Figure 4.2 Converting moles, grams, molarity, and liters.

Example:

How many grams of solid sodium carbonate are in a sample if it takes 30.5 mL of 0.254 M hydrochloric acid to completely react with the sample?

Solution:

Write and balance a chemical equation, convert mL to L by dividing by 1000, and then follow the road map to the solution.

$$2HCl(aq) + Na_2CO_3(s) \longrightarrow CO_2(g) + H_2O(l) + 2NaCl(aq)$$

30.5 mL = ? g $Na_2CO_3(s)$

.0305 L

× 0.254 M   × 106 g/mol

× 1 mol Na_2CO_3

moles   2 mol HCl   mol Na_2CO_3
HCl

$$x \ g \ Na_2CO_3 = (30.5 \ mL \ HCl)(1000 \ mL/L)(0.254 \ mol/L)$$
$$(1 \ mol \ Na_2CO_3/2 \ mol \ HCl)(106 \ g/mol) = 0.411 \ g \ Na_2CO_3$$

A **titration** is an analytical technique used to determine the unknown concentration of a solution by reacting it with a solution of known concentration called a standard solution.

The **equivalence point** of the titration is the point at which the moles of substance dissolved in the unknown solution completely react with the moles of substance in the standard solution.

The **endpoint** is the point at which an indicator changes color. The endpoint is designed to coincide closely to the equivalence point. From the results of the experiment the concentration of the unknown solution can be calculated.

Example:

The percentage of hydrogen peroxide is to be determined by titration with a standard solution of potassium permanganate. The standard solution is prepared by dissolving 20.65 g of $KMnO_4$ in enough water to make 500 mL of solution. Exactly 25.00 mL of this solution is titrated with an unknown solution of hydrogen peroxide. The endpoint is reached upon addition of 34.05 mL of H_2O_2. The density of the H_2O_2 solution is 1.05 g per milliliter. The reaction is:

$$5H_2O_2(aq) + 2MnO_4^-(aq) + 6H^+(aq) \rightarrow 5O_2(g) + 2Mn^{2+}(aq) + 8H_2O(l)$$

a. *What is the molar concentration of the standard $KMnO_4$ solution?*
b. *What is the molar concentration of the H_2O_2 solution?*
c. *How many grams of H_2O_2 are used in the experiment?*
d. *What is the percent of hydrogen peroxide in the solution?*

Solution:

a. *Molarity of $KMnO_4$ solution = moles of $KMnO_4$/liters solution*
   = (20.65 g/158.0 g/mol)/0.5000 L = 0.2614 M $KMnO_4$
b. *Follow the mole road from 25.00 mL of $KMnO_4$ solution to molarity of H_2O_2 solution:*

$$5H_2O_2(aq) + 2MnO_4^-(aq) + 6H^+(aq) \longrightarrow 5O_2(g) + 2Mn^{2+}(aq) + 8H_2O(l)$$

25.00 mL

? g

$\times$ 1 L $\div$ 1000 mL

L

$\times$ 34.0 g/mol $\times$ 0.2614 mol/L   (M)

$\times$ 5 mol

mol $\longleftarrow$ ——— mol

2 mol

$\div$ 0.03405 L

? M

Molarity of H_2O_2 =
   (25.00 mL/1000 mL/L)(0.2614 mol/L)(5 mol H_2O_2/
   2 mol MnO_4^-)/(0.03405 L) = 0.4798 M
c. *On the road map, go from moles of H_2O_2 to grams of H_2O_2.*
   (25.00/1000)(0.2614)(5/2) mol H_2O_2 (34.0 g/mol) = 0.555 g H_2O_2
d. *g solution = 34.05 mL × 1.05 g/mL = 35.8 g*
   % H_2O_2 = (0.555 g H_2O_2/35.8 g solution)(100) = 1.55% H_2O_2

Multiple Choice Questions

1. Which of the following elements should react most readily with acid?

   A) potassium

   B) calcium

   C) gold

   D) copper

2. The collection of ions, all of whose members do not commonly form precipitates, is

   A) $Hg_2^{2+}, Ag^+, Pb^{2+}, Ba^{2+}$

   B) $PO_4^{3-}, OH^-, S^{2-}, CO_3^{2-}$

   C) $NO_3^-, Na^+, K^+, NH_4^+$

   D) $SO_4^{2-}, Cl^-, Br^-, I^-$

3. Which substance will NOT form a gas upon mixing with an aqueous acid?

   A) $NaHCO_3(s)$

   B) $Mg(s)$

   C) $Al_2O_3(s)$

   D) $K_2CO_3(s)$

4. Which metal will NOT react with aqueous hydrochloric acid?

   A) Fe

   B) Al

   C) Cu

   D) K

5. How many milliliters of 0.40 M $FeBr_3$ solution would be necessary to precipitate all of the Ag^+ from 30 mL of a 0.40 M $AgNO_3$ solution?

   $$FeBr_3(aq) + 3AgNO_3(aq) \rightarrow Fe(NO_3)_3(aq) + 3AgBr(s)$$

   A) 10

   B) 20

   C) 30

   D) 60

6. How many grams of baking soda, sodium hydrogen carbonate, are required to completely neutralize 1.00 L of 6.00 M sulfuric acid that has been spilled on the floor?

   A) (1/6.00) (2/1) (84.0)

   B) (6.00) (84.0)

   C) (6.00) (2/1)/(84.0)

   D) (6.00) (2/1) (84.0)

7. It takes 37.50 mL of 0.152 M sodium chromate to titrate 25.00 mL of silver nitrate. What is the molarity of the silver nitrate solution?

A) (2) (37.50) (0.152) (25.00)

B) (25.00)/(37.50) (0.152) (2)

C) (2) (37.50) (0.152)/(25.00)

D) (37.50) (0.152)/(25.00)

8. Which substance will react with acid, at room temperature and pressure, to produce carbon dioxide gas?

A) Mg

B) $NaHCO_3$

C) CH_3COOH

D) NaOH

9. What is the net ionic equation for the reaction of aqueous solutions of $CaCl_2$ and Na_2CO_3?

A) $Ca^{2+}(aq) + 2Cl^-(aq) + 2Na^+(aq) + CO_3^{2-}(aq) \rightarrow CaCO_3(s) + 2Na^+(aq) + 2Cl^-(aq)$

B) $Cl^-(aq) + Na^+(aq) \rightarrow NaCl(s)$

C) $Ca^{2+}(aq) + CO_3^{2-}(aq) \rightarrow CaCO_3(s)$

D) $Ca^{2+}(aq) + Na_2CO_3(aq) \rightarrow CaCO_3(s) + 2Na^+(aq)$

10. Magnesium burns in carbon dioxide to produce carbon and magnesium oxide. What is the ratio of carbon to magnesium oxide in the products?

A) 1:1

B) 2:1

C) 1:2

D) 2:3

Questions 11–15 refer to the following aqueous solutions.

A) 0.1 M Na_3PO_4

B) 0.2 M NH_4Cl

C) 0.1 M CH_3CH_2OH

D) 0.1 M HNO_3

11. Which solution has a pH of approximately 7?

12. Which solution will cause a solution of sodium hydrogen carbonate to effervesce?

13. Which solution is basic?

14. Which solution will react with an equal molar amount of hydrochloric acid to form a weakly basic solution?

15. Which solution will form a water-soluble gas upon reaction with sodium hydroxide?

Free Response Questions

1. *A student accidentally spills a 1.00 L bottle of concentrated 18.0 M sulfuric acid on the floor of the laboratory. She attempts to neutralize the spill by pouring a 5.00 kg box baking soda, sodium hydrogen carbonate, onto the acid.*

   a. *Write a balanced net ionic equation for the reaction. Assume the concentrated sulfuric acid is 100% pure and not in aqueous solution.*

   b. *What is the limiting reactant?*

   c. *How many grams of sodium hydrogen carbonate are required to neutralize all the acid?*

   d. *How many moles of excess reactant remain after all the limiting reactant has been consumed?*

   e. *Would a floor consisting of bare concrete require more, less, or the same amount of baking soda to neutralize the spill? Explain.*

2. *Three unknown metals are labeled A, B, and C. One is silver, one is zinc, and the other is nickel. Using only aqueous solutions of 0.50 M iron(II) nitrate and 1.0 M hydrochloric acid, write a short, concise experimental procedure, the results of which will be sufficient to identify each of the unknown metals. Tell what you would expect to see and what it means. Write net ionic equations to illustrate your answers.*

Multiple Choice Answers and Explanations

1. *A. Because they are near the top of the activity series, alkali metals are highly reactive with acid. Alkaline earth metals are less reactive. Copper and gold do not react with acid.*

   $$2K(s) + 2H^+(aq) \rightarrow 2K^+(aq) + H_2(g)$$

2. *C. NO_3^-, Na^+, K^+, and NH_4^+ form no common precipitates.*

3. *C. Upon reaction with acids:*

   Carbonates and hydrogen carbonates produce carbon dioxide gas:

   $$HCO_3^-(aq) + H^+(aq) \rightarrow CO_2(g) + H_2O(l)$$
   $$CO_3^{2-}(aq) + 2H^+(aq) \rightarrow CO_2(g) + H_2O(l)$$

   Active metals (above H_2 on the activity series) produce hydrogen gas:

   $$Ca(s) + 2H^+(aq) \rightarrow H_2(g) + Ca^{2+}(aq)$$

   Metal oxides are usually bases:

   $$Al_2O_3(s) + 6H^+(aq) \rightarrow 2Al^{3+}(aq) + 3H_2O(l)$$

4. *C. Metals above hydrogen on the activity series will react with H^+ in aqueous acids to give hydrogen gas and a corresponding metal ion.*

   $$M(s) + 2H^+(aq) \rightarrow H_2(g) + M^{2+}(aq)$$

Metals below hydrogen on the same table will not react with H^+. Copper is the only metal listed that is below hydrogen on the activity series or the table of standard reduction potentials.

5. **A.** *$FeBr_3$ delivers three Br^- ions per mole of $FeBr_3$, so it would take one-third of the volume of $AgNO_3$ to completely precipitate the Ag^+ ions.*
   $1/3 \times 30\ mL = 10\ mL$. (Note: No calculators are permitted on the multiple choice section, and a calculator is not needed to solve this simple ratio.)

   Using the mole road: $mL\ FeBr_3 = (30\ mL\ AgNO_3/1000\ mL/L)(0.40\ mol/L)$
   $(1\ mol\ FeBr_3/3\ mol\ AgNO_3)(1\ L/0.40\ mol)(1000\ mL/L) = 1/3 \times 30\ mL$

6. **D.** *The balanced equation and the corresponding mole road solution are:*

   $$H_2SO_4(aq) + 2NaHCO_3(s) \longrightarrow CO_2(g) + H_2O(l) + Na_2SO_4(aq)$$

   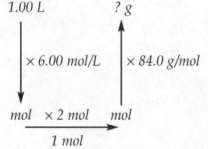

   $g\ NaHCO_3(s) = (1.00\ L)(6.00\ mol/L)(2\ mol/1\ mol)(84.0\ g/mol)$

7. **C.** *The balanced equation and the mole road solution are:*

   $$2AgNO_3(aq) + Na_2CrO_4(aq) \longrightarrow Ag_2CrO_4(s) + 2NaNO_3(aq)$$

   ? M   37.50 mL

   $\uparrow \div 25.00\ mL$ $\downarrow \times 0.152\ mmol/mL$

   $mmol\ \times 2\ mmol\ \ mmol$
   ──────────
   $1\ mmol$

   $M\ AgNO_3 = (37.50\ mL)(0.152\ mmol/mL)(2\ mmol\ /1\ mmol)/(25.00\ mL)$

8. **B.** $NaHCO_2(aq) + H^+(aq) \rightarrow CO_2(g) + H_2O(l)$

   Metal hydrides react with water to form metal hydroxides and hydrogen gas. Group 1 and 2 metals and other active metals react with acid to form hydrogen gas. Acetic acid will not react with acid. Sodium hydroxide reacts with acid to form water.

9. **C.** *Both solutions are aqueous, and the spectator ions are Cl^- and Na^+ so the reactants are written $Ca^{2+}(aq) + CO_3^{2-}(aq)$. Carbonates commonly form precipitates so the product is $CaCO_3(s)$.*

10. **C.** *The balanced equation is $2Mg(s) + CO_2(g) \rightarrow C(s) + 2MgO(s)$.*

11. C. *Ethanol, a covalent substance, is a nonelectrolyte and does not ionize in water so the pH is approximately 7.*

12. D. *Acids react with carbonates to form carbon dioxide gas and water:*
$$H^+(aq) + HCO_3^-(aq) \longrightarrow CO_2(g) + H_2O(l)$$

13. A. *Generally, anions are basic except anions of strong acids. Phosphate is a base:*
$$PO_4^{3-}(aq) + H_2O(l) \longrightarrow HPO_4^{2-}(aq) + OH^-(aq)$$

14. A. *Phosphate ion reacts with acid to form hydrogen phosphate, a base.*
$$PO_4^{3-}(aq) + H^+(aq) \longrightarrow HPO_4^{2-}(aq)$$

(Note: Hydrogen phosphate ion is amphoteric and without more information, it might be an acid in aqueous solution. However, sodium phosphate is the only substance listed that has a possibility to be basic when acid is added.)

15. B. *Ammonium ion reacts with hydroxide ion to form ammonia, a water-soluble gas and water:*
$$NH_4^+(aq) + OH^-(aq) \longrightarrow NH_3(aq) + H_2O(l)$$

Free Response Answers

1. a. $H_2SO_4(l) + 2NaHCO_3(s) \rightarrow 2CO_2(g) + 2H_2O(l) + 2Na^+(aq) + SO_4^{2-}(aq)$

    b.

H_2SO_4	$+$	$2NaHCO_3$	$\longrightarrow$
1.0 L		5000 g	

    $\downarrow \times 18.0$ mol/L $\downarrow \div 84.0$ g/mol

    mol   mol

    $\downarrow \div 1$ mol $\downarrow \div 2$ mol

    (1.0 L)(18.0 mol/L)/1 mol = 18.0   (5000 g)/84.0 g/mol/2 mol = 29.8
    Sulfuric acid is limiting.

H_2SO_4	$+$	$2NaHCO_3$	$\longrightarrow$
1.0 L		? g	

    $\downarrow \times 18.0$ mol/L $\uparrow \times 84.0$ g/mol

    mol $\xrightarrow{\hspace{2cm}}$ mol
    2 mol NaHCO$_3$/1 mol H$_2$SO$_4$

    c. *x g* $NaHCO_3 = (1.00\ L\ H_2SO_4) \times (18.0\ mol/L)$
    $(2\ mol\ NaHCO_3/1\ mol\ H_2SO_4) \times (84.0\ g/mol) = 3020\ g.$

    d. *x mol* $NaHCO_3$ *initially* $= 5000\ g \div 84.0\ g/mol$
    $= 59.5\ mol\ NaHCO_3\ initially.$

    x mol $NaHCO_3$ *consumed* $= 1.00\ L \times 18.0\ mol/L \times$
    $2\ mol/1\ mol = 36.0\ mol\ NaHCO_3\ consumed.$

    Moles $NaHCO_3$ *remaining* $= 59.5 - 36.0 = 23.5\ mol.$

    e. *A concrete floor would require less baking soda to neutralize the spill because concrete contains significant amounts of calcium and other carbonates that would neutralize some of the sulfuric acid.*

2. *Add one drop of acid to each metal and observe the results.*

Silver is the only metal of the three that will not react. The other two metals will produce bubbles of hydrogen gas.

$$Zn(s) + 2H^+(aq) \rightarrow Zn^{2+}(aq) + H_2(g)$$
$$Ni(s) + 2H^+ \rightarrow Ni^{2+} + H_2(g)$$

Because both zinc and nickel are above H_2 on the activity series, both metals will react with $H^+(aq)$. Silver will not react with aqueous acid because it is below hydrogen on the activity series.

Add a drop of iron(II) nitrate to freshly clean pieces of the other two metals. The nickel will not react but the zinc will oxidize and the iron will reduce. A dark coating of iron metal will appear on the zinc metal.

$$Zn(s) + Fe^{2+}(aq) \rightarrow Zn^{2+}(aq) + Fe(s)$$

Because zinc is above iron on the activity series, zinc metal will react with aqueous iron(II) ions. Nickel will not react with the iron(II) nitrate because nickel is below iron on the activity series.

Your Turn Answers

4.1. $HCl(g) \rightarrow H^+(aq) + Cl^-(aq)$

4.2. *$CaCl_2$ and $(NH_4)_2SO_4$ are strong electrolytes because they are ionic compounds. HCN is not on the list of strong acids, so it is a weak acid and therefore a weak electrolyte. Glucose is a covalent molecule that is neither an acid nor a base, so it is a nonelectrolyte.*

4.3. $Ni(NO_3)_2(s) + CO_3^{2-}(aq) \rightarrow NiCO_3(s) + 2NO_3^-(aq)$

4.4. $OH^-(aq) + CH_3COOH(aq) \rightarrow H_2O(l) + CH_3COO^-(aq)$

4.5. $2H^+(aq) + Li_2CO_3(s) \rightarrow CO_2(g) + H_2O(l) + 2Li^+(aq)$

4.6. $2Al(s) + 3Ni^{2+} \rightarrow 2Al^{3+} + 3Ni(s)$

Metals toward the top of the activity are more likely to be oxidized. Aluminum is above nickel so aluminum metal loses electrons and Ni^{2+} gains electrons.

4.7. $K = 1-, Al = 3+, S = 6+, O = 2-$

THERMOCHEMISTRY

The content in this topic is the basis for mastering Learning Objectives 5.1 to 5.8 as found in the Curriculum Framework.

When you finish reviewing this topic, be sure you are able to:

- Explain how and why potential energy varies with distance between atoms in covalent bonds and intermolecular forces (see also Section 9.7)
- Explain how temperature relates to molecular motion using particle views (see also Section 10.7)
- Use molecular collisions to explain or predict the transfer of heat between systems
- Use the law of conservation of energy to explain energy transfer, including heat and work between systems
- Explain the quantity of energy change that occurs when two substances of different temperatures interact
- Calculate or estimate enthalpy changes associated with chemical reactions
- Calculate or estimate energy changes associated with temperature changes using heat capacity
- Calculate or estimate energy changes associated with physical changes including phase changes using heats of fusion or vaporization
- Use results of a constant pressure calorimetry experiment to determine the change in enthalpy of a chemical or physical process
- Use bond energies to calculate or estimate enthalpies of reaction (see also Section 8.8)

Section 5.1

The Nature of Energy

Thermodynamics is the study of energy and its transformations.

Thermochemistry is the study of the relationships between energy changes involving heat and chemical reactions.

Energy is the capacity to do work or to transfer heat.

Heat is the energy transferred from one object to another because of a difference in temperature.

A **calorie** is an informal but still used unit for heat energy. One calorie is the amount of energy required to raise the temperature of one gram of water by one degree Celsius. The large Calorie (spelled with a capital C) is used to measure food energy. 1 Cal = 1000 cal.

A **joule** is the SI unit of energy. One calorie is equal to 4.184 joules. 1 cal = 4.184 J.

Common misconception: Commonly, the energy values of various foods are expressed as follows: for fats, 9 Cal/g; for carbohydrates, 4 Cal/g; for protein, 4 Cal/g. These caloric values are large calories and each refers to 1000 cal or 1 kcal.

Energy changes involve the transfer of heat between the **system**, that portion of the universe we single out for study, and the **surroundings**, everything else.

The First Law of Thermodynamics   Section 5.2

The **first law of thermodynamics**, also called the **law of conservation of energy**, states that energy is conserved. The energy of the universe is constant. Energy can be neither created nor destroyed, but it can be changed to other forms.

An **exothermic** process is a process that releases heat to the surroundings. Heat flows out of the system and into the surroundings. The temperature of the surroundings increases.

Common misconception: An exothermic process releases heat, but this does not mean that the system cools off. The word "release" essentially means that potential energy of the system is converted to heat energy so the surroundings increase in temperature during an exothermic process.

An **endothermic** process absorbs heat from the surroundings. Heat flows into the system from the surroundings. The temperature of the surroundings decreases.

Common misconception: An endothermic process absorbs heat, but this does not mean that the temperature of the system increases. The word "absorb" essentially means that heat energy from the surroundings is changed to potential energy of the system, and the temperature of the surroundings decreases.

Your Turn 5.1

⟵————————————————————

Imagine an ice cube melting in your hand. Is the melting of ice endothermic or exothermic? Explain using the terms system and surroundings. Write your answer in the space provided.

_____

All chemical and physical changes involve some form of energy change. Because atoms are composed of electrical particles, electrostatic forces between atoms and molecules form the basis of those energy changes. Figure 5.1 illustrates the forces that exist between charged particles. Opposite charges attract releasing energy (Figure 5.1a). Like charges repel and release energy when they do so (Figure 5.1b).

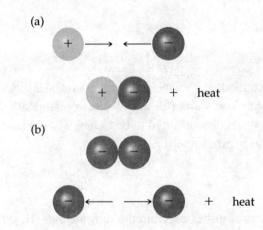

Figure 5.1 Opposite charges attract (a) and like charges repel (b).

Coulomb's law says that the force acting between two charged particles is related to their charges and the distance between them: $F = kQ_1Q_2/d^2$.

Because energy is force times distance, multiplying both sides by d (distance) gives a similar relationship for energy: $E = kQ_1Q_2/d$.

When two opposite charges attract as in Figure 5.1a, the process is exothermic. The difference in energy is the heat released by the system. Attractive interactions are always exothermic while the separation of opposite charges is always endothermic.

When two like charges repel as in Figure 5.1b, the process is also exothermic. The difference in energy is the heat released by the system. Repulsive interactions are always exothermic, whereas it requires energy to move like charges together.

Your Turn 5.2

Imagine warming your hands near a campfire. Is a campfire an endothermic or exothermic process? Justify your answer. Write your answer in the space provided.

Temperature in Kelvin is proportional to the average kinetic energy of the particles in a sample. Figure 5.2 illustrates two samples of gas particles at two different temperatures. Each arrow indicates the relative kinetic energy of each particle.

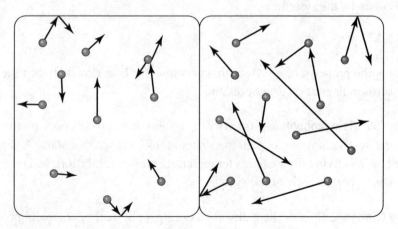

Figure 5.2 Gas particles at two different temperatures.

Which gas has the higher temperature? Justify your answer.

Section 5.3

Enthalpy

Pressure–volume work (P–V work) is the work involved in the expansion or compression of gases at constant pressure. Figure 5.3 shows how a chemical reaction can both release heat *and* do work on its surroundings. Because the reaction produces a gas, the piston moves and pushes back on the atmosphere.

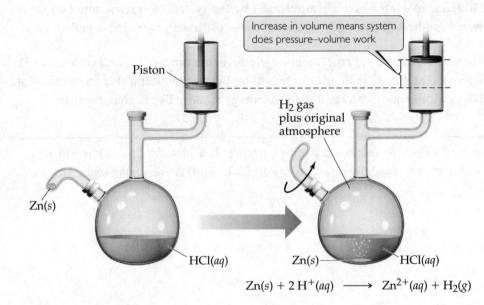

Increase in volume means system does pressure–volume work

Piston

H₂ gas plus original atmosphere

Zn(s)

HCl(aq)   Zn(s)   HCl(aq)

$$Zn(s) + 2\,H^+(aq) \longrightarrow Zn^{2+}(aq) + H_2(g)$$

Figure 5.3 A system that does work on its surroundings.

P–V work done by the system is given by the equation: $w = -P\Delta V$, where w is work, P is constant pressure, and ΔV is the change in volume of the system. The negative sign shows the direction of the work. That is, the work is done by the system.

The **internal energy**, ΔE, of the system is the sum of the heat changed, q, and the work, w, done by the system:

$$\Delta E = q + w$$

Enthalpy is the property of a system that accounts for heat flow between the system and the surroundings at constant pressure.

Enthalpy is a **state function**, a property of a system that depends only on the present state of the system, not on the path the system took to reach that state. A state is determined by specifying the system's temperature, pressure, location, and other conditions that are characteristic of the system.

Enthalpy change, ΔH, is the heat absorbed during a physical or chemical process.

ΔH is positive for an endothermic process, one that absorbs heat.

ΔH is negative for an exothermic process, one that releases heat.

Common misconception: The total change in internal energy for all systems is the change in enthalpy plus the work done by the system at constant pressure: $\Delta E = \Delta H - P\Delta V$. However, for most reactions, $P\Delta V$ is very small so it is satisfactory to use ΔH as a measure of energy change during most chemical processes: $\Delta E = \Delta H$.

Enthalpies of Reaction   Section 5.4

Enthalpy changes are usually expressed in kJ or kJ/mol. For endothermic changes, the heat absorbed is always a positive number because endothermic changes absorb heat. For an exothermic reaction, ΔH is negative because exothermic changes liberate (the opposite of absorb) heat.

Enthalpy change, ΔH, can be applied to either a physical or a chemical change.

Common misconception: It is important to understand that the concept of enthalpy change, ΔH, is the same idea for a wide variety of processes. To distinguish specific types of change, ΔH takes on various subscripts.

Table 5.1 lists examples of various types of enthalpy changes. Each subscript for ΔH denotes a specific kind of process.

Table 5.1 Enthalpy changes for various types of processes with examples.

Symbol	Type of Process	Definition of Process with Example
ΔH_{rxn} $AgNO_3(aq) + HCl(aq) \rightarrow AgCl(s) + HNO_3(aq)$	Heat of reaction	Enthalpy change for any chemical reaction $\Delta H_{rxn} = -68$ kJ
ΔH_{comb} $CH_4(g) + 2O_2(g) \rightarrow CO_2(g) + 2H_2O(g)$	Heat of combustion	Enthalpy change for a combustion reaction $\Delta H_{comb} = -802$ kJ
ΔH_{fus} $H_2O(s) \rightarrow H_2O(l)$	Heat of fusion	Heat change when a solid melts $\Delta H_{fus} = +6.0$ kJ
ΔH_{vap} $H_2O(l) \rightarrow H_2O(g)$	Heat of vaporization	Heat change when a liquid vaporizes $\Delta H_{vap} = +44$ kJ

Table 5.1 *(Continued)*

ΔH_{BDE} $H_2(g) \rightarrow H(g) + H(g)$	Bond dissociation energy	Heat required to break a chemical bond $\Delta H_{BDE} = +436 \text{ kJ}$
ΔH_f $H_2(g) + \frac{1}{2}O_2(g) \rightarrow H_2O(l)$	Heat of formation	Heat change when one mole of a substance is formed from its elements $\Delta H_f = -285.83 \text{ kJ}$
ΔH_{soln} $LiCl(s) \rightarrow Li^+(aq) + Cl^-(aq)$	Heat of solution	Heat change when solute dissolves in a solvent $\Delta H_{soln} = -37.4 \text{ kJ}$

The magnitude of the enthalpy change, ΔH, for any chemical or physical change is directly proportional to the amount of reactants and products involved in the change. For example, if one mole of methane burns in air to produce -802 kJ of energy, then two moles of methane will produce twice the energy.

$$CH_4(g) + 2O_2(g) \rightarrow CO_2(g) + 2H_2O(g) \qquad \Delta H_{comb} = -802 \text{ kJ}$$

$$2CH_4(g) + 4O_2(g) \rightarrow 2CO_2(g) + 4H_2O(g) \qquad \Delta H_{comb} = -1604 \text{ kJ}$$

Common misconception: The AP test commonly employs the units of kJ/mol$_{rxn}$ for thermodynamic quantities linked to balanced chemical equations. However, most college texts use the units of kJ and assume the fact that the given number of kJ is directly proportional to the number of moles of reactants and products in the specified balanced equation. Whenever you see it, be sure to translate "X kJ per mol$_{rxn}$" to "X kJ per the given balanced equation."

Because it is directly proportional to the number of moles in a balanced equation, enthalpy change, ΔH, for any amount of reactant or product can be calculated using the mole road.

Example:

How many kJ of heat are absorbed when 25.0 g of methane burn in air?

Solution:

$$x \, kJ = (25.0 \text{ g } CH_4)/(16.0 \text{ g/mol}) \times (-802 \, kJ/mol) = -1250 \, kJ$$

$$CH_4(g) + 2O_2(g) \longrightarrow CO_2(g) + 2H_2O(g) \qquad \Delta H_{comb} = -802 \, kJ/mol$$

25.0 g

$\downarrow$ ÷ 16.0 g/mol

mol $\xrightarrow{\qquad \times -802 \, kJ/mol \qquad}$? kJ

The sign of ΔH depends on the direction of the reaction. The magnitude of the enthalpy change for a forward reaction is the same as that of a reverse reaction but it differs in sign. For example, if it takes $+6\, kJ$ to melt a mole of solid water, then one mole of liquid water releases $-6\, kJ$ of energy upon freezing.

$$H_2O(s) \rightarrow H_2O(l) \qquad \Delta H = +6.0\, kJ$$

$$H_2O(l) \rightarrow H_2O(s) \qquad \Delta H = -6.0\, kJ$$

Common misconception: The sign of ΔH indicates the direction of energy flow, not a positive or negative value for energy. A positive sign indicates that heat is absorbed by the system. A negative sign means that heat is released by the system. Often the absolute value of ΔH is used in the context of sentences and its sign is implied. For example, when heat is said to be "absorbed," the sign of ΔH is positive. When heat is "liberated," the sign is negative.

Your Turn 5.3

What scientific law requires that the magnitude of the heat change for forward and reverse processes be the same with opposite signs? Explain. Write your answer in the space provided.

Phase transitions from solid to liquid and from liquid to gas always absorb heat. They are endothermic. Phase transitions from gas to liquid and from liquid to solid always liberate heat. They are exothermic.

$$H_2O(l) \rightarrow H_2O(g) \quad \Delta H_{vap} = \ +44\ kJ$$
$$H_2O(g) \rightarrow H_2O(l) \quad \Delta H_{vap} = \ -44\ kJ$$

Your Turn 5.4

Why are phase changes from solid to liquid and from liquid to gas always endothermic? Is the process of sublimation (changing directly from a solid to a gas) endothermic or exothermic? Explain. Write your answer in the space provided.

Section 5.5

Calorimetry

Calorimetry is the measurement of heat flow. A **calorimeter** is an apparatus that measures heat flow. A constant pressure calorimeter is shown in Figure 5.4.

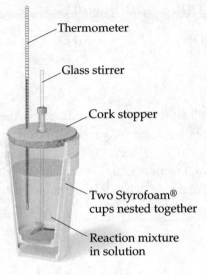

Thermometer

Glass stirrer

Cork stopper

Two Styrofoam®
cups nested together

Reaction mixture
in solution

Figure 5.4 Coffee-cup calorimeter. This simple apparatus is used to measure temperature changes of reactions at constant pressure.

Heat capacity, C, is the heat required to raise the temperature of an object by 1 K. The units for heat capacity are J/K (or J/°C).

Common misconception: Remember that 1 K is the same size as 1 °C (even though they are 273 degrees apart on their respective scales). Kelvin and degrees Celsius are often used interchangeably in various units.

Molar heat capacity, C_{molar}, is the amount of heat absorbed by one mole of a substance when it experiences a one degree temperature change. The units of C_{molar} are J/mol K (or J/mol °C).

Specific heat capacity, c, is the heat capacity of one gram of a substance. The units are J/g K (or J/g °C). Table 5.2 shows the specific heats of some common substances.

Table 5.2   Specific heat capacities of various substances.

Substance	Specific Heat, J/g°C	Substance	Specific Heat, J/g°C
aluminum	0.90	liquid water	4.184
iron	0.46	ice	2.1
silver	0.24	steam	1.9
mercury	0.14	ethanol	2.4

The specific heat of water is worth remembering: $1\ \text{cal/g K} = 4.184\ \text{J/g K}$.

Explain why the value of the specific heat of water is 1 cal/g K or 4.184 J/g K.
Write your answer in the space provided.

Your Turn 5.5

Heat capacities, temperature, energy, moles, and grams are related by an analogy to the mole road as shown in Figure 5.5.

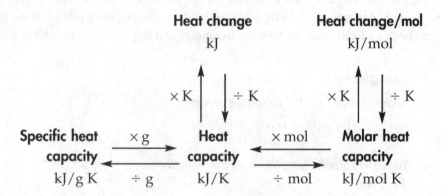

Figure 5.5 Mole road analogy for heat capacity calculations.

Calorimetry is often used to measure enthalpy changes in chemical reactions. For example, the heat of combustion of ethanol, CH_3CH_2OH, can be measured by placing a measured quantity of ethanol and excess oxygen in a bomb calorimeter having a known heat capacity. The ethanol is ignited, the temperature change of the calorimeter is observed, and the heat released by the combustion reaction is calculated from the heat capacity of the calorimeter.

A student performs an experiment to determine the heat of fusion of ice. In a coffee
cup calorimeter, the student adds an ice chip to 4.735 g of water at 44.0 °C. Upon
mixing, the temperature of the system drops to 16.0 °C at the point where all the ice
has melted. The total mass of the water is 6.097 g.

a. Calculate the amount of heat lost by the water.
b. Calculate the mass of the ice.

Your Turn 5.6

c. *How much heat did the ice gain?*

d. *Assume all the ice was liquid water at 0.0 °C. How much heat did this liquid water gain?*

e. *Use this data to calculate the heat of fusion of ice in kJ/mol.*

f. *If the accepted value is 6.02 kJ/mol, calculate the percentage error of the experiment.*

Section 5.6

Hess's Law

Hess's law states that if a reaction is carried out in a series of steps, ΔH of the overall reaction is equal to the sum of the ΔH's for each individual step. Hess's law is useful in calculating enthalpies of reactions that are difficult or impossible to measure directly. The formation of sulfur trioxide by the reaction of sulfur with oxygen, for example, does not proceed directly under normal conditions, but the heat of the reaction can be calculated from the heats of the individual steps that lead to the reaction.

Example:

Calculate ΔH for the following reaction,

$$2S(s) + 3O_2(g) \rightarrow 2SO_3(g)$$

from the enthalpies of these related reactions.

Reaction	ΔH_{rxn}
$S(s) + O_2(g) \rightarrow SO_2(g)$	$-296.9 \, kJ$
$2SO_2(g) + O_2(g) \rightarrow 2SO_3(g)$	$-196.6 \, kJ$

Solution:

The given reactions can be manipulated like algebraic quantities to yield the reaction in question. Their enthalpy values are mathematically manipulated in the same way.

Reaction	ΔH_{rxn}
$2[S(s) + O_2(g) \rightarrow SO_2(g)]$	$2(-296.9 \, kJ)$
$+ \, 2SO_2(g) + O_2(g) \rightarrow 2SO_3(g)$	$-196.6 \, kJ$
$2S(s) + 3O_2(g) \rightarrow 2SO_3(g)$	$-790.4 \, kJ$

Hess's law says that the enthalpy of the reaction is calculated by manipulating the enthalpy quantities in the same way as we manipulated the corresponding reactions.

Common misconception: Be sure to manipulate the ΔH values in the same *way you manipulate the reactions. That is, if you multiply a reaction by 2, you must multiply its ΔH value by 2. If you reverse a reaction, you must change the sign of its ΔH value. Always be careful of signs.*

Figure 5.6 shows an enthalpy diagram illustrating Hess's law for the combustion of methane.

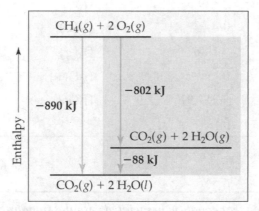

Figure 5.6   An enthalpy diagram illustrating Hess's law. The quantity of heat generated in any chemical reaction is independent of the pathway of the reaction.

Enthalpies of Formation   Section 5.7

A **formation reaction** is a reaction that produces one mole of a substance from its elements in their most stable thermodynamic state. For example, the formation reaction for gaseous hydrogen iodide, HI, includes only one mole of HI as the sole product, and the elements hydrogen and iodine in their most stable forms as the only reactants:

$$\frac{1}{2}H_2(g) \;+\; \frac{1}{2}I_2(s) \rightarrow HI(g) \quad \Delta H = +25.94\,\text{kJ}$$

Gaseous diatomic hydrogen and solid diatomic iodine are the most stable thermodynamic states of those elements at 25 °C.

The **standard heat of formation,** ΔH_f°, is the heat absorbed when one mole of a substance is formed from its elements in their standard states at 25 °C and 1 atmosphere pressure. A heat of formation is ΔH for a formation reaction. For example, the standard enthalpy of formation, ΔH_f°, of HI is the enthalpy of the formation reaction for HI. Its value is +25.94 kJ. Table 5.3 gives the standard heats of formation of some selected substances. Appendix C of *Chemistry: The Central Science* provides a comprehensive table of ΔH_f° values. Keep in mind that each substance listed is the sole product of a formation reaction and that the corresponding ΔH_f° value listed is the enthalpy of that formation reaction under standard conditions.

Table 5.3 Standard enthalpies of formation, ΔH_f°, for selected substances.

Substance	ΔH_f° (kJ/mol)	Substance	ΔH_f° (kJ/mol)
$AlCl_3(s)$	−705.6	$MnO_4^-(aq)$	−541.4
$Br_2(g)$	+30.71	$NH_3(aq)$	−80.29
$Br_2(l)$	0	$NH_3(g)$	−46.19
$Ca(g)$	+179.3	$O(g)$	+247.5
$Ca(s)$	0	$O_2(g)$	0
$C(s, \text{diamond})$	+1.88	$O_3(g)$	+142.3
$C(s, \text{graphite})$	0	$H_2O(g)$	−241.82
$H(g)$	+217.97	$H_2O(l)$	−285.83
$H_2(g)$	0		

Your Turn 5.7

Write the thermochemical equation associated with the standard heat of formation of $AlCl_3(s)$ listed in Table 5.3. Write your answer in the space provided.

Notice that the substances in Table 5.3 include elements, compounds, and ions. Notice also that the heat of formation of any element in its most stable thermodynamic state is zero. For example, the ΔH_f° values for solid monatomic calcium, liquid diatomic bromine, and gaseous diatomic oxygen are all zero because these are the most stable forms of these elements at 25 °C and 1 atmosphere pressure.

Your Turn 5.8

Considering the definition of a formation reaction, justify why the standard heat of formation of an element in its most stable thermodynamic state is zero. Write a chemical equation to illustrate your answer. Write your answer in the space provided.

Hess's law allows us to use a relatively small number of measurements to calculate ΔH for a vast number of reactions. Using data from Table 5.3 or from Appendix C of *Chemistry: The Central Science*, the standard enthalpy of many reactions can be calculated from the enthalpies of the reactants and products.

The standard enthalpy of any reaction, ΔH°_{rxn}, is equal to the sum of the standard enthalpies of formation of products minus the sum of standard enthalpies of formation of reactants. The values for n and m in the following equation represent the coefficients of the balanced equation.

$$\Delta H^{\circ}_{rxn} = \sum n \, \Delta H^{\circ}_{f \, products} - \sum m \, \Delta H^{\circ}_{f \, reactants}$$

Example:

Calculate the standard enthalpy change for the combustion of one mole of liquid ethanol.

Solution:

Write and balance the equation. Use Appendix C in Chemistry: The Central Science *to determine the standard enthalpies of formation for reactants and products. Apply the summation equation. Be sure to multiply each ΔH°_f value by the corresponding coefficient that balances the equation.*

$$CH_3CH_2OH(l) + 3O_2(g) \rightarrow 2CO_2(g) + 3H_2O(g)$$

From Appendix C: $\Delta H^{\circ}_f = -238.6 \text{ kJ} \quad 0 \text{ kJ} \quad\quad -393.5 \text{ kJ} \quad -241.82 \text{ kJ}$

$\Delta H^{\circ}_{rxn} = \sum n \, \Delta H^{\circ}_{f \, products} - \sum m \, \Delta H^{\circ}_{f \, reactants}$

$\Delta H^{\circ}_{rxn} = 2(-393.5 \text{ kJ}) + 3(-241.82 \text{ kJ}) - (-238.6 \text{ kJ}) - 3(0 \text{ kJ})$

$\Delta H^{\circ}_{rxn} = -1273.9 \text{ kJ}$

Common misconception: The hardest part of this type of problem is the arithmetic. Especially be careful to manipulate the $+$ and $-$ signs correctly.

Reexamine Table 5.3. Notice that there is a difference between the ΔH°_f values for liquid water and gaseous water. The difference represents the molar heat of vaporization of water. The equation is:

$$H_2O(l) \quad \rightarrow \quad H_2O(g)$$

$\Delta H^{\circ}_f = -285.83 \text{ kJ} \quad\quad -241.82 \text{ kJ}$

$\Delta H^{\circ}_{rxn} = \Delta H^{\circ}_{vap} = \Delta H^{\circ}_f [H_2O(g)] - \Delta H^{\circ}_f [H_2O(l)]$

$\Delta H^{\circ}_{vap} = -241.82 \text{ kJ} - (-285.83 \text{ kJ}) = 44.01 \text{ kJ}$

Your Turn 5.9

Calculate (a) the enthalpy of sublimation of solid calcium. (b) The heat of solution of gaseous ammonia (c) The bond dissociation energy of hydrogen gas (d) The heat change when gaseous bromine condenses to a liquid. Where can you find the data needed to solve these problems? Write chemical equations to illustrate your answers. Write your answers in the space provided.

Multiple Choice Questions

1. The standard enthalpy of formation (ΔH_f°) for potassium chloride is the enthalpy change for the reaction

   A) $K(g) + \frac{1}{2}Cl_2(g) \rightarrow KCl(g)$

   B) $K^+(s) + Cl^-(g) \rightarrow KCl(s)$

   C) $2K(s) + Cl_2(g) \rightarrow 2KCl(s)$

   D) $K(s) + \frac{1}{2}Cl_2(g) \rightarrow KCl(s)$

2. For which of these processes is the value of ΔH expected to be negative?

   I.   The temperature increases when calcium chloride dissolves in water.

   II. Steam condenses to liquid water.

   III. Water freezes.

   IV. Dry ice sublimes.

   A) IV only

   B) I, II, and III

   C) I only

   D) II and III only

3. Which is expected to not have a ΔH_f° value of zero?

   A) $F_2(g)$

   B) $Br_2(g)$

   C) $I_2(s)$

   D) $C(s, graphite)$

4. For which of the following equations is the change in enthalpy at 25 °C and 1 atmosphere pressure equal to ΔH_f° of $CH_3OH(l)$?

   A) $CH_3OH(l) + \frac{3}{2}O_2(g) \rightarrow CO_2(g) + 2H_2O(l)$

   B) $CH_3OH(l) + \frac{3}{2}O_2(g) \rightarrow CO_2(g) + 2H_2O(g)$

   C) $2CH_3OH(l) + 3O_2(g) \rightarrow 2CO_2(g) + 4H_2O(l)$

   D) $C(s) + 2H_2(g) + \frac{1}{2}O_2(g) \rightarrow CH_3OH(l)$

5. Which change will result in an increase in enthalpy of the system?

   A) burning a candle

   B) freezing water

   C) evaporating alcohol

   D) condensing steam

6. The standard enthalpy of formation of $Cl(g)$ is $+242 \, kJ/mol$. What is the dissociation energy of a $Cl—Cl$ bond?

   A) $+242 \, kJ/mol$

   B) $-242 \, kJ/mol$

   C) $+484 \, kJ/mol$

   D) $+121 \, kJ/mol$

7. For which process is the sign of ΔH negative?

   A) Photosynthesis

   B) $CO_2(g) \rightarrow C(s) + O_2(g)$

   C) $N_2(g) \rightarrow 2N(g)$

   D) $NaOH(s) \rightarrow Na^+(aq) + OH^-(aq) + heat$

8. Given the following data, what is the heat of formation of methane gas?

   I. $CH_4(g) + 2O_2(g) \rightarrow CO_2(g) + 2H_2O(g)$ $\qquad \Delta H = -803 \, kJ$

   II. $H_2(g) + \frac{1}{2}O_2(g) \rightarrow H_2O(g)$ $\qquad \Delta H = -242 \, kJ$

   III. $C(s) + O_2(g) \rightarrow CO_2(g)$ $\qquad \Delta H = -394 \, kJ$

   IV. $C(s) + \frac{1}{2}O_2(g) \rightarrow CO(g)$ $\qquad \Delta H = -111 \, kJ$

   A) $-803 \, kJ/mol$

   B) $-75 \, kJ/mol$

   C) $+167 \, kJ/mol$

   D) $+208 \, kJ/mol$

9. The standard heat of formation of gaseous sulfur trioxide is $-396 \, kJ/mol$. What is the enthalpy of reaction represented by the following balanced equation?

   $2SO_3(g) \rightarrow 2S(s) + 3O_2(g)$

   A) $-396 \, kJ$

   B) $+396 \, kJ$

   C) $+792 \, kJ$

   D) $-792 \, kJ$

10. Given only the following data, what can be said about the following reaction?

$$3H_2(g) + N_2(g) \rightarrow 2NH_3(g) \qquad \Delta H = -92 \, kJ$$

   A) The enthalpy of products is greater than the enthalpy of reactants.

   B) The total bond energies of products are greater than the total bond energies of reactants.

   C) The reaction is very fast.

   D) Nitrogen and hydrogen have very stable bonds compared to the bonds of ammonia.

11. For the following reaction, $\Delta H = -400 \, kJ$.

$$2K(s) + 2H_2O(l) \rightarrow 2KOH(aq) + H_2(g)$$

   What is ΔH for this reaction?

$$KOH(aq) + \tfrac{1}{2} H_2(g) \rightarrow K(s) + H_2O(l)$$

   A) $-400 \, kJ$

   B) $+400 \, kJ$

   C) $-200 \, kJ$

   D) $+200 \, kJ$

Use the data in Table 5.3 to answer Questions 12–15.

12. Estimate the heat of formation for $O(g)$.

   A) $+250 \, kJ/mol$

   B) $-250 \, kJ/mol$

   C) $+500 \, kJ/mol$

   D) $-500 \, kJ/mol$

13. Estimate the bond dissociation energy of $H_2(g)$ in kJ/mol.

   A) 0

   B) $+218$

   C) -218

   D) $+436$

14. Estimate the electrical energy required to produce one mole of oxygen gas from liquid water.

   A) $+143$

   B) $+286$

   C) -286

   D) $+572$

15. *Estimate the heat of solution of ammonia gas.*

    A) −34.10

    B) −46.19

    C) −80.29

    D) −126.48

Free Response Questions

1. *The heat of combustion of gaseous butane is −2658 kJ/mol and the heat of combustion of liquid butane is −2635 kJ/mol when, in both cases, all products are gases.*

    a. *Write a balanced chemical equation for the combustion of gaseous butane.*

    b. *How many grams of gaseous butane combust when 1550 kJ of heat are produced?*

    c. *What is the magnitude and sign of the molar heat of vaporization of butane? Explain your reasoning using Hess's law. Is your sign for the heat of vaporization realistic? Explain.*

2. *When 15.00 g of propane are burned in air to produce all gaseous products, 730.0 kJ of heat are produced.*

    a. *Calculate the molar heat of combustion of propane.*

    b. *When 15.00 g of propane are combusted in air to produce gaseous carbon dioxide and liquid water, 790.0 kJ of heat are produced. Explain why the amount of heat available from the combustion of propane depends on the phase of the products.*

    c. *Calculate the heat of vaporization of water in units of kJ/g.*

Multiple Choice Answers and Explanations

1. D. The enthalpy of formation of a substance is the enthalpy change for the formation of one mole of that substance from its elements in their most stable thermodynamic forms at 25 °C and 1 atmosphere pressure. Solid potassium and gaseous diatomic chlorine are the most stable forms of those elements.

2. B. A negative ΔH value is characteristic of an exothermic process, one that releases heat to its surroundings. Exothermic processes increase the temperature of their surroundings. Phase changes from gas to liquid and from liquid to solid are all exothermic processes. The opposite processes are endothermic. Sublimation is the process by which a solid changes directly into a gas, also an endothermic process.

3. B. By definition, the standard heats of formation of elements in their most stable thermodynamic state at 25 °C and 1 atmosphere pressure is zero. Bromine is a liquid at 25 °C and 1 atmosphere pressure. Solid graphite is the most stable form of carbon.

4. D. Although the direct formation of methanol from its elements is improbable, the heat of formation of methanol is defined as the enthalpy change for this reaction. Answers A, B, and C are all combustion reactions of methanol.

5. C. An increase in enthalpy is associated with an endothermic process, one that absorbs energy from its surroundings. Phase changes from solid to liquid or gas and from liquid to gas are always endothermic. Combustion reactions are always exothermic as are phase changes from gas to liquid and from liquid to solid.

6. C. The bond dissociation of chlorine gas is the enthalpy change for this reaction: $Cl_2(g) \rightarrow 2Cl(g)$. Bond dissociation energies always have positive values because bond breaking is always endothermic, so the sign of the heat change is always positive. The formation reaction for $Cl(g)$ is $\frac{1}{2}Cl_2(g) \rightarrow Cl(g)$. Notice that the formation equation is exactly half the reaction in question. So the bond dissociation energy is twice the enthalpy of formation.

7. D. ΔH is negative for exothermic processes and positive for endothermic processes. Exothermic processes release heat to their surroundings. Photosynthesis involves absorbing energy from sunlight and is endothermic. Combustion reactions are always exothermic and Answer B is the reverse of a combustion reaction so it is endothermic. Bond breaking is always endothermic and bond making is always exothermic. The process of forming nitrogen atoms from nitrogen molecules requires bond breaking.

8. B. The heat of formation of methane gas is the heat change for the formation reaction: $C(s) + 2H_2(g) \rightarrow CH_4(g)$. One way to solve the problem is to notice that Equation 1 represents the combustion of methane. The other given equations are the formation reactions for the reactants and products of the combustion reaction. (Equation 4 is extraneous.) Apply the corresponding heats to the summation equation and solve for the unknown quantity, the heat of formation of methane.

$$\Delta H°_{rxn} = \sum n\,\Delta H°_{f\,products} - \sum m\,\Delta H°_{f\,reactants}$$
$$\Delta H°_{comb} = 2\Delta H°_f[H_2O] + \Delta H°_f[CO_2] - \Delta H°_f[O_2] - \Delta H°_f[CH_4]$$
$$-803 = 2(-242)+(-394) - 0 - \Delta H°_f CH_4$$
$$\Delta H°_f[CH_4] = -75\,kJ/mol$$

Another approach is to use Hess's law and mathematically manipulate the given equations to yield the formation reaction for methane. Apply the same mathematical manipulations to the given heats to find the heat of the formation reaction. (This approach is the essence of the summation equation used in the first approach.)

1. $-[CH_4(g) + 2O_2(g) \rightarrow CO_2(g) + 2H_2O(g)]$
$$\Delta H = -803\,kJ \times (-1) = +803$$

2. $+2[H_2(g)+\frac{1}{2}O_2(g) \rightarrow H_2O(g)]$ $\quad \Delta H = -242\,kJ \times (+2) = -484\,kJ$

3. $+[C(s)+O_2(g) \rightarrow CO_2(g)]$ $\qquad \Delta H = -394\,kJ = -394$

$C(s) + 2H_2(g) \rightarrow CH_4(g)$ $\qquad \Delta H = -75\,kJ/mol$

9. C. The standard heat of formation of gaseous sulfur trioxide is heat change for the formation reaction: $S(s) + 3/2\, O_2(g) \rightarrow SO_3(g)$. Recognize that the reaction in question is double the formation reaction and the reverse of it. The heat change for the reaction in question is:

    $$-2(-396) = +792\ kJ$$

10. B. Bond making is always exothermic and bond breaking is always endothermic. The reaction is exothermic, one that releases energy to its surroundings, because the sign of the heat change is negative. The bonds formed by the products are more stable than those broken in the reactants leaving a net energy released to the surroundings.

11. D. The reaction in question is the reverse of the given reaction and balanced with half the coefficients. The change in enthalpy of the reaction in question is half the value of the given reaction with a change in sign from negative to positive.

12. A. The formation reaction is $\frac{1}{2}\, O_2(g) \rightarrow O(g)$. One half mole of $O{=}O$ bonds are broken so the heat of formation is $\frac{1}{2}\,(+500)\ kJ/mol$.

13. D. The reaction is $H_2(g) \rightarrow 2H(g)$. ΔH for this reaction is $2(+218) = +436\ kJ$.

14. D. The reaction is $2H_2O(l) \rightarrow 4H_2(g) + O_2(g)$.
    $\Delta H = -2(-285.83) = +572\ kJ$.

15. A. The reaction is $NH_3(g) \rightarrow NH_3(aq)$.
    $\Delta H = -80.29 - (-46.19) = -34.10\ kJ$.

Free Response Answers

1. a. Butane is the alkane hydrocarbon containing four carbon atoms. Alkanes have all single carbon–carbon bonds and have the general formula, C_nH_{2n+2}. Water and carbon dioxide are the products of the combustion of hydrocarbons.

    $$C_4H_{10}(g) + {}^{13}\!/_2\, O_2(g) \rightarrow 4CO_2(g) + 5H_2O(g)$$

    (Double coefficients are acceptable.)

    b. The amount of heat in a thermochemical equation is proportional to the amount of reactants and products. Use the mole road to convert 1550 kJ to grams.

    $C_4H_{10}(g) + 13/2\, O_2(g) \longrightarrow 4CO_2(g) + 5H_2O(g) + 1550\ kJ$

    ? g

    $\uparrow$ × 58.0 g/mol $\qquad\qquad\qquad\qquad\qquad\qquad\qquad$ $\downarrow$

    $\div\ 2658\ kJ/mol\ C_4H_{10}(g)$

    mol $\longleftarrow\!$ 1550 kJ

    $x\, g = (1550\ kJ)(58.0\ g/mol)/(2658\ kJ/mol\ C_4H_{10}(g))$

    $\quad = 33.8\ g\ C_4H_{10}(g)$

c. *The molar heat of vaporization of butane is the difference between the heats of combustion of liquid and gaseous butane. Subtracting the equation for the combustion of gaseous butane from the equation for the combustion of liquid butane yields the equation for the vaporization of butane. Subtracting the corresponding heats yields the heat of vaporization of butane. Vaporization processes are always positive.*

$$C_4H_{10}(l) + \tfrac{13}{2}O_2(g) \rightarrow 4CO_2(g) + 5H_2O(g) \qquad \Delta H = -2635 kJ/mol$$
$$-[C_4H_{10}(g) + \tfrac{13}{2}O_2(g)\Delta \rightarrow 4CO_2(g) + 5H_2O(g)] \; \Delta H = -(-2658 kJ/mol)$$
$$\overline{C_4H_{10}(l) \rightarrow C_4H_{10}(g) \qquad\qquad\qquad\qquad \Delta H = +23 kJ/mol}$$

2. a. *Use the mole road and the balanced chemical equation to calculate the number of kJ burned in one mole of propane. Propane is the alkane hydrocarbon having three carbon atoms.*

$$C_3H_8(l) + 5O_2(g) \longrightarrow 3CO_2(g) + 4H_2O(g) \qquad \Delta H = ?$$

1.000 mol

$\downarrow$ $\times\ 44.00\ g/mol$

g $\xrightarrow{\quad\times -730.0\ kJ/15.00\ g\quad}$ kJ

x kJ = 1.000 mol(44.0 g/mol)(–730 kJ/15.0 g) = –2141 kJ

b. *Upon combustion of the same amount of butane, more heat is liberated when liquid water forms than when gaseous water forms because heat is released when water vapor condenses. That is, water vapor possesses more enthalpy (potential energy) than liquid water, and when gas changes to liquid, the heat is released.*

c. *Apply the same mole road approach to calculate the molar heat of combustion of propane when liquid water forms. The difference is the heat of vaporization of four moles of water because the balanced equation contains four moles of water. Divide by four and by the molar mass of water to obtain the heat of vaporization of water in kJ/g.*

$$x\ kJ/g = 1.000\ mol(44.0\ g/mol)(-792.9\ kJ/15.0\ g) = -2326\ kJ/mol$$

$$C_3H_8(l) + 5O_2(g) \rightarrow 3CO_2(g) + 4H_2O(g) \qquad \Delta H = -2141\ kJ/mol$$
$$-[C_3H_8(l) + 5O_2(g) \rightarrow 3CO_2(g) + 4H_2O(l)] \qquad \Delta H = -(-2326\ kJ/mol)$$
$$\overline{4H_2O(l) \rightarrow 4H_2O(g) \qquad\qquad\qquad\qquad \Delta H = +185\ kJ}$$

$$\Delta H = +185\ kJ/4\ mol = 46.25\ kJ/mol$$

$$x\ kJ/g = (46.25\ kJ/mol)/(18.0\ g/mol) = 2.57\ kJ/g$$

Your Turn Answers

5.1. *Melting of ice (the system) is endothermic as evidenced by the cooling of your hand (the surroundings) as the ice melts. Endothermic processes cool the surroundings by taking heat away from the surroundings, and converting it to potential energy of the system.*

5.2. *A campfire (the system) is an exothermic process. It releases heat to your hands (the surroundings). Potential energy of the system is converted to heat energy, and your hands feel the heat coming from the campfire.*

5.3. *The law of conservation of energy says that the energy of the universe is constant. Energy is neither created nor destroyed so the amount of energy that flows into a forward process will be the same as that flowing out of a reverse process. The value for ΔH will be the same for both processes but will have opposite signs. The sign of ΔH indicates the direction of heat flow.*

5.4. *It requires energy to melt a solid or to vaporize a liquid to overcome the strong forces of attraction between particles that exist in solids and liquids. This energy is released when gases change to liquids, and liquids change to solids. Sublimation is always an endothermic process because it requires energy to overcome strong forces of attraction in solids and liquids.*

5.5. *The value of the specific heat of water derives from the original and modern definitions of a calorie. One calorie is the amount of heat necessary to change one gram of water by one degree Celsius (or Kelvin). One calorie is 4.184 J.*

5.6. a. *Heat gained = mass $\times$ specific heat $\times$ temperature change*

$$q = m \times c \times \Delta T = 4.735 \text{ g} \times 4.184 \text{ J/g} \,^\circ\text{C} \times (16.0 \,^\circ\text{C} - 44.0 \,^\circ\text{C}) = -555 \text{ J}$$

The negative sign denotes the direction of heat flow, away from the hot water.

b. *Mass of ice = total mass − mass of hot water*
     = 6.097 g−4.735 g = 1.362 g

c. *Heat gained by ice =−heat lost by hot water = +555 J*

d. $q = m \times c \times \Delta T = 1.362 \text{ g} \times 4.184 \text{ J/g} \,^\circ\text{C} \times (16.0 \,^\circ\text{C} - 0 \,^\circ\text{C})$
     $= +91.2 \text{ J}$

e. *The heat of fusion of ice is calculated by subtracting the heat required to melt the ice from the total heat change of the system.*

   555 J − 91.2 J = 463.8 J

   x kJ/mol = 463.8 J (1 kJ/1000 J)(18.0 g/mol)/(1.362 g) = 6.13 J/mol

f. *% error = (accepted value − experimental value)/(accepted value)*
     $\times$ 100 =

   (6.13 − 6.02)/6.02 $\times$ 100 = 1.83% error

5.7. $Al(s) + 3/2 \, Cl_2(g) \rightarrow AlCl_3(s)$

5.8. *The formation of a stable form of an element from that element represents no net change so there is no heat change.*

$$Ca(s) \rightarrow Ca(s) \quad \Delta H_{rxn} = 0$$

5.9. a. $Ca(s) \rightarrow Ca(g) \quad \Delta H°_f = +179.3 \, kJ - 0 \, kJ = +179.3 \, kJ/mol$

b. $NH_3(g) \rightarrow NH_3(aq) \, \Delta H°_{soln} = -80.29 \, kJ - (-46.19 \, kJ)$
$$= -34.10 \, kJ/mol$$

c. $H_2(g) \rightarrow 2H(g) \quad \Delta H°_{BDE} = 2(+217.97 \, kJ) - 0 \, kJ = +435.94 \, kJ/mol$

d. $Br_2(g) \rightarrow Br_2(l) \quad \Delta H°_{cond} = 0 \, kJ - (+30.71 \, kJ) = -30.71 \, kJ/mol$

Table 5.3 or Appendix C in Chemistry: The Central Science *has the thermodynamic data to calculate the enthalpies of hundreds of processes.*

TOPIC 6

ELECTRONIC STRUCTURE OF ATOMS

The content in this topic is the basis for mastering Learning Objectives 1.5, 1.6, 1.7, 1.8, 1.12, 1.13, and 1.15 as found in the Curriculum Framework.

When you finish reviewing this topic, be sure you are able to:

- Calculate wave properties including frequency, wavelength, and energy of a photon
- Write ground state electron configurations of atoms using the periodic table as a guide
- Explain the photoelectric effect and photoelectron spectroscopy (PES)
- Describe electron structure using photoelectron spectroscopy, ionization energy data, and Coulomb's law
- Analyze data that relate ionization energies to electron configurations
- Explain electron configurations using Coulomb's law
- Identify and distinguish between paramagnetic and diamagnetic electron configurations

Section 6.1   The Wave Nature of Light

Electromagnetic radiation (also called radiant energy or light) is a form of energy having both wave and particle characteristics. It propagates through a vacuum at the speed of light, 3.00×10^8 m/s.

Wavelength, λ, is the distance between two adjacent peaks of the wave.

Frequency, ν, is the number of wavelengths (or cycles) that pass a given point in a second.

The **electromagnetic spectrum** includes all the wavelengths of radiant energy from short gamma rays to long radio waves (see Figure 6.1).

The **visible spectrum** is that part of the electromagnetic spectrum that we can see, generally with wavelengths ranging between about 400 and 700 nm.

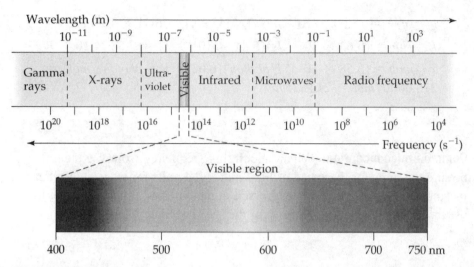

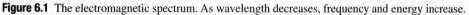

Figure 6.1 The electromagnetic spectrum. As wavelength decreases, frequency and energy increase.

Quantized Energy and Photons   Section 6.2

A **quantum** (also called a **photon**) is a specific particle of light energy that can be emitted or absorbed as electromagnetic radiation. The energy of a photon is described by the equation, $E = h\nu$. **All energy is quantized.** That is, matter is allowed to emit or absorb energy only in discrete amounts, whole number multiples of $h\nu$.

The **speed of light**, c, in a vacuum is 3.00×10^8 m/s.

Table 6.1 shows how the wavelength, frequency, and energy of a single photon of light are related mathematically.

Table 6.1 Mathematical relationships regarding electromagnetic radiation.

$\nu = c/\lambda$	$E = h\nu$	$E = hc/\lambda$
λ = wavelength in nm ν = frequency in 1/s or hertz; 1 Hz = 1 s^{-1}	E = energy of a single photon in joules	
c = speed of light = 3.00×10^8 m/s = 3.00×10^{17} nm/s; 1 nm = 10^{-9} m	h = Planck's constant = 6.63×10^{-34} J-s	

Example:

What is the frequency, the energy of a single photon, and the energy of a mole of photons of light having a wavelength of 555 nm?

Solution:

First, calculate the frequency from the wavelength using $\nu = c/\lambda$. Then, use your answer to calculate the energy of a single photon using $E = h\nu$. Finally, multiply the resulting energy by Avogadro's number of photons per mole to obtain the energy of a mole of photons.

$$\nu = c/\lambda = (3.00 \times 10^{17}\,nm/s)/(555\,nm) = 5.41 \times 10^{14}\,1/s$$
$$E = h\nu = (6.63 \times 10^{-34}\,Js)(5.41 \times 10^{14}\,1/s) = 3.58 \times 10^{-19}\,J$$
$$x\,J/mol = (3.58 \times 10^{-19}\,J/photon)(6.02 \times 10^{23}\,photons/mol) =$$
$$216{,}000\,J/mol = 216\,kJ/mol$$

Common misconception: When calculating frequency from wavelength, be sure the units for the speed of light match the units for wavelength. For instance, when wavelength is expressed in nanometers, it is convenient to use the value of 3.00×10^{17} nm/s for the speed of light.

Your Turn 6.1

Explain why the units for frequency are reciprocal seconds, 1/s. Write your answer in the space provided.

The **photoelectric effect** is the emission of electrons from a metal surface that is induced by light energy. Figure 6.2 illustrates the photoelectric effect.

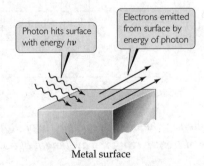

Photon hits surface with energy $h\nu$

Electrons emitted from surface by energy of photon

Metal surface

Figure 6.2 The photoelectric effect: Light energy striking a metal causes the surface to emit electrons.

Each type of metal requires a different minimum energy of light to cause the surface to emit electrons because each metal has a unique energy binding its electrons to the surface.

Line Spectra and the Bohr Model   Section 6.3

An **atomic emission spectrum** (or line spectrum) is a pattern of discrete lines of different wavelengths when the light energy emitted from energized atoms is passed through a prism or diffraction grating. Each element produces a characteristic and identifiable pattern. Figure 6.3 shows the atomic emission spectrum of hydrogen.

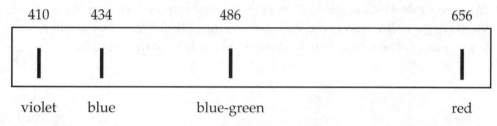

Figure 6.3 The atomic emission spectrum of hydrogen showing the colors and wavelengths of the visible lines.

The Bohr model of the atom (developed by Danish physicist Niels Bohr) explains the origin of the lines of the atomic emission spectrum of hydrogen. Adopting the idea that energies are quantized, Bohr proposed that electrons move in circular, fixed energy orbits around the nucleus. He postulated that each circular orbit corresponds to an "allowed" stable energy state. The ground state is the lowest energy state. Excited states are states of higher energy than the ground state. Energy, in the form of a photon, is emitted or absorbed by an electron only when it changes from one allowed energy state to another. The lines of the atomic emission spectrum of hydrogen result when an electron falls from a higher allowed state to a lower allowed state. The increment between each allowed state is proportional to Planck's constant, the speed of light, and the Rydberg constant, R_H (see Figure 6.4).

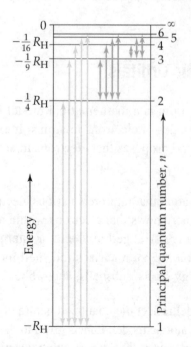

Figure 6.4 Energy levels in the hydrogen atom from the Bohr model. The four transitions with $n = 2$ as the lower state represent the four lines in the atomic emission spectrum of hydrogen.

The energy transition from allowed states $n = 3$ to $n = 2$ in Figure 6.4 gives rise to the 656 nm line in the atomic emission spectrum of hydrogen. The three transitions immediately to the right of the $n = 3$ to $n = 2$ transition correspond to the other three lines seen in the hydrogen spectrum.

Your Turn 6.2

←————————————————————————————————————

The energy transitions shown in Figure 6.4 correspond to which colors and wavelengths of the visible lines of the hydrogen spectrum? Which line corresponds to the largest energy change? Explain. Write your answer in the space provided.

Section 6.4

The Wave Behavior of Matter

Like light, electrons have characteristics of both waves and particles. Because a wave extends in space, its location is not precisely defined.

The **uncertainty principle**, applied to electrons in an atom, states that it is inherently impossible to simultaneously determine the exact position and momentum of an electron. The best that can be done is to calculate a probability of finding an electron in a certain region of space.

Section 6.5

Quantum Mechanics and Atomic Orbitals

The **quantum mechanical model** of the atom is a mathematical model that incorporates both wave and particle characteristics of electrons in atoms. It explains the atomic emission spectrum of hydrogen and proposes that electrons in atoms are arranged with certain energies.

The **shell model** is a simple model of the atom that interprets various electronic energies within an atom. Experimental evidence shows that electrons within atoms have different energies and that the electrons are arranged in **shells** or **energy levels** at varying distances from the nucleus. Table 6.2 summarizes the shell model of the atom with electrons arranged within energy shells, subshells, and orbitals.

The energy shells of the simple shell model reflect the quantized nature of the energy levels inherent in the quantum mechanical atomic model. Labels given to the atomic orbitals are examples of the quantum numbers used to label the resulting quantized states.

Table 6.2. The shell model of the atom.

Principal Energy Shell, n	Subshell Designation	Number of Orbitals	Number of Electrons
1	$1s$	1	2
2	$2s$	1	2
	$2p$	3	6
3	$3s$	1	2
	$3p$	3	6
	$3d$	5	10
4	$4s$	1	2
	$4p$	3	6
	$4d$	5	10
	$4f$	7	14
5	$5s$	1	2
	$5p$	3	6
	$5d$	5	10
	$5f$	7	14
	$5g$	9	18

A **principal energy shell** is designated 1, 2, 3, 4, 5, and so on. Principal energy shell 1 contains electrons that are located closest to the nucleus.

Energy subshells exist within principal energy shells. Subshells are designated s, p, d, f, g, and so on. Energy shell 1 has only an s subshell. Energy shell 2 has two subshells, s and p. Energy shell 3 contains s, p, and d subshells. Energy shell 4 has subshells s, p, d, and f; and so on.

An **orbital** is a region of space where an electron of a given energy is likely to be found. Each subshell contains one or more orbitals. Each orbital can contain a maximum of two electrons.

Your Turn 6.3

How many electrons can occupy the following energy shells and subshells?
$n = 4, 3d, 5s$, *and 5f? Write your answers in the space provided.*

Section 6.6   **Representations of Orbitals**

An **orbital** (or the square of a wave function) is a calculated probability of finding an electron of a given energy in a region of space. Figure 6.5 shows the electron probability distributions of various orbitals.

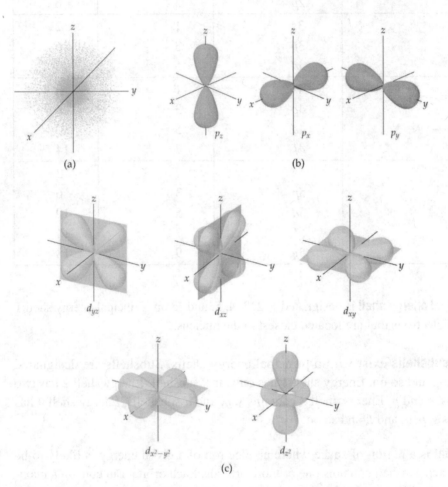

Figure 6.5 Electron-density distributions of an *s* orbital (a), three *p* orbitals (b), and five *d* orbitals (c).

Common misconception: An orbital is not the same as an orbit. An orbital is not a defined path of an electron. Rather it is a three-dimensional probability density distribution where an electron is likely to be found in the space surrounding the nucleus of an atom.

Many-Electron Atoms   Section 6.7

In many-electron atoms (atoms other than hydrogen), electron–electron repulsions cause different subshells to have different energies. Figure 6.6a shows the relative energy shells in many-electron atoms. Figure 6.6b is a convenient device for determining the relative energies, from lowest to highest of each subshell of a many-electron atom.

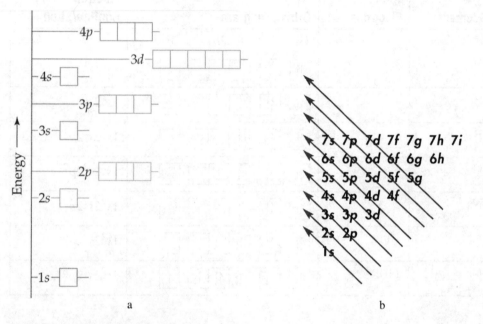

Figure 6.6 (a) Orbital energy shells in many-electron atoms. (b) A device to determine the relative energies of subshells. The lower energy subshells start at the bottom of the chart and increase in energy in the direction of the arrows, tail to head.

Your Turn 6.4

List the first 16 energy subshells shown in Figure 6.6 in order of increasing energy. Write your answer in the space provided.

Section 6.8

Electron Configurations

An **electron configuration** is a distribution of electrons among various orbitals of an atom. Table 6.3 shows the electron configurations of some lighter elements.

Table 6.3 Electron configurations of several lighter elements.

Element	Total Electrons	Orbital Diagram	Electron Configuration
		$1s$ $2s$ $2p$ $3s$	
Li	3	↑↓ ↑ ☐☐☐ ☐	$1s^2 2s^1$
Be	4	↑↓ ↑↓ ☐☐☐ ☐	$1s^2 2s^2$
B	5	↑↓ ↑↓ ↑☐☐ ☐	$1s^2 2s^2 2p^1$
C	6	↑↓ ↑↓ ↑↑☐ ☐	$1s^2 2s^2 2p^2$
N	7	↑↓ ↑↓ ↑↑↑ ☐	$1s^2 2s^2 2p^3$
Ne	10	↑↓ ↑↓ ↑↓↑↓↑↓ ☐	$1s^2 2s^2 2p^6$
Na	11	↑↓ ↑↓ ↑↓↑↓↑↓ ↑	$1s^2 2s^2 2p^6 3s^1$

Paramagnetic is a term referring to an atom having one or more unpaired electrons. Table 6.3 shows that lithium, boron, carbon, nitrogen, and sodium are all paramagnetic.

Diamagnetic means that all electrons in an atom are paired.

Your Turn 6.5 ⟵ ─────────────────────────────────────

Which of the elements listed in Table 6.3 are diamagnetic? Explain. Write your answer in the space provided.

Figure 6.6a or 6.6b can be used to write the ground-state electron configurations of most atoms.

Rules for writing ground-state electron configurations for atoms using Figure 6.6a or 6.6b are the following:

1. Fill the lowest energy shell first. Electrons in the same orbital must have opposite spins (different spin quantum numbers). The total number of electrons to be used is the atomic number of the element.

2. Place no more than two electrons per orbital to satisfy the Pauli exclusion principle.

3. Do not pair electrons in degenerate (same energy) orbitals until each orbital has one electron of the same spin. (This is called Hund's rule.)

4. Write the electron configuration by using subshell designations and superscripts to designate the number of electrons in each subshell.

Example:

Write the electron configuration for iron.

Solution:

The atomic number of iron is 26. Fill 26 electrons in the orbital diagram like this:

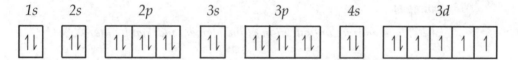

Write the corresponding ground-state electron configuration like this:

$1s^2 2s^2 2p^6 3s^2 3p^6 4s^2 3d^6$

An **excited-state configuration** has higher energy than the **ground-state configuration**. Excited-state configurations have one or more electrons occupying higher-energy levels than would be predicted from Figure 6.6. For example, one of many possible excited-state configurations for iron arises when an electron moves from a 4s subshell to a 3d subshell. The excited state orbital diagram looks like this:

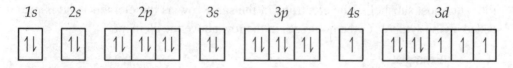

$1s^2 2s^2 2p^6 3s^2 3p^6 4s^1 3d^7$ is an excited-state electron configuration.

Section 6.9   **Electron Configurations and the Periodic Table**

The shell model of the atom is a useful model that can qualitatively explain and/or predict many atomic properties and trends in atomic properties. The arrangement of electrons into shells and subshells is reflected in the structure of the periodic table and in the periodicity of many atomic properties.

The periodic table is organized so that elements with similar electron configurations are arranged in columns as shown in Figure 6.7. Electron configurations of most elements can be determined by their location on the periodic table using Figure 6.7.

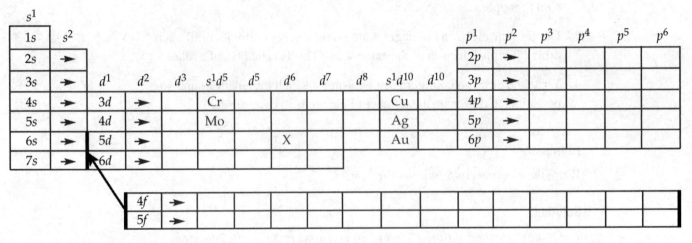

Figure 6.7 Elements on the periodic table are largely arranged according to electron configurations.

Example:

Write the electron configuration of the element marked by the "X."

Solution:

Element "X" is located in the row labeled 5d and the column labeled d^6, so there are six electrons in the 5d subshell, the highest occupied subshell. The electron configuration for element X ends in $5d^6$. Write the complete electron configuration by starting at the top left and working left to right and top to bottom until the element X is reached:

$$1s^2 2s^2 2p^6 3s^2 3p^6 4s^2 3d^{10} 4p^6 5s^2 4d^{10} 5p^6 6s^2 4f^{14} 5d^6$$

A **condensed electron configuration** for an element shows only electrons occupying the outermost subshells (the electrons in the same row as the element) and is preceded by the symbol for the noble gas in the row above the element.

Example:

Write the condensed electron configuration for element X.

Solution:

Element X has these subshells occupied in its row: $6s^2 4f^{14} 5d^6$ and the noble gas in the row above is xenon, Xe. The condensed configuration is (Xe) $6s^2 4f^{14} 5d^6$.

Your Turn 6.6

In a condensed electron configuration, what does the symbol (Xe) represent? Write your answer in the space provided.

Common misconception: Aufbau assumes that each individual element has a fixed set of orbital energies and that these energies are the same for different elements. Although both assumptions are invalid, Aufbau provides a good approximation for fixed energy levels and correctly predicts many electron configurations, especially those of *s* and *p* block elements. However, it fails to predict configurations of many *d* and *f* block elements because the energies of atomic orbitals are not fixed. Rather they are affected by each atom's or ion's electrons and protons.

The positive nucleus of an atom attracts its negative electrons and this attraction is the basis for the shell model. The energies of atomic orbitals determine the stabilities of atoms and how atoms react.

Coulomb's law is a way to estimate the relative forces of attraction between two charged particles such as a nucleus and an electron. Coulomb's law states that the **force of attraction** between two charged particles is related to the **magnitude of their charges** and the **distance** between them:

$$F = kQ_1Q_2/d^2$$

where

F is the force of attraction
Q_1 and Q_2 are the charges of the particles
d is the distance between the particles
k is a constant

It is not appropriate to use Coulomb's law to calculate interactions of electrons because Coulomb's law is a classical model and electrons are governed by quantum mechanics. However, we can use the equation to guide our thinking about the relative magnitudes of forces between charged particles. Because we rationalize these forces of attraction using Coulomb's law, we call them **coulombic forces**.

The greater the charges of the particles, the greater the coulombic forces between them. Also the closer the particles are to each other, the greater the attraction.

A similar equation describes the **energy** between the particles:

$$E = kQ_1Q_2/d$$

Ionization energy of an electron in an atom is the energy required to remove the electron from the atom. Coulomb's law indicates that the farther an electron is from the nucleus, the lower the energy required to remove that electron. Electrons close to the nucleus are held with a greater force than those that are more distant from the nucleus. Also, higher positive nuclear charges draw electrons closer to the nucleus and hold them with greater force.

Photoelectron Spectroscopy (PES)

Photoelectron spectroscopy is an experimental method used to measure the energies of electrons in atoms. These energies, called binding energies or ionization energies, give direct experimental evidence of the shell model of the atom.

Ionization energy is the energy required to remove an electron from the ground state of a gaseous atom.

Photoelectron spectroscopy works like the photoelectric effect except that the sample is in the gas phase. When a very high-energy ultraviolet photon of a known energy bombards a gaseous atom in a vacuum, the photon ejects an electron from the atom. The spectrometer measures the kinetic energy of the ejected electron. The ionization energy (also called the binding energy) of the electron is calculated using the following equation:

Ionization energy = energy of the photon minus the kinetic energy of the electron.

A typical photoelectron spectrometer uses high-energy photons of about 12,000 kJ/mol. Any ionization energy less than the bombarding photons can be measured by the spectrometer.

A **photoelectron spectrum** of an atom is a graph showing energy on the x-axis and relative number of electrons on the y-axis. The photoelectron spectra of the elements having atomic numbers 1 through 5 are shown in Figure 6.8.

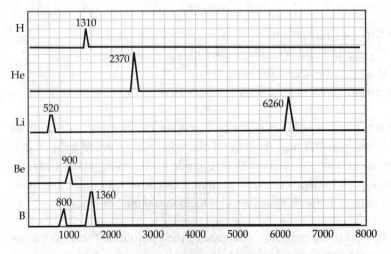

Figure 6.8 Photoelectron spectra of elements 1–5. The numbers are in kJ/mol.

Each signal or peak in a photoelectron spectrum represents the energy of one or more electrons in a given energy subshell. For example, lithium displays two peaks in its photoelectron spectrum, indicating that its electrons are distributed among two subshells.

The intensity of each signal at a given energy is interpreted as the relative number of electrons in that energy level. The 6260 kJ signal in the lithium photoelectron spectrum is twice the size as the 520 kJ peak. This means that there are twice as many electrons in one subshell compared to the other. The larger energy peak corresponds to 2 electrons in the $1s$ subshell because they are close to the nucleus and held with a larger force than the one electron in the $2s$ sublevel represented by the 520 kJ signal.

PES provides direct evidence for the shell model of the atom and is a useful means to rationalize and explain periodic properties and trends.

Electron configurations of atoms with multiple electrons can be inferred from photoelectron spectra. Table 6.4 uses data from the photoelectron spectra in Figure 6.8 to infer the electron configurations of hydrogen, helium, lithium, beryllium, and boron.

Table 6.4 Electron configurations from photoelectron ionization energies of lighter elements.

Atom	Electron Configuration	Ionization Energy, kJ/mol
H	$1s^1$	1310
He	$1s^2$	2370
Li	$1s^2$	6260
	$2s^1$	520
Be	$1s^2$	*
	$2s^2$	900
B	$1s^2$	*
	$2s^2$	1,360
	$2p^1$	800

*Because of the relatively high nuclear charges of beryllium and boron, the ionization energies of their $1s$ electrons are higher than the 12,000 kJ/mol photons typically used by photoelectron spectrometers to eject electrons. Thus, photoelectron spectra do not show corresponding signals for these electrons. This is true for the inner electrons of most heavy atoms. A higher energy technique, called x-ray photoelectron spectroscopy (XPS) is used to probe inner-core electrons on solid surfaces.

Your Turn 6.7

a.   *Explain what the peaks signify in the photoelectron spectra shown in Figure 6.8.*

b.   *For each signal in the photoelectron spectra shown in Figure 6.8, assign an orbital designation from the electron configuration of each atom.*

c.   *Use Coulomb's law to explain why the signal in the helium spectrum is at higher energy than the signal in the hydrogen spectrum.*

Write your answers in the space provided.

Table 6.5 shows photoelectron spectra values of orbital ionization energies in *kJ/mol* for elements 11–21.

Table 6.5   Photoelectron spectra values of orbital ionization energies for elements 11–21.

	Na	Mg	Al	Si	P	S	Cl	Ar	K	Ca	Sc
2s	6840	9070									
2p	3670	5310	7790								
3s	500	740	1090	1460	1950	2050	2440	2820	3930	4650	5440
3p			580	790	1010	1000	1250	1520	2380	2900	3240
3d											770
4s									420	590	630

Your Turn 6.8

a.   *Why are the values for the 1s electrons missing?*

b.   *Why are the values for the 2s electrons from aluminum through scandium missing, whereas they exist for sodium and magnesium?*

c.   *Use Coulomb's law to explain why sodium's 3s energy value is lower than its 2s subshell.*

d.   *How do the values listed for magnesium give evidence for the shell model of the atom?*

e.   *Predict the relative intensities of the three peaks corresponding to the energy values given for the aluminum atom. Justify your answer.*

f.   *Determine the trend in energy values from left to right along the row corresponding to the 3s subshell.*

g.   *Suggest a plausible reason for your answer to part f.*

h.   *Why does only scandium show an energy value for the 3d subshell?*

Write your answers in the space provided.

Spectroscopy

Spectroscopy is the study of the interaction of light with matter. Matter interacts differently with light of different energies. Thus, various methods of spectroscopy use different wavelengths of light to study different properties of matter. We have already seen applications of spectroscopy.

Mass spectrometry uses high-energy electrons, rather than light, to knock electrons from atoms and molecules producing positive ions that separate in a magnetic field according to their masses. Mass spectrometry is useful in determining **atomic and molar masses** and studying **isotope ratios**.

Atomic emission spectroscopy provides a basis for **identifying elements**. It uses high-energy photons, usually in the ultraviolet range, to excite electrons into higher atomic energy states. When an electron returns to a lower atomic energy state, it gives off a photon of light corresponding to the difference in energy between the states. Hydrogen and all other elements exhibit characteristic fingerprints: their unique atomic emission spectra.

A practical use of atomic emission is in fluorescent lighting. Fluorescent tubes, containing gases such as mercury vapor, neon, and argon, become excited by a high-voltage electrical discharge. As the excited electrons return to the ground state, they emit light that is absorbed and reemitted by a phosphorescent coating on the inside of the tube.

Photoelectron spectroscopy uses ultraviolet photons to remove valence-shell electrons from gaseous atoms. The measured energy of the ejected electron is used to calculate **ionization energy**. A higher energy technique, called XPS photoelectron spectroscopy (XPS) is used to probe inner-core electrons on solid surfaces.

Infrared spectroscopy probes the **vibrations of bonds within molecules** and gives evidence for various types of covalent bonds (discussed in Topics 8 and 9, respectively). Bonds in molecules vibrate with energies that correspond to the energies of infrared light, making infrared spectroscopy a valuable tool for determining the types of bonds in molecules.

Ultraviolet and visible radiation promote **electronic transitions** within atoms and molecules and give information about **atomic and molecular structure**. As the electrons vibrate with near ultraviolet and visible energies, they absorb light. By measuring light absorption, we can deduce molecular structure and measure the concentrations of the absorbing molecules as shown in Figure 6.9.

For example, a schematic of a typical visible spectrophotometer is shown in Figure 6.9.

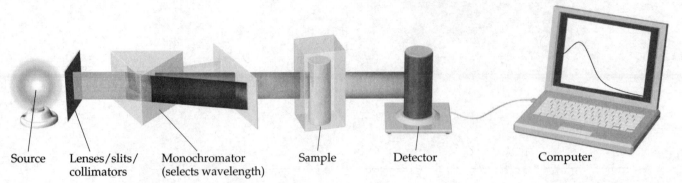

| Source | Lenses/slits/ collimators | Monochromator (selects wavelength) | Sample | Detector | Computer |

Figure 6.9 Components of a spectrometer.

A light source passes through a slit and is separated into its component wavelengths. A specific wavelength passes through a colored sample that absorbs the light in proportion to its concentration. The detector records the result and a computer graphs the data. Figure 6.10 illustrates the absorption of different concentrations of iodine over a range of wavelengths.

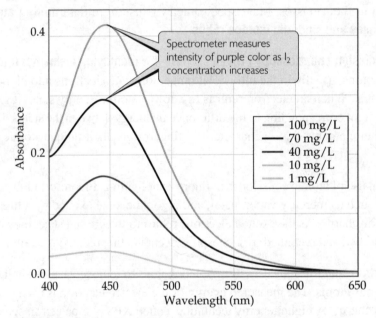

Figure 6.10 Visible spectra of I_2 at different concentrations

Beer's law relates the amount of light absorbed to the concentration of the absorbing species.

A = abc

A = the absorbance

a = the extinction coefficient or molar absorptivity, a characteristic of the substance at a given wavelength

b = the path length through which the light passes

c = the concentration of the absorbing species.

→ *Your Turn 6.9*

Examine Figure 6.10 to answer the following:

a. *Estimate the approximate wavelength at which iodine displays a maximum absorbance. Justify your answer.*

b. *Estimate the concentration of iodine that would display a maximum absorbance of 0.2 under the same conditions of the data illustrated. Explain your reasoning.*

c. *Estimate the approximate maximum absorbance of an iodine solution having a concentration of 20 mg/L under the conditions of the experiment. Explain how you arrived at your answer.*

Write your answers in the space provided.

Multiple Choice Questions

1. *Gaseous atoms of which of the following elements have electron configurations that are paramagnetic in their ground states?*

   I. Na   II. Mg   III. Al   IV. P

   A) *I, II, III, and IV*

   B) *I, II, and III only*

   C) *I, III, and IV only*

   D) *II only*

2. *What is the wavelength of light that has a frequency of $6.0 \times 10^{14} Hz$?*

   A) *$2.0 \times 10^6 nm$*

   B) *2000 nm*

   C) *500 nm*

   D) *200 nm*

3. *What is the maximum number of electrons that can occupy the 5f subshell?*

   A) *2*

   B) *5*

   C) *10*

   D) *14*

4. What is the maximum number of orbitals in a 4d subshell?

   A) 2

   B) 5

   C) 10

   D) 14

5. X: $1s^2 2s^2 2p^3$ Y: $1s^2 2s^1$

   Atoms X and Y have the ground-state electronic configuration shown above. The formula for the compound most likely formed from X and Y is

   A) YX.

   B) Y_2X.

   C) Y_3X.

   D) YX_3.

6. A blue line in the atomic emission spectrum of hydrogen has a wavelength of 434 nm. Which of the following calculates the energy of this light per mole of photons?

   A) $(10^6)(6.63)(3.00)(6.02)/(434)$ kJ/mol

   B) $(10^3)(6.63)(3.00)(6.02)/(434)$ kJ/mol

   C) $(10^6)(6.63)(3.00)(6.02)(434)$ J/mol

   D) $(10^3)(6.63)(3.00)(6.02)(434)$ J/mol

7. The wavelength of electromagnetic radiation is longer when

   A) its energy is small and its frequency is large.

   B) its energy is small and its frequency is small.

   C) its energy is large and its frequency is large.

   D) its energy is large and its frequency is small.

8. Which pair consists of species that have the same electron configuration?

   A) K and K^+

   B) K^+ and Ar

   C) Cl^+ and Ar

   D) Cl^- and K

9. Which are directly proportional?

   a.   frequency and wavelength

   b.   wavelength and energy

   c.   energy and frequency

A) *a only*

B) *b only*

C) *c only*

D) *a and b only*

10. *Which is an excited-state electron configuration?*

A) $1s^2 2s^2 2p^6 3s^1$

B) $1s^2 2s^2 2p^6 3s^2$

C) $1s^2 2s^2 2p^5 3s^1$

D) $1s^2 2s^2 2p^6 3s^2 3p^1$

11. *Which is the ground-state electron configuration for the Mn^{3+} ion?*

A) $[Ar]4s^2 3d^2$

B) $[Ar]4s^2 3d^5$

C) $[Ar]4s^0 3d^4$

D) $[Ar]4s^1 3d^3$

12. *Which species is paramagnetic in the ground state?*

A) N^{3-}

B) Zn^{2+}

C) Cu^{2+}

D) O^{2-}

Use Figure 6.10 to answer Questions 13–16. The figure shows data a student collected to determine the concentrations of violet-colored iodine in various solutions.

13. *If the highest peak represents a solution with a concentration of 100 mg/L of iodine, what is the approximate concentration of the solution represented by the second highest peak?*

A) *100 mg/L*

B) *70 mg/L*

C) *50 mg/?*

D) *25 mg/L*

14. *If a known solution containing 33 mg/L of iodine were measured under the same conditions, what would be its approximate absorbance?*

A) *445*

B) *0.25*

C) *0.14*

D) *0.10*

15. If the cell path length is 1.00 cm, estimate the approximate extinction coefficient under the condition of the experiment. (Ignore the units for the extinction coefficient.)

    A) 0.004

    B) 0.003

    C) 0.002

    D) 0.001

16. If the path length of the sample cell is doubled and all other parameters remain the same, the corresponding absorbances will

    A) remain the same.

    B) double.

    C) half.

    D) quadruple.

Free Response Questions

1. A line having a wavelength of 656 nm exists in the atomic emission spectrum of hydrogen.

    a. For the line, calculate the following values and specify their units:

        i.   frequency

        ii.   energy of a photon

        iii. energy of a mole of photons

    b. What color is the line? Explain your reasoning.

    c. Discuss the origin of the line, citing the Bohr theory of the atom. Specify any energy transitions that are applicable.

2. Molecules of oxygen are converted to atomic oxygen in the upper atmosphere by absorbing photons having wavelengths of 240 nm and shorter.

    a. Write the electron configuration of oxygen and tell why atomic oxygen is diamagnetic or paramagnetic.

    b. Write the electron configuration of the oxide ion.

    c. Calculate the energy equivalent of a photon of wavelength 240 nm in units of kJ/mol.

Multiple Choice Answers and Explanations

1. *C. Paramagnetic is a term referring to an atom having one or more unpaired electrons. Diamagnetic means that all electrons in an atom are paired. In orbital diagram form, the electron configurations of each of the elements listed are:*

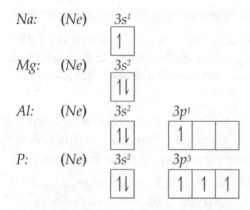

Na: *(Ne)* $3s^1$

Mg: *(Ne)* $3s^2$

Al: *(Ne)* $3s^2$ $3p^1$

P: *(Ne)* $3s^2$ $3p^3$

All the electrons in the neon core are paired and the 3s electrons of magnesium are paired. Na, Al, and P all have one or more unpaired electrons.

2. *C. Wavelength and frequency of light are related by the equation, $v = c/\lambda$, where v is the frequency in Hz (or 1/s), λ is the wavelength, and c is the speed of light. Rearranging the equation and solving:*

$$\lambda = c/v$$

$$\lambda = (3.00 \times 10^{17}nm/s)/(6.0 \times 10^{14}1/s) = 500nm$$

3. *D. Any f subshell contains seven orbitals, each of which can contain two electrons for a total of fourteen electrons maximum. The number of orbitals and maximum number of electrons in the other subshells are s, 1, 2; p, 3, 6; and d, 5, 10. The key to this question is to interpret a 5f subshell as a set of seven orbitals.*

4. *B. Any d subshell contains a set of five orbitals. The key to this question is to understand that it asks for the number of orbitals, not electrons.*

5. *C. Atom X is nitrogen and atom Y is lithium. Lithium will lose one electron to form a 1+ ion and nitrogen will gain three electrons to form a 3− ion.*

6. *B. The energy of a single photon is given by the following equation: $E = hc/\lambda$. Solving for E in J/photon and multiplying by 6.02×10^{23} photons/mol:*

$$E = (6.63 \times 10^{-34}\,Js)(3.00 \times 10^{17}\,nm/s)$$
$$(6.02 \times 10^{23}\,photons/mol)\,/(434\,nm)$$

$$= (6.63)(3.00)(6.02)(10^{-34})(10^{17})(10^{23})/(434)\,J/mol$$

$$= (6.63)(3.00)(6.02)(10^{6})/(434)\,J/mol$$

$$= (6.63)(3.00)(6.02)(10^{3})/(434)\,kJ/mol$$

Be careful to convert joules to kilojoules to match the units of the answer.

7. *B. Wavelength is inversely proportional to both energy and frequency as seen by the equations $\nu = c/\lambda$ and $E = hc/\lambda$. Small energies and frequencies are associated with large wavelengths.*

8. *B. Both have 18 electrons and an electron configuration of $(Ne)3s^2 3p^6$.*

9. *C. The energy of a photon is given by the following equations: $E = h\nu = hc/\lambda$.*

10. *C. A partially filled inner subshell indicates an excited-state configuration.*

11. *C. A manganese atom has 25 electrons because its atomic number is 25. Mn changes to Mn^{3+} with the loss of three electrons, two from the 4s subshell and one from the 3d subshell. Transition metals lose their highest "s" electrons before their highest "d" electrons.*

12. *C. A paramagnetic species is one that has one or more unpaired electrons. Cu^{2+} ion has the electron configuration: $[Ar]3d^9$. Four of the five redundant d orbitals are filled leaving one unpaired electron in the remaining orbital.*

13. *B. The absorbance of a species in solution is directly proportional to its concentration according to Beer's law. If a 100 mg/L solution absorbs at slightly more than 0.4, a slightly less than 0.3 absorbance would indicate a concentration of slightly less than ¾ of the original concentration.*

14. *C. Figure 6.10 shows that a solution having a concentration of 100 mg/L has an absorbance of approximately 0.42. Because absorbance is proportional to concentration the absorbance of a 33 mg/L solution will be:*

    A = (33 mg/L/100 mg/L)(0.42) = 0.14

15. *A.*

    A = abc

    0.42 = a (1.00 cm)(100 mg/ L)

    a = 0.0042

16. *B. With double the path length the light will interact with double the number of absorbing particles as it passes through the cell. This will double the absorbance.*

Free Response Answers

1. a. i. *Wavelength and frequency are related by the equation, $\nu = c/\lambda$*
       Substituting:
       $\nu = c/\lambda$
       $\nu = (3.00 \times 10^{17}\, nm/s)/656\, nm = 4.57 \times 10^{14}\, 1/s$

   ii. *The energy of a single photon is related to its frequency by the equation, $E = h\nu$.*
       $E = h\nu$
       $E = (6.63 \times 10^{-34}\, Js)(4.57 \times 10^{14}\, 1/s)$
       $= 3.03 \times 10^{-19}\, J/photon$

iii. *The energy of a mole of photons is the number of joules of one photon* $(3.03 \times 10^{-19} J/photon)$ *times Avogadro's number of photons:*

$$x \, J/mol = (3.03 \times 10^{-19} J/photon)(6.02 \times 10^{23} \, photons/mol)$$
$$= 182{,}000 \, J/mol = 182 \, kJ/mol$$

b. *The 656 nm line is red. The visible spectrum ranges from a short wavelength of about 400 nm for violet to a long wavelength of about 650 nm for red.*

c. *The red 656 nm line originates when an electron gives off a photon of corresponding energy upon making a transition from the $n = 3$ level to the $n = 2$ level in the Bohr model.*

2. a. $1s^2 2s^2 2p^4$

   Atomic oxygen is paramagnetic because two of its 2p electrons are unpaired.

   b. *The oxide ion has two more electrons than the oxygen atom. The electron configuration of the oxide ion, O^{2-}, is $1s^2 2s^2 2p^6$.*

   c. *For a photon of wavelength 240 nm, $\lambda = 240$ nm. Convert 240 nm to kJ/mol:*

   $$E = hc/\lambda = (6.63 \times 10^{-34} \, Js)(3.00 \times 10^{17} \, nm/s)/240 \, nm$$
   $$= 8.28 \times 10^{-19} \, J/photon$$
   $$(8.28 \times 10^{-19} \, J/photon)(6.02 \times 10^{23} \, photons/mol)(1 \, kJ/1000 \, J)$$
   $$= 499 \, kJ/mol$$

Your Turn Answers

6.1. *The unit for frequency is 1/s because frequency of light is measured in complete wavelengths per second or, more generally, complete cycles of anything per second.*

6.2. *Blue-green line, $n = 4$ to $n = 2$; blue line, $n = 5$ to $n = 2$; violet line, $n = 6$ to $n = 2$.*

   The violet line represents the largest energy change because violet light is the most energetic visible light.

6.3. *No matter what the principal energy shell is, all s subshells contain one orbital that can have two electrons. All p subshells contain three orbitals having six electrons. All d subshells can have ten electrons occupying five orbitals. Fourteen electrons can occupy all f subshells in seven orbitals. Principal energy shell 4 contains four subshells: 4s, 4p, 4d, and 4f with a maximum of two, six, ten, and fourteen electrons occupying each subshell respectively, for a total of thirty-two electrons.*

6.4. *1s, 2s, 2p, 3s, 3p, 4s, 3d, 4p, 5s, 4d, 5p, 6s, 4f, 5d, 6p, 7s.*

6.5. *Table 6.3 shows that Be and Ne are diamagnetic because all the electrons in their respective configurations are paired.*

6.6. *The symbol (Xe) represents the electron configuration of Xe:*
   $1s^2 2s^2 2p^6 3s^2 3p^6 4 s^2 3d^{10} 4p^6 5s^2 4d^{10} 5p^6$.

6.7. a. *Each peak in a photoelectron spectrum represents the relative number of electrons and the energy they have in the shell model of the atom.*

  b. *Hydrogen: The peak at 1310 kJ/mol represents one electron in the 1s subshell.*

  Helium: The peak at 2370 kJ/mol represents two electrons in the 1s subshell.

  Lithium: The peak at 520 kJ/mol represents one electron in the 2s subshell.

  Lithium: The peak at 6260 kJ/mol represents two electrons in the 1s subshell.

  Beryllium: The peak at 900 kJ/mol represents two electrons in the 2s subshell.

  Boron: The peak at 800 kJ/mol represents one electron in the 2p subshell.

  Boron: The peak at 1360 kJ/mol represents two electrons in the 2s subshell.

  c. *The electrons in the 1s subshell of helium are held more strongly by the nucleus than the electron in the 1s subshell of hydrogen because helium has a higher nuclear charge. Coulomb's law predicts that the force of attraction for electrons by the nucleus is proportional to the magnitude of the charges: $F = kQ_1Q_2/d^2$.*

6.8. a. *The 1s electrons are held so tightly to the nucleus for elements with nuclear charges 11–21 that the method of photoelectron spectroscopy will not measure the very high ionization energies. Typically, a photoelectron spectrometer will use a high-energy photon of about 12,000 kJ/mol to ionize an atom. Any electron with a binding (ionization) energy greater than 12,000 kJ/mol will not be ejected and its energy will not appear on the spectrum.*

  b. *The nuclear charge of aluminum and those of higher atomic numbers are greater than that for sodium and magnesium, so the ionization energies of the closely held electrons in the 2s subshell are greater than the energy of the ionizing photons of the experiment.*

  c. *The 3s electron is farther from the 11+ nuclear charge than are the 2s electrons. Coulomb's law states that the energy between the nuclear charge and the electrons is inversely proportional to the distance between them. $E = kQ_1Q_2/d$. The greater the distance from the nucleus, the lower the ionization energy.*

  d. *In magnesium and in all the atoms, the ionization energies decrease as the subshells increase from 2s, 2p, 3s, and so on. The data show that the electron ionization energies fall into different energy levels or shells.*

  e. *The electron configuration of aluminum is $1s^2 2s^2 2p^6 3s^2 3p^1$. Each energy value listed represents the orbital ionization energy of a particular subshell: 2p, 3s, and 3p. The intensity of each peak in the photoelectron spectrum represents the number of electrons in that particular subshell. Subshell 2p (representing six electrons) will have an intensity three times as great as subshell 3s (two electrons); and six times as large as subshell 3p (one electron).*

    f. From left to right along any row, the orbital ionization values increase with increasing nuclear charge.

    g. As the nuclear charge gets larger, the energy of attraction for electrons becomes greater according to Coulomb's law: $E = kQ_1Q_2/d$.

    h. Of the elements in Table 6.5, only scandium has a 3d electron in its ground-state electron configuration.

6.9. *a. Iodine displays a maximum absorbance at approximately 440 nm on the peaks of the graphs in Figure 6.10.*

    b. At an absorbance of 0.2, an iodine solution would have a concentration of about 50 mg/mL. On the graph an absorbance of 0.2 is approximately one-third the distance between the peaks for 40 mg/L and 70 mg/L.

    c. A sample having a concentration of 20 mg/L would display a maximum absorbance of twice that of the 10 mg/L sample which is approximately 0.08.

PERIODIC PROPERTIES OF THE ELEMENTS

The content in this topic is the basis for mastering Learning Objectives 1.7, 1.9, 1.10, and 1.11 as found in the Curriculum Framework.

When you finish reviewing this topic, be sure you are able to:

- Explain how the properties of elements vary across the periodic table using Coulomb's law and effective nuclear charge
- Explain the role that electron configurations play in determining periodic properties
- Know trends in atomic radius, ionic radius, and ionization energy and rationalize them by applying the ideas of Coulomb's law, effective nuclear charge, and the shielding effect
- Identify and explain the anomalies in the trends of first ionization energy
- Write balanced equations for the common reactions of Group 1 and 2 metals
- Apply periodic properties to chemical reactivity

Recall that a **Coulombic force** is the force of attraction between two charged particles. A Coulombic force increases with increasing charge and/or decreasing distance between the charged particles as described by Coulomb's law: $F = kQ_1Q_2/d^2$.

A similar relationship exists for energy: $E = kQ_1Q_2/d$.

Although we rarely calculate values using Coulomb's law, it is a useful relationship to guide our thinking about the relative forces between two charged particles.

Valence electrons are electrons in the outermost orbitals of atoms, those farthest from the nucleus.

Core electrons are inner electrons and include noble gas core electrons and electrons in completely full d orbitals.

Section 7.2   ## Effective Nuclear Charge

Effective nuclear charge is the net positive charge experienced by an electron in an atom. This charge is not the full nuclear charge because core electrons closer to the nucleus shield (cancel) part of the positive nuclear charge. As a result, valence electrons experience less than the full nuclear charge.

The **shielding effect** (also called the **screening effect**) is the reduction of the full nuclear charge experienced by an outer electron as a result of screening by inner core electrons. Inner core electrons always shield valence electrons but valence electrons shield one another ineffectively. The shielding effect arises from core electrons within the atom screening part of the positive nuclear charge.

A simple relationship between effective nuclear charge, Z_{eff}, and the number of protons in the nucleus, Z, is:

$$Z_{eff} = Z - S$$

S is the screening constant. The value of S, for comparison purposes, can be taken as approximately the total number of core electrons in the atom.

Effective nuclear charge increases from left to right across any period of the periodic table. Although the number of shielding core electrons remains constant in any period, the nuclear charge increases, and thus, the effective nuclear charge increases.

Compare electron configurations of sodium, magnesium, and aluminum and their corresponding effective nuclear charges.

$_{11}$Na: $1s^2 2s^2 2p^6 3s^1$ or $(Ne\text{-}10)3s^1$. $Z_{eff} = Z - S = 11 - 10 = +1$.

$_{12}$Mg: $1s^2 2s^2 2p^6 3s^2$ or $(Ne\text{-}10)3s^2$. $Z_{eff} = Z - S = 12 - 10 = +2$.

$_{13}$Al: $1s^2 2s^2 2p^6 3s^2 3p^1$ or $(Ne\text{-}10)3s^2 3p^1$. $Z_{eff} = Z - S = 13 - 10 = +3$.

All three elements contain ten noble gas core electrons that shield (cancel the charge of) ten protons in the nucleus. Because they each have a different total nuclear charge, the outer electrons in each element experience a different effective nuclear charge. As a consequence, the valence electrons of aluminum are drawn more closely to the nucleus and are held more tightly than the valence electron of sodium. (Remember, the valence electrons typically do not shield one another effectively.)

The shielding effect leads to periodic properties of elements as the effective nuclear charge varies across the periodic table. Those properties include atomic and ionic size and ionization energy.

The effective nuclear charge remains fairly constant going down a group of the periodic table. This is because the number of valence electrons within a group is constant while an increasing number of protons balance an increasing number of shielding noble gas core electrons. For example, compare the electron configurations of sodium, potassium, and rubidium.

$_{11}$Na: $1s^2 2s^2 2p^6 3s^1$ or $(Ne\text{-}10)3s^1$. $Z_{eff} = 11 - 10 = +1$.

$_{19}$K: $1s^2 2s^2 2p^6 3s^2 3p^6 4s^1$ or $(Ar\text{-}18)4s^1$. $Z_{eff} = 19 - 18 = +1$.

$_{37}$Rb: $1s^2 2s^2 2p^6 3s^2 3p^6 4s^2 3d^{10} 4p^6 5s^2$ or $(Kr\text{-}36)5s^1$. $Z_{eff} = 37 - 36 = +1$.

Your Turn 7.1

What is the approximate effective nuclear charge of scandium? Would you expect that its valence electrons are held more or less tightly than those of potassium? Use scandium's electron configuration to explain your answer. Write your answer in the space provided.

Section 7.3   Sizes of Atoms and Ions

Atomic radius is an estimate of the size of an atom. According to the quantum mechanical model, atoms do not have sharply defined boundaries because of the inherent uncertain distributions of electrons within atomic orbitals. Definite sizes are not obtainable, and although atomic size is defined in different ways based on the distances between atoms in various situations, comparisons of the relative size of atoms are instructive.

Within a period, atomic size increases from right to left. Atoms get smaller left to right because shielding remains roughly constant as nuclear charge increases. Coulomb's law tells us that as the effective nuclear charge, Q_1, increases, the force of attraction increases between the nucleus and the outermost electron whose charge is Q_2. This greater force draws the electron closer to the nucleus.

$$F = kQ_1Q_2/d^2$$

Your Turn 7.2

Use effective nuclear charge and Coulomb's law to order the relative sizes of sodium, magnesium, and aluminum. Explain your reasoning. Write your answer in the space provided.

Within a group, atomic size increases from top to bottom of the periodic table. Atoms get larger down a group because valence electrons occupy orbitals having higher principal quantum numbers and, thus, have greater probabilities of being farther from the nucleus. Coulomb's law states that as the distance, d, from the nucleus gets larger, the force of attraction for the outermost electron decreases.

Common misconception: Do not confuse a trend with an explanation for a trend. For example, if asked why the atomic radius of argon is smaller than that of chlorine, it is not acceptable to say that argon is farther to the right than is chlorine on the periodic table. That is a statement of the trend, not an answer to the question. The correct explanation is that argon's higher effective nuclear charge draws its valence electrons closer to the nucleus. Both atoms have ten core electrons screening their respective nuclei but argon has one more proton than does chlorine, giving argon the higher effective nuclear charge.

Figure 7.1 shows the relative sizes of some parent atoms and their ions.

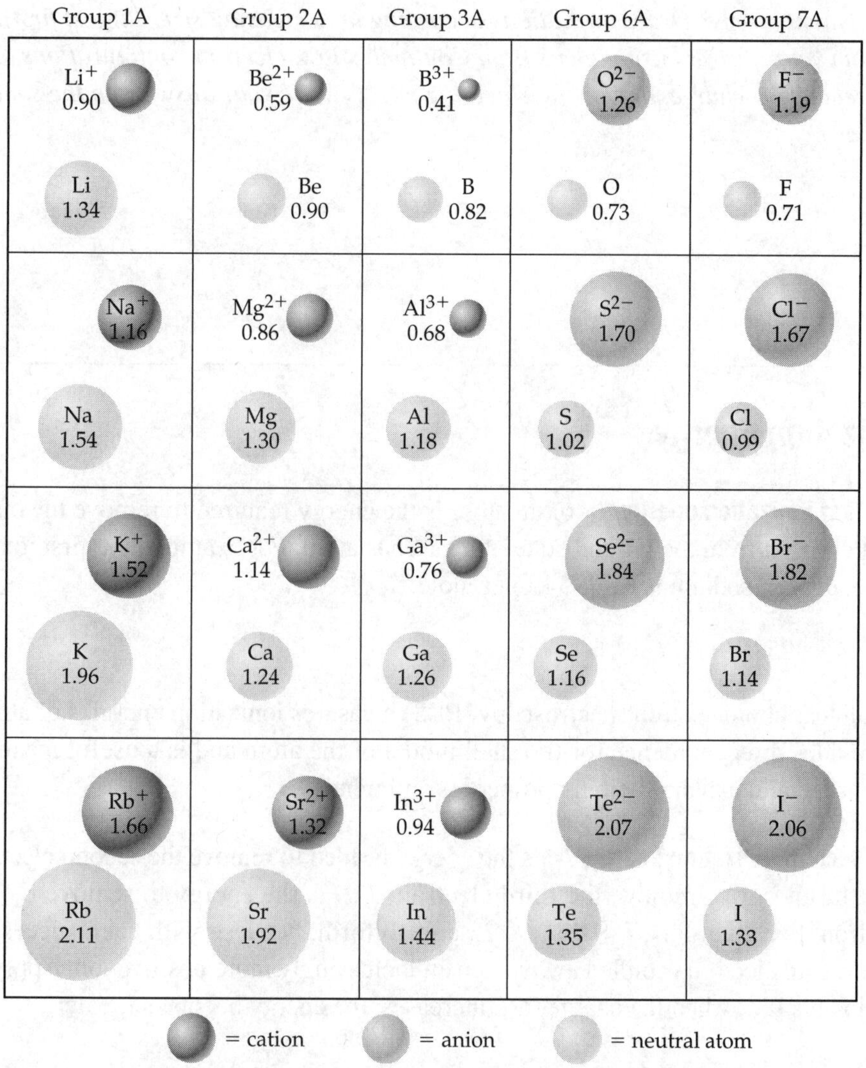

Group 1A	Group 2A	Group 3A	Group 6A	Group 7A
Li^+ 0.90	Be^{2+} 0.59	B^{3+} 0.41	O^{2-} 1.26	F^- 1.19
Li 1.34	Be 0.90	B 0.82	O 0.73	F 0.71
Na^+ 1.16	Mg^{2+} 0.86	Al^{3+} 0.68	S^{2-} 1.70	Cl^- 1.67
Na 1.54	Mg 1.30	Al 1.18	S 1.02	Cl 0.99
K^+ 1.52	Ca^{2+} 1.14	Ga^{3+} 0.76	Se^{2-} 1.84	Br^- 1.82
K 1.96	Ca 1.24	Ga 1.26	Se 1.16	Br 1.14
Rb^+ 1.66	Sr^{2+} 1.32	In^{3+} 0.94	Te^{2-} 2.07	I^- 2.06
Rb 2.11	Sr 1.92	In 1.44	Te 1.35	I 1.33

= cation   = anion   = neutral atom

Figure 7.1 The relative sizes of atoms and ions in angstroms, Å. 1 Å = 10^{-10} m.

Cations are always smaller than their parent atoms because the electrons lost upon the formation of a cation vacate the outermost orbitals. Underlying core electrons, which are not as well shielded from the nucleus, experience a greater effective nuclear charge so they are held closer to the nucleus. Additionally, there are fewer electron–electron repulsions. Thus, the size of a cation is always smaller than its parent atom.

Anions are always larger than their parent atoms because additional electrons within the valence shell produce increased electron–electron repulsions, causing the electrons to spread out more in space.

For ions carrying the same charge, the trend in size is the same as that for neutral atoms. The size of both cations and anions increases down a group and increases from right to left along a period.

Your Turn 7.3

Are the cations of sodium, magnesium, aluminum, and silicon smaller or larger than their parent atoms? Order the cations according to decreasing size (largest first). Explain your answers using ideas from Coulomb's law, electron configurations, effective nuclear charge, and/or the shielding effect. Write your answers in the space provided.

Section 7.4   Ionization Energy

The **first ionization energy,** I_1, of an atom is the energy required to remove the outermost electron from the ground state of a gaseous atom. For example, the first ionization energy of sodium is $+495$ kJ per mole:

$$495 \text{ kJ} + \text{Na} \longrightarrow \text{Na}^+ + \text{e}^-$$

Recall that photoelectron spectroscopy (PES) measures ionization energies of atoms. It provides direct evidence for the shell model of the atom and is a useful means to rationalize and explain periodic properties and trends.

The **second ionization energy,** I_2, is the energy needed to remove the second electron; I_3 is the energy to remove the third electron; $I(n)$ is the energy to remove the nth electron. For all atoms, $I_1 < I_2 < I_3$, and so forth, because with each successive removal, an electron is pulled away from an increasingly more positive ion. Applying Coulomb's law, when the charge, Q_1, increases, the energy becomes greater.

$$E = kQ_1Q_2/d$$

Figure 7.2 shows that first ionization energy increases from left to right along a period and from bottom to top within a group on the periodic table. Generally, the smaller atoms have the higher first ionization potentials. Outer electrons in smaller atoms are closer to the nucleus, less shielded, and held more tightly.

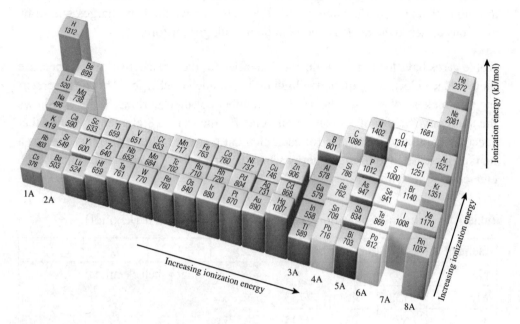

Figure 7.2 Trends in first ionization energy.

Subtle anomalies exist in the trend for first ionization energies between atoms of Groups 2A and 3A and between atoms of Groups 5A and 6A.

First ionization energies decrease from Be to B, Mg to Al, Zn to Ga, and Cd to In because electrons in filled *s* or *d* orbitals provide limited screening for electrons in the *p* subshells.

First ionization energies also decrease from N to O, P to S, and As to Se because of repulsion of paired electrons in the p^4 configuration of the Group 6A atoms.

Your Turn 7.4

Arrange the Period 3 elements in order of increasing first ionization energy, lowest to highest. Justify your answer noting and explaining any anomalies. Write your answer in the space provided.

Coulomb's law can guide our thinking about ionization energy, effective nuclear charge, and atomic size. Ionization energy of an electron in an atom is the energy required to remove the electron from the atom. Coulomb's law states that the farther an electron is from the nucleus, the lower the energy required to remove that electron. Electrons close to the nucleus will be held with a greater force than those that are more distant from the nucleus. Also, higher positive nuclear charges will draw electrons closer to the nucleus and hold them with greater force.

Noble gases have the highest ionization energies for their respective periods because their valence electrons experience high effective nuclear charges. This poor screening also makes noble gases the smallest members of their periods. Table 7.1 shows the successive values of ionization energies for the Period 3 elements. Notice that successive ionization energies for each element increase. Notice also that there is a marked increase in ionization energy when the first noble gas core electron for each element is removed.

Table 7.1   Values for ionization energies, I, for Na through Ar (kJ/mol).

Element	I_1	I_2	I_3	I_4	I_5	I_6	I_7
Na	495	4562	(inner-shell electrons)				
Mg	738	1451	7733				
Al	578	1817	2745	11,577			
Si	786	1577	3232	4356	16,091		
P	1012	1907	2914	4964	6274	21,267	
S	1000	2252	3357	4556	7004	8496	27,107
Cl	1251	2298	3822	5159	6542	9362	11,018
Ar	1521	2666	3931	5771	7238	8781	11,995

Section 7.5   Electron Affinity

Electron affinity, ΔH_{ea}, is the energy change when an electron is added to a gaseous atom.

$$F(g) + e^- \rightarrow F^-(g) \quad \Delta H_{ea} = -328 \, \text{kJ/mol}$$

When most atoms attract electrons, energy is released so the sign of ΔH_{ea} is negative. Electron affinity generally increases in magnitude (becomes more negative) from left to right along a period and from bottom to top within a group. The valence shells of smaller atoms are less shielded and attract electrons more readily. Fluorine is an anomaly because its smaller size causes electron–electron repulsion making it less likely to attract an electron than chlorine. Figure 7.3 shows the electron affinities of the representative elements.

1A	2A	3A	4A	5A	6A	7A	8A
H −73							He >0
Li −60	Be >0	B −27	C −122	N >0	O −141	F −328	Ne >0
Na −53	Mg >0	Al −43	Si −134	P −72	S −200	Cl −349	Ar >0
K −48	Ca −2	Ga −30	Ge −119	As −78	Se −195	Br −325	Kr >0
Rb −47	Sr −5	In −30	Sn −107	Sb −103	Te −190	I −295	Xe >0

Figure 7.3 Electron affinity in kJ/mol for selected s- and p-block elements.

Common misconception: It is important to recognize the difference between ionization energy and electron affinity. Ionization energy measures the energy change when an atom loses an electron, whereas electron affinity measures the energy change when an atom gains an electron. Ionization energies are usually endothermic (with positive energies) and electron affinities are usually exothermic (with negative energies). Keep in mind, that the more negative the electron affinity, the larger its magnitude. The sign of the energy value tells what direction the energy flows, not how large the energy is.

Figure 7.3 shows that the trends for electron affinity are not as evident as they are for ionization energy. The group 8A noble gases all have positive electron affinities because an electron added to a noble gas would reside in a higher energy s subshell that is well screened by a noble gas core. Be and Mg also have positive electron affinities because an added electron would reside in a higher energy p subshell. The electron affinities of the group 5A elements are more positive than expected because the added electron would experience an electron–electron repulsion upon forming a p^4 configuration.

Tables 7.2 and 7.3 summarize the trends of important periodic properties and their anomalies with explanations.

Table 7.2   Related properties and trends on the periodic table.

Periodic Property	Trend: Increases Across the Table	Explanation for Trends
Atomic size Ionic size	 ← – – – – – – – – ↓	As effective nuclear charge increases left to right, outer electrons are held more closely and more strongly to the nucleus.
First ionization energy, I_1	 ↑ – – – – – – →	Top to bottom, outer electrons are in larger atomic orbitals and farther from the nucleus. As size decreases, attraction for electrons increases, increasing first ionization energy.

Table 7.3 Periodic "anomalies" and explanations.

Periodic Property	Periodic Anomalies	Explanation
Atomic size	None	—
First ionization energy, I_1	B < Be, Al < Mg, Ga < Zn, In < Cd	Partial shielding by s and d valence electrons decreases Z_{eff}, thus decreasing ionization energy.
First ionization energy, I_1	O < N, S < P, Se < As, Te < Sb	Electron–electron repulsion in p^4 configurations of Group 6A atoms decreases ionization energy.

Section 7.6   Metals, Nonmetals, and Metalloids

Metals tend to have low ionization energies and lose electrons readily. Metals tend to form positive ions. A metal typically has well-screened valence electrons that experience relatively low effective nuclear charges.

Metals exhibit luster, conduct heat and electricity, are malleable (can be hammered into thin sheets), and ductile (can be drawn into wires).

The simple electron-sea model explains the properties of metals. Metals exist as an array of metal cations in a sea of loosely held electrons. Electrostatic attractions confine the mobile electrons to the metal and they are uniformly distributed throughout the structure. These mobile electrons explain the electrical and thermal conductivity of metals because the electrons can readily flow through the solid (electricity) and transfer kinetic energy (heat). The deformation of metals (malleability and ductility) arises because as the metal reshapes, the sea of electrons readily redistributes itself about the metal. Figure 7.4 shows the electron-sea model of metallic solids.

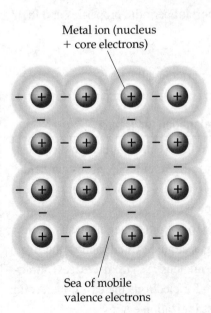

Metal ion (nucleus + core electrons)

Sea of mobile valence electrons

Figure 7.4 Electron-sea model of metallic bonding. The valence electrons delocalize to form a sea of mobile electrons that surrounds and binds together an extended array of metal ions.

Metallic character is a reflection of the extent to which elements exhibit the physical and chemical properties of metals. Generally, metallic character increases right to left along a period and top to bottom within a group.

The **reactivity** of a metal relates directly to the electron configuration of its atoms, its effective nuclear charge, its ionization energy, and its placement on the periodic table. For example, metals with the highest reactivity are those that lose electrons most readily. They have low ionization energies, low effective nuclear charges with effective screening of valence electrons, and large size. It is no coincidence that metals having these characteristics are found on the extreme left side of the periodic table. Of those, the ones toward the bottom are more reactive than those at the top of their respective groups.

Most oxides of Group 1 and 2 metals are basic. These oxides are called "base anhydrides" (bases without water).

They react with water to produce bases:

$$CaO(s) + H_2O(l) \rightarrow Ca^{2+}(aq) + 2OH^-(aq)$$
$$Li_2O(s) + H_2O(l) \rightarrow 2Li^+(aq) + 2OH^-(aq)$$

Nonmetals tend to have high ionization energies so they do not lose electrons readily. Rather, nonmetals tend to attract electrons from other atoms to form negative ions. A nonmetal gains electrons because its valence shell experiences a relatively high effective nuclear charge.

Nonmetals do not readily conduct heat or electricity. Many are gases or brittle solids. Bromine is a liquid at room temperature. Compounds composed entirely of nonmetals are molecular substances.

Most nonmetal oxides are acidic and are called "acid anhydrides." They react with water to produce acids. Usually, the nonmetal retains its oxidation number.

$$SO_2(g) + H_2O(l) \rightarrow H_2SO_3$$
$$SO_3(g) + H_2O(l) \rightarrow H^+(aq) + HSO_4^-(aq)$$
$$CO_2(g) + H_2O(l) \rightarrow H_2CO_3$$
$$Cl_2O_7(s) + H_2O(l) \rightarrow 2H^+(aq) + 2ClO_4^-(aq)$$
$$P_2O_5(s) + 3H_2O(l) \rightarrow 2H_3PO_4(aq)$$
$$Cl_2O_3(s) + H_2O(l) \rightarrow 2HClO_2(aq)$$
$$2NO_2(g) + H_2O(l) \rightarrow HNO_2(aq) + H^+(aq) + NO_3^-(aq)$$

Notice that strong acids are shown in ionic form and weak acids are shown in molecular form. When nitrogen dioxide reacts with water, both nitrous and nitric acids are formed.

Metalloids have properties intermediate between those of metals and nonmetals. They do not exhibit luster and are poor conductors of heat and electricity.

Section 7.7   Trends of Group 1A and Group 2A Metals

The **alkali metals** (Group 1A) are soft, metallic solids. They all have s^1 valence electron configurations and lose one electron to form $1+$ cations. Generally, reactivity of metals depends on their low ionization energies. Because the size of the alkali metals increases down the group, their ionization energies decrease. Thus, alkali metals become more reactive down the group because they lose their weakly held valence electron (react) more readily.

Reactivity of the alkali metals (Group 1): $Li < Na < K < Rb < Cs$.

Your Turn 7.5

Which metal is more reactive, sodium or lithium? Use Coulomb's law, electron configuration, effective nuclear charge, and ionization energy to justify your answer. Write your answer in the space provided.

All alkali metals react with water to produce hydrogen gas because they are above hydrogen on the activity series (see Section 4.4):

$$2Na(s) + 2H_2O(l) \rightarrow 2Na^+(aq) + 2OH^-(aq) + H_2(g)$$

All alkali metals react with most nonmetals:

$$2Li(s) + H_2(g) \rightarrow 2LiH(s)$$

$$2K(s) + S(s) \rightarrow K_2S(s) \qquad 2Rb(s) + Cl_2(g) \rightarrow 2RbCl(s)$$

$$6Li(s) + N_2(g) \rightarrow 2Li_3N(s) \quad 4Li(s) + O_2(g) \rightarrow 2Li_2O(s)$$

Common misconception: Know the difference between the oxide ion, O^{2-}, the peroxide ion, O_2^{2-}, and the superoxide ion, O_2^-.

Your Turn 7.6

Write and balance a chemical equation to describe what happens when solid potassium is added to water. Classify the reaction as acid–base, redox, or precipitation. Describe what you would observe when the reaction takes place. Justify why potassium is more reactive than sodium toward water. Write your answer in the space provided.

All **alkaline earth metals** (Group 2A) have s^2 valence electron configurations and lose two electrons to form 2+ cations. They all have low ionization energies but each is higher than the corresponding alkali metal of the same period. These higher ionization energies make the alkaline earth metals less reactive than the alkali metals. Like the alkali metals, the alkaline earth metals become more reactive as they progress down the group because as their sizes become larger, their corresponding ionization energies become smaller.

Reactivity of the alkaline earth metals (Group 2): Be < Mg < Ca < Sr < Ba.

Calcium and the elements below it react with liquid water:

$$Ca(s) + 2H_2O(l) \rightarrow H_2(g) + Ca^{2+}(aq) + 2OH^-(aq)$$

Because magnesium is not as reactive as calcium, it does not react with liquid water but reacts with steam:

$$Mg(s) + H_2O(g) \rightarrow H_2(g) + MgO(s)$$

All alkaline earth metals react with nonmetals:

$$Sr(s) + H_2(g) \rightarrow SrH_2(s) \qquad 2Ca(s) + O_2(g) \rightarrow 2CaO(s)$$
$$3Mg(s) + N_2(g) \rightarrow Mg_3N_2(s) \quad Ba(s) + Cl_2(g) \rightarrow BaCl_2(s)$$

Your Turn 7.7

Write and balance a chemical equation to describe what happens when solid barium is added to water. Classify the reaction as acid–base, redox, or precipitation. Would you expect barium or cesium to be more reactive toward water? Justify your answer. Write your answers in the space provided.

Section 7.8   Trends for Selected Nonmetals

Hydrogen's $1s^1$ electron configuration places it in Group 1A above the alkali metals. However, hydrogen has many unique properties and does not belong to any particular group. The ionization energy of hydrogen is extremely high (1312 kJ/mol) because of the complete lack of shielding of its single electron. Its high ionization energy, its ability to gain an electron to form the hydride ion, H^-, and its tendency to share electrons to form covalent bonds are the basis for classifying hydrogen as a nonmetal.

Allotropes are different forms of the same element in the same state. For example, several members of the carbon, nitrogen, and oxygen families can exist as allotropes as shown in Table 7.4.

Table 7.4   Allotropes are different forms of the same element in the same physical state.

Element	Allotropes
Carbon	$C(s, \text{graphite})$, $C(s, \text{diamond})$
Phosphorus	$P_4 (s, \text{white})$, $P_4 (s, \text{red})$
Oxygen	Dioxygen, $O_2(g)$, Ozone, $O_3(g)$
Sulfur	$S(s)$, $S_8(s)$

The **halogens** (Group 7A) exist as diatomic molecules. Fluorine, $F_2(g)$, and chlorine, $Cl_2(g)$, are gases. Bromine, $Br_2(l)$, is a liquid at room temperature and Iodine, $I_2(s)$, is a solid that readily sublimes (changes directly from a solid to a gas) at room temperature. All share the s^2p^5 valence electron configuration and each gains one electron to form a 1− anion. Artists use hydrofluoric acid, HF, to etch glass. Chlorine is commonly used as a disinfectant in drinking water and swimming pools:

$$Cl_2(g) + H_2O(l) \rightarrow H^+(aq) + Cl^-(aq) + HOCl(aq)$$

Common misconception: The above reaction is a redox reaction called a disproportionation, where chlorine is both oxidized and reduced. Notice that the strong acid, HCl, is written in ionized form.

The **noble gases** (Group 8A) are all nonmetallic monatomic gases at room temperature. They all have completely filled s and p subshells and form a limited number of compounds: XeF_2, XeF_4, XeF_6, KrF_2, and HArF.

Multiple Choice Questions

Questions 1–4 refer to the following data:
The first five ionization energies, in kJ/mol, for element E are shown below.

I_1	I_2	I_3	I_4	I_5
578	1817	2745	11,577	16,091

1. *The element is likely to form ionic compounds in which its charge is*

   A) 1+

   B) 2+

   C) 3+

   D) 4+

2. *The most likely formula for the oxide of element E is*

   A) E_2O

   B) E_3O_2

   C) EO_2

   D) E_2O_3

3. *The most probable ground state electron configuration for element E is*

   A) $1s^2 2s^2 2p^6 3s^2 3p^1$

   B) $1s^2 2s^2 2p^6 3s^2 3p^2$

   C) $1s^2 2s^2 2p^6 3s^2 3p^3$

   D) $1s^2 2s^2 2p^6 3s^2$

4. *The identity of element E is most probably:*

   A) *phosphorus*

   B) *magnesium*

   C) *aluminum*

   D) *silicon*

Questions 5–7 refer to the following:
Consider second period elements having atomic numbers 4–8.

5. *Which sequence is arranged in order of increasing first ionization energies?*

   A) *Be, B, C, N, O*

   B) *B, Be, C, O, N*

   C) *Be, B, C, O, N*

   D) *B, Be, C, N, O*

6. Which of these elements would probably have the lowest third ionization energy?

    A) Be

    B) B

    C) C

    D) N

7. Which sequence is arranged in order of increasing atomic size?

    A) Be, B, C, N, O

    B) B, Be, C, O, N

    C) Be, B, C, O, N

    D) O, N, C, B, Be

Questions 8–10 refer to the following elements: Be, Mg, Ca, Sr, Ba.

8. Which sequence is arranged in order of increasing atomic size?

    A) Be, Mg, Ca, Sr, Ba

    B) Ba, Sr, Ca, Mg, Be

    C) Be, Ca, Ba, Mg, Sr

    D) Be, Ba, Ca, Mg, Sr

9. Which element has an electron that experiences the highest effective nuclear charge?

    A) Be

    B) Mg

    C) Ca

    D) Sr

10. Which element has the largest number of screening electrons?

    A) Ba

    B) Mg

    C) Ca

    D) Sr

11. Which atom in the ground state is paramagnetic?

    A) He

    B) Be

    C) Ba

    D) C

12. Which is not true of nonmetals?

   A) Most of their oxides are acidic.

   B) They are poor conductors of heat.

   C) They are poor conductors of electricity.

   D) Most tend to lose electrons readily.

Questions 13 and 14 refer to the following sets of elements:

   I.   Mg and Al
   II. As and Se
   III. Zn and Ga
   IV. P and S

13. Which show a reversal in the trend for first ionization energy because of electron–electron repulsion?

   A) I only

   B) I and III only

   C) I and II only

   D) II and IV only

14. Which show a reversal in the trend for first ionization energy because of screening by full orbitals?

   A) I only

   B) I and III only

   C) I and II only

   D) II and IV only

15. Which element has the smallest first ionization energy?

   A) Ca

   B) Ga

   C) Ge

   D) As

16. Graphite and diamond

   A) are both sp^3 hybridized.

   B) have the same crystal structure.

   C) are isotopes.

   D) are the same element, but two different substances.

17. Which are not a set of allotropes?

    A) O_2 and O_3

    B) graphite and diamond

    C) white and red phosphorus

    D) uranium-235 and uranium-238

Questions 18–20 refer to the following elements.

    A) Cl

    B) Ba

    C) F

    D) Ne

18. Which element has the largest difference between the second and third ionization energies?

19. Which element has the largest electron affinity?

20. Which element has the most oxidation states?

Free Response Questions

1. Use Coulomb's law and/or the screening effect and details of the modern atomic theory and periodicity to explain why:

    a. atomic radii become larger as the atomic number within a family gets larger.

    b. atomic radii become smaller as the atomic number within a period gets larger.

    c. the radius of an oxide ion is larger than the radius of an oxygen atom.

    d. the first ionization energy of aluminum is larger than the first ionization energy of magnesium.

    e. the third ionization energy of an element is always larger than its second ionization energy.

2. Answer the following questions using the data in Table 7.1, Coulomb's law, the shielding effect, electron configurations, and/or photoelectron spectroscopy.

    a. What evidence exists for the number of valence electrons in each of the Period 3 elements?

    b. Rationalize the three ionization energies of magnesium shown in Table 7.1.

    c. Explain how the data predict that the aluminum ion will carry a 3+ charge.

    d. How does the data in Table 7.1 support the shell model of the atom?

    e. Of the Period 3 metals, which is the most reactive? Justify your answer.

    f. Write the most probable formula for the oxide of each of these elements: Na, Mg, Al, Si. Justify your answers.

Multiple Choice Answers and Explanations

1. C. The marked difference between ionization energies I_3 and I_4 indicates that the fourth electron to be ionized is a poorly screened core electron, probably a noble gas core electron. Thus, the three valence electrons will be lost relatively easily, but the fourth electron will not, resulting in a 3+ ion.

2. D. Because the charge of an ionic compound is zero, a 3+ ion, E^{3+}, will combine with an oxide ion, O^{2-}, to form E_2O_3.

3. A. Element E has three valence electrons in the outer s and p subshells, which will be lost upon forming a 3+ ion.

4. C. Aluminum is in Group 3A, indicating that it has three valence electrons and forms an ion with a 3+ charge.

5. B. Answer D reflects the general trend that ionization energy increases left to right along any period to parallel the general increase in effective nuclear charge. However, B has a lower ionization energy than Be because the $2s^2$ electrons of B partially shield the $2p^1$ electron. Also the electron–electron repulsion of the two paired electrons in the $2p^4$ configuration of oxygen makes the ionization energy of oxygen slightly lower than that of nitrogen.

6. B. Boron in Group 3A has three valence electrons, all of which will be lost relatively easily because they are screened from the nuclear charge by core electrons. The third electron in carbon, nitrogen, and oxygen is also screened by core electrons but they each have higher effective nuclear charges than does boron.

7. D. The effective nuclear charge generally increases from left to right along a period. This means that the positive charge experienced by the outermost valence electron increases from left to right. Coulomb's law tells us that the force acting between the nucleus and the outermost electron is directly proportional to the effective nuclear charge. The higher the force, the closer the electron is drawn to the center of the atom and the smaller is its size.

8. A. From top to bottom of any group, the valence electrons of atoms reside in increasingly larger orbitals (shells) having higher principal quantum numbers. The outer electrons are farther from the nucleus as the atoms proceed down a group and their size increases.

9. D. The electron that experiences the highest effective nuclear charge for any given atom is the innermost 1s electron because it is not shielded from the nuclear charge by any other electrons. Thus, the atom with the electron that feels the highest effective nuclear charge is the one with the most protons; in this case, strontium.

10. A. Barium has an electron configuration of $1s^2 2s^2 2p^6 3s^2 3p^6 3d^{10} 4s^2 4p^6 4d^{10} 5s^2 4p^6 6s^2$ or $(Xe)6s^2$. It has 2 valence electrons and 54 core electrons. Core electrons screen (shield) valence electrons.

11. D. Paramagnetic means that one or more electrons are unpaired. The electron configuration of carbon contains two unpaired electrons. The electron configurations of all the other elements listed show that all the electrons are paired, a condition termed diamagnetic.

12. D. Nonmetals tend to have large effective nuclear charges, which give them high electron affinities and high ionization energies, so they tend to gain electrons readily. Metals have low effective nuclear charges, causing them to lose electrons readily because of their relatively low ionization energies.

13. D. First ionization energy generally increases from left to right along any period. However, selenium has two paired electrons in its $4p^4$ subshell. They repel each other, giving Se a lower ionization energy than As, which has only three electrons in the 4p sublevel, all of which are unpaired. Sulfur also has four p electrons, two of which are paired, in its valence shell compared to three unpaired p electrons for phosphorus. Therefore, sulfur has a lower ionization energy than phosphorus.

14. B. The $3s^2$ configuration of aluminum partially shields its $3p^1$ electron, giving aluminum a lower than expected first ionization energy. Similarly, gallium's 4p electron is effectively shielded from the nucleus by its ten 3d electrons giving it a lower ionization energy than zinc.

15. B. Generally, first ionization energy increases from left to right along any period because the effective nuclear charge increases. However, gallium's 3p electron is screened by the 4s level and the 3d level giving gallium a slightly smaller effective nuclear charge than calcium.

16. D. Graphite and diamond are allotropes, two different forms of the same element in the same physical state. Even though they are both carbon, they are different substances. Graphite is sp^2 hybridized while diamond is sp^3 hybridized.

17. D. U-235 and U-238 are isotopes, atoms having the same number of protons but different number of neutrons. Allotropes are different forms of the same element in the same phase.

18. B. Group 2 atoms have relatively low first and second ionization energies because their two valence electrons are well screened from the nuclear charge. However, their third ionization energies are relatively high because the third electron comes from a poorly screened inner noble gas core.

19. A. Generally, electron affinity increases from left to right along a period and from bottom to top within a group. However, chlorine has a higher electron affinity than fluorine because fluorine's small size contributes to considerable electron–electron repulsion.

20. A. Chlorine displays oxidation states of 1−, 0, 1+, 3+, 5+ and 7+.

Free Response Answers

1. a. Atomic radii become larger as the atomic number within a family gets larger because down a group, the outer electrons occupy larger and larger orbitals and have greater probability of being farther from the nucleus.

    b. Because the number of shielding electrons remains constant along any period, the effective nuclear charge increases as the atomic number increases. Coulomb's law tells us that the increased effective nuclear positive charge tends to draw negative valence electrons closer to the nucleus, thus decreasing the size of the atoms.

c. A 2− oxide ion has two more electrons in the valence level than does a neutral oxygen atom and these added electrons increase electron–electron repulsion expanding the region they occupy in the oxide ion.

d. The $3s^2$ electron configuration of aluminum partially shields from the nucleus the outermost $3p^1$ aluminum electron making that electron more loosely held than the outermost $3s^2$ electrons of magnesium, which do not shield each other. The result is that aluminum has a smaller first ionization energy than magnesium.

e. The third ionization energy of an element is always larger than its second ionization energy because the third electron is pulled away from a 2+ ion, whereas the second electron is pulled away from a 1+ ion. Coulomb's law tells us that the higher nuclear charge of the 2+ ions holds the remaining electrons with more force. $F = kQ_1Q_2/d^2$, where Q_1 is the effective nuclear charge. The larger the charge, the higher the force of attraction for an electron.

2. a. The relatively low ionization energy values left of the stair-step line in Table 7.1 represent the ionization energies of the valence electrons for each element of Period 3. Each value immediately right of the line shows a marked increase in energy from the value before it, indicating that it is the ionization energy for a poorly screened inner-core electron. The left-hand values are relatively low, indicating that they are ionization energies of well-screened valence electrons. From left to right along the period, the number of relatively low values of ionization energy increases to equal the group number and the number of valence electrons of each element.

b. For magnesium, $I_1 = 738, I_2 = 1451,$ and $I_3 = 7733\,kJ/mol$. The two lower values represent ionization energies of magnesium's two valence electrons, which are well-screened from the nuclear charge. $1s^22s^22p^63s^2$. $Z_{eff} = 12p^+ - 10e^- = 2+$. Both valence electrons experience a relatively low 2+ effective nuclear charge. The very high third ionization energy represents a poorly screened inner-core electron. $Z_{eff} = 12p^+ - 2e^- = 10+$. Because of the high effective nuclear charge, this electron is held much more strongly to the nucleus according to Coulomb's law: $F = kQ_1Q_2/d^2$. I_2 for magnesium is greater than I_1 because once the first electron is lost, the second electron is held by a net 1+ charge of the nucleus.

c. The first three values for the successive ionization of aluminum are relatively low, whereas the fourth is very large. This indicates that aluminum has three valence electrons that will be readily lost forming a 3+ ion.

d. The shell model depicts electrons in atoms grouped in shells according to their relative energies. Each shell contains electrons of similar energy. The data in Table 7.1 show that each atom has one or more electrons of relatively low ionization energy and at least one electron of a very different and very high ionization energy.

e. Sodium is the most reactive Period 3 metal as evidenced by its very low first ionization energy. A low ionization energy means that the electron will be readily lost in a chemical reaction.

f. The formulas for the most probable oxides are Na_2O, MgO, Al_2O_3, SiO_2. Oxide ion, O^{2-}, has a 2– charge, having gained two electrons in its valence shell. The data show that the number of low values of ionization energies for Na, Mg, Al, and Si are 1, 2, 3, and 4, respectively. This means that 1, 2, 3, and 4 electrons will be lost, respectively, making these ions: Na^+, Mg^{2+}, Al^{3+}, and Si^{4+}. They combine with oxygen in the ratios above to form compounds of zero charge.

Your Turn Answers

7.1. $_{21}Sc$: $1s^2 2s^2 2p^6 3s^2 3p^6 4s^2 3d^1$ or $(Ar)4s^2 3d^1$ $Z_{eff} = 21-18 = +3$. Scandium's 18 noble gas core electrons shield 18 of 21 protons, giving it an effective nuclear charge of about +3. As a result of its increased Z_{eff}, scandium's valence electrons are held closer to the nucleus and more tightly than those of potassium. Therefore scandium is smaller than potassium and scandium has a higher first ionization energy.

7.2. Aluminum is smaller than magnesium, which is smaller than sodium. Each atom has ten core electrons screening ten nuclear protons. However, aluminum has three unscreened protons, so its outermost electron experiences an effective nuclear charge of approximately 3 ($Z_{eff} = 13$ protons $- 10$ electrons $= 3$), while magnesium's Z_{eff} is 2 and sodium's is 1. Coulomb's law tells us that the higher the effective nuclear charge felt by a valence electron, the closer it will be held to the nucleus.

7.3. All monatomic cations are smaller than their parent atoms. Cations have lost their valence electrons. The next inner shell, which defines the size of cations, is less well-screened from the nuclear charge, so those inner electrons are held more tightly and closer to the nucleus. The size of the cations varies like this: $Si^{4+} < Al^{3+} < Mg^{2+} < Na^+$. Each ion has ten electrons and the outer eight s and p core electrons are shielded only by the $1s^2$ electrons, $1s^2 2s^2 2p^6$. Thus, they experience a greater effective nuclear charge than the valence electrons and are held more closely to the nucleus.

7.4. First ionization energies: Na < Al < Mg < Si < S < P < Cl < Ar. Generally, first ionization energies increase from left to right along a period because the effective nuclear charge increases, drawing valence electrons more tightly to the nucleus. Aluminum has a lower ionization energy than magnesium because its s^2 valence electrons partially screen the nucleus making the effective nuclear charge smaller. Sulfur has a lower ionization energy than phosphorus because electron–electron repulsion in sulfur's p^4 valence configuration aids the removal of a p electron.

7.5. *Sodium is more reactive than lithium because sodium has a smaller first ionization energy. Both have an effective nuclear charge of +1. However, sodium is larger than lithium so sodium's $3s^1$ electron is farther from the nucleus than is lithium's $2s^1$ valence electron. Coulomb's law predicts that the farther an electron is from the nuclear charge, the less tightly it is held and the lower will be the ionization energy.*

7.6. $2K(s)+2H_2O(l) \rightarrow 2K^+(aq)+2OH^-(aq)+H_2(g)$. *The chemical equation represents a redox reaction. Bubbles of hydrogen are visible as the potassium dissolves. The hydrogen might catch fire. Potassium is more reactive than sodium because potassium loses electrons more readily because of its larger size and lower first ionization energy.*

7.7. $Ba(s)+2H_2O(l) \rightarrow Ba^{2+}(aq)+2OH^-(aq)+H_2(g)$. *The chemical equation represents a redox reaction. Electrons are transferred from barium to hydrogen. Cesium is more reactive than barium. Reactivity of metals has to do with how easily they lose electrons. Cesium's ionization energy is less than that of barium because cesium's lower effective nuclear charge holds its valence electron less tightly than those of barium. Thus, cesium is larger and loses its electron more readily.*

TOPIC

8

BASIC CONCEPTS OF CHEMICAL BONDING

The content in this topic is the basis for mastering Learning Objectives 2.1, 2.17, 2.18, 2.21, and 5.8 as found in the Curriculum Framework.

When you finish reviewing this topic, be sure you are able to:

- Write both octet and non-octet Lewis structures for atoms, ions, and molecules
- Predict properties of binary compounds based on their chemical formulas
- Provide explanations of bonding properties based on particle views
- Predict bonding type in binary compounds based on element positions on the periodic table
- Rank bond polarity using electronegativity values of the bonded atoms and/ or their positions on the periodic table
- Draw resonance structures and interpret the nature of their delocalized electrons
- Correlate bond multiplicity to bond length and strength
- Calculate enthalpies of reactions from bond dissociation energies
- Use formal charge to evaluate the suitability of different octet resonance structures

Section 8.1

Lewis Symbols and the Octet Rule

A **chemical bond** is a strong force of attraction that holds two atoms together. Chemical bonding involves the valence electrons of atoms. Chemical bonds within compounds are significantly stronger than the intermolecular forces of attraction between molecules (see Topic 11).

An **ionic bond** is an attractive force between ions of opposite charges, often a **metal** cation and a **nonmetal** anion. Ionic bonds are the strong Coulombic attractions between ions in an ionic solid (see Topic 12).

A **covalent bond** results from sharing electrons between two atoms, usually **two nonmetal** atoms.

A **metallic bond** occurs when the nuclei of a collection of metal atoms simultaneously attract their collective electrons. Metallic bonds are characterized by a sea of delocalized valence electrons surrounding atomic nuclei of metals (see Topic 12).

Your Turn 8.1

Classify the following compounds as ionic or covalent:
KBr, SO_2, H_2SO_4, CH_3COOH, Na_3PO_4, $CaCO_3$. On what do you base your answer?
Which compounds contain both ionic and covalent bonds? Write your answers in the
space provided.

A **Lewis symbol** shows the valence electrons as dots around the symbol for the element as seen in Table 8.1. The number of valence electrons for a representative element is the same as its group number on the periodic table.

Table 8.1 Lewis symbols.

Group	Element	Electron Configuration	Lewis Symbol	Element	Electron Configuration	Lewis Symbol
1A	Li	$[He]2s^1$	Li·	Na	$[Ne]3s^1$	Na·
2A	Be	$[He]2s^2$	·Be·	Mg	$[Ne]3s^2$	·Mg·
3A	B	$[He]2s^22p^1$	·Ḃ·	Al	$[Ne]3s^23p^1$	·Äl·
4A	C	$[He]2s^22p^2$	·Ċ·	Si	$[Ne]3s^23p^2$	·Ṡi·
5A	N	$[He]2s^22p^3$	·N̈:	P	$[Ne]3s^23p^3$	·P̈:
6A	O	$[He]2s^22p^4$	:Ö:	S	$[Ne]3s^23p^4$	:S̈:
7A	F	$[He]2s^22p^5$	·F̈:	Cl	$[Ne]3s^23p^5$	·C̈l:
8A	Ne	$[He]2s^22p^6$	:N̈e:	Ar	$[Ne]3s^23p^6$	:Är:

The **octet rule** states that representative elements tend to gain, lose, or share electrons until they are surrounded by eight valence electrons (an octet). An octet of electrons gives an atom a noble gas configuration with completely full *s* and *p* subshells. Noble gas configurations are stable because they are poorly shielded from the nucleus. Hydrogen provides an exception to the octet rule because it requires only two electrons to attain a noble gas configuration.

Common misconception: When an atom gains or loses electrons to attain an octet of valence electrons, it does not become a noble gas. For example, chloride ion, Cl^-, has the same electron configuration as argon, but it is not argon. Chloride ion is isoelectronic (the same number of electrons) with argon, but chloride has one fewer proton.

Section 8.2

Ionic Bonding

Ions form when electrons transfer from an atom of low ionization energy (usually a metal) to an atom of high electron affinity (usually a nonmetal). The electrostatic attraction between two oppositely charged ions constitutes an ionic bond.

A **lattice** is a stable, ordered, solid three-dimensional array of ions associated with ionic compounds. Figure 8.1 shows a lattice of sodium and chloride ions.

 = Na^+ = Cl^-

Each Na^+ ion surrounded by six Cl^- ions

Each Cl^- ion surrounded by six Na^+ ions

Figure 8.1 The crystal structure of sodium chloride.

Lattice energy, $\Delta H_{lattice}$, is the energy required to completely separate a mole of a solid ionic compound into its gaseous ions. For example, the lattice energy of potassium fluoride is 808 kJ/mol.

$$KF(s) \rightarrow K^+(g) + F^-(g) \quad \Delta H_{lattice} = +808 \text{ kJ/mol}$$

Table 8.2 lists the lattice energies of some common ionic compounds. Lattice energy increases with smaller, more highly charged ions. The potential energy of two interacting charged particles is given by the equation, $E = kQ_1Q_2/d$, where Q_1 and Q_2 are the charges on the ions, d is the distance between them and k is a proportionality constant.

Table 8.2 Lattice energies for some ionic compounds.

Compound	Lattice Energy (kJ/mol)	Compound	Lattice Energy (kJ/mol)
LiF	1030	$MgCl_2$	2326
LiCl	834	$SrCl_2$	2127
LiI	730		
NaF	910	MgO	3795
NaCl	788	CaO	3414
NaBr	732	SrO	3217
NaI	682		
KF	808	ScN	7547
KCl	701		
KBr	671		
CsCl	657		
CsI	600		

Your Turn 8.2

Use Coulomb's law to justify why lithium fluoride has higher lattice energy than sodium chloride. Why does magnesium oxide have higher lattice energy than sodium fluoride? Write your answers in the space provided.

Ionic compounds tend to have high lattice energies, which tend to make ionic compounds hard and brittle with relatively high melting points.

The charge of a monatomic ion is determined by the number of valence electrons of the parent atom. Representative metals in Groups 1, 2, or 3 will typically lose all of their valence electrons when forming monatomic cations. Because ionization energies increase rapidly for each successive electron removed, metals tend not to form monatomic ions having charges greater than 3+. (Common exceptions are tin, lead, and titanium, which form 4+ cations.) Similarly, nonmetals gain only enough electrons to complete an octet. Because of electron–electron repulsion, nonmetals rarely form monatomic anions having charges more negative than 3−.

Transition metals lose their valence level s electrons first and then one or two d orbital electrons. Having two outermost s electrons is the major reason why many transition metals commonly form 2+ ions in addition to ions of other charges. For example, the electron configurations of Fe, Fe^{2+}, and Fe^{3+} are shown below:

Fe: $(Ar)3d^6 4s^2$

Fe^{2+}: $(Ar)3d^6 4s^0$ or $(Ar)3d^6$

Fe^{3+}: $(Ar)3d^5 4s^0$ or $(Ar)3d^5$

Common misconception: When writing electron configurations for transition metals, the outer s levels are filled before the outer d levels. However, when writing electron configurations for transition metal ions, remove the outer s electrons before removing the d electrons. (Note that often electron configurations are written so that the outer s sublevel comes before outer d sublevel.)

Lead and tin commonly form monatomic cations having 2+ and 4+ charges. For example, the electron configurations of Pb, Pb^{2+}, and Pb^{4+} are shown below:

Pb: $(Xe)4f^{14}5d^{10}6s^2 6p^2$

Pb^{2+}: $(Xe)4f^{14}5d^{10}6s^2 6p^0$ or $(Xe)4f^{14}5d^{10}6s^2$

Pb^{4+}: $(Xe)4f^{14}5d^{10}6s^0 6p^0$ or $(Xe)4f^{14}5d^{10}$

Your Turn 8.3

Write the electron configurations of Cr^{3+} and Sn^{4+}. Write your answer in the space provided.

Covalent Bonding   Section 8.3

A **covalent bond** is formed between two atoms that share one or more pairs of electrons.

Lewis structures for covalent molecules often show shared pairs of electrons (bonding pairs) as lines and unshared electron pairs (nonbonding pairs) as lines or dots. For example, the Lewis structure for carbon dioxide is represented as:

$$\ddot{O} = C = \ddot{O} \quad \text{or} \quad \bar{\overline{O}} = C = \bar{\overline{O}}$$

Bond Polarity and Electronegativity   Section 8.4

A **nonpolar covalent bond** is one in which the electrons are shared equally between two atoms.

A **polar covalent bond** is a bond in which one atom attracts the pair of electrons more strongly than the other atom.

Electronegativity is the relative ability of an atom to attract a pair of electrons. Electronegativity generally increases from left to right along a period and from bottom to top within a group as shown in Figure 8.2.

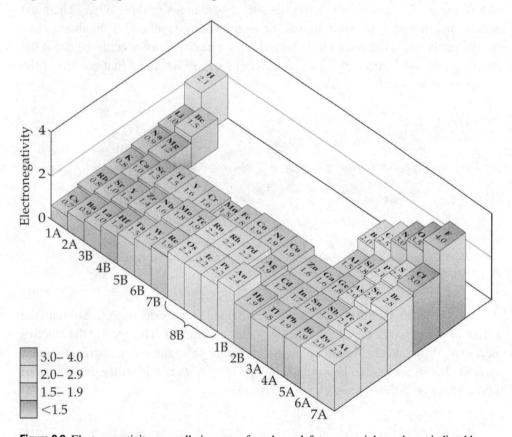

Figure 8.2 Electronegativity generally increases from lower left to upper right on the periodic table.

The trend in electronegativity can be understood through the shell model of atomic structure and Coulomb's law. Recall that the number of protons increases from left to right along any period, but the number of inner shell electrons remains constant. Thus, the effective nuclear charge increases. The trend in increasing electronegativity parallels increasing effective nuclear charge from left to right along a period. Increasing Z_{eff} increases an atom's tendency to attract electrons because by Coulomb's law, the larger the charge, the greater the force of attraction. Within a group, smaller atoms attract electrons better because the forces of attraction increase with decreasing distance from the nucleus.

Fluorine has the highest electronegativity of all the reactive atoms and francium has the lowest.

Common misconception: Noble gases have relatively high electronegativities. However, because noble gases do not make many covalent bonds, their electronegativities are not usually considered.

The difference between ionic bonds and covalent bonds is not distinct. Rather, it is a continuum based, in part, on the difference in electronegativities of the two bonded atoms. Figure 8.3 shows the electron-density distributions of three binary chemical species and illustrates the continuum. The nonpolar covalent bond of F_2 shares electrons equally while the polar HF bond has more electron density centered about the fluorine atom. The extremely polar (ionic) bond of LiF has most (but not all) of the electrons centered about the fluorine atom.

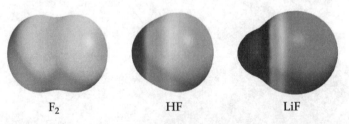

F_2 HF   LiF

Figure 8.3 Electron-density distribution. This computer-generated rendering shows the calculated electron-density distribution on the surface of the F_2, HF, and LiF molecules.

The **electronegativity difference** between two bonded atoms is used to estimate the extent of polarity of a covalent bond along this continuum. The greater the electronegativity difference between two atoms, the more polar the bond. Extremely polar covalent bonds are said to be ionic. Table 8.3 describes the arbitrary definitions of bonds based on differences in electronegativities.

Table 8.3   Arbitrary characterizations of chemical bonds.

If the electronegativity difference is:	the bond is:	example	(difference)
0–0.4	nonpolar covalent	Cl–Cl	(0.0)
0.4–1.0	polar covalent	H–Cl	(0.9)
1.0–2.0	very polar covalent	H–F	(1.9)
> 2.0	ionic	NaCl	(2.1)

While electronegativity differences can be used to predict whether a bond is covalent or ionic, the properties of ionic and covalent compounds (see Topic 12) are better indications of the type of bond.

A **bond dipole** is a molecule with one end having a slightly positive charge and the other end having a slightly negative charge because of differences in electronegativity. For example, HF is a dipole and is often represented as:

$$\delta+ \qquad\qquad \delta-$$
$$H \quad\longrightarrow\quad F$$

where the Greek letter delta, δ, means "partial" and the arrow represents a polar bond and points toward the higher electron concentration (the more electronegative element). The greater the difference in electronegativity, the greater the bond dipole and the more polar the bond. Figure 8.4 illustrates the charge separation in the hydrogen halides. Note: the darker areas indicate high electron density.

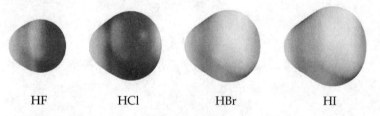

HF   HCl   HBr   HI

Figure 8.4 Charge separation in the hydrogen halides. In HF, the strongly electronegative F pulls much of the electron density away from H (darker shades). In HI, the I, being much less electronegative than F, does not attract the shared electrons as strongly, and consequently, there is far less polarization of the bond.

A **dipole moment** is a quantitative measure of the magnitude of a dipole. The higher the dipole moment, the more polar the molecule.

Drawing Lewis Structures   Section 8.5

Lewis structures use valence electrons to aid our understanding of the bonding in molecules and ions.

Rules for drawing Lewis structures of molecules and ions are the following:

1. Total the valence electrons of all bonded atoms.

2. Use one pair of electrons to bond each outer atom to the central atom (usually the atom in least abundance).

3. Complete the octets around all outer atoms.

4. Place any remaining electrons on the central atom.

5. If there are not enough electrons to give the central atom an octet, make multiple bonds.

 **Common misconception:** Hydrogen can never be a central atom because it needs only two electrons to attain a noble gas configuration. In oxyacids and oxyanions, hydrogen bonds to oxygen, not to the central atom.

Examples:

Write the Lewis structure for the nitrate ion, NO_3^-.

Solution:

1. *The group numbers of nitrogen (5) and oxygen (6) tell us how many valence electrons each atom contributes to the Lewis structure. The negative charge means to add one extra electron. The total number of valence electrons is $5+6+6+6+1=24$ electrons.*

2. *Nitrogen is the central atom:*

$$
\begin{array}{c}
O \\
| \\
O - N - O
\end{array}
$$

3. *Each oxygen needs three more pairs to complete its octet:*

$$
\begin{array}{c}
.. \\
:O: \\
.. \quad | \quad .. \\
:O - N - O: \\
.. \quad\quad ..
\end{array}
$$

4. *Nitrogen still does not have an octet and we have used all 24 electrons.*

5. *Make a double bond:*

$$
\left[
\begin{array}{c}
.. \\
:O: \\
\quad || \\
.. \quad\quad .. \\
:O - N - O: \\
.. \quad\quad ..
\end{array}
\right]^{1-}
$$

Section 8.6

Resonance Structures

Resonance structures are two or more Lewis structures that are equally good representations of the bonding in a molecule or ion. Resonance structures usually differ only in the positions of multiple bonds or single, unpaired electrons. For example, the nitrate ion is represented by three equally good Lewis structures differing only in the placement of the double bond:

$$
\begin{bmatrix}
\quad :\ddot{O}: \\
\quad \ \| \\
:\ddot{O}-N-\ddot{O}:
\end{bmatrix}^{1-}
\longleftrightarrow
\begin{bmatrix}
\quad :\ddot{O}: \\
\quad \ | \\
:\ddot{O}=N-\ddot{O}:
\end{bmatrix}^{1-}
\longleftrightarrow
\begin{bmatrix}
\quad :\ddot{O}: \\
\quad \ | \\
:\ddot{O}-N=\ddot{O}:
\end{bmatrix}^{1-}
$$

Common misconception: Once atoms and nonbonding pairs of electrons are placed, it is not correct to move an atom, or a nonbonding pair, to represent a different resonance structure.

Keep in mind that no individual resonance Lewis structure adequately represents the bonding in a molecule. Resonance structures indicate that there is a **blending of electron density** among the atoms that show double bonds. For example, Figure 8.5 depicts the two resonance structures of ozone. Neither structure has a distinct O—O single bond and a truly double bond. Rather, the bonding is a blend of the two resonance structures. Both O—O bonds are identical having the electrons distributed equally between them.

Resonance structure   Resonance structure

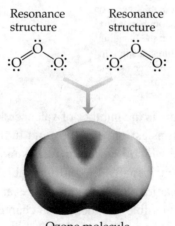

Ozone molecule

Figure 8.5 The ozone molecule is a blend of two resonance structures. The electrons are distributed equally about the oxygen atoms.

Your Turn 8.4

The structure of sodium chloride is depicted as a large collection of many atoms in Figure 8.1, yet its chemical formula is NaCl. The structure of ozone is depicted in Figure 8.5 showing three atoms and its formula is O_3. Distinguish between the different kinds of formulas and why they are used. Write your answer in the space provided.

Similarly, the resonance structures of benzene depict alternating double and single bonds, whereas the molecule is a blend of the two resonance structures (Figure 8.6).

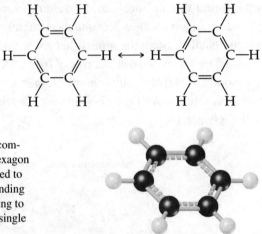

Figure 8.6 Benzene, an "aromatic" organic compound. The benzene molecule is a regular hexagon of carbon atoms with a hydrogen atom bonded to each one. The dashed lines represent the blending of two equivalent resonance structures, leading to C—C bonds that are intermediate between single and double bonds.

The **formal charge** of an atom is the number of valence electrons in an isolated atom minus the number of electrons assigned to the atom in the Lewis structure. Formal charge is used to determine which Lewis structure is most suitable to represent the bonding in a molecule or ion. Usually, the most suitable Lewis structure is the one whose atoms bear formal charges closest to zero. For example, three resonance structures of carbon dioxide are possible and the formal charges are assigned:

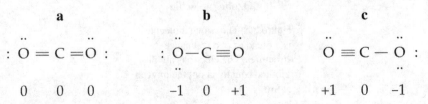

To calculate the formal charge for an atom in a Lewis structure use the following equation:

formal charge = total valence electrons in an isolated atom − nonbonding electrons assigned − ½ bonding electrons assigned

Ö = C = Ö	Using structure **a** as an example:
−4 0 −4	minus nonbonding electrons assigned to an atom
$\frac{4}{2}$ $\frac{8}{2}$ $\frac{4}{2}$	minus $^1/_2$ bonding electrons assigned to an atom
+6 +4 +6	plus valence electrons in isolated atom
0 0 0	= formal charge

Lewis structure **a** for carbon dioxide is the most suitable representation of bonding because its atoms all bear zero formal charge.

Exceptions to the Octet Rule   Section 8.7

There are many common exceptions to the octet rule for writing Lewis structures. These exceptions are summarized as follows:

1. When the species contains an odd number of electrons, one atom will have only seven electrons around it.

    Examples: NO, NO_2.

2. When the species contains a central atom from Group 2 or 3, the number of electrons around the central atom will be twice the group number.

    Examples: BeI_2, BCl_3, GaF_3.

3. When a central atom has more than four other atoms bonded to it, it will have more than eight electrons around it. This "expanded octet" usually occurs with larger nonmetal central atoms in Period 3 and beyond because a large central atom can accommodate more atoms surrounding it. The size of the surrounding atoms is also important. Expanded octets occur most often when large central atoms bond to small, electronegative atoms such as F, Cl, and O.

    Examples: PCl_5, SF_6, AsF_6^-.

4. An expanded octet may also occur for many species, where the total number of valence electrons divided by the number of atoms attached to the central atom is greater than eight.

    Examples: SF_4, BrI_3, I_3^-, XeF_4, XeF_2, ICl_4^-

(Note: Correct octet structures exist for species such as PCl_3, AsF_3 SO_2, and SCl_2. which also conform to Exception 4.)

Section 8.8

Strengths of Covalent Bonds

Bond enthalpy or bond dissociation energy, ΔH_{BDE}, is the enthalpy change for the breaking of bonds in one mole of a gaseous substance. Table 8.4 shows the average bond enthalpies of selected bonds.

Common misconception: Keep in mind that bond enthalpies are always positive values because they represent breaking of bonds. Bond breaking is always endothermic and bond making is always exothermic.

Table 8.4   Average bond enthalpies (kJ/mol).

Single Bonds							
C—H	413	N—H	391	O—H	463	F—F	155
C—C	348	N—N	163	O—O	146		
C—N	293	N—O	201	O—F	190	Cl—F	253
C—O	358	N—F	272	O—Cl	203	Cl—Cl	242
C—F	485	N—Cl	200	O—I	234		
C—Cl	328	N—Br	243			Br—F	237
C—Br	276			S—H	339	Br—Cl	218
C—I	240	H—H	436	S—F	327	Br—Br	193
C—S	259	H—F	567	S—Cl	253		
		H—Cl	431	S—Br	218	I—Cl	208
Si—H	323	H—Br	366	S—S	266	I—Br	175
Si—Si	226	H—I	299			I—I	151
Si—C	301						
Si—O	368						
Si—Cl	464						
Multiple Bonds							
C=C	614	N=N	418	O₂	495		
C≡C	839	N≡N	941				
C=N	615	N=O	607	S=O	523		
C≡N	891			S=S	418		
C=O	799						
C≡O	1072						

Common misconception: The bond enthalpy of a multiple bond is not an integer multiple of the bond enthalpy of a single bond. For example, the bond enthalpy of a $C=C$ double bond is not double that of a $C-C$ single bond. Nor is the bond enthalpy of a $C\equiv C$ triple bond three times that of a $C-C$ single bond. Each type of bond has its own enthalpy value.

The enthalpy change of any reaction, ΔH_{rxn}, is estimated as the sum of the bond enthalpies of the broken bonds minus the sum of the bond enthalpies of the bonds formed:

$$\Delta H_{rxn} = \Sigma \text{ (bond enthalpies of broken bonds)}$$
$$-\Sigma \text{ (bond enthalpies of bonds formed)}$$

Example:

Use average bond enthalpies to estimate the enthalpy change of the following reaction:

$2H_2O \rightarrow 2H_2 + O_2$

Solution:

Draw Lewis structures of all the reactants and products, identify all the bonds that are broken and formed, and apply the bond enthalpies from Table 8.3 to the summation equation.

$2H_2O \rightarrow 2H_2 + O_2 = H-O-H + H-O-H \rightarrow H-H + H-H + O_2$

The following bond enthalpies apply:
$H-O = +463\,kJ/mol, H-H = +436\,kJ/mol,$
and $O_2 = +495\,kJ/mol.$
$\Delta H_{rxn} = 4(+463)-2(+436)-(+495) = +485\,kJ/mol$

Because the enthalpy is positive, the reaction is endothermic.

Multiple bonds are shorter and stronger than single bonds. Table 8.5 shows that bond length decreases from single to double to triple bonds involving the same atoms. The more electrons involved in bonding, the more closely and tightly the atoms are held together.

Table 8.5 Average bond lengths for some single, double, and triple bonds.

Bond	Bond Length (Å)	Bond	Bond Length (Å)
C—C	1.54	N—N	1.47
C═C	1.34	N═N	1.24
C≡C	1.20	N≡N	1.10
C—N	1.43	N—O	1.36
C═N	1.38	N═O	1.22
C≡N	1.16		
		O—O	1.48
C—O	1.43	O═O	1.21
C═O	1.23		
C≡O	1.13		

Multiple Choice Questions

1. Which pair of atoms should form the most polar bond?

   A) F and B

   B) C and O

   C) F and O

   D) N and F

2. Which pair of ions should form the ionic lattice with the highest energy?

   A) Na^+ and Br^-

   B) Li^+ and F^-

   C) Cs^+ and F^-

   D) Li^+ and O^{2-}

3. The electrostatic force of attraction is greatest in which compound?

   A) BaO

   B) MgO

   C) CaS

   D) MgS

4. Which molecule has the weakest bond?

   A) CO

   B) O_2

   C) NO

   D) Cl_2

5. For which species are octet resonance structures necessary and sufficient to describe the bonding satisfactorily?

   A) BCl_3

   B) SO_2

   C) CO_2

   D) BeF_2

6. How are the bonding pairs arranged in the best Lewis structure for ozone?

   A) $O\!-\!O\!-\!O$

   B) $O\!=\!O\!-\!O$

   C) $O\!\equiv\!O\!-\!O$

   D) $O\!\equiv\!O\!=\!O$

7. Which species has the shortest bond length?

    A) CN^-

    B) O_2

    C) SO_2

    D) SO_3

8. Which species requires the least amount of energy to remove an electron from the outermost energy level?

    A) Na^+

    B) He

    C) F^-

    D) O^{2-}

9. Which species has a valid non-octet Lewis structure?

    A) $GeCl_4$

    B) SiF_4

    C) NH_4^+

    D) $SeCl_4$

10. The Lewis structure for SeS_2 has a total of

    A) two bonding pairs and seven nonbonding pairs.

    B) two bonding pairs and six nonbonding pairs.

    C) three bonding pairs and six nonbonding pairs.

    D) four bonding pairs and five nonbonding pairs.

11. The neutral atom with the largest electronegativity is

    A) Na

    B) Al

    C) P

    D) Cl

12. For which pair of atoms is the electronegativity difference the greatest?

    A) Al, Si

    B) Li, Br

    C) Rb, Cl

    D) Se, S

13. Which one of the following does not have a valid octet Lewis structure?

   A) $SeCl_4$

   B) CCl_4

   C) NO_3^-

   D) PF_3

14. Which of the following diatomic molecules has the strongest bond?

   A) N_2

   B) O_2

   C) F_2

   D) Cl_2

15. Which compounds contain both ionic and covalent bonds?

   I. NH_4NO_3 II. $KAl(SO_4)_2$ III. CH_3COOH

   A) II only

   B) II and III only

   C) I and II only

   D) I and III only

   E) I, II, and III

Free Response Questions

1. Answer the following questions using the data in Table 8.2.

   a. Which binary compound in Table 8.2 has the highest lattice energy? Explain using Coulomb's law.

   b. Rank the compounds having the three highest lattice energies, highest to lowest, in Column 1 of Table 8.2. Use Coulomb's law to explain the data.

   c. Predict the approximate lattice energy of RbF. Explain your reasoning. Predict whether CsF will have a larger or smaller lattice energy than RbF.

   d. Which ionic compound in Table 8.2 has the least ionic character? Explain.

   e. Rank the four sodium compounds in Table 8.2 according to decreasing lattice energy. Explain the ranking using Coulomb's law.

2. Consider the following chemical species: the nitrogen molecule, the nitrite ion, and the nitrate ion.

   a. Write the chemical formulas for each of the species and identify the oxidation number of the nitrogen atom in each formula.

   b. Draw Lewis structures for each of the species. Where appropriate, draw resonance structures for each.

c. List the chemical species in order of increasing N—O bond length, the formula with the shortest bond first. Justify your answer.

d. Write a balanced net ionic equation for the reaction of nitrogen dioxide with water. Comment on the molecular and/or ionic species that are formed.

e. Draw each of the resonance structures for nitrogen monoxide.

3. Carbon dioxide gas is bubbled into water.

   a. Write and balance a chemical equation to describe the process.

   b. Draw the Lewis structures of the reactants and products. Include any valid resonance structures.

   c. Given the following bond enthalpies, estimate the enthalpy of the reaction.

Bond	Bond Enthalpy (kJ/mol)
H—H	436
H—O	463
O—O	146
C—O	358
C = O	799
C≡O	1072

   d. Compare the carbon-oxygen bond strengths in the reactant to those in the product. Are the reactant carbon-oxygen bonds stronger or weaker than those in the product? Explain your reasoning. Is your explanation consistent with the sign of the enthalpy change you estimated? Explain.

   e. Excess aqueous sodium hydroxide is added to the solution. Write and balance a net ionic equation for the resulting reaction.

Multiple Choice Answers and Explanations

1. A. Bond polarity increases with an increasing difference in electronegativity of the bonded atoms. Generally, electronegativity increases from left to right along a period and from bottom to top within a group. Electronegativity differences are generally largest for those elements that are farther apart on the periodic table.

2. D. Lattice energy is largest for ions of small size and large charge. Charge generally has a greater effect on lattice energy than does size. Lithium ion is the smallest cation listed and oxide has the largest negative charge.

3. B. A strong electrostatic force of attraction between two ions is dependent on large charge and small size. All of the responses are compounds having 2+ cations and 2− anions. The size of cations and anions increases top to bottom within a group. Magnesium ion is the smallest cation represented and oxide is the smallest anion.

4. D. The strength of covalent bonds increases with increasing multiplicity and decreasing length. Triple bonds are stronger than double bonds, which are stronger than single bonds. Lewis structures show that CO has a triple bond, O_2 and NO have double bonds, and Cl_2 has a single bond.

5. B. Valid resonance structures for SO_2 are $|\underline{O} = S—\underline{\ddot{O}}|$ and $|\underline{\ddot{O}}—S = \underline{O}|$. The Lewis structure for CO_2 is $|\underline{O} = C = \underline{O}|$, where the formal charge of each atom is zero. Two possible resonance forms can be eliminated because the formal charges on the oxygens are $+1$ and -1: $|O{\equiv}C—\underline{\ddot{O}}|$ and $|\underline{\ddot{O}}—C{\equiv}O|$.

6. B. The Lewis structure for ozone is $|\underline{O} = \underline{O}—\underline{\ddot{O}}|$.

7. A. Triple bonds are shorter and stronger than double bonds. Double bonds are shorter and stronger than single bonds. The Lewis structure for CN^- has a triple bond. Double bonds exist in O_2, SO_2, and SO_3.

8. D. All four are isoelectronic. Each of the species is shielded by two inner core electrons. Oxide ion has the least number of protons and the smallest effective nuclear charge.

9. D. The Lewis structure of each of the species includes four single bonds to the central atom. In $SeCl_4$, the central atom has an additional nonbonding pair of electrons. Because of their small size, central atoms from Period 2 cannot form expanded octets. Atoms from Period 3 and beyond can form expanded octets especially if they bond to small highly electronegative outer atoms such as F and O.

10. C. The Lewis structure for SeS_2 is $|\underline{S} = \underline{Se}—\underline{\overline{S}}|$.

11. D. Generally, electronegativity increases from left to right along a period. The noble gases do not attract electron pairs and are not included in the trend.

12. C. Generally, electronegativity increases from the lower left to the upper right of the periodic table. Elements that are farthest apart along the diagonal from lower left to upper right probably have the largest difference in electronegativity. Li and Br also have a large difference but Rb has a lower electronegativity than does Li and chlorine's electronegativity is larger than that of bromine.

13. A. Se has 10 electrons around it, 4 bonding pairs and 2 nonbonding pairs. Octet structures can be written for all the others.

14. A. Lewis structures show that the nitrogen molecule has a triple bond, the oxygen molecule has a double bond, and all the rest have single bonds. Generally, triple bonds are stronger and shorter than double bonds which are stronger and shorter than single bonds.

15. C. Generally, an ionic bond is formed between a metal and a nonmetal. A covalent bond is formed between two nonmetals. However, an ionic bond can be formed when a polyatomic cation, such as ammonium ion, has only nonmetals.

Free Response Answers

1. a. *ScN has the highest lattice energy of all the compounds in Table 8.2. Coulomb's law states that the energy between charged particles is directly proportional to their charges: $E = kQ_1Q_2/d$. Sc^{3+} and N^{3-} have the largest positive and negative charges of the ions represented in Table 8.2.*

   b. *Rank of lattice energies: LiF > NaF > KF. Coulomb's law states that the energy between charged particles is inversely proportional to the distance between them. Li^+ is the smallest ion represented and K^+ is the largest. So the fluoride ion will be closest to the lithium ion and farthest from the potassium ion.*

   c. *RbF will have lattice energy of about 700 kJ/mol, smaller than KF because the Rb^+ ion is larger than the K^+ ion. CsF will have a lattice energy even smaller than RbF because the Cs^+ ion is larger than the Rb^+ ion.*

   d. *CsI is the least polar compound in Table 8.1. CsI has the lowest lattice energy and both Cs and I have very low and, therefore, similar electronegativities.*

   e. *Rank of lattice energies: NaF > NaCl > NaBr > NaI. The lattice energy ranking follows the inverse order of the size of the anions. Coulomb's law states that the closer the ions, the larger the energy. Fluoride ion is the smallest ion so it will be closer to the sodium ion and there will be a greater energy between the particles.*

2. a. *Nitrogen = N_2, oxidation number = 0; nitrite ion = NO_2^-, oxidation number = 3+; nitrate ion = NO_3^-, oxidation number = 5+.*

   b. $: N \equiv N :$

   c. *$N_2 < NO_2^- < NO_3^-$*

   Multiple bonds are shorter and stronger than single bonds. The Lewis structure for N_2 shows that it has a triple bond. The resonance structures for nitrite show that each N—O bond has some double bond character. The resonance structures for nitrate show that each N—O bond has less double bond character than does nitrite.

d. $2\,NO_2(g)+H_2O(l) \rightarrow H^+(aq)+NO_3^-(aq)+HNO_2(aq)$

Nitric acid is a strong electrolyte so it is written in ionic form. Nitrous acid is a weak electrolyte so it is written in molecular form.

e.

$$: \overset{\cdot\cdot}{N} = \overset{\cdot\cdot}{O} \cdot \quad \longleftrightarrow \quad \cdot\, \overset{\cdot\cdot}{N} = \overset{\cdot\cdot}{O} :$$

$$\;\;\; -1 \quad\;\; +1 \qquad\qquad 0 \quad\; 0$$

3. a. $CO_2(g)+H_2O(l) \rightarrow H_2CO_3(aq)$ *(Carbonic acid is a weak acid so it is written in molecular form.)*

b.

$$H - \overset{\cdot\cdot}{\underset{\cdot\cdot}{O}} - H$$

$$: \overset{\cdot\cdot}{O} = C = \overset{\cdot\cdot}{O} :$$

$$H - \overset{\cdot\cdot}{\underset{\cdot\cdot}{O}} - \overset{\overset{\textstyle :\,O\,:}{\textstyle \|}}{C} - \overset{\cdot\cdot}{\underset{\cdot\cdot}{O}} - H$$

c. *Two H—O bonds are broken but two more H—O bonds are formed for a net gain or loss of energy of about zero. One C=O bond is broken and two C—O bonds are formed.*

$$\Delta H_{rxn} = +799 - (2)(+358) = +83\,kJ/mol$$

d. *The C—O bonds in CO_2 are stronger than they are in H_2CO_3. Multiple bonds are stronger and shorter than single bonds. The Lewis structures show that both C—O bonds are double bonds in CO_2, whereas in H_2CO_3, the resonance structures show that the C—O bonds have more single bond character. The enthalpy change is positive indicating that the reaction is endothermic. The bond energy of one C=O bond is greater than the total bond energies of two C—O bonds, which means that it requires more energy to break the bond in the reactant than is delivered by the bonds forming in the product.*

e. $H_2CO_3(aq)+2OH^-(aq) \rightarrow 2H_2O(l)+CO_3^{2-}(aq).$

Your Turn Answers

8.1. *KBr, Na_3PO_4, and $CaCO_3$ are ionic compounds. They contain metals and nonmetals.*

SO_2, H_2SO_4, and CH_3COOH are covalent compounds. They contain only nonmetals.

Na_3PO_4 and $CaCO_3$ have both ionic and covalent bonds. Phosphate and carbonate ions form ionic bonds with their cations but also have covalent bonds within each ion.

8.2. *The lattice energy of LiF is higher than that of NaCl because the lithium cation is smaller than the sodium cation and the fluoride anion is smaller than the chloride anion. Smaller ions will be closer together than larger ions. In the equation for Coulomb's law, $F = kQ_1Q_2/d^2$, d is smaller for LiF than for NaCl so the corresponding force of attraction is larger. MgO has a higher lattice energy than NaF because Mg and O carry a 2^+ and 2^- charge, respectively, whereas Na and F have charges of 1^+ and 1^-.*

8.3. Cr^{3+}: $(Ar)\, 3d^3 4s^0$ or $(Ar)\, 3d^3$; Sn^{4+}: $(Kr)\, 4d^{10} 5s^0 5p^0$ or $(Kr)\, 4d^{10}$.

8.4. *NaCl and almost all ionic compounds consist of large collections of ions arranged in a regular three-dimensional array called a lattice. For convenience, empirical formulas are used for ionic compounds because they show only the smallest whole-number ratio of combined atoms. Ozone and most all covalent compounds consist of individual molecules. Molecular formulas are used to depict only the exact number and kind of atoms in each individual molecule. When you see an ionic formula (it usually contains a metal) visualize a large collection of atoms in a lattice. When you see a molecular formula, visualize a collection of individual molecules, each having only as many atoms as dspicted by the fromula.*

MOLECULAR GEOMETRY AND BONDING THEORIES

The content in this topic is the basis for mastering Learning Objective 2.21 as found in the Curriculum Framework.

When you finish reviewing this topic, be sure you are able to:

- Distinguish between electron domain geometry and molecular geometry
- Apply VSEPR theory to predict geometries of both octet and non-octet Lewis structures of ions and molecules
- Predict molecular geometries and bond angles of molecules
- Predict sp, sp^2, and sp^3 hybridization from the geometries of molecules
- Determine the polarity of molecules from their geometries and atomic electronegativities
- Visualize covalent bond formation as the overlap of atomic orbitals
- Distinguish between sigma and pi bonds
- Explain why sigma bonds have larger bond energies than pi bonds
- Use Lewis structures to identify formulas that have delocalized electrons
- Use bond order to predict relative bond energies

The VSEPR Model   Section 9.2

The **valence-shell electron-pair repulsion** (VSEPR) model is a way to use Lewis structures to determine the geometries of molecules. It is based on the natural repulsive forces that electron pairs exhibit within a molecule.

The **geometry** of a molecule refers to the arrangement of its atoms in three-dimensional space.

A **bond angle** is an angle made by the lines joining the nuclei of atoms in a molecule.

An **electron domain** is a region around an atom in which electrons will most likely be found. An electron domain is produced by a nonbonding pair, a single bond, a double bond, or a triple bond.

An **electron domain geometry** is the three-dimensional arrangement of electron domains around the central atom of a molecule.

A **molecular geometry** is the arrangement of only the atoms in the molecule.

Tables 9.1 and 9.2 show the common electron domain and molecular geometries of atoms.

Table 9.1   Electron domain geometries and molecular geometries for molecules with two, three, and four electron domains.

Number of Electron Domains	Electron- Domain Geometry	Bonding Domains	Nonbonding Domains	Molecular Geometry	Example
2	Linear	2	0	Linear	$\ddot{O}=C=\ddot{O}$
3	Trigonal planar	3	0	Trigonal planar	BF_3
		2	1	Bent	$[NO_2]^-$
4	Tetrahedral	4	0	Tetrahedral	CH_4
		3	1	Trigonal pyramidal	NH_3
		2	2	Bent	H_2O

Table 9.2 Electron domain geometries and molecular geometries for molecules with five and six electron domains.

Number of Electron Domains	Electron-Domain Geometry	Bonding Domains	Nonbonding Domains	Molecular Geometry	Example
5	Trigonal bipyramidal	5	0	Trigonal bipyramidal	PCl_5
		4	1	Seesaw	SF_4
		3	2	T-shaped	ClF_3
		2	3	Linear	XeF_2
6	Octahedral	6	0	Octahedral	SF_6
		5	1	Square pyramidal	BrF_5
		4	2	Square planar	XeF_4

Rules for determining geometry from VSEPR theory are the following:

1. Draw the Lewis structure.

2. Count the number of electron domains around the central atom. Count each nonbonding pair, single bond, double bond, and triple bond as one domain.

3. Arrange the domains of electrons as far away in three-dimensional space as possible. Use the geometries in Tables 9.1 and 9.2 that correspond to the electron domains around the central atom. Examples are given in Table 9.3.

Table 9.3   Examples of geometries obtained from the VSEPR model. Notice that the existence of nonbonding electrons affects the name of the molecular geometry.

Electron Domains, Nonbonding Pairs	Electron Domain Geometry	Molecular Geometry	Bond Angles	Orbital Hybridization	Examples
2,0	Linear	Linear	180°	sp	BeI_2, CO_2, HCN, OCN^-
3,0	Trigonal planar	Trigonal planar	120°	sp^2	BF_3, SO_3, PCl_3, NO_3^-, CO_3^{2-}
3,1	Trigonal planar	Nonlinear	<120°	sp^2	SO_2, O_3, NO_2^-
4,0	Tetrahedral	Tetrahedral	109.5°	sp^3	CH_4, SO_4^{2-}, ClO_4^-, NH_4^+
4,1	Tetrahedral	Trigonal pyramidal	<109°	sp^3	NH_3, SO_3^{2-}, ClO_3^-
4,2	Tetrahedral	Nonlinear	<109°	sp^3	H_2O, OF_2
5,0	Trigonal bipyramidal	Trigonal bipyramidal	90° 120°	—	PCl_5
5,1	Trigonal bipyramidal	Seesaw	<90° <180°	—	SF_4
5,2	Trigonal bipyramidal	T-shape	<90° <120°	—	ClF_3
5,3	Trigonal bipyramidal	Linear	180°	—	I_3^-, XeF_2
6,0	Octahedral	Octahedral	90°	—	SF_6
6,1	Octahedral	Square pyramidal	<90° <180°	—	BrF_5
6,2	Octahedral	Square planar	90° 180°	—	XeF_4

Common misconception: The vital and subtle difference between an electron domain geometry and a molecular geometry is the presence of one or more nonbonding pairs of electrons around the central atom. When no nonbonding pair is present, the electron domain geometry has the same name as the molecular geometry. When one or more nonbonding pairs exist on the central atom, the name changes for the molecular geometry to describe only the locations of the atoms and not the nonbonding pair(s).

Common misconception: Except for the 109.5° angles in tetrahedral geometries, most bond angles need not be memorized. Most bond angles can be deduced from the electron domain geometries using basic geometrical principles.

Any nonbonding pairs on a five-electron domain geometry occupy the radial (or equatorial) positions, not the axial positions as seen in Figure 9.1. Because nonbonding pairs have greater repulsion, the radial positions offer fewer 90° interactions with other domains. In the axial position, a nonbonding pair experiences three 90° interactions. By contrast, the equatorial position offers only two 90° interactions.

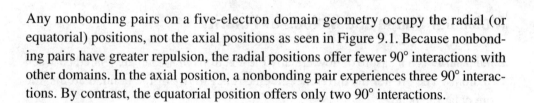

Axial bond

Equatorial bond

Figure 9.1   The trigonal bipyramidal geometry showing equatorial and axial bonds.

Your Turn 9.1

Examine Tables 9.1 and 9.2 and deduce the bond angles for the following electron domain geometries: linear, trigonal planar, trigonal bipyramidal, octahedral. Write your answers in the space provided.

Electron domains for nonbonding electron pairs and double bonds exert greater repulsive forces on adjacent domains and thus tend to compress the bond angles. Table 9.4 lists several examples of molecules having slightly smaller bond angles than predicted by VSEPR model.

Table 9.4   Molecules having smaller than normal bond angles because of nonbonding electron pairs or double bonds.

Molecule	Electron Domain Geometry	Molecular Geometry	Actual Bond Angle
NH_3	Tetrahedral	Trigonal pyramid	107°
H_2O	Tetrahedral	Nonlinear	104.5°
SF_4	Trigonal bipyramidal	Seesaw	116°
$Cl_2O = O$	Trigonal planar	Trigonal planar	111.4° (Cl−C−Cl)
SO_2	Trigonal planar	Nonlinear	116°

Section 9.3

Molecular Shape and Molecular Polarity

Bond polarity is a measure of how equally the electrons in a bond are shared between two atoms. The greater the difference in electronegativity of the bonded atoms, the more polar the bond.

Dipole moment is a quantitative measure of the charge separation in a molecule.

A **bond dipole** is the dipole moment for a particular bond in a molecule.

An **overall dipole moment** of a molecule is the vector sum of all of its bond dipoles. For a molecule that consists of more than two atoms, the dipole moment depends on both the polarities of the individual bonds and the geometry of the molecule. Figure 9.2 illustrates how bond polarity and geometry affect the polarity of a molecule.

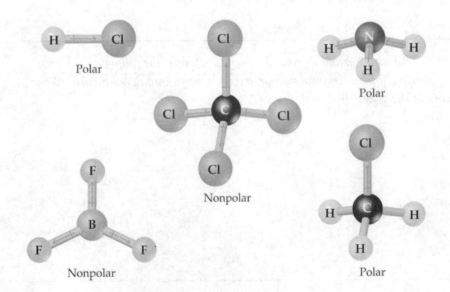

Figure 9.2   Geometry affects whether a molecule containing polar bonds will be polar.

Explain why the molecules shown in Figure 9.2 are polar or nonpolar. Write your answer in the space provided.

Hybrid Orbitals   Section 9.5

Valence-bond theory defines a covalent bond as an **overlap** of orbitals allowing two electrons of opposite spin to share a common region of space between the nuclei. Figure 9.3 illustrates bonding by orbital overlap in the molecules H_2, HCl, and Cl_2.

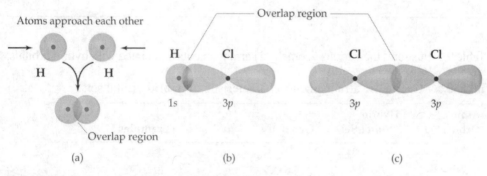

Figure 9.3 Orbitals overlap to form covalent bonds.

Hybrid orbitals result from the mathematical mixing of two or more atomic "unhybridized" atomic orbitals. The shape of any hybrid orbital is different from the shapes of the original unhybridized orbitals and explains the geometries of molecules. For example, the mixing of the valence $2s$ and $2p$ orbitals of carbon can result in sp^3, sp^2, or sp hybridized orbitals as shown in Figure 9.4.

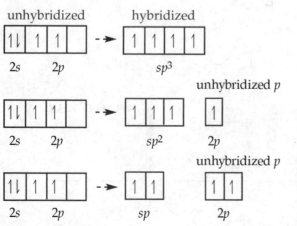

Figure 9.4 Mixing one s and three p orbitals results in an sp^3 hybrid. Mixing one s and two p orbitals creates an sp^2 hybrid. Mixing one s and one p orbital yields an sp hybrid.

Common misconception: Remember that the number of orbitals mixed always equals the number of hybrid orbitals produced. Leftover orbitals that are unhybridized often take part in bonding, especially with double and triple bonds.

Your Turn 9.3

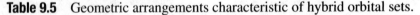

Use a diagram like that in Figure 9.4 to show the valence unhybridized and sp³ hybridized orbitals of the oxygen atom. Write your answer in the space provided.

Table 9.5 illustrates the various geometrical arrangements associated with hybrid orbitals.

Table 9.5 Geometric arrangements characteristic of hybrid orbital sets.

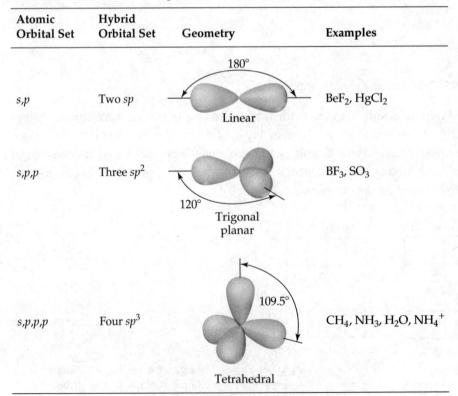

Atomic Orbital Set	Hybrid Orbital Set	Geometry	Examples
s,p	Two sp	180° Linear	BeF_2, $HgCl_2$
s,p,p	Three sp^2	120° Trigonal planar	BF_3, SO_3
s,p,p,p	Four sp^3	109.5° Tetrahedral	CH_4, NH_3, H_2O, NH_4^+

Multiple Bonds   Section 9.6

A **sigma** (σ) **bond** is formed by the **end-to-end overlap** of orbitals. All single bonds are sigma bonds.

A **pi** (π) **bond** results from a **side-to-side overlap** of orbitals. A **double bond** consists of one sigma and one pi bond. A **triple bond** results from one sigma and two pi bonds.

Sigma bonds are stronger than pi bonds. Sigma bonds have most of their electron density concentrated between and, therefore, closer to the nuclei of the bonded atoms. The pi bond sideways orientation of p orbitals does not produce as effective overlap as the sigma orientation, so sigma bonds are stronger.

Figure 9.5 illustrates the difference between a sigma and a pi bond.

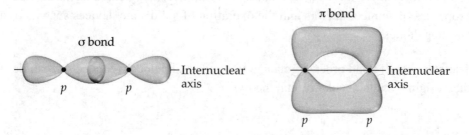

Figure 9.5 Comparison of a sigma and a pi bond. Note that the two regions of overlap in the pi bond, above and below the internuclear axis, constitute a single pi bond.

Bond order can be taken as the multiplicity of the bond. That is, a double bond has a bond order of two and a triple bond has a bond order of three.

Delocalized electrons are spread out over a number of atoms in a molecule rather than localized between a pair of atoms. Delocalized pi bonding electrons are characteristic of molecules that have resonance structures involving double bonds. For example, benzene, C_6H_6, is a ring of six carbons, each bonded to the next by a sigma bond. Delocalized pi bonds blend the two resonance structures into a single structure as shown in Figure 9.6.

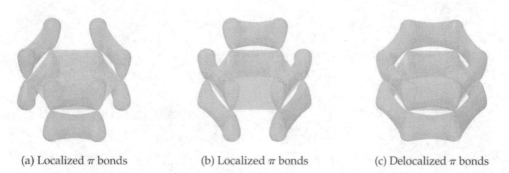

(a) Localized π bonds   (b) Localized π bonds   (c) Delocalized π bonds

Figure 9.6 Two resonance structures of benzene (a and b) showing localized pi bonds differ from a more accurate representation (c) showing delocalized pi bonds.

Section 9.7

Molecular Orbitals

Molecular orbital (MO) theory is a more sophisticated bonding model that visualizes electrons in orbitals associated with an entire molecule, rather than orbitals confined to a single atom. It uses electron distributions over entire molecules to explain bonding systems that valence bond theory or Lewis structures cannot.

For example, an octet Lewis structure of dioxygen predicts that it contains a double bond and that all electrons are paired. However, liquid oxygen displays paramagnetism indicating that its structure has two unpaired electrons. Molecular orbital theory correctly predicts a bond order of two and two unpaired electrons, which explains dioxygen's bond length and its magnetic properties.

Molecular orbital theory also explains the excited states of molecules and why they absorb light. It also explains the bonding in metals and many properties of metals that the electron-sea model does not. In addition, MO theory explains the conductive properties of semiconductors and the operation of solid state devices such as light-emitting diodes.

The concepts of bond order, sigma and pi bonds and delocalized electrons all derive their origin from molecular orbital theory.

Multiple Choice Questions

1. *Which of these molecules is not polar?*

   A) H_2O

   B) CO_2

   C) NO_2

   D) SO_2

2. *Which species contains a central atom with sp^2 hybridization?*

   A) C_2H_2

   B) SO_3^{2-}

   C) O_3

   D) BrI_3

3. *For ClF_3, the electron domain geometry of Cl and the molecular geometry are, respectively,*

   A) *trigonal planar and trigonal planar.*

   B) *trigonal planar and trigonal bipyramidal.*

   C) *trigonal bipyramidal and trigonal planar.*

   D) *trigonal bipyramidal and T-shaped.*

4. *The size of the H—N—H bond angles of the following species increases in which order?*

   A) $NH_3 < NH_4^+ < NH_2^-$

   B) $NH_3 < NH_2^- < NH_4^+$

   C) $NH_2^- < NH_3 < NH_4^+$

   D) $NH_4^+ < NH_3 < NH_2^-$

5. *What is the molecular geometry and polarity of the BF_3 molecule?*

   A) *trigonal pyramidal and polar*

   B) *trigonal pyramidal and nonpolar*

   C) *trigonal planar and polar*

   D) *trigonal planar and nonpolar*

6. *In which species is the F—X—F bond angle the smallest?*

   A) NF_3

   B) BF_3

   C) CF_4

   D) BrF_3

7. Which set does not contain a linear species?

    A) CO_2, SO_2, NO_2

    B) H_2O, HCN, BeI_2

    C) OCN^-, C_2H_2, OF_2

    D) H_2S, ClO_2^-, NH_2^-

8. The hybrid orbitals of nitrogen in N_2O_4 are

    A) sp

    B) sp^2

    C) sp^3

    D) sp and sp^3

9. How many sigma and pi bonds are in

$$\overset{\displaystyle O}{\overset{\displaystyle \|}{CH_2 = CHCH_2CCH_3}}?$$

    A) five sigma and two pi

    B) eight sigma and four pi

    C) eleven sigma and two pi

    D) thirteen sigma and two pi

10. What is the best estimate of the H—O—H bond angle in H_3O^+?

    A) 109.5°

    B) 107°

    C) 104.5°

    D) 120°

11. The hybrid orbitals of carbon in CO_3^{2-} are

    A) sp

    B) sp^2

    C) sp^3

    D) sp^2 and sp^3

12. When the following species are arranged according to increasing $O-S-O$ bond angle, what is the correct order?

A) $SO_2 < SO_3 < SO_4^{2-} < SO_3^{2-}$

B) $SO_3 < SO_4^{2-} < SO_2 < SO_3^{2-}$

C) $SO_3^{2-} < SO_4^{2-} < SO_2 < SO_3$

D) $SO_3 < SO_2 < SO_4^{2-} < SO_3^{2-}$

E) $SO_4^{2-} < SO_3^{2-} < SO_2 < SO_3$

13. Which set contains all trigonal pyramidal species?

A) NH_3, SO_3, NO_3^-

B) $NF_3, CO_3^{2-}, SO_3^{2-}$

C) BF_3, H_3O^+, NH_3

D) SO_3, NO_3^-, CO_3^{2-}

E) NF_3, SO_3^{2-}, H_3O^+

14. What is the correct order of increasing bond energy?

A) $Br-Br < Br-Cl < Br-F$

B) $Br-F < Br-Cl < Br-Br$

C) $Br-Cl < Br-Br < Br-F$

D) $Br-F < Br-Br < Br-Cl$

E) $Br-Br < Br-F < Br-Cl$

15. What geometrical arrangement is associated with orbitals that are sp^2 hybridized?

A) linear

B) octahedral

C) trigonal bipyramidal

D) trigonal planar

E) tetrahedral

Free Response Questions

1. Consider the chemical species IF_5 and IF_4^+.

   a. Draw the Lewis structure and make a rough three-dimensional sketch of each species.

   b. Identify the electron domain geometry and the molecular geometry of each structure.

   c. Identify the approximate bond angles of each species.

   d. Predict which, if any, is a polar species. Justify your answer.

   e. Predict the most probable oxidation number of the iodine atom in each species. Give an example of another chemical species with iodine having the same oxidation number as IF_4^+.

   f. Would you expect the conversion of IF_5 to IF_4^+ to be exothermic or endothermic? Explain.

2. Consider each of these molecules: C_3H_4, C_3H_6, and C_3H_8.

   a. Draw the Lewis structure for each molecule and identify the orbital hybridization of each carbon atom.

   b. Specify the geometry of each central carbon atom.

   c. Write a balanced chemical equation for the complete combustion of each molecule.

   d. Use the following bond enthalpies to determine the heat of combustion of each molecule. Specify your answer in kJ/mol.

Bond	kJ/mol	Bond	kJ/mol
$C-H$	413	$O-H$	463
$C-C$	348	O_2	495
$C=C$	614	$C=O$	799
$C\equiv C$	839	$C-O$	358

Multiple Choice Answers and Explanations

1. B. The bond dipoles in linear CO_2 cancel leaving the molecule with a zero dipole moment. H_2O, NO_2, and SO_2 are all nonlinear and have a net dipole moment.

2. C. A trigonal planar electron domain geometry exhibited by O_3 is characteristic of the sp^2 hybrid set. C_2H_2 is linear and sp hybridized; SO_3^{2-} is tetrahedral and sp^3; BrI_3 is trigonal bipyramidal.

3. D. ClF_3 has five pairs of electrons surrounding the central chlorine atom, three bonding pairs, and two nonbonding pairs, giving it a trigonal bipyramidal electron domain geometry. Nonbonding pairs orient themselves in the radial

positions because the number of close interactions with other domains is less than in the axial positions. The result is a T-shaped molecular geometry.

4. *C. All three species have a tetrahedral electron domain geometry. NH_4^+ has no nonbonding pairs and has a tetrahedral molecular geometry with bond angles of 109.5°. NH_3 has one nonbonding pair that repels more than the bonding pairs making the bond angle about 107°. NH_2^- has two nonbonding pairs that repel even more than one nonbonding pair making the bond angle about 105°.*

5. *D. BF_3 has a non-octet Lewis structure and VSEPR analysis shows that it is a trigonal planar molecule having bond angles of 120°. The three B—F bond dipoles are oriented toward the corners of an equilateral triangle and cancel each other to give the molecule a zero dipole moment.*

6. *D. VSEPR analysis shows that BrF_3 is a T-shaped molecule having bond angles of about 90°. NF_3 is trigonal pyramidal having bond angles of 107°; CF_4 is tetrahedral, 109.5°.*

7. *D. Lewis structures and VSEPR analysis show that the following are all linear: CO_2, HCN, OCN^-, I_3^-, and SCN^-. (Notice that CO_2, OCN^-, and SCN^- are isoelectronic and, therefore, have the same Lewis structure and geometry.)*

8. *B. Each N is the center of a trigonal plane in the Lewis structure of N_2O_4. The sp^2 hybrid set is characteristic of trigonal planar geometry.*

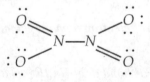

9. *D. Each single bond is a sigma bond and each double bond consists of one sigma bond and one pi bond. There are eight C—H sigma bonds, four C—C sigma bonds, and one C—O sigma bond. There is one C—C pi bond and one C—O pi bond.*

10. *B. The electron domain geometry of the hydronium ion, H_3O^+, is tetrahedral. However, its Lewis structure shows that it has one nonbonding pair of electrons making the molecular geometry trigonal pyramidal. The lone pair of electrons exerts a more repulsive force than the bonding pairs forcing a slight decrease in the bond angles. Hydronium ion is isoelectronic with ammonia, NH_3.*

11. *B. Carbonate is a planar ion which is associated with sp^2 hybridization.*

12. *C. Lewis structures show that the electron domain geometry of sulfite is tetrahedral having a nonbonding pair of electrons, which decreases the bond angle to less than 109°. Sulfate is tetrahedral having bond angles of 109°. Sulfur dioxide is trigonal planar having a nonbonding pair of electrons, which decreases the bond angle to less than 120°. Sulfur trioxide is also trigonal planar having bond angles of 120°.*

13. E. The NH_3 molecule is also trigonal pyramidal owing to its nonbonding pair of electrons on the central atom. All the other species represented are isoelectronic having trigonal planar geometries.

14. A. Generally, the bond energies of similar covalently bonded atoms increase with decreasing atomic size. Fluorine is smaller than chlorine which is smaller than bromine.

15. D. Generally, linear electron domain geometries are associated with sp hybridization, trigonal planar with sp^2, and tetrahedral with sp^3.

Free Response Answers

1. a.

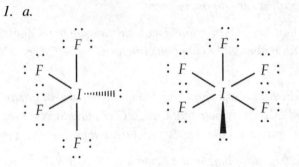

b. IF_4^+ has a trigonal bipyramidal electron domain geometry and a seesaw molecular geometry.

   IF_5 has an octahedral electron domain geometry and a square pyramidal molecular geometry.

c. The radial F—I—F bond angle in IF_4^+ is about $120°$ or slightly less due to a larger repulsive force exerted by the radial nonbonding pair. Axial F—I—F bond angle is $180°$.

   All the bond angles in IF_5 are $90°$.

d. Both species are polar. Each I—F bond is polar due to a large difference in electronegativity of the two atoms. The three-dimensional arrangement of bond dipoles in both species contributes to a net molecular dipole.

e. The oxidation number of iodine is probably $5+$ in both species. Iodine in the iodate ion, IO_3^-, also has an oxidation number of $5+$.

f. The reaction: $IF_5 \rightarrow IF_4^+ + F^-$ would be endothermic. The reaction requires that an I—F bond be broken. Bond breaking is always endothermic.

2. a. $CH_3C\equiv CH$ $CH_3CH=CH_2$ $CH_3CH_2CH_3$
        sp^3, sp, sp sp^3, sp^2, sp^2 all sp^3

b. All sp hybridized carbons are linear, all sp^2's are trigonal planar, and all sp^3's are tetrahedral.

c. $C_3H_4(g) + 4O_2(g) \rightarrow 3CO_2(g) + 2H_2O(l)$

$C_3H_6(g) + 9/2O_2(g) \rightarrow 3CO_2(g) + 3H_2O(l)$

$C_3H_8(g) + 5O_2(g) \rightarrow 3CO_2(g) + 4H_2O(l)$

d. *For C_3H_4:*

$\Delta H_{comb} = \sum \Delta H_{BDE}$ *bonds broken* $- \sum \Delta H_{BDE}$ *bonds formed*

$= 4(O_2) + 4(C-H) + 1(C \equiv C) + 1(C \equiv C) - 6(C=O)$

$-4(H-O) = +4(495) + 4(413) + 839 + 348 - 6(799)$

$-4(463) = -1827 \ kJ/mol$

For C_3H_6:

$= 9/2(O_2) + 6(C-H) + 1(C=C) + 1(C-C)$

$-6(C=O) - 6(H-O) = +4.5(495) + 6(413) + 614$

$+348 - 6(799) - 6(463) = -1905 \ kJ/mol$

For C_3H_8:

$= 5(O_2) + 8(C-H) + 2(C-C) - 6(C=O) - 8(H-O)$

$= +5(495) + 8(413) + 2(348) - 6(799) - 8(463)$

$= -2023 \ kJ/mol$

Your Turn Answers

9.1. *Linear = 180°; trigonal planar = 120°; trigonal bipyramidal = 90° and 120°; octahedral = 90°.*

9.2. *The nonpolar molecules have bonds geometrically oriented so that their bond dipoles cancel. The bond dipoles of the polar molecules do not cancel.*

9.3.

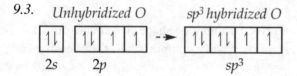

10

GASES

The content in this topic is the basis for mastering Learning Objectives 2.4, 2.5, 2.6, 2.12, and 5.2 as found in the Curriculum Framework.

When you finish reviewing this topic, be sure you are able to:

- Use kinetic-molecular theory and Maxwell–Boltzmann distribution to explain and make predictions about the macroscopic behavior of the properties of gases: pressure, volume, the number of particles, and temperature
- Construct particle representations of the gas phase that explain the macroscopic properties of gases
- Calculate temperature, pressure, and volume from given data for an ideal gas
- Interpret the graphical representations of pressure, volume, and temperature and explain how absolute zero can be determined experimentally
- Explain the deviations of real gases from ideal behavior using the structure of atoms and molecules and the forces acting between them

Section 10.7

The Kinetic-Molecular Theory of Gases

A **gas** is a form of matter that has no fixed volume or shape. It expands to fill the volume and shape of its container. A gas is readily compressible, flows easily, and diffuses into another gas quickly.

Kinetic-molecular theory (the theory of moving molecules), or KMT, is an atomic-level view of gases that explains their macroscopic properties. Figure 10.1 illustrates a particle view of gases.

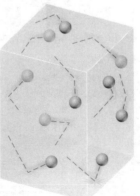

Figure 10.1 Gas particles are far apart, and are in rapid, random motion, and their intermolecular forces are negligible.

These statements summarize the kinetic-molecular theory:

1. Gases consist of atoms or molecules in continuous rapid, random motion.

2. The particles are far apart and their volumes are negligible compared to the volume of the container.

3. Attractive and repulsive forces between gas molecules are negligible.

4. Molecular collisions are perfectly elastic (they happen without loss of energy).

5. The average kinetic energy of the particles is proportional to the absolute temperature. At any given temperature all gases have the same average kinetic energy.

Pressure   Section 10.2

The KMT explains why **a gas exerts a pressure** on its container. Pressure is caused by collisions that molecules make with the container walls (Figure 10.2). How often and how forcefully the particles strike the walls determines the magnitude of the pressure.

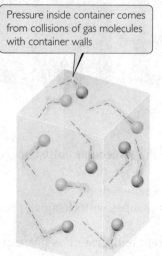

Pressure inside container comes from collisions of gas molecules with container walls

Figure 10.2 Pressure originates from collisions of gas molecules on the walls of the container.

Pressure is the force that acts on a given area: Pressure = force/area. Gases exert a pressure on any surface on which they come in contact.

Standard pressure corresponds to a typical pressure that the gases of the atmosphere exert at sea level. The SI value and unit for standard pressure are 1.01×10^5 Pa.

Pressure units most commonly used in chemistry and their relationships are:

$$1 \text{ atm} = 760 \text{ mmHg} = 760 \text{ torr} = 1.01 \times 10^5 \text{ Pa} = 101 \text{ kPa}$$

Standard temperature is 0 °C = 273 K.

Common misconception: In all gas law calculations, temperature units must be expressed in Kelvin. K = 273 + °C. Even though 1 °C is the same size as 1K, the two units are 273° apart on their respective temperature scales. All the gas equations are proportional to Kelvin temperature but not Celsius temperature.

Section 10.3   The Gas Laws

The KMT explains why **the pressure of a gas changes with volume** at constant temperature. If the volume of a fixed amount of gas decreases, the pressure increases and vice versa (Figure 10.3).

Figure 10.3 The pressure of a gas increases when the volume decreases at constant temperature because the surface area of the container decreases, $P = F/A$.

Low pressure   High pressure

When the volume of the container decreases, the molecular collisions occur on a smaller surface area, increasing the pressure. $P = F/A$.

Boyle's law tells how much the volume of a gas changes with changing pressure:

The volume of a fixed quantity of gas at constant temperature is inversely proportional to the pressure.

$$P_1V_1 = P_2V_2$$

Figure 10.4 graphically illustrates how the volume of a gas depends on the pressure at constant temperature.

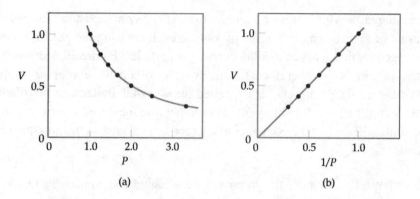

Figure 10.4 Boyle's law states that the volume of a gas decreases with increasing pressure. (a) Volume vs. pressure, (b) volume vs. $1/P$.

Your Turn 10.1

If the pressure of a fixed amount of gas doubles at constant temperature, what happens to its volume? Write your answer in the space provided.

The KMT explains why **the volume of a gas changes with temperature** at constant pressure. If the temperature of a fixed amount of gas increases at constant pressure, the volume increases and vice versa.

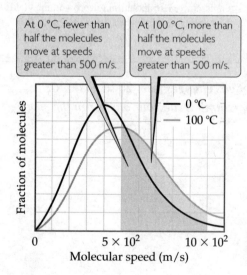

Figure 10.5 Higher temperature increases the speed of gas molecules and, therefore, their kinetic energies.

Volume increases with increasing temperature at constant pressure. Temperature is a measure of average kinetic energy of molecules. Increasing temperature increases the average kinetic energy of a collection of gas particles. Figure 10.5 shows the distribution of speeds and, therefore, kinetic energies of a collection of gas molecules at two different temperatures. This is called the **Maxwell–Boltzmann distribution.** If the gas is confined in a flexible-walled container, the increased forces of collisions on the walls will expand the container to a larger surface area so the pressure remains constant.

Charles's law tells how much the volume of a gas changes with changing temperature:

The volume of a fixed amount of gas at constant pressure is directly proportional to the absolute temperature.

$$V_1/T_1 = V_2/T_2$$

Figure 10.6 shows how volume decreases with decreasing temperature. Notice how extrapolation of the graph to a theoretical zero volume gives the value of absolute zero temperature (0 K or −273 °C).

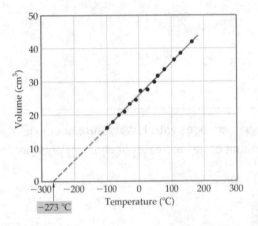

Figure 10.6 Charles's law states that the volume of an enclosed gas increases with increasing temperature. Extrapolation to zero volume yields the value of absolute zero.

Your Turn 10.2

When the temperature of a fixed amount of gas changes from 20 °C to 40 °C, what happens to the volume at constant pressure? Write your answer in the space provided.

Your Turn 10.3

→

A corollary to Charles's law relates the pressure of a fixed volume of gas to the temperature: the pressure of a fixed amount of gas increases with increasing temperature at constant volume. Explain this statement using ideas from the kinetic-molecular theory. Write your answer in the space provided.

Avogadro's hypothesis states that equal volumes of gases under the same conditions of temperature and pressure contain equal numbers of molecules.

The KMT explains Avogadro's hypothesis because it assumes that all individual gas molecules occupy essentially zero volume and have essentially zero attractive and repulsive forces. (All gas molecules are pinpoint dots that move freely and independently.) Therefore, the same number of particles of all gases, no matter their chemical identity, will behave in the same way.

Figure 10.7 shows that volumes of equal moles of gases at the same temperature and pressure are independent of the identity of the gas.

	He	N$_2$	CH$_4$
Volume	22.4 L	22.4 L	22.4 L
Pressure	1 atm	1 atm	1 atm
Temperature	0 °C	0 °C	0 °C
Mass of gas	4.00 g	28.0 g	16.0 g
Number of gas molecules	6.02 × 10^{23}	6.02 × 10^{23}	6.02 × 10^{23}

Figure 10.7 Avogadro's hypothesis states that equal number of moles of any gas at the same temperature and pressure occupy equal volumes.

Avogadro's law states that the volume of a gas at constant temperature and pressure is directly proportional to the number of moles of the gas.

$$V_1/n_1 = V_2/n_2$$

Since volume is directly proportional to moles, the coefficients that balance chemical equations for gas reactions can be taken as ratios of moles or liters at constant temperature and pressure.

Example:

How many liters of water vapor can be obtained from the complete combustion of 24 L of methane gas? Assume temperature and pressure are such that all the water formed will be in the gas phase.

Solution:

$$CH_4(g) + 3O_2(g) \rightarrow CO_2(g) + 2H_2O(g)$$

$$24\ L\ CH_4(g) \xrightarrow{\times 2\,L\,H_2O(g)/1\,L\,CH_4(g)} ?L\ H_2O(g)$$

$$x\ liters\ H_2O(g) = 24\ L\ CH_4\ (2\ L\ H_2O/1\ L\ CH_4) = 48\ L\ H_2O(g)$$

Section 10.4

The Ideal-Gas Equation

The **ideal-gas equation** combines Boyle's, Charles's, and Avogadro's laws:

$$PV = nRT$$

P = pressure in atmospheres

V = volume in liters

n = amount of substance in moles

T = absolute temperature in Kelvin

R = 0.0821 L-atm/mol-K

 **Common misconception:** When using the ideal-gas equation, pressure, volume, amount of substance, and temperature must always be expressed in atmospheres, liters, moles, and Kelvin, respectively, when the constant R has those units. In the other equations, volume and pressure may be expressed in any units as long as they are consistent.

An **ideal gas** is a hypothetical gas whose pressure, volume, and temperature behavior is completely described by the ideal-gas equation.

Common misconception: No gas is an ideal gas. All gases are real gases. However, at temperatures at or above 25 °C and pressures at or below 1 atm, generally most real gases behave ideally. A real gas deviates from ideal behavior at high pressure and/or low temperature, especially near the condensation point. This is because at relatively low pressures, the individual gas particles are very far apart. This makes the volumes of the individual molecules of a gas and their attractive and/or repulsive forces negligible. Both are key assumptions of the kinetic-molecular theory. But at high pressure, the gas molecules are close together, making their particle volumes significant, and they collide more frequently, making their interactive forces significant. Also at low temperature, the molecules move more slowly, increasing the significance of their interactive forces.

Further Applications of the Ideal-Gas Equation   Section 10.5

The ideal-gas equation is useful in stoichiometry calculations involving gases.

Example:

Gasoline is a mixture of many hydrocarbon compounds but its chemical formula can be approximated as C_8H_{18}. How many liters of carbon dioxide gas are formed at 25.0 °C and 712 torr when 1.00 gallon of liquid gasoline is burned in excess air? Liquid gasoline has a density of 0.690 g/mL. One gallon is 3.80 L.

Solution:

First, write and balance the equation. Then, calculate the number of moles of CO_2 using the mole road. Finally, use the ideal-gas equation to convert moles of CO_2 to volume in liters at the given temperature and pressure. Be sure to convert °C to K and torr to atmospheres.

$$2C_8H_{18}(l) + 25O_2(g) \longrightarrow 16CO_2(g) + 18H_2O(l)$$

1 gallon   ? L

$\times$ | 3.80 L/gal

liters

$\times$ | 690 g/L $V = nRT/P$

grams

$\div$ | 114 g/mol $\times$ 16 mol

mols ————————————→ mols = n
              2 mol

$$x \; mol \; CO_2 = 1.00 \; gal(3.80 \; L/gal)(690 \; g/L)(1 \; mol/114 \; g)$$
$$(16 \; mol \; CO_2/2 \; mol \; C_8H_{18}) = 184 \; moles \; CO_2.$$

$$V = nRT/P = (184\ mol)\ (0.0821\ L\text{-}atm/mol\text{-}K)(25 + 273\ K)$$
$$/(712\ torr/760\ torr/atm) = 4810\ L.$$

The **density of a gas** at any given temperature and pressure is directly proportional to its molar mass:

$$d = PM/RT$$

where d is density in grams per liter and M is the molar mass in grams per mole.

Example:

What is the density of sulfur dioxide gas at 35 °C and 1270 torr?

Solution:

The molar mass of SO_2 is 64.0 g/mol. Use the equation for density. Make sure temperature is in Kelvin and pressure is in atmospheres.

$$d = PM/RT =$$
$$(1270\ torr/760\ torr/atm)\ (64.0\ g/mol)/(0.0821\ L\text{-}atm/mol\text{-}K)$$
$$(35 + 273K) = 4.23\ g/L.$$

Common misconception: Because the densities of most gases are so low, they are commonly expressed in units of g/L rather than g/mL or g/cm^3. At common temperatures and pressures, most gas densities fall between about 1 and 10 g/L.

Section 10.6

Gas Mixtures and Partial Pressures

A partial pressure of a gas is the pressure exerted by an individual gas in a mixture of gases. Water vapor pressure is a partial pressure.

Dalton's law of partial pressures states that the total pressure of a mixture of gases equals the sum of the pressures that each gas would exert if it were present alone.

$$P_{total} = P_1 + P_2 + P_3 + \cdots$$

where P_{total} is the total pressure of a mixture of gases and P_1, P_2, and P_3 are the **partial pressures** of the individual gases in the mixture.

The **mole fraction**, X_g, of a gas in a mixture is the ratio of moles of that gas to the total moles of gas in the mixture.

$$X_g = n_g/n_{total}$$

Each gas in a mixture of gases behaves independently of all the other gases in the mixture. Hence, each ideal gas in a mixture obeys the ideal-gas law and all other gas laws. Each gas can be treated separately from the other gases in any mixture. Table 10.1 summarizes some equations that are useful in partial pressure calculations.

Table 10.1 Some useful equations involving partial pressure.

	Equation	Comments
Dalton's law	$P_{total} = P_1 + P_2 + P_3 + \cdots$	$P_{total} = $ total pressure of the mixture, P_1, P_2, and $P_3 = $ partial pressures of the individual gases
Mole fraction, X	$X_1 = n_1/n_t$	$n_1 = $ number of moles of an individual gas, $n_t = $ total moles of the gas
Ideal-gas equation	$P_1 = n_1 RT/V$	$P_1 = $ partial pressure of an individual gas, $n_1 = $ number of moles of that gas
Partial pressure	$P_1 = (n_1/n_t)(P_t)$	A convenient way to calculate partial pressure from total pressure

Example:

A mixture of 9.00 g of oxygen, 18.0 g of argon, and 25.0 g of carbon dioxide exerts a pressure of 2.54 atm. What is the partial pressure of argon in the mixture?

Solution:

First, calculate the number of moles of each gas. Then, calculate the mole fraction of argon and multiply it by the total pressure to get the partial pressure of argon.

Moles of oxygen = 9.00 g/32.0 g/mol = 0.281 mol O_2.

Moles of argon = 18.0 g/39.9 g/mol = 0.451 mol Ar.

Moles of carbon dioxide = 25.0 g/44.0 g/mol = 0.568 mol CO_2.

Mole fraction of Ar = X_{Ar} = moles of Ar/total moles of gases =

$n_{Ar}/n_t = 0.451/(0.281 + 0.451 + 0.568) = 0.451/1.30 = 0.347$.

Partial pressure of Ar = $P_{Ar} = (X_{Ar})(P_t) = 0.347 \times 2.54$ atm
$= 0.881$ atm.

For convenience in the laboratory, gases are often collected by bubbling them through water. This process causes the collected gas to be "contaminated" with water vapor. That is, the collected gas and the water vapor both exert their own partial pressures. The total pressure inside the collection vessel (usually the atmospheric pressure) is equal to the combined partial pressures of the gas and the water vapor.

$$P_{total} = P_{gas} + P_{water}$$

Example:

Hydrogen is produced by the action of sulfuric acid on zinc metal and collected over water in a 255 mL container at 24.0 °C and 718 torr. The vapor pressure of water at 24 °C is 22.38 torr. How many moles of hydrogen gas are produced and how many grams of zinc react?

Solution:

First, write and balance the equation. Then, subtract the vapor pressure of water (given in the question or obtained from Appendix B of Chemistry: The Central Science) from the atmospheric pressure to obtain the partial pressure of hydrogen gas. Finally, calculate the number of moles of hydrogen using the ideal-gas equation. Any time you use the value of R, be sure to convert pressure to atmospheres and volume to liters.

$$Zn(s) + 2H^+(aq) \rightarrow Zn^{2+}(aq) + H_2(g)$$

$$P_{H_2} = P_{atm} - P_{water} = 718\ torr - 22.38\ torr = 696\ torr$$

$$nH_2 = PV/RT = (696\ torr/760\ torr/atm)(0.255\ L)$$
$$/(0.0821\ L\text{-}atm/mol\text{-}K)(24 + 273\ K) = 0.00958\ mol\ H_2$$

The balanced equation tells us that the number of moles of hydrogen produced is equal to the number of moles of zinc reacted.

$$x\ g\ Zn = 0.00958\ mol\ Zn \times 65.4\ g/mol = 0.627\ g.$$

Your Turn 10.4

←————————————————————————

Use kinetic-molecular theory to explain why the pressure increases when the temperature of a fixed volume of gas increases. Write your answer in the space provided.

Molecular Effusion and Diffusion   Section 10.8

Effusion is the escape of gas molecules through a tiny hole into an evacuated space.

Diffusion is the spread of one substance through space or through another substance.

Both effusion and diffusion occur faster at higher temperatures because the average speed of the molecules is greater. This is because the absolute temperature of a gas is a measure of the average kinetic energy of the particles. Molecular motion increases with increasing temperature.

At the same temperature, the average kinetic energy of gas molecules is the same. Thus, particles of smaller molar mass move faster on average than larger ones (see Figure 10.8).

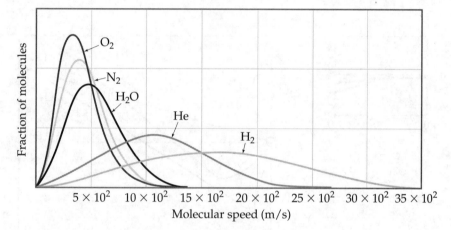

Figure 10.8 The effect of molar mass on molecular speed at 25 °C.

Real Gases: Deviations from Ideal Behavior   Section 10.9

Real gases differ from **ideal gases** largely because the volumes of real gas particles are finite and their attractive forces and repulsive forces are nonzero.

A real gas does not behave ideally at high pressure because the finite volume of its particles is significant compared to the volume of its container (see Figure 10.9). Also attractive forces come into play at short distances when gas particles are crowded together.

Low pressure   High pressure

Figure 10.9 Gases behave more ideally at low pressure than at high pressure. The combined volume of the molecules can be neglected at low pressure but not at high pressure.

A real gas does not behave ideally at low temperature, especially near its condensation point, because its nonzero attractive forces are significant at low kinetic energy. Eventually, as the temperature (average kinetic energy) drops, attractive forces cause the gas to condense to a liquid.

Deviations from ideal behavior for gases generally increase with increasing molecular complexity and increasing mass. Mass is directly related to molecular volume, and molecular complexity is associated with both volume and attractive forces.

Figure 10.10 shows the deviations from ideal behavior of four real gases at various pressures. Notice that at low pressures the deviations are negative and at high pressures they are positive.

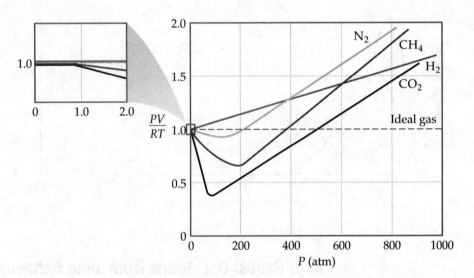

Figure 10.10 The effect of pressure on the behavior of several real gases. Data for 1 mol of gas in all cases. Data for N_2, CH_4, and H_2 are at 300 K; for CO_2 data are at 313 K because under high pressure CO_2 liquefies at 300 K.

Your Turn 10.5

Which of the noble gases deviate the most from ideal behavior? Explain your reasoning. Write your answer in the space provided.

Your Turn 10.6

Arrange the following gases in order of increasing deviation from ideality:
H_2O, CH_4, *Ne. Justify your answer. Write your answer in the space provided.*

Table 10.2 summarizes the important gas laws.

Table 10.2   Summary of the gas laws and their equations.

Gas Law	Statement	What Is Constant	Equation
Boyle's law	The volume of a fixed quantity of gas at constant temperature is inversely proportional to the pressure	n, T	$P_1V_1 = P_2V_2$
Charles's law	The volume of a fixed amount of gas at constant pressure is directly proportional to the absolute temperature	n, P	$V_1/T_1 = V_2/T_2$
Gay-Lussac's law	The pressure of a fixed quantity of gas at constant volume is directly proportional to the absolute temperature	n, V	$P_1/T_1 = P_2/T_2$
Avogadro's law	The volume of a gas at constant temperature and pressure is directly proportional to the number of moles	T, P	$V_1/n_1 = V_2/n_2$
Ideal-gas law	Combines the above laws into one equation	$R = 0.0821$ L-atm/mol-K	$PV = nRT$
Dalton's law of partial pressures	The total pressure of a mixture of gases equals the sum of the partial pressure of each component		$P_t = P_1 + P_2 + P_3 + \cdots$

Multiple Choice Questions

1. Hydrogen peroxide, H_2O_2, in the presence of a catalyst decomposes into water and oxygen gas. How many liters of O_2 at STP are produced from the decomposition of 34.0 g of H_2O_2?

   A) 1.00

   B) 5.60

   C) 11.2

   D) 22.4

2. A mixture of 6.02×10^{23} molecules of $NH_3(g)$ and 3.01×10^{23} molecules of $H_2O(g)$ has a total pressure of 6.00 atm. What is the partial pressure of NH_3?

   A) 1.00 atm

   B) 2.00 atm

   C) 3.00 atm

   D) 4.00 atm

   Questions 3–5 apply to these gases at $0°C$ and 1 atm:

   A) H_2

   B) He

   C) Rn

   D) Kr

3. Which gas deviates the most from ideality?

4. Which gas has a density of 3.74 g/L?

5. Which gas has the highest average molecular speed?

6. Which increases as a gas is heated at constant volume?
   I.   Pressure
   II. Kinetic energy of molecules
   III. Attractive forces between molecules

   A) I only

   B) II only

   C) III only

   D) I and II only

7. At room temperature and 1 atm pressure, the molecules are farthest apart in

    A) fluorine.

    B) bromine.

    C) iodine.

    D) mercury.

8. What is the name of the process? $H_2O(s) \rightarrow H_2O(g)$

    A) condensation

    B) evaporation

    C) fusion

    D) sublimation

9. Which statement is true of a measured pressure of a sample of hydrogen gas collected over water at constant temperature?

    A) The measured pressure is greater than the pressure of dry hydrogen.

    B) The measured pressure is less than the pressure of dry hydrogen.

    C) The measured pressure is equal to the pressure of dry hydrogen.

    D) The measured pressure varies inversely with the pressure of dry hydrogen.

10. In which instance is a gas most likely to behave as an ideal gas?

    A) At low temperatures, because the molecules are always far apart.

    B) When the molecules are highly polar, because intermolecular forces are more likely.

    C) At room temperature and pressure, because intermolecular interactions are minimized and the particles are relatively far apart.

    D) At high pressures, because the distance between molecules is likely to be small in relation to the size of the molecules.

11. Methanol, CH_3OH, burns in oxygen to form carbon dioxide and water. What volume of oxygen is required to burn 6.00 L of gaseous methanol measured at the same temperature and pressure?

    A) 4.00 L

    B) 8.00 L

    C) 9.00 L

    D) 12.0 L

12. The physical behavior of an ideal gas is dependent on all the following except:

   A) temperature

   B) volume

   C) chemical composition

   D) number of moles

13. Gases tend to exhibit nonideal behavior under conditions of

   A) low temperature and low pressure.

   B) low temperature and high pressure.

   C) high temperature and high pressure.

   D) high temperature and low pressure.

14. Which gas deviates the most from ideal behavior?

   A) H_2

   B) Ne

   C) H_2O

   D) CH_4

15. Which gas will have the smallest average velocity at the same temperature?

   A) He

   B) SO_2

   C) Ar

   D) CO_2

Free Response Questions

1. Equal masses (0.500 g each) of hydrogen and oxygen are placed in an evacuated 4.00 L flask at 25.0 °C. The mixture is allowed to react to completion and the flask is returned to 25.0 °C and allowed to come to equilibrium. The equilibrium vapor pressure of water at 25 °C is 23.76 torr.

   a. Write and balance a chemical equation for the reaction.

   b. What is the total pressure inside the flask before the reaction begins?

   c. What is the mass of water vapor in the flask at equilibrium?

   d. How many grams of which reactant gas remains at equilibrium?

   e. What is the total pressure inside the flask at equilibrium?

   f. After the reaction, is there any liquid water present? If so, how many grams? If not, why not?

2. A 2.00 L flask at 27 °C contains 3.00 g each of Ar(g), SO₂(g), and He(g). Answer the following questions about the gases, and in each case, explain your reasoning.

   a. Which gas has particles with the highest average kinetic energy?

   b. Which gas has particles with the highest average velocity?

   c. Which gas has the highest partial pressure?

   d. Which gas will deviate the most from ideal behavior?

   e. Which substance will have the highest boiling point?

   f. What changes in temperature and pressure will increase the deviations of all the gases from ideal behavior?

Multiple Choice Answers and Explanations

1. C. The balanced equation is: $H_2O_2 \rightarrow H_2O + \frac{1}{2}O_2$. One mole of hydrogen peroxide produces one-half mole of oxygen gas. One mole of H_2O_2 is 34.0 g because the molar mass of hydrogen peroxide is 34.0 g/mol. If 1 mol of gas at STP occupies 22.4 L, then one-half mole has a volume of 11.2 L.

2. D. Because there are twice as many molecules of ammonia than of water, there are twice as many moles of ammonia. The mole fraction of ammonia is 2/3. The partial pressure of ammonia is given by:

$$P_{NH_3} = X_{NH_3} \times P_t = 2/3 \times 6.00 \, atm = 4.00 \, atm.$$

3. C. All five are nonpolar but radon has the largest molar mass and the largest volume.

4. D. Even without a calculator, the product of $(3.74 \, g/L)(22.4 \, L/mol)$ can be estimated to be about 80 g/mol $(4 \times 20 = 80)$. The molar mass of krypton from the periodic table is 83.8 g/mol while the closest other noble gases are argon (39.9 g/mol) and xenon (131 g/mol).

5. A. Average molecular speed varies inversely with the molar mass. At the same temperature, the lightest gas will move faster on average.

6. D. Heating causes the temperature to increase, and temperature is a measure of kinetic energy. The faster moving molecules strike the walls of the container more frequently and with greater force increasing the pressure. Intermolecular forces are a function of the structures of the molecules present and not of the temperature or pressure.

7. A. Kinetic-molecular theory states that liquids and solids are in close contact with each other because of the attractive forces between molecules. Gases have little or no attractive forces and the molecules are far apart. This question is really asking, "Which of the following is a gas?" Fluorine, at room temperature and 1 atm, is the only gas on the list.

8. D. Sublimation is the process by which a solid changes directly to a gas.

9. A. Whenever a gas is collected over water, the gas is contaminated with water vapor. The measured pressure is equal to the pressure of the dry gas plus the partial pressure of water vapor at a given temperature: $P_{total} = P_{H_2} + P_{H_2O}$. The pressure of the hydrogen sample is greater than the pressure of the dry gas.

10. C. Gases behave ideally at low pressures because the molecular volumes are small compared to the volume of the container and at high temperature because the kinetic energy overcomes the intermolecular forces making them insignificant. Most gases behave as ideal gases at room temperature and pressure.

11. C. The balanced equation is $2CH_3OH(g) + 3O_2(g) \rightarrow 2CO_2(g) + 4H_2O(g)$. The coefficients for gases that balance an equation are ratios of liters as well as moles at constant temperature and pressure. If 2 L of methanol requires 3 L of oxygen, then 6 L of methanol requires 9 L of oxygen.

    $x\,L\,O_2 = 6\,L\,CH_3OH\,(3\,L\,O_2/2\,L\,CH_3OH) = 9.00\,L$

12. C. Ideal gases are assumed to be composed of tiny particles having no attractive forces. Therefore, the chemical composition will have no affect on their behavior.

13. B. Nonideal gases are real gases with significant attractive forces between particles and significant particle volumes. Low temperatures slow the particles sufficiently so that the attractive forces become more dominant. High pressures crowd the particles so that their volumes become significant.

14. C. Ideal gases have insignificant volumes and no attractive forces. Deviations from ideal behavior become greater for larger molecules with high attractive forces. Water is a polar molecule with very large dipole–dipole interactions and hydrogen bonds.

15. E. Gases at the same temperature will have the same average kinetic energy. The gas with the greatest molar mass will, on average, move more slowly than the other gases.

Free Response Answers

1. a. $2H_2(g) + O_2(g) \rightarrow 2H_2O$

   b. $mol\,H_2 = 0.500\,g/2.00\,g/mol = 0.250\,mol\,H_2$
   $mol\,O_2 = 0.500\,g/32.0\,g/mol = 0.0156\,mol\,O_2$
   $P_{total} = n_{total}RT/V = (0.250 + 0.0156\,mol)(0.0821\,L\text{-}atm/mol\text{-}K)$
   $(25 + 273\,K)/(4.00\,L) = 1.62\,atm$

   c. $n = PV/RT = (23.76\,torr/760\,torr/atm)(4.00L)/(0.0821\,L\text{-}atm/mol\text{-}K)$
   $(298\,K) = 0.00511\,mol\,H_2O\,vapor$
   $0.00511\,mol \times 18.0\,g/mol = 0.0920\,g\,H_2O\,vapor.$

   d. O_2 is limiting because 0.250 mol of hydrogen would require 0.125 mol of oxygen to react and there are only 0.0156 mol of oxygen.

   Twice as many moles of hydrogen react:
   $2 \times 0.0156\,mol = 0.0312\,mol\,H_2\,react$
   $0.250 - 0.0312\,mol = 0.219\,mol\,H_2\,remain$
   $0.219\,mol \times 2.00\,g/mol = 0.438\,g\,H_2\,remain$

e. $P_{H_2} = (n_{H_2})RT/V$

$(0.219 \ mol)(0.0821 \ L\text{-}atm/mol\text{-}K)(298 \ K)/4.00 \ L) = 1.34 \ atm$

$P_t = P_{H_2O} + P_{H_2}(23.76 \ torr/760 \ torr/atm) + 1.34 \ atm = 1.37 \ atm$

f. *Yes, liquid water remains in the flask.*

0.0312 mol of hydrogen will produce 0.0312 mol of water. There are only 0.00511 mol of water vapor present, so the rest is liquid.

0.0312 mol − 0.00511 mol = 0.0261 mol of water is liquid

0.0261 mol × 18.0 g/mol = 0.470 g liquid water

2. a. *All three gases have the same average kinetic energy because the temperature is the same for each and temperature is a measure of average kinetic energy.*

b. *The helium atoms will have the highest average velocity because they are the smallest. At the same temperature, the square of the velocity of any gas varies inversely with its molar mass.*

c. *Helium has the highest partial pressure because partial pressure is proportional to the number of moles of gas present and the number of moles increases with decreasing molar mass.*

d. *Sulfur dioxide will display the greatest deviation from ideal behavior because SO_2 molecules are the largest and most complex of the three different kinds of gas particles. It is also polar and will have the highest attractive forces.*

e. *Sulfur dioxide will have the highest boiling point because its polarity provides higher attractive forces.*

f. *Decreasing the temperature and increasing the pressure will increase deviations from ideal behavior for all gases.*

Your Turn Answers

10.1. *The volume of a fixed amount of gas halves when its pressure is doubled at constant temperature.*

10.2. *The volume of a fixed amount of gas at constant pressure rises by a factor of $(40 + 273)/(20 + 273)$ when the temperature increases from $20\,°C$ to $40\,°C$.*

10.3. *At constant volume, the pressure of a gas increases with increasing temperature because the molecular collisions on the walls of the container happen with greater force. Temperature is a measure of average kinetic energy. Increasing temperature increases the speed of the molecules and their average kinetic energy. At constant volume, faster moving molecules strike the walls of the container with greater force increasing the pressure.*

10.4. *Increasing temperature increases the average kinetic energy and, therefore, velocity of the molecules. Pressure increases because the faster moving molecules strike the walls of the container more often and with greater energy.*

10.5.   *Of the noble gases, radon will deviate the most from ideal behavior because it is the heaviest and has the largest finite volume for its particles.*

10.6.   *Expected deviation from ideal behavior: Ne $<$ CH_4 $<$ H_2O. All have similar molar masses but neon is the simplest in complexity, followed by methane that has perfect tetrahedral geometry, and water that is nonlinear. Water is also very polar and forms hydrogen bonds, causing its attractive forces to be much greater than the two nonpolar species.*

LIQUIDS AND INTERMOLECULAR FORCES

The content in this topic is the basis for mastering Learning Objectives 2.1, 2.3, 2.8, 2.11, 2.13, 2.14, 2.15, 2.16, 5.9, and 5.10 as found in the Curriculum Framework.

When you finish reviewing this topic, be sure you are able to:

- Distinguish among intermolecular forces and explain with examples how they affect the properties of molecules
- Compare the macroscopic differences between solids, liquids, and gases using their molecular structures and behaviors and the forces that hold them together
- Use particle representations to rationalize the differences between solids, liquids, and gases
- Use intermolecular forces to explain the properties of liquids such as melting point, boiling point, vapor pressure, viscosity, and surface tension
- Use the structures of molecules to predict the types of intermolecular forces that exist between them
- Describe the relationships between the structures of polar molecules and their dipole–dipole intermolecular forces
- Use London dispersions to justify properties of nonpolar atoms and molecules

A Molecular Comparison of Gases, Liquids, and Solids   Section 11.1

The three phases of matter are solids, liquids, and gases. The phase of a substance depends largely on the balance between the kinetic energies of the particles, which keep the particles moving, and the attractive forces between them, which hold the particles together. The differences in the atomic- and molecular-level structures of solids, liquids, and gases explain their differences in macroscopic properties. Figure 11.1 illustrates macroscopic and molecular views of solids, liquids, and gases.

Figure 11.1 Gases, liquids, and solids. Chlorine, bromine, and iodine are all made up of diatomic molecules as a result of covalent bonding. However, because of differences in the strength of the intermolecular forces, they exist in three different states at room temperature and standard pressure: Cl_2 is gaseous, Br_2 is liquid, and I_2 is solid.

In **crystalline solids**, the particles are packed closely together in a regular three-dimensional structure called a **crystal**. The close spacing and the relatively strong attractive forces between the individual particles limit their motion. The particles can vibrate in place but do not change positions with respect to each other. Figure 11.2 shows the well-ordered crystalline structure of sodium chloride.

Figure 11.2 Crystal structure of sodium chloride.

Amorphous solids differ from crystalline solids because they are not arranged in a regular ordered crystal pattern. Like crystalline solids, the particles of amorphous solids are packed closely together with motion limited to vibrations in place.

Liquids differ from solids because the forces of attraction in a liquid do not hold the particles in rigid positions. Particles in a liquid are constantly moving and colliding, changing locations as they slip and slide past each other. Like solids, liquids have particles that are close together.

Typically, when a substance changes from solid to liquid, its volume usually changes little because of the relatively close packing in both phases.

In **gases,** the particles are far apart, in rapid, random motion, and their intermolecular forces are negligible.

Table 11.1 compares the macroscopic properties of gases, liquids, and solids.

Table 11.1   Some characteristic properties of the states of matter.

Gas	Assumes both volume and shape of its container
	Expands to fill its container
	Is compressible
	Flows readily
	Diffusion within a gas occurs rapidly
Liquid	Assumes shape of portion of container it occupies
	Does not expand to fill its container
	Is virtually incompressible
	Flows readily
	Diffusion within a liquid occurs slowly
Solid	Retains own shape and volume
	Does not expand to fill its container
	Is virtually incompressible
	Does not flow
	Diffusion within a solid occurs extremely slowly

Your Turn 11.1

Use the particle nature of matter shown in Figure 11.1 to explain the following properties of solids, liquids, and gases listed in Table 11.1.

    a. Compressibility

    b. Volume and shape

    c. Diffusion

Write your answer in the space provided.

Section 11.2

Intermolecular Forces

Intramolecular forces are the attractive forces **within** molecules that we call chemical bonds. Intramolecular forces cause many of the chemical properties of molecules.

Intermolecular forces are the forces that exist **between** molecules. They are largely responsible for the physical properties of solids and liquids.

The physical state of a substance depends largely on the balance between the kinetic energies of the particles and the intermolecular attractive forces between the particles. For example, a gas condenses to a liquid at low temperature because the kinetic energy of the particles decreases to a point where the intermolecular attractive forces become significant. Figure 11.3 illustrates the molecular-level differences between solids, liquids, and gases.

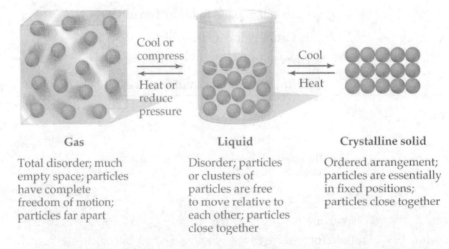

Gas	Liquid	Crystalline solid
Total disorder; much empty space; particles have complete freedom of motion; particles far apart	Disorder; particles or clusters of particles are free to move relative to each other; particles close together	Ordered arrangement; particles are essentially in fixed positions; particles close together

Figure 11.3 Each phase of a substance—solid, liquid, gas—differs in kinetic energy. Higher temperatures impart higher kinetic energy, which makes attractive forces less significant.

Generally, the greater the intermolecular forces, the higher the melting points of solids and the higher the boiling points of liquids.

Ion–dipole forces exist between an ion and a polar molecule. For example, when sodium chloride dissolves in water (see Figure 11.4), the partial negative end of the water molecule and the positive sodium ion are held together by an ion–dipole force of attraction.

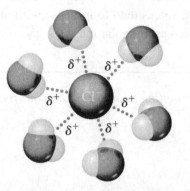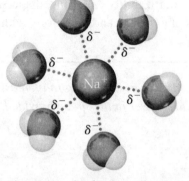

Positive ends of polar molecules are oriented toward negatively charged anion

Negative ends of polar molecules are oriented toward positively charged cation

Figure 11.4 Ion–dipole forces between water molecules and sodium chloride ions.

When an ionic substance dissolves in water, the ionic bonds break as the ions separate. Water molecules attract the ions to form ion–dipole interactions. Bond breaking is endothermic and bond making is exothermic. If the energy absorbed when the solid crystal comes apart is less than the energy released when ion–dipole interactions form, the ionic compound will dissolve exothermically.

Dipole–dipole forces exist between neutral polar molecules in the liquid or solid state as illustrated in Figure 11.5.

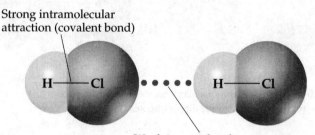

Strong intramolecular attraction (covalent bond)

H——Cl • • • • • H——Cl

Weak intermolecular attraction

Figure 11.5 The positive end of an HCl molecule attracts the negative end of another, exhibiting a dipole–dipole intermolecular force.

London dispersion forces are the result of attractions between **induced dipoles**. Even though no dipole–dipole forces exist between nonpolar atoms or molecules, they do have attractive forces because they do form liquids and solids. In close proximity, an induced or temporary dipole forms between nonpolar atoms and molecules when the positive nucleus of one atom or molecule attracts the electrons of another atom or molecule. London dispersion forces exist in all matter because all atoms and molecules have electrons. The greater the number of electrons, the greater the probability that a temporary dipole will form. Dispersion forces, although the weakest of intermolecular forces, are often the dominant forces of attraction.

Polarizability refers to the degree to which a dipole can be induced in a nonpolar species. Polarizability and, thus, dispersion forces tend to increase with increasing numbers of electrons and, therefore, with increasing molar mass.

Your Turn 11.2

←——————————————————————————————————

Order the halogens according to increasing boiling points. Explain your reasoning. Write your answer in the space provided.

_____

Figure 11.6 illustrates the various kinds of intermolecular forces.

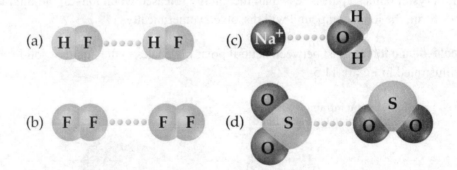

Figure 11.6 Four major intermolecular forces: (a) hydrogen bonding, (b) London dispersion, (c) ion–dipole, and (d) dipole–dipole.

Hydrogen bonding is an especially strong form of a dipole–dipole force. Hydrogen bonding exists only between hydrogen atoms bonded to F, O, or N of one molecule and F, O, and N of another molecule. The small size of electropositive hydrogen allows it to approach and form a strong force of attraction with a nonbonding electron pair on very electronegative F, O, or N atoms. Figure 11.7 shows some examples of hydrogen bonding.

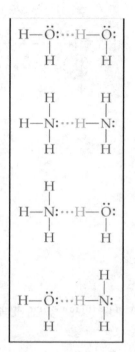

Figure 11.7 Hydrogen bonding exists between electropositive hydrogen atoms and nonbonding pairs of electrons on electronegative oxygen, nitrogen, or fluorine atoms.

Hydrogen bonding accounts for many unique properties of water. For example, Figure 11.8 illustrates the exceptionally high boiling point of water and Figure 11.9 shows the open, hexagonal arrangement of ice, which causes solid water to float on liquid water.

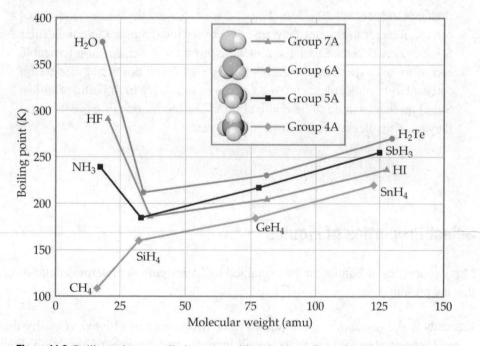

Figure 11.8 Boiling point generally increases with molar mass. Strong hydrogen bonding in water accounts for its unusually high boiling point.

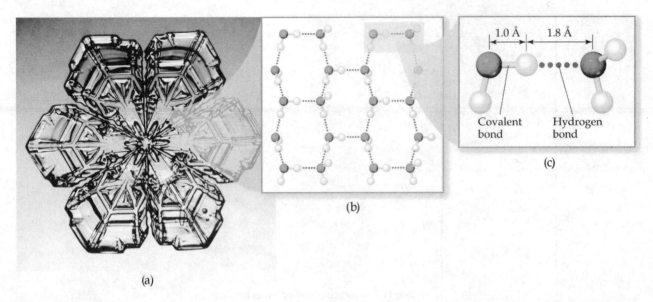

(a)

(b)

(c)

Figure 11.9 The hexagonal geometry of snowflakes (a) and the open, low-density structure of ice (b) result from strong hydrogen bonding of water molecules (c).

Generally for molecules of similar size and mass, intermolecular forces of attraction increase like this: Dispersion forces < dipole–dipole forces < hydrogen bonding < ion–dipole forces.

Common misconception: Even though dispersions are the weakest individual forces, in larger molecules they are collectively the dominant intermolecular forces. This is because a large molecule has a large number of polarizable electrons over its entire surface. Because of these dominant dispersion forces, larger molecules tend to be solids or relatively high boiling liquids. Small molecules tend to be relatively low boiling liquids or gases because they have smaller collective dispersion forces.

Section 11.3   Select Properties of Liquids

Many properties of liquids can be explained by identifying the intermolecular forces that are present.

Viscosity is the resistance of a liquid to flow. Molasses has a higher viscosity than water. Viscosity increases with increased intermolecular forces of attraction. For a series of related nonpolar compounds, viscosity increases with molar mass because larger molecules have more electrons so they are more polarizable and hence have stronger London dispersions.

Surface tension is the energy required to increase the surface area of a liquid by a unit amount. Surface tension is caused by an imbalance of intermolecular forces at the surface of the liquid. Water, which has very strong hydrogen bonding, has an unusually large surface tension.

Cohesive forces are intermolecular forces that bind similar molecules to one another, such as the hydrogen bonding in water.

Adhesive forces are intermolecular forces that bind a substance to a surface. For example, water placed in a glass tube adheres to the glass because the adhesive forces between the water and the glass are stronger than the cohesive forces between the water molecules. The curved upper surface that forms a meniscus in burets results from the high surface tension of water.

Capillary action is the rise of a liquid up a narrow tube. The adhesive forces between the liquid and the walls of the tube increase the surface area of the liquid. The surface tension responds by reducing the surface area and the liquid is pulled up the tube. The rise will continue until the force of gravity acting on the liquid balances the adhesive and cohesive forces.

Phase Changes   Section 11.4

A heating curve is a graph of the temperature of a system versus the amount of heat added as illustrated in Figure 11.10.

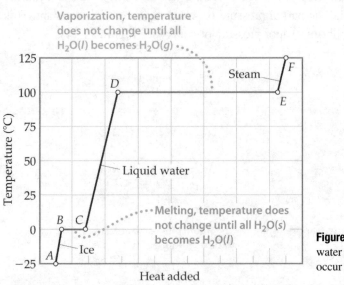

Figure 11.10 The heating curve for water shows that phase changes occur at constant temperature.

The **heat of fusion**, ΔH_{fus}, is the energy required to melt one mole of a substance at constant temperature.

The **heat of vaporization**, ΔH_{vap}, is the energy required to vaporize one mole of a substance at constant temperature.

The horizontal lines of a heating curve represent the heat of fusion, ΔH_{fus}, and heat of vaporization, ΔH_{vap}, of the substance. Notice that the temperature does not change during melting or vaporization. The nearly vertical lines represent the heat required to effect the corresponding temperature change of a single phase.

The **critical temperature** of a substance is the highest temperature at which a liquid can exist. At temperatures higher than the critical temperature, the kinetic energy of the molecules is so great that the substance can only be in the gas phase.

The **critical pressure** is the pressure required to cause liquefaction at the critical temperature. This is the pressure necessary to bring the molecules sufficiently close together, so that the forces of attraction between them can operate at the critical temperature.

Nonpolar substances and those with low molar masses (few electrons) tend to have low intermolecular forces of attraction and correspondingly low critical temperatures and pressures. Polar substances and substances with higher molar masses (many electrons) have higher critical temperatures and pressures because they are more polarizable and have higher intermolecular forces of attraction.

Section 11.5   Vapor Pressure

Vapor pressure is the partial pressure exerted by a vapor in a closed system when it is in equilibrium with its liquid or solid phase. For example, water placed in a closed container will evaporate at a constant rate and produce a partial pressure in the gas phase above the liquid. The partial pressure of water vapor will increase until the rate of evaporation equals the rate of condensation. The system is said to be in a state of **dynamic equilibrium** at this point and the partial pressure of water vapor remains constant. This partial pressure is the equilibrium vapor pressure of water (see Figure 11.11).

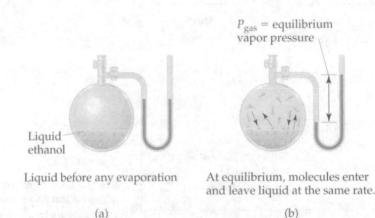

P_{gas} = equilibrium vapor pressure

Liquid ethanol

Liquid before any evaporation   At equilibrium, molecules enter and leave liquid at the same rate.

(a)   (b)

Figure 11.11 Equilibrium vapor pressure arises when a liquid in a closed container (a) evaporates producing a partial pressure of vapor above the liquid. (b) At equilibrium, the rate of evaporation equals the rate of condensation.

Nonpolar liquid substances having low molar masses, and therefore few electrons, usually have weak intermolecular forces and tend to have high vapor pressures.

Your Turn 11.3

Place the following compounds in order of increasing vapor pressure:
CCl₄, CI₄, CBr₄. Justify your answer. Write your answer in the space provided.

Increasing temperature will increase vapor pressure of a liquid or solid as shown in Figure 11.12. Higher temperatures provide greater kinetic energy of molecules, which gives them higher energies to overcome the attractive forces that hold them together.

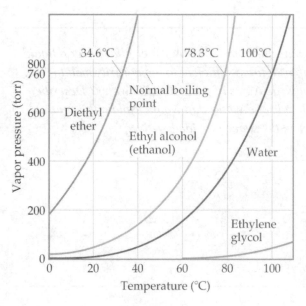

Figure 11.12 Vapor pressure of liquids increase with increasing temperature. The normal boiling point of a liquid is the temperature at which the vapor pressure reaches 760 torr.

The **boiling point** of a liquid is the temperature at which the vapor pressure of the liquid equals the external pressure acting on the liquid surface.

The **normal boiling point** of a liquid is the temperature at which the vapor pressure equals 1 atm.

Your Turn 11.4

Predict whether glycerol, $C_3H_5(OH)_3$, or 1-propanol, C_3H_7OH, will have the higher: (a) viscosity, (b) vapor pressure, and (c) boiling point. Justify your reasoning. Write your answers in the space provided.

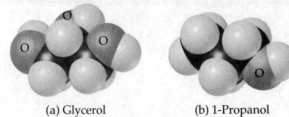

(a) Glycerol   (b) 1-Propanol

Your Turn 11.5

Ice skaters demonstrate that ice melts under pressure. A skater glides over a liquid surface of water as her blades impart a force sufficient to temporarily melt the ice. What does this say about the relative densities of ice and liquid water? Describe the molecular structures of liquid and solid water that would explain this unusual property of ice. Write your answer in the space provided.

Your Turn 11.6

Examine Figure 11.12 and list the four liquids in order of increasing vapor pressure at any given temperature and give their formulas. Justify the trend citing the intermolecular forces acting in each liquid. Write your answer in the space provided.

Multiple Choice Questions

1. *Which compound is most likely to form intermolecular hydrogen bonds?*

    A) C_4H_{10}

    B) NaH

    C) C_2H_5OH

    D) C_2H_5SH

2. *Which best explains why bromine is soluble in mineral oil?*

    A) *Both substances are liquids.*

    B) *Both substances have similar densities.*

    C) *Both substances are made up of nonpolar molecules.*

    D) *One substance is made up of polar molecules and the other substance is made up of nonpolar molecules.*

3. *Generally, the strongest interaction with water molecules in aqueous solution is for ions that have*

    A) *large charge and large size.*

    B) *large charge and small size.*

    C) *small charge and large size.*

    D) *small charge and small size.*

For questions 4–7, consider the following intermolecular forces of attraction. Choose which type of interaction best explains each statement. You may use a response once, more than once, or not at all.

    A) *London dispersions*

    B) *dipole–dipole interactions*

    C) *hydrogen bonds*

    D) *covalent bonds*

4. *This force is the strongest interaction between hexane and iodine.*

5. *Water and ethanol are completely miscible.*

6. *Dry ice sublimes endothermically.*

7. *The strongest intermolecular forces present in acetone, $(CH_3)_2C{=}O$, a volatile, flammable liquid, whose central carbon is sp^2 hybridized.*

8. A container is half filled with a liquid and sealed at room temperature and atmospheric pressure. What happens inside the container?

   A) Evaporation stops.

   B) Evaporation continues for a time and then stops.

   C) The pressure in the container remains constant.

   D) The pressure inside the container increases for a time and then remains constant.

9. Which factor(s) affect the vapor pressure of a liquid at equilibrium?

   I.   Intermolecular forces of attraction within the liquid.

   II.   The volume and/or surface area of liquid present.

   III. The temperature of the liquid.

   A) I only

   B) II only

   C) III only

   D) I and III only

10. The molar masses of a series of similar polar molecules increase in this order: A < B < C < D. The boiling points, in degrees Celsius, of molecules A, B, C, and D are 20°, 50°, 150°, and 100°, respectively. Which molecule is likely to form hydrogen bonds?

    A) A

    B) B

    C) C

    D) D

11. The relatively low boiling point of ethyl ether shown in Figure 11.12 is due to the lack of which type of force of attraction?

    A) London dispersions

    B) Ion-dipoles

    C) Hydrogen bonds

    D) Covalent bonds

12. How would the ion-dipole forces of dissolved potassium bromide compare to those of sodium chloride shown in Figure 11.4?

    A) They would be equal because all the charges are of equal magnitude.

    B) They would be larger for KBr because potassium ion is larger than sodium ion and bromide ion is larger than chloride ion.

C) They would be smaller for KBr because potassium ion is larger than sodium ion and bromide ion is larger than chloride ion.

D) They would be larger for NaCl because potassium ion is smaller than sodium ion and bromide ion is smaller than chloride ion.

13. Which is the best explanation for the fact that at 20 °C and 1.0 atm, chlorine is a gas, bromine is a liquid, and iodine is a solid?

A) Dispersion forces become greater as the number of electrons increases.

B) Iodine sublimes and bromine evaporates.

C) Dipole–dipole interactions are greater for lower mass particles.

D) The covalent bonds in iodine molecules are stronger than in bromine which are stronger than in chlorine.

14. The energy absorbed when dry ice sublimes is required to overcome which type of interaction?

A) covalent bonds

B) ion–dipole forces

C) dipole–dipole forces

D) dispersion forces

15. Upon swabbing on the back of your hand, which substance would create the most cooling effect at room temperature?

A) methanol, CH_3OH

B) ethanol, CH_3CH_2OH

C) 1-propanol, $CH_3CH_2CH_2OH$

D) 1-butanol, $CH_3CH_2CH_2CH_2OH$

Free Response Questions

1. Use concepts of chemical bonding and/or intermolecular forces to account for each of the following observations:

a. The boiling points of water, ammonia, and methane are 100 °C, −33 °C, and −164 °C, respectively.

b. At 25 °C and 1.0 atm, chlorine is a gas, bromine is a liquid, and iodine is a solid.

c. Calcium oxide melts at a much higher temperature (2615 °C) than does potassium chloride (770 °C).

d. Propane is a gas and ethanol is a liquid, even though they have similar molar masses.

2. Answer the following questions about water using principles of solids, liquids, and gases and intermolecular forces.

   a. Why does water boil at a lower temperature in Denver, Colorado, than in New York City?

   b. For substances of similar molar mass, why does water have unusually high values for boiling point, heat of vaporization, and surface tension?

   c. What structural features of ice cause it to float on liquid water?

   d. Why does calcium chloride dissolve exothermically in water?

3. Use Coulomb's law to qualitatively explain two reasons why hydrogen bonds, which are especially strong dipole–dipole forces of attraction, form only between hydrogen on one molecule and either nitrogen, oxygen, or fluorine on another.

4. List the substances CCl_4, CBr_4 and CH_4 in order of increasing boiling point (lowest first). Use ideas of intermolecular forces to justify your answer.

Multiple Choice Answers and Explanations

1. C. Hydrogen bonding occurs between molecules that have $H{-}O$, $H{-}N$, or $H{-}F$ bonds. The hydrogen atom on one molecule attracts a nonbonding electron pair on an O, N, or F atom of another molecule.

2. C. The adage, "Like dissolves like," means that polar substances will dissolve other polar substances and nonpolar substances will dissolve other nonpolar substances. Polar substances dissolve in each other because of strong dipole–dipole interactions. Nonpolar substances dissolve in each other because of London dispersions. Polar substances generally do not dissolve in nonpolar substances because dipole–dipole interactions among the polar molecules exclude the nonpolar molecules.

3. B. The equation, $F = kQ_1Q_2/d^2$, where Q_1 and Q_2 are ionic charges and d is the distance between ions, describes the force of attraction between two charged particles. It is also useful in estimating the relative strengths of ion–dipole interactions, such as those between polar water molecules and an aqueous ion. The larger the charge and the smaller the ion, the stronger the intermolecular force.

4. A. Hexane, $CH_3CH_2CH_2CH_2CH_2CH_3$, and iodine, I_2, are both nonpolar molecules. The strongest intermolecular forces acting between them are London dispersion forces. London dispersion forces arise when a positive nucleus of one molecule attracts the electrons of another molecule, inducing an instantaneous dipole, a momentary shift in electron density.

5. C. Water and ethanol, CH_3CH_2OH, are both small molecules and both have $O{-}H$ bonds. The hydrogen atoms on one molecule attract nonbonding electron pairs on an oxygen atom of another molecule, forming an especially strong dipole–dipole interaction called a hydrogen bond.

6. A. Carbon dioxide molecules are nonpolar. They are held together only by London dispersion forces. Sublimation is the process where a solid changes directly into a gas. Energy is required to overcome the forces of attraction that hold the molecules together in the solid phase.

7. B. The C=O bond in trigonal planar acetone is very polar making the molecule a strong dipole. The absence of H−O bonds rules out hydrogen bonding but strong dipole–dipole interactions exist.

8. D. The liquid will continue to evaporate without stopping. The pressure will rise until the partial pressure of the vapor equals the vapor pressure of the liquid at the given temperature. Then, a dynamic equilibrium is established when the rate of evaporation equals the rate of condensation.

9. D. Intermolecular forces and temperature both affect the vapor pressure of a liquid but vapor pressure is independent of volume and surface area.

10. C. Because of increased dispersion forces, the boiling points of a series of similar molecules will increase regularly with increasing molar mass. Molecule C is lighter than molecule D, yet it has a higher boiling point. This can be explained by especially strong dipole–dipole forces called hydrogen bonding in molecule C.

11. C. Ethyl ether, $CH_3CH_2OCH_2CH_3$, cannot hydrogen bond because it lacks a covalent bond between hydrogen and oxygen.

12. C. Because potassium ion and bromide ion are larger than sodium ion and chloride ion, respectively, the coulombic forces between water molecules and the ions of KBr will be smaller.

13. A. Because of the non-polar bonds in chlorine, bromine and iodine, the only intermolecular forces in effect are dispersion forces, also called instantaneous dipoles. Larger atoms have more electrons and are more polarizable. Thus larger atoms have greater instantaneous dipoles and stronger intermolecular attractions.

14. D. Carbon dioxide is a nonpolar molecule, held together only by London dispersion forces. Sublimation is the process where a solid changes directly into a gas. Energy is required to overcome the forces of attraction that hold the molecules together in the solid phase.

15. A. Evaporation is an endothermic process that absorbs heat, thus cooling its surroundings. All the alcohols are held together by hydrogen bonding. Methanol, with fewest electrons, is least polarizable. Therefore, it has fewer dispersion forces than the others causing it to have the highest vapor pressure and it evaporates the most readily.

Free Response Answers

1. a. *Water, H_2O, and ammonia, NH_3, both have higher boiling points than methane, CH_4, because water and ammonia form hydrogen bonds among their molecules and methane does not. Hydrogen bonds are relatively strong intermolecular attractive forces, which tend to hold molecules together in liquids, thus requiring more energy to separate them. Water has a much higher boiling point than ammonia because water has two nonbonding pairs of electrons per molecule versus one nonbonding pair for ammonia. Additionally, oxygen is more electronegative than nitrogen. These facts work together to allow stronger and much greater hydrogen bonding in water than in ammonia.*

    b. *Chlorine, bromine, and iodine are all nonpolar diatomic molecules held together by London dispersion forces. The dispersion forces become greater as the number of electrons increase. Iodine has the highest molar mass, the most electrons, and the largest dispersion forces, large enough to hold the molecules together in a molecular solid. Bromine has weaker dispersion forces but still strong enough to hold the molecules together in a liquid. Chlorine has the weakest dispersion forces, too weak to hold the molecules together, so it is a gas.*

    c. *To melt a solid, the temperature must be sufficient to overcome the attractive forces holding the solid together. Calcium oxide, CaO, is composed of small ions of relatively large charge, so they are held together with relatively large attractive forces requiring a high temperature to melt. Potassium chloride is composed of larger ions of smaller charge requiring a relatively low temperature to provide sufficient kinetic energy to overcome the relatively low attractive forces.*

    d. *Propane, $CH_3CH_2CH_3$, is a nonpolar molecule held together by relatively weak London dispersion forces. Ethanol, CH_3CH_2OH, is a polar molecule held together by London dispersion forces, dipole–dipole forces, and hydrogen bonding. Hydrogen bonding is a much stronger force of attraction than the London dispersion forces in propane.*

2. a. *Boiling point is the temperature at which the vapor pressure of a liquid equals the external pressure. Vapor pressure increases with increasing temperature. Because of its relatively high elevation above sea level, the atmospheric (external) pressure in Denver is lower than that in New York. Consequently, a lower temperature is required to reach the vapor pressure equal to the lower pressure in Denver.*

    b. *Water forms very strong hydrogen bonds between molecules, which hold the molecules together in the liquid phase much more readily than liquids having only weaker dipole–dipole or dispersion attractive forces.*

    c. *The hydrogen bonding in water causes ice to form a relatively open hexagonal structure that is less dense than the more disorganized liquid molecules.*

    d. *The process of dissolving an ionic substance in water breaks the ion–ion bonds (bond breaking is always endothermic) and forms ion–dipole interactions (bond formation is always exothermic) with water. The fact that*

$CaCl_2$ *dissolves exothermically means that the ion–dipole interactions formed in the solution are stronger than the ion–ion interactions of the solid ionic lattice.*

3. *Coulomb's law says that the force of attraction between two particles is directly proportional to their charges and inversely related to the square of the distance between them. The small sizes of N, O, and F allow them to get very close to H, another small atom, thus minimizing the distance between them which increases the force. Also nitrogen, oxygen, and fluorine are highly electronegative, whereas hydrogen is electropositive making the charges relatively large and the force large.*

4. *The boiling points are in order:* $CH_4 < CCl_4 < CBr_4$. *Polarizability increases with increasing numbers of electrons and thus, molecular size and molar mass. The relative strengths of the dispersion forces of these nonpolar molecules determine the order of boiling points. The smallest, lightest molecule having the fewest electrons is held together most weakly and boils at the lowest temperature.*

Your Turn Answers

11.1. a. *Gases are readily compressible because there is abundant space between particles. Solids and liquids are incompressible because their particles are very close together.*

   b. *Gases expand to the volume and shape of their container because their particles have complete freedom to move, rapidly and randomly.*

   c. *Gases diffuse quickly because of the space between the particles and their rapid, random motion. Liquids diffuse much more slowly because of their close packing and more limited motion. Solids hardly diffuse at all because their particles are virtually locked in place.*

11.2. *The boiling points of the halogens will increase in this order:* $F_2 < Cl_2 < Br_2 < I_2 < At$. *As the number of electrons increases, the polarizability of the molecules increases causing greater induced dipoles and stronger London dispersion forces that hold the molecules together.*

11.3. *The vapor pressures increase in this order:* $CI_4 < CBr_4 < CCl_4$. *Higher molar mass substances have more electrons and higher dispersion forces and are held together more strongly than are lower molar mass substances.*

11.4. *Glycerol has a higher viscosity, a higher boiling point, and a lower vapor pressure than 1-propanol. Glycerol contains three* −OH *groups, which form very strong hydrogen bonds with neighboring molecules and hold the molecules together very strongly. While 1-propanol also forms hydrogen bonds, it has only one* −OH *group per molecule. This results in a relatively high viscosity for glycerol. Because it takes energy to overcome the intermolecular forces in a liquid to evaporate, higher intermolecular forces require more energy. Thus, the vapor pressure of glycerol is smaller and its boiling point is higher.*

11.5.   *Ice is less dense than liquid water. Usually, liquids and solids have similar densities because their structures have closely packed atoms or molecules. Because water forms very strong hydrogen bonds, when it solidifies its molecules pack in a relatively open crystal lattice held apart by hydrogen bonds with more spaces between the molecules than in the liquid form (see Figure 11.9).*

11.6.   *Ethylene glycol, CH_2OHCH_2OH < water, H_2O < ethyl alcohol, CH_3CH_2OH < diethyl ether, $CH_3CH_2OCH_2CH_3$.*
Ethylene glycol has two hydroxyl groups which can form strong hydrogen bonds holding the molecules in the liquid phase. Water molecules are also strongly held by very effective hydrogen bonding. However, more electrons in the higher molar mass ethylene glycol molecules cause them to have stronger dispersion forces than water molecules. Ethanol can also form a hydrogen bond but because each of its molecules has only one hydroxyl group, the hydrogen bonding is not as effective. Diethyl ether molecules are held together only by relatively weak dispersion forces because it is not very polar.

SOLIDS AND MODERN MATERIALS

The content in this topic is the basis for mastering Learning Objectives 2.1, 2.19, 2.20, and 2.22 through 2.32 as found in the Curriculum Framework.

When you finish reviewing this topic, be sure you are able to:

- Construct atomic-level visual representations for the structural features of the major classes of solids: ionic, metallic, covalent-network, and molecular

- Predict characteristic properties and structure of solids based on their chemical formulas

- Distinguish and explain the forces that bind the atoms and molecules of each type of solid

- Use three-dimensional representations and the interaction of particles to explain the common macroscopic properties of each class of solid

- Rationalize how the electron-sea model of a metal with its delocalized electrons explains common metallic properties

- Describe an alloy and explain how its structure and properties compare to that of a pure metallic solid

- Distinguish the structures of substitutional alloys and interstitial alloys

- Use chemical formulas to associate and recognize the classification, structure, and bonding of solid substances

- Design a plan to collect or interpret data to classify a solid substance based on its observable properties

Classifications of Solids   Section 12.1

The structures of solids and their physical properties are determined by the types of bonds that hold their atoms in place. Classification of solids is based on bonding type. Often classification can be deduced from the chemical formula. Figure 12.1 illustrates the three-dimensional nature of the four bonding types. Table 12.1 summarizes the bonding and properties of different types of solid materials.

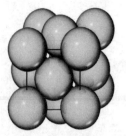

Metallic solids

Extended networks of atoms held
together by metallic bonding (Cu, Fe)

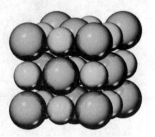

Ionic solids

Extended networks of ions held together
by ion–ion interactions (NaCl, MgO)

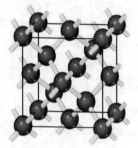

Covalent-network solids

Extended networks of atoms held
together by covalent bonds (C, Si)

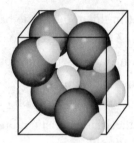

Molecular solids

Discrete molecules held together by
intermolecular forces (HBr, H_2O)

Figure 12.1 Classifications of solids according to predominant bonding type.

Table 12.1 Summary of the four bonding types in solids.

Solid	Recognizing a Formula with Examples	Structure and Bonding	Properties
Ionic solids	Compounds of metal cations and nonmetal anions: NaCl, Al_2O_3, K_2SO_4, FeS	Three-dimensional crystal lattice of ions locked in place by relatively strong ionic bonds	Brittle, high melting non-conductors (insulators) in pure form, conductors in water solution
Metallic solids	Metal atoms only: Al, Fe, Cr, Ni	Three-dimensional arrays of metal ions surrounded by a uniform sea of delo-calized valence electrons	Good conductors of heat and electricity, malleable and ductile; mixtures of metals form alloys
Covalent-network solids	C (graphite and diamond); metalloids: Si, Ge; and compounds of metalloids: SiO_2, SiC, BN	An extended network of covalent bonds	Hard, brittle, high melting, poor conductiv-ity or semiconductors
Molecular solids	Compounds of nonmetals only: $H_2O(s)$, P_2O_5, $C_6H_{12}O_6$	Individual covalently bonded molecules held together by weak intermo-lecular forces	Soft, low melting nonconductors

---

Your Turn 12.1

Classify each of the following chemical solids according to bonding type: $CBr_4(s)$, $GaAs$, Na_3PO_4, Mg. Explain your answers. Write your answers in the space provided.

Metallic Bonding   Section 12.4

Metallic solids consist entirely of metal atoms. Bonding in metallic solids arise because of attractions of metal nuclei to **delocalized electrons** throughout the solid. The **electron-sea model** pictures a metal as an array of metal cations immersed in a sea of delocalized valence electrons as shown in Figure 12.2.

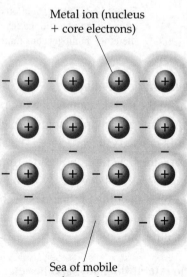

Metal ion (nucleus + core electrons)

Sea of mobile valence electrons

Figure 12.2 Electron-sea model of metallic bonding. The valence electrons delocalize to form a sea of mobile electrons that surrounds and binds together an extended array of metal ions.

Because the electrons in metals are delocalized, none of them belongs to any metal cation. Rather, they are dispersed throughout the metal structure. These loosely held electrons are highly mobile.

High electrical conductivity in metals results from loosely held, highly mobile electrons. An electrical current can easily move through the electron sea.

High thermal conductivity of metals results because the mobile electrons can readily transfer kinetic energy (heat) through the solid.

This model also explains why metals deform. Metals are **malleable** (they can be shaped) and **ductile** (they can be drawn into thin wires). Mobile electrons easily redistribute themselves when reshaping of the metal causes changes in atomic positions.

An **alloy** has the characteristic properties of a pure metal but contains two or more elements. Alloys are useful because they impart desirable properties to the metal. For example, pure gold is too soft to be used as jewelry but small amounts of added silver make it much harder. The structure of an alloy resembles that of the electron-sea model of a pure metal. Figure 12.3 shows the structures of two common alloys, both solid solutions.

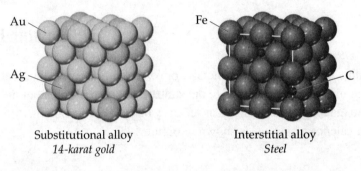

Substitutional alloy
14-karat gold

Interstitial alloy
Steel

Figure 12.3 The distribution of solute and solvent atoms in a substitutional alloy and an interstitial alloy. Both types of alloys are solid solutions and, therefore, homogeneous mixtures.

A **substitutional alloy** is a solid solution where atoms of another element replace some of the metal atoms. For example, silver atoms, which are about the same size as gold atoms, and copper atoms, which are only slightly smaller, readily replace atoms of gold in its crystal structure. The slightly different-sized replacement atoms deform the crystal structure enough to improve strength and hardness because the crystal cannot break or bend easily along nonuniform planes. Also, a substitutional alloy takes on some of the properties of the substituted metal. For example, silver is harder than gold and copper modifies its color, so a gold alloy is harder than pure gold and has a different color.

In an **interstitial alloy**, another element occupies the "holes" between the metal atoms. Typically, an interstitial element is a nonmetal with a much smaller bonding radius than the metal. Its atoms fit into the spaces between the metal atoms and form covalent bonds with the metal. These extra bonds cause the metal lattice to become harder, stronger, and less malleable and ductile. Steel, an interstitial alloy of iron and carbon that forms covalent iron carbide, is a good example.

(Note: Except for alloys, you need NOT know the structural details of solids described in Sections 12.2 and 12.3 of *Chemistry: The Central Science*.)

Your Turn 12.2

Describe the atomic-level structures of iron and steel and explain why steel is much harder and stronger than iron. Write your answer in the space provided.

Ionic Solids   Section 12.5

Ionic solids consist of cations and anions locked together by ionic bonds in a three-dimensional regularly ordered **crystal lattice** structure as shown in Figure 12.4. High melting points and boiling points of ionic solids indicate that these ionic bonds are very strong.

Coulomb's law guides our thinking to determine relative strengths of ionic bonds. Recall that the strength of an ionic bond depends on the size and charge of each ion.

$$F = kQ_1Q_2/d^2$$

Small ions with large charges will produce very strong forces of attraction. Larger ions with smaller charges will be less tightly bonded.

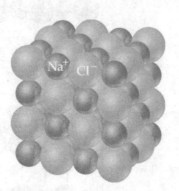

Figure 12.4 The crystal lattice structure of sodium chloride, an ionic solid.

Unlike metallic solids, ionic substances are insulators rather than conductors.

The valence electrons in ionic solids are confined, so they do not carry an electric current in the solid phase. However, when melted, the ions are free to move and conduct electricity. Aqueous solutions of ionic compounds also conduct electricity because the dissolving process breaks down the lattice and frees the ions to move throughout the solution. Ionic compounds do not dissolve in nonpolar solvents because the ionic bonds in the solid are much stronger than the attractive forces of the nonpolar solute.

Ionic solids are brittle because of repulsive forces of ions of like charge. Figure 12.5 shows that when a stress is applied to an ionic solid, a fracture occurs between planes of ions. Movement along a plane shifts the alignment of ions from an attractive cation–anion–cation–anion arrangement to a repulsive cation–cation and anion–anion configuration. This causes the planes to break away from each other resulting in a brittle property.

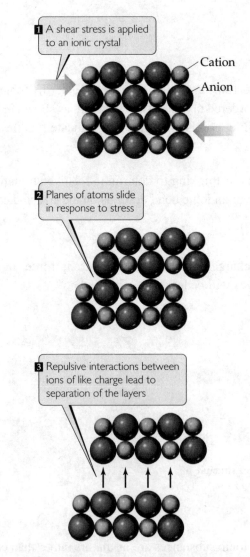

Figure 12.5 Brittleness in ionic crystals.

When ionic solids dissolve in water, the ionic bonds break and the ions attach themselves to water molecules as they dissociate into the aqueous solution (Figure 12.6). Such an ionic compound is called an **electrolyte** because its aqueous solution conducts electricity. On dissolving, the ions are no longer locked into place. The charged particles are free to move about the solution to carry a charge.

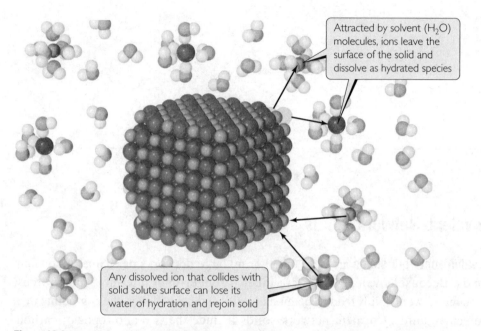

Attracted by solvent (H₂O) molecules, ions leave the surface of the solid and dissolve as hydrated species

Any dissolved ion that collides with solid solute surface can lose its water of hydration and rejoin solid

Figure 12.6 Dynamic equilibrium in a saturated solution with excess ionic solute.

Molecular Solids   Section 12.6

Molecular solids usually consist of discrete molecules made up of exclusively nonmetals having covalent bonds. Molecular solids are held together by weak dipole–dipole, London dispersions, and/or hydrogen bonds. Because of these relatively weak intermolecular forces, molecular solids tend to be soft, low-melting substances. Because their electrons are confined to strong covalent bonds, molecular solids are nonconductors. Common examples include sucrose (common table sugar, Figure 12.7), candle wax ($C_{20}H_{42}$), and aspirin ($C_9H_8O_4$). Low molar mass molecular substances such as water, carbon dioxide, and argon tend to be liquids or gases at room temperature and form molecular solids only at cold temperatures.

Figure 12.7 Sucrose forms discrete molecules that are held in a solid structure by relatively weak intermolecular forces of attraction.

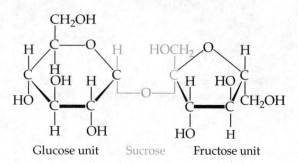

Glucose unit   Sucrose   Fructose unit

Your Turn 12.3   ←————————————————————————————

Examine the structure of sucrose. Tell what kinds of intermolecular forces likely hold sucrose molecules together. Predict whether sucrose has a relatively high or low melting point compared to table salt (NaCl) and other molecular solids. Justify your answers. Write your answers in the space provided.

Section 12.7   ## Covalent-Network Solids

Covalent-network solids are held together by large networks or chains of covalent bonds. Because covalent bonds are much stronger than intermolecular forces, covalent-network solids tend to be much harder and have higher melting points than molecular solids. Covalent-network solids include the two allotropes of carbon, diamond and graphite, as well as metalloids such as silicon and germanium and compounds of metalloids such as quartz (SiO_2), silicon carbide (SiC), and boron nitride (BN). The structures of diamond and graphite are shown in Figure 12.8.

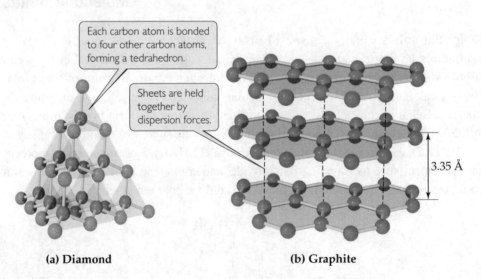

Figure 12.8 The structures of two covalent-network solids: (a) diamond and (b) graphite. Notice the planar structure of graphite and the tetrahedral structure of diamond.

Doping is the process of adding small amounts of impurities to the crystal lattice of a material to influence its electrical conductivity.

An **n-type semiconductor**, one that can carry a negative charge, is made by replacing a few atoms of pure silicon, each of which contains four valence electrons, with atoms of phosphorus, which contain five valence electrons. The "extra" valence electrons greatly increase the conductivity of silicon.

A **p-type semiconductor** consists of silicon doped with a Group 3A element having three valence electrons. The resulting material has a deficiency of valence electrons called **holes**. A hole can be thought of as having a positive charge. Conductivity is increased because electrons can jump from hole to hole as they move through the material. The junction of an n-type semiconductor and a p-type semiconductor is the basis for many electronic devices such as diodes, transistors, and solar cells.

Your Turn 12.4

Examine Figure 12.8 and predict the hybridization of carbon in diamond and in graphite. Justify your answers. Write your answers in the space provided.

Your Turn 12.5

What characteristics of the electron-sea model account for the malleable and ductile properties of metals and their thermal and electrical conductivity? Explain your answer. Write your answers in the space provided.

Multiple Choice Questions

Questions 1–4 refer to the following information.
A solid is a poor conductor of electricity, is very hard, has a high melting point, and is non-brittle.

1. The solid is probably

   A) metallic.

   B) covalent network.

   C) ionic.

   D) molecular.

2. The solid might be

   A) quartz.

   B) tin.

   C) rock salt.

   D) table sugar.

3. The solid could have the chemical formula:

   A) $CaSO_4$

   B) Pb

   C) $C_{20}H_{42}$

   D) SiC

4. The properties of this solid can be attributed to

   A) an interlocking pattern of atoms.

   B) intermolecular hydrogen bonding.

   C) the electron-sea model.

   D) strong ion–ion interactions.

   Examine the atomic-level structures of graphite and diamond in Figure 12.8 and answer Questions 5–8.

5. The orbital hybridization of graphite and diamond, respectively, are

   A) sp^3 and sp^3.

   B) sp^2 and sp^2.

   C) sp^3 and sp^2.

   D) sp^2 and sp^3.

6. *Which contains delocalized electrons?*

    A) *Neither graphite nor diamond*

    B) *Graphite only*

    C) *Diamond only*

    D) *Both graphite and diamond*

7. *Which conducts electricity?*

    A) *Neither graphite nor diamond*

    B) *Graphite only*

    C) *Diamond only*

    D) *Both graphite and diamond*

8. *Graphite is characterized by all of the following except*

    A) *adjacent layers that can slide past each other easily.*

    B) *London dispersions that hold the layers together.*

    C) *strong covalent bonds between the carbon atoms.*

    D) *a low melting, relatively hard material.*

9. *The best explanation that solid naphthalene is insoluble in water but is soluble in mineral oil is because naphthalene is a(n)*

    A) *ionic solid*

    B) *molecular solid*

    C) *metallic solid*

    D) *covalent-network solid*

10. *Which of the following elements has the greatest electrical conductivity?*

    A) *Ga*

    B) *Si*

    C) *P*

    D) *As*

11. *All the following statements are true. Which best explains why ionic solids are brittle?*

    A) *Ionic solids have relatively large coulombic attractions.*

    B) *Planes of strongly attracted ions can reposition so coulombic attractions repel.*

    C) *Polar water molecules can pull apart three-dimensional lattices of cation–anion coulombic attractions.*

    D) *Ionic solids have relatively large lattice energies due to coulombic attractions.*

12. Which of the following statements DOES NOT explain why alloys are generally harder and stronger than pure metals?

A) Different-sized replacement atoms deform the lattice creating nonuniform planes.

B) Some alloys contain nonmetal atoms that form strong covalent bonds with the metal atoms.

C) The atoms of intermetallic compounds are more ordered than in metals.

D) The more perfectly ordered crystal gives strength and stability to an alloy.

13. The solid structure of sucrose, shown in Figure 12.7, is held together by which of the following forces?

I.   Dispersion.

II. Dipole-dipole

III. Hydrogen bonds

IV. Ion-dipole

A) I only

B) I and II only

C) I, II and III only

D) III and IV only

14. Which substance is likely to be a hard, brittle, nonconductor?

A) K_2SO_4

B) SiO_2

C) $C_{12}H_{22}O_{11}$

D) brass

15. Below are four properties of metals, each followed by an explanation using the electron-sea model. Which explanation DOES NOT explain the property preceding it?

A) High thermal conductivity: loosely held electrons readily transfer kinetic energy

B) High electrical conductance: current easily moves through the electron sea

C) Malleability: mobile electrons easily redistribute themselves

D) Ductility: electrons readily reflect light

Free Response Questions

1. Using some common laboratory equipment and materials, devise a plan to deduce the type of bonding in a sample of unknown solid. Specify the tests you would perform and discuss what the results mean.

2. a. Draw an atomic representation of a binary ionic solid. Use the interactions of the particles to justify the structure and stability of the solid.

   b. Use your model to explain these macroscopic properties of ionic solids:
      i. Melting point
      ii. Conductivity
      iii. Solubility

   c. Make a two-dimensional drawing of the solid showing at the atomic level why it is brittle.

3. Draw a molecular depiction of the structure of ice. Label and name the major forces of attraction between the molecules and tell why these forces operate.

4. a. Draw an atomic representation of a metal and describe the relative positions of atoms and the electrons.

   b. Use your depiction to explain on an atomic level the following macroscopic properties of metals:
      i. Electrical conductivity
      ii. Malleability
      iii. High thermal conductivity

5. Draw a model of an interstitial alloy showing the relative positions of the atoms and the electrons. Explain the composition of a steel alloy and why it is harder and stronger than pure iron.

Multiple Choice Answers and Explanations

1. B. Covalent-network solids are good insulators, have high melting points, and are very hard. Ionic solids have the same characteristics but they are brittle. Metallic solids and alloys are good conductors of heat and electricity and molecular solids typically have relatively low melting points ($< 200\,^\circ C$).

2. A. Quartz is a very hard covalent-network solid. Tin is a metal element, table sugar is sucrose, a molecular substance, and rock salt is the ionic solid, sodium chloride.

3. D. Silicon carbide is a very hard, high melting nonconductor with covalent-network bonding. Recognize it as such because it contains a metalloid. $CaSO_4$ is an ionic solid recognized by the fact that its formula contains both metals and nonmetals. Pb is a metal. $C_{20}H_{42}$ is molecular as its formula contains only nonmetals.

4. A. Covalent-network solids such as SiC, diamond, and quartz are good insulators, are very hard, and have high melting points because they have large networks of covalent bonds that interlock in a regular, ordered geometric pattern.

5. D. The geometry of graphite appears in the diagram to be planar, indicating that its carbon atoms are sp^2 hybridized. The three-dimensional structure of diamond appears to be tetrahedral, which correlates to sp^3 hybridization.

6. B. Graphite with its planar geometry and its sp^2 orbital hybridization has delo-calized electrons occupying the hybridized p orbitals between the planes of the structure.

7. B. Graphite conducts electricity because of the delocalized pi electrons between the hexagonal planes. Diamond has a very hard three-dimensional interlocking tetrahedral structure with no delocalized electrons through which a current can flow.

8. D. Graphite is soft because its crystalline structure consists of adjacent hex-agonal layers that can easily slide by each other because they are held in place mainly by weak London dispersions. It has a high melting point because the covalent C—C bonds are relatively strong.

9. B. Nonpolar molecular solids are soluble in nonpolar solvents like mineral oil but not in polar water.

10. A. From its position on the periodic table we can predict that gallium is a metal with loosely held, highly mobile electrons that can conduct electricity.

11. B. The strong coulombic attractions change to strong repulsions when planes of atoms slide in response to stress.

12. D. A perfectly ordered crystal of a pure metal allows it to bend and break easily. Substitutional alloys contain metal atoms of slightly different size that deform the planes of the crystal creating nonuniform planes so it does not bend or break as easily. Interstitial alloys contain nonmetal atoms that form very strong covalent bonds. Because intermetallic compounds are not mixtures, they are ordered rather than randomly distributed.

13. C. All molecular solids contain dispersion forces. Polar molecules like sucrose contain polar covalent bonds such as carbon–oxygen bonds which produce dipole-dipole interactions between molecules. The abundant hydroxyl groups can form relatively strong intermolecular hydrogen bonds. Sucrose contains no ions.

14. A. Ionic compounds, recognized by their formulas because they usually contain a metal and a nonmetal, typically have those properties. Silicon dioxide is a hard, nonbrittle, nonconducting covalent-network solid. Sucrose is a relatively soft molecular solid and brass is a conducting alloy of copper and zinc.

15. D. The properties of metals; high thermal and electrical conductivity, malle-ability, and ductility all can be explained by the electron-sea model of mobile, delocalized electrons. Both malleability and ductility are due to mobile elec-trons redistributing themselves when reshaping the metal causes changes in atomic positions.

Free Response Answers

1. *Test the sample for conductivity. If it conducts electricity, it is either a metal or a covalent-network solid. If it has a high conductivity, it is probably a metal.*

   Add water to a portion, and if it dissolves, it is probably an ionic or molecular solid. Test the solution for conductivity. Ionic solids in water conduct electricity, whereas molecular solids do not.

   Determine the melting point. Molecular solids usually melt well below 200 °C. Add acid to a portion. Some metals will dissolve in acid with the evolution of a gas.

2. a. *The drawing will resemble Figure 12.4. Each cation (smaller spheres) attracts multiple anions (larger spheres) to form strong ionic bonds creating a very rigid, stable crystal lattice.*
   b. i. *Ionic solids have very high melting points because the ionic bonds are very strong requiring large amounts of heat to overcome the forces of attraction that hold the crystal together.*
      ii. *Each ion is locked into place with respect to the other ions by the strong ionic bonds, so the ions cannot move to conduct an electrical current.*
      iii. *Ionic compounds will dissolve only if the ions have relatively low charges and corresponding low forces of attraction.*

   c. *(The drawings will look much like Figure 12.4.) When a stress causes slippage along a plane, the ions realign in a cation–cation and anion–anion arrangement. This results in repulsive forces that cause the crystal to break abruptly.*

3. *The drawing will look like the center hexagonal structure depicted in Figure 11.9. The dotted lines represent hydrogen bonds that hold the structure together. A hydrogen bond between two water molecules is an especially strong dipole–dipole interaction between an electropositive hydrogen atom of one water molecule and an electronegative oxygen atom of an adjacent molecule.*

4. a. *The model will look like Figure 12.2. A metallic model shows an ordered array of metal atoms surrounded by a sea of mobile, delocalized electrons.*
   b. i. *A metal conducts electricity well because its delocalized electrons are mobile, not held tightly to any one metal atom. If a voltage is applied to a metal, the negative electrons will flow toward the positive end.*
      ii. *A metal deforms easily because its mobile, delocalized, loosely held electrons easily redistribute themselves as the positions of the atoms change.*
      iii. *A metal has the property of high thermal conductivity because heat applied to one end of the metal will be transferred throughout the metal by the kinetic energy of its loosely held, mobile electrons.*

5. *The model will look like the model in the right side of Figure 12.3. Steel is an alloy in which small atoms of carbon fit into the spaces between larger iron atoms. The nonmetal carbon atoms form covalent bonds with the iron atoms making the crystal structure harder and stronger.*

Your Turn Answers

12.1. $CBr_4(s)$ *is a molecular solid. Most molecular solids have chemical formulas containing only covalently bonded nonmetals. GaAs is a covalent-network solid. Most covalent-network solids are metalloids or compounds of metalloids.* Na_3PO_4 *is an ionic solid. It consists of a metal cation bonded to a polyatomic anion containing nonmetals. Mg is a metallic solid because it is a metal element.*

12.2.   *Steel is an interstitial alloy of the nonmetal carbon and the metal iron. The atoms of iron occupy a three-dimensional lattice surrounded by a sea of loosely held, mobile, delocalized electrons. Steel has essentially the same structure except that small atoms of carbon occupy the spaces between the iron atoms. Steel is stronger and harder than iron because the carbon atoms form covalent bonds with the iron atoms. These added covalent bonds impart added hardness and strength to the metal lattice.*

12.3.   *Sucrose molecules are likely to be held together by weak London dispersions and relatively strong hydrogen bonds. Sucrose will have a relatively high melting point compared to other molecular solids because there are six OH groups per molecule that can form relatively strong hydrogen bonds. Compared to table salt, sucrose will have a low melting point because the intermolecular forces of attraction that hold sucrose in the solid phase are weak as compared to ionic bonds in ionic solids such as NaCl.*

12.4.   *Figure 12.8 illustrates a tetrahedral structure of diamond indicating that carbon is* sp^3 *hybridized. Graphite contains* sp^2 *hybridized carbon as evidenced by its planar geometry.*

12.5.   *Electrons in the electron-sea model of metals are loosely held, delocalized and mobile. When a metal deforms, the relative positions of its atoms change and the electrons can easily redistribute themselves to accommodate the change.*

PROPERTIES OF SOLUTION

The content in this topic is the basis for mastering Learning Objectives 2.1, 2.7, 2.8, 2.9, 2.10, 2.14, 2.15, and 6.24 as found in the Curriculum Framework.

When you finish reviewing this topic, be sure you are able to:

- Describe and interpret the interactive forces between solute and solvent ions and molecules
- Construct visual representations of solute and solvent particles in solution
- Apply enthalpy and entropy principles to justify the factors that affect solubility of solutes
- Explain solubility data of ionic substances in water and justify with considerations of energy and entropy
- Use chemical formulas to predict the solubilities of compounds in water and other solvents
- Calculate molarity and construct visual models to demonstrate different molar concentrations
- Explain how the technique of chromatography uses intermolecular attractions to separate mixtures

The Solution Process   Section 13.1

A **solution** is a homogeneous mixture of one or more solutes dispersed uniformly throughout a solvent, normally the substance in greatest amount. The concentration of the solute(s) and the intermolecular forces among the components determine the physical properties of a solution.

Entropy is a state of randomness or disorder of a system. An increase in entropy is associated with the mixing that occurs when a solution forms. The driving force of most solution processes is the natural tendency for systems to increase in entropy. (A more detailed discussion of entropy appears in Section 19.2.)

Energetically, the solution process involves three kinds of intermolecular interactions. Recall that bond breaking (or separating attracted particles) is endothermic and bond making (or attracting particles) is exothermic.

When a solute dissolves in a solution:

Solute–solute interactions between solute particles **break** (endothermic).

Solvent–solvent interactions between solvent molecules **break** (endothermic).

Solvent–solute interactions **form** (exothermic).

A solution process is exothermic when solvent–solute interactions release more energy than is required to break both the solvent–solvent and solute–solute forces.

Recall that solvent–solute and solvent–solvent interactions are the intermolecular attractive forces discussed in Topic 11:

Dispersion forces act between particles of a nonpolar solvent and a nonpolar solute.

Dipole–dipole forces, including **hydrogen bonding**, act between particles of a polar solvent and a polar solute.

Ion–dipole forces act between a polar solute and ions in solution.

Figure 13.1 illustrates examples of solvent–solute forces in solution.

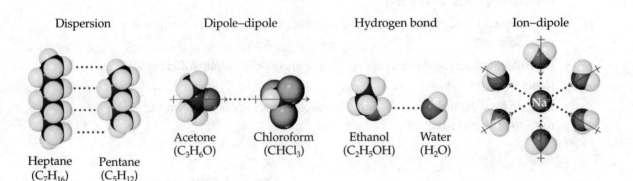

| Dispersion | Dipole–dipole | Hydrogen bond | Ion–dipole |

Heptane (C₇H₁₆) Pentane (C₅H₁₂) Acetone (C₃H₆O) Chloroform (CHCl₃) Ethanol (C₂H₅OH) Water (H₂O)

$$\text{Heptane } (C_7H_{16}) \quad \text{Pentane } (C_5H_{12}) \quad \text{Acetone } (C_3H_6O) \quad \text{Chloroform } (CHCl_3) \quad \text{Ethanol } (C_2H_5OH) \quad \text{Water } (H_2O)$$

Figure 13.1 Intermolecular interactions involved in solutions.

Figure 13.2 illustrates what happens when sodium chloride dissolves in water. Solute–solute forces (ionic bonds) between sodium ions and chloride ions in the ionic solid break. Solvent–solvent forces between the water molecules break. Ion–dipole forces between the ions and water form. The positive ends of water dipoles attract anions while cations are attracted to the negative ends of water dipoles.

Hydrated ions are ions attracted to water molecules by ion–dipole intermolecular forces.

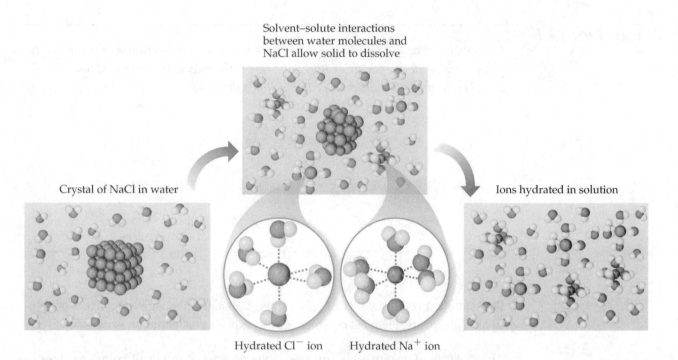

Solvent–solute interactions between water molecules and NaCl allow solid to dissolve

Crystal of NaCl in water

Ions hydrated in solution

Hydrated Cl⁻ ion   Hydrated Na⁺ ion

Figure 13.2 Hydrated Na⁺ and Cl⁻ ions form ion–dipole interactions with water molecules when sodium chloride dissolves.

The solute–solute forces in ionic solids are ionic bonds. Solubility of ionic solids in water depends, in part, on the strength of the ionic bonds.

Hydration forces are a measure of the strength of the ion–dipole forces that keep dissociated ions hydrated minus the forces required to overcome the solute–solute interactions.

When the ion–dipole forces are **greater than** the ionic bonds, the ionic compound **dissolves exothermically**, with the release of heat to the solution.

Most ionic compounds **dissolve endothermically** because the energy required to break the ionic bonds is usually greater than the energy released when the ion–dipole interactions are formed in the solution. The heat required for the process comes from the solution as it cools. The driving force of an endothermic dissolving process is the increase in entropy of the system.

A few ionic compounds dissolve exothermically when the ion–dipole forces formed in the solution are greater than the forces required to overcome the ionic bonds of the solid and the attractions between solvent particles. Exothermic processes tend to be thermodynamically favored. The amount of released heat is essentially the difference in the energies.

Your Turn 13.1

Calcium chloride dissolves in water with an increase in temperature of the water. Is this process endothermic or exothermic? Use intermolecular forces and ionic bonding to explain. Write your answer in the space provided.

Concentration is the quantity of solute present in a given quantity of solvent or solution. In chemistry, the most common way to express concentration is molarity.

The **molarity** of a solute in a solution is the number of moles of solute per liter of solution: **molarity = M = mol solute/L soln**

Examples:

Calculate the molarity of a solution made by dissolving 25.0 g of $CuSO_4 \cdot 5H_2O$ in a total volume of 500.0 mL.

Solution:

$x \, mol/L = (25.0 \, g \, CuSO_4 \cdot 5H_2O/0.5000 \, L)$
$(1 \, mol/249.5 \, g)$
$= 0.200 \, M$

Your Turn 13.2

Copper sulfate pentahydrate, $CuSO_4 \cdot 5H_2O$, is a light blue ionic solid that readily dissolves in water to form a blue solution.

a. *Compare the appearances of two 500.0 mL solutions, one contains 12.5 g of $CuSO_4 \cdot 5H_2O$ and the other contains 25.0 g of solute. Explain your answer.*

b. *Draw particle representations of the two solutions in Part a. Use a small x to represent each 0.01 M of solution. Write your answers in the space provided.*

Saturated Solutions and Solubility   Section 13.2

As a solute dissolves in a solvent, its concentration increases. This increases the chance that dissolved solute particles will collide with the surface of the solid and recrystallize. Dissolving and crystallization are opposite processes.

Dynamic equilibrium is the condition in which two opposite processes occur at the same rate.

$$\text{Solute} + \text{solvent} \overset{\text{Dissolving}}{\underset{\text{Crystallization}}{\rightleftharpoons}} \text{solution}$$

Figure 13.3 shows an example of a dynamic equilibrium.

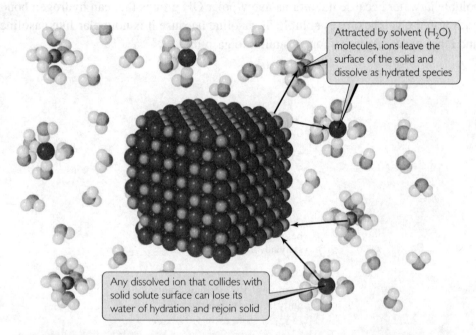

Attracted by solvent (H_2O) molecules, ions leave the surface of the solid and dissolve as hydrated species

Any dissolved ion that collides with solid solute surface can lose its water of hydration and rejoin solid

Figure 13.3 Dynamic equilibrium in a saturated solution with excess ionic solute.

A **saturated solution** is one in which dissolved solute is in dynamic equilibrium with undissolved solute.

Solubility is the amount of solute needed to form a saturated solution in a given amount of solvent. The units of solubility for an aqueous solution are usually grams of solute per 100 mL of water, g solute/100 mL water.

An **unsaturated solution** contains less solute than a saturated solution.

A **supersaturated solution** contains more solute than a saturated solution. Supersaturation can be achieved because many substances are more soluble at high temperatures than they are at low temperatures. If a hot, saturated solution is slowly cooled, an unstable supersaturated solution often forms.

Section 13.3   Factors Affecting Solubility

Solubility increases with increasing strength of attractions between solvent and solute particles.

Substances with similar intermolecular attractive forces tend to be soluble in one another. An easily remembered adage is, **"Like dissolves like."**

Polar solutes tend to dissolve in polar solvents. Nonpolar solutes tend to dissolve in nonpolar solvents. Polar substances do not dissolve in nonpolar substances. Polar solvents, because of their relatively strong dipole–dipole forces, tend to exclude nonpolar substances with their relatively weak dispersion forces.

Figure 13.4 shows the chemical structures of cyclohexane and glucose. Glucose is soluble in water because it contains many polar OH groups that can hydrogen bond with water. Cyclohexane is soluble in gasoline because it is nonpolar like gasoline and it has weak dispersion forces similar to gasoline.

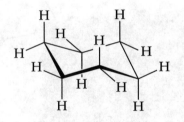

Cyclohexane, C_6H_{12}, which
has no polar OH groups, is
essentially insoluble in water

OH groups enhance the aqueous
solubility because of their ability
to hydrogen bond with H_2O

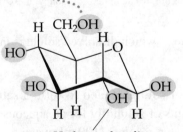

Hydrogen-bonding
sites

Glucose, $C_6H_{12}O_6$, has
five OH groups and is
highly soluble in water

Figure 13.4 Structure and solubility.

Miscible liquids are pairs of liquids that dissolve in all proportions. They do so because their attractive forces are similar, either both polar or both nonpolar. Ethanol, CH_3CH_2OH, and water, HOH, are completely miscible because they both strongly hydrogen bond. Hexane and benzene are also completely miscible because both molecules have only weak London dispersion forces.

Immiscible liquids are those that do not dissolve in each other. Their attractive forces are dissimilar, one is polar and the other is nonpolar.

Table 13.1 shows the solubilities of several alcohols in water and in hexane.

Table 13.1   Solubilities of some alcohols in water and in hexane.*

Alcohol	Solubility in H_2O	Solubility in C_6H_{14}
CH_3OH (methanol)	∞	0.12
CH_3CH_2OH (ethanol)	∞	∞
$CH_3CH_2CH_2OH$ (propanol)	∞	∞
$CH_3CH_2CH_2CH_2OH$ (butanol)	0.11	∞
$CH_3CH_2CH_2CH_2CH_2OH$ (pentanol)	0.030	∞
$CH_3CH_2CH_2CH_2CH_2CH_2OH$ (hexanol)	0.0058	∞

*Expressed in mol alcohol/160 g solvents at 20 °C. The infinity symbol (∞) indicates that the alcohol is completely miscible with the solvent.

Notice that all alcohols have OH groups that can hydrogen bond with water. However, only the alcohols with short carbon–carbon chains are readily soluble in water and only those with longer C—C chains are readily soluble in the hydrocarbon, hexane. As the number of nonpolar C—C bonds increases, the OH group becomes a smaller part of the molecule and the molecule behaves like a nonpolar hydrocarbon. As a result, the short-chain alcohols dissolve in water while the long-chain molecules dissolve more readily in hydrocarbons.

Your Turn 13.3

Explain using intermolecular forces why gasoline and water do not mix. Write your answer in the space provided.

Gases tend to be more soluble in liquids at higher pressure and at lower temperature. The solubility of a gas increases in direct proportion to its partial pressure above the solution.

Your Turn 13.4

←————————————————————————

Why do bubbles appear in a plastic soda bottle when the cap is removed? Justify your answer by discussing the intermolecular forces that interact between the solute and the solvent.

Write your answer in the space provided.

_____

Chromatography

Chromatography is a versatile and powerful method used extensively in chemistry to separate and purify substances. In the three common types of chromatography—gas, liquid, and paper—a mobile solution phase carries a mixture of compounds over a stationary insoluble phase. As the mixture moves, the compounds separate because they bind differently through weak intermolecular forces with the stationary phase.

In **gas chromatography**, the mobile phase is a gas and the stationary phase is a liquid bound to a solid support. Both **liquid** and **paper chromatography** employ a liquid mobile phase and a solid stationary phase.

The rates of movement of the compounds in the mixture depend on their relative strengths of attraction for the mobile phase and the stationary phase. For example, if the mobile phase is less polar than the stationary phase, polar groups of the stationary phase strongly attract polar compounds in the mobile phase and slow their movement. Nonpolar compounds, which are not as strongly attracted to the stationary phase, move more quickly. If the stationary phase is less polar than the mobile phase, then the less polar compounds will move more slowly.

The differential rate of movement of the compounds due to their relative attractions to the stationary phase is the basis for their separation. Chromatography is versatile because a chemist can vary the phases to match the compounds he or she wishes to separate.

A typical separation of food dyes by paper chromatography illustrates the technique. Figure 13.5 shows a paper chromatogram of a mixture of three food dyes. A liquid mixture of three dyes, A, B, and C, is applied near the bottom of the paper and the paper is placed in a solvent. As the solvent (mobile phase) climbs the paper (stationary phase) by capillary action, the three dyes separate. Just before the solvent front reaches the top, the paper is removed and dried. The result is a chromatogram shown in Figure 13.5.

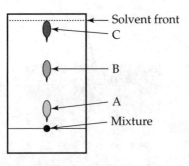

Figure 13.5 A paper chromatogram of a mixture of three food dyes.

The three dyes separate because they each have different affinities for a relatively nonpolar solvent and the polar paper. The differences in polarity cause each dye to bind differently to the solvent and to the paper. Dye A is the most polar and relatively strong intermolecular forces of attraction bind Dye A to the paper and slow its rate of ascent. Dye C is the least polar, so it spends the most time in the nonpolar solvent and moves quickly up the paper. Dye B is of intermediate polarity. The different rates at which each dye ascends effect a clean separation.

Common misconception: Most sources commonly misidentify the stationary phase in paper chromatography as only the paper. In reality, the stationary phase consists of an intimate relationship between the cellulose of the paper and water molecules hydrogen bonded to the cellulose. Experiments show that under the same conditions, papers of different water content produce very different separations.

Your Turn 13.5

Figure 13.6 shows how a solution can be diluted with water to make a less concentrated solution. Use a molecular-level interpretation to explain why one solution appears darker than the other. Write your answer in the space provided.

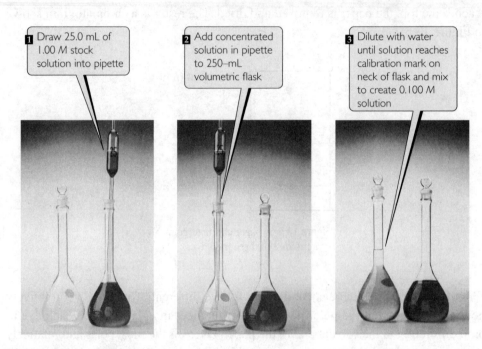

1 Draw 25.0 mL of 1.00 *M* stock solution into pipette

2 Add concentrated solution in pipette to 250–mL volumetric flask

3 Dilute with water until solution reaches calibration mark on neck of flask and mix to create 0.100 *M* solution

Figure 13.6 Preparing 250.0 mL of 0.100 *M* CuSO$_4$ by dilution of 1.00 *M* CuSO$_4$

Explain why only some of the alcohols shown in Table 13.1 are completely miscible in water yet they all contain –OH groups that can hydrogen bond with water. Justify your answer with evidence. Write your answer in the space provided

Multiple Choice Questions

1. The aqueous solution of which salt will have the strongest cation–dipole interactions?

    A) NaCl

    B) $MgCl_2$

    C) K_2SO_4

    D) $CaSO_4$

2. Enough water is added to 11.5 g of ethanol to make 2.00 L of solution. What is the molarity of the ethanol?

    A) 0.125

    B) 0.250

    C) 0.500

    D) 5.75

3. Which pairs of substances will dissolve in each other:

    I. CH_3OH

    II. C_6H_6

    III. CH_3CH_3

    A) I and II only

    B) II and III only

    C) I and III only

    D) I and II, II and III

4. All the following substances will dissolve in water EXCEPT:

    A) CH_3CH_2OH

    B) $AlCl_3$

    C) $Ca(NO_3)_2$

    D) C_6H_6

    Use the structures of cyclohexane and glucose in Figure 13.4 and pentane and acetone in Figure 13.1 to answer Questions 5–7.

5. Pentane is most soluble in

    A) glucose only.

    B) glucose and acetone.

    C) glucose, acetone, and cyclohexane.

    D) cyclohexane only.

6. When glucose dissolves in water, the strongest intermolecular forces in the solution are

   A) dispersions.

   B) ion–dipoles.

   C) hydrogen bonds.

   D) covalent.

7. Which of these molecules will not dissolve in water?

   A) acetone

   B) cyclohexane

   C) pentane

   D) cyclohexane and pentane

8. Which 0.10 M aqueous solution exhibits the highest electrical conductivity?

   A) NH_3

   B) $NaHCO_3$

   C) CH_3COOH

   D) CH_3CH_2OH

9. Which substance is most likely readily soluble in BOTH water and benzene, C_6H_6?

   A) $CH_3CH_2CH_2CH_3$

   B) K_2CO_3

   C) CH_3COOH

   D) $CH_3CH_2CH_2OH$

10. Examine Figure 13.1 and tell which SINGLE interaction shown in dotted lines is probably the strongest?

   A) dispersion

   B) dipole–dipole

   C) hydrogen bond

   D) ion–dipole

11. Which substance is the most soluble in water?

   A) CH_4

   B) CH_3Cl

   C) O_2

   D) HF

12. *If the dye mixture in Figure 13.5 were separated using a solvent of dilute sodium chloride solution rather than a nonpolar solvent, predict which is most likely.*

   A) *All dyes will separate but in reverse order.*

   B) *All dyes will separate in the same order but they all will run faster.*

   C) *All dyes will separate in the same order but they will run more slowly.*

   D) *The appearance of the chromatogram will remain unchanged.*

13. *The phrase "like dissolves like" refers to solutes and solvents of similar*

   A) *molar masses.*

   B) *polarities.*

   C) *phases.*

   D) *bonding.*

14. *Most ionic compounds dissolve _____, with a(n)_____ in _____.*

   A) *exothermically, decrease, enthalpy*

   B) *exothermically, increase, entropy*

   C) *endothermically, increase, entropy*

   D) *endothermically, decrease, enthalpy*

15. *A container is half filled with a liquid and sealed at room temperature and atmospheric pressure. What happens inside the container?*

   A) *Evaporation stops.*

   B) *Evaporation continues for a time then stops.*

   C) *The pressure in the container remains constant.*

   D) *The pressure inside the container increases for a time and then remains constant.*

Free Response Questions

1. *Answer the following questions about these laboratory observations.*

   Solid ammonium chloride dissolves in water with a marked decrease in temperature. Solid calcium chloride dissolves in water with a marked increase in temperature. Little or no temperature change is observed when solid sodium chloride dissolves in water.

   a. *Write an equation that describes the dissolving process of ammonium chloride.*

   b. *Is the dissolving of calcium chloride endothermic or exothermic? Explain.*

   c. *Describe the opposing forces of attraction that are at work in the dissolution of calcium chloride. Which are greater? Why?*

d. What can be said about opposing forces of attraction when sodium chloride dissolves in water? Why?

e. Use the observation for ammonium chloride to discuss these seemingly contradictory statements:

Exothermic processes tend to be thermodynamically favored.

Most processes are thermodynamically favored when there is an increase in entropy.

2. Two important vitamins are shown in Figure 13.7.

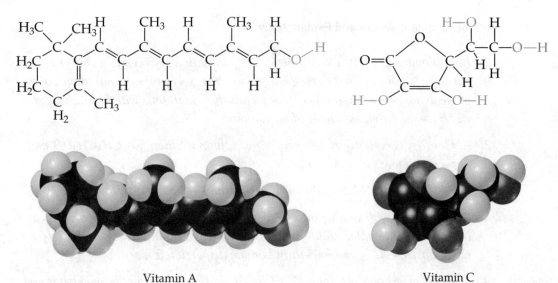

Vitamin A   Vitamin C

Figure 13.7 Vitamins A and C.

a. Tell whether each vitamin is more likely to be water soluble or fat soluble. Justify your reasoning.

b. What is the principal intermolecular force acting when a nonpolar substance dissolves in a nonpolar solvent?

c. Describe the principal intermolecular force(s) acting when a water-soluble vitamin dissolves in water?

d. Identify one aspect that the space-filling models in the figure represent accurately and one aspect that limits their usefulness.

e. Identify one aspect that the structural formulas represent accurately and one aspect that limits their usefulness.

3. *Figure 13.3 shows the process of an ionic salt dissolving in water.*

   a. *Describe the forces that must be overcome for the salt to dissolve.*

   b. *Are the larger ions depicted most likely cations or anions? Give two reasons for your answer.*

   c. *Describe the principal force that holds the ions in solution.*

   d. *Under what conditions will this system never reach equilibrium? Explain.*

   e. *Comparing a salt solution to pure water with both systems containing the same amount of water, which system will require more heat to completely evaporate the system to dryness? Explain.*

Multiple Choice Answers and Explanations

1. B. *Coulomb's law tells us that the force of attraction between two charged particles is proportional to the charges and inversely proportional to the square of the distances between them. That means that small ions with large charges will have the strongest forces of attraction.*

2. A. *Molarity is moles of solute per liter of solution. Ethanol is CH_3CH_2OH and has a molar mass of 46.0 g/mol.*

   $$M = (11.5 \text{ g ethanol})/(46.0 \text{ g/mol}) \div 2\,L = 0.125\,M.$$

3. B. *Substances with similar intermolecular attractive forces will dissolve in each other. CH_3OH is polar and forms hydrogen bonds. Both C_6H_6 and CH_3CH_3 are nonpolar molecules and only form London dispersion forces.*

4. D. *Benzene has only nonpolar C—C and C—H bonds so, unlike water, it is nonpolar. Water is a polar molecule that forms strong ion–dipole forces, so it dissolves many salts and it can hydrogen bond with compounds containing OH groups.*

5. D. *Like dissolves like. Both pentane and cyclohexane are nonpolar, so dispersion forces will cause them to dissolve. Glucose and acetone are polar.*

6. C. *The presence of OH groups in glucose will form very strong hydrogen bonds with water.*

7. D. *Water is polar while both pentane and cyclohexane are nonpolar.*

8. B. *Sodium hydrogen carbonate is the only ionic compound listed. It dissociates completely in water so it is a strong electrolyte. Ammonia and ethanoic acid are weak electrolytes and ethanol is a nonelectrolyte.*

9. D. *1-Propanol has an OH group that can hydrogen bond to water AND a relatively long nonpolar chain that can form dominant dispersion forces with benzene.*

10. D. *The ion–dipole interaction is the strongest because it involves a polar water molecule attracting a fully charged ion. Coulomb's law says that the force of attraction is directly dependent on the magnitude of the charges.*

11. D. *Water is a polar solvent and will readily dissolve polar molecules. All the species are nonpolar except HF.*

12. A. *"Reverse-phase" chromatography employs a mobile phase solvent that is more polar than the stationary phase. Thus the dyes will separate but the most polar dye will run fastest because its intermolecular forces will attract the more polar moving solvent more than the less polar stationary phase.*

13. B. *A solute will likely dissolve in a solvent if both species are either polar or nonpolar. Because water is a very polar compound it will dissolve polar solutes, even many ionic compounds.*

14. C. *Most chemical and physical systems tend toward a minimum enthalpy and a maximum entropy. The driving force of endothermic dissolution is the increase of randomness of the solution compared to the solid ionic solid.*

15. D. *The liquid will continue to evaporate without stopping. The pressure will rise until the partial pressure of the vapor equals the vapor pressure of the liquid at the given temperature. Then a dynamic equilibrium is established where the rate of evaporation equals the rate of condensation.*

Free Response Answers

1. a. $NH_4Cl(s) \rightarrow NH_4^+(aq) + Cl^-(aq)$

   b. *The dissolving of calcium chloride in water is exothermic as evidenced by the increase in temperature of the water. In the dissolving process, heat flows out of the system (calcium chloride) and into the surroundings (water).*

   c. *Ionic bonds are electrostatic forces of attraction between ions of opposite charge. These ionic bonds are broken when calcium chloride dissolves in water. When calcium chloride dissolves in water, ion–dipole forces exist between a Ca^{2+} ion and the negative end of a water molecule, and between a Cl^- ion and the positive end of a water molecule. Forming the ion–dipole interactions releases more energy than it takes to break the ionic bonds in calcium chloride. As a result, a net amount of heat is released to the system.*

   d. *Because NaCl dissolves with no apparent change in temperature, it can be said that the ion–dipole forces between water molecules and sodium and chloride ions are about equal to the ionic bonds in NaCl.*

   e. *The process of ammonium chloride dissolving in water is endothermic based on the observed decrease in temperature. However, the dissolving process occurs with an increase in entropy or randomness of the system. In the case of ammonium chloride and most ionic salts that dissolve in water, the drive toward increasing entropy outweighs the drive toward minimum enthalpy. As a result, the endothermic process is thermodynamically favored.*

2. a. *Vitamin C, with its many OH groups, will be soluble in water because it can readily form hydrogen bonds. Vitamin A will be soluble in nonpolar fats because most of the molecule is nonpolar.*

   b. *Dispersion forces are the principal intermolecular forces acting when a nonpolar solute dissolves in a nonpolar solvent.*

    c. *Hydrogen bonding (see Answer a).*

    d. *The space-filling model well represents the three-dimensional shape of the molecule. It does not show the polarity of the molecule or the nature of the delocalized electrons.*

    e. *Structural formulas give a clear picture of which atoms are present and how they are attached to other atoms. They do not accurately depict the geometric shape of molecules or their electronic natures.*

3. a. *The ionic bonds bind the solid crystal and the hydrogen bonds hold the water molecules together.*

    b. *The larger ions are anions. Anions tend to be larger than cations because of electron–electron repulsion of the extra electrons in the valence shell. Also, the larger ions are shown attracted to the positive ends of water molecules.*

    c. *Ion–dipole forces, the attraction of the ions to the dipoles of water molecules, hold the particles in solution.*

    d. *The system will never reach equilibrium if the dissolving process is exothermic. Entropy increases as an ionic substance dissolves because the very ordered crystal lattice of the ionic solid becomes dispersed throughout the liquid. Increasing entropy drives change. The tendency of a system to move toward lower potential energy also drives change. If the system is exothermic, the driving forces of increased entropy and decreased potential energy work together, so equilibrium will never be achieved.*

    e. *A salt solution requires more heat to evaporate than does pure water because extra heat is required to break the relatively strong solute–solvent interactions, in this case ion–dipole forces.*

Your Turn Answers

13.1.   *Calcium chloride dissolving with an increase in temperature is an exothermic process, releasing heat to the water. The ion–dipole forces in the solution release more energy than is required to break the ionic bonds of calcium chloride. The excess heat warms the water.*

13.2.   a. *The solution containing 25.0 g would be darker than the less concentrated solution. There are twice as many ions in the more concentrated solution, so they absorb more light.*

    b. *The drawing would have two solutions side by side with 10 x's in the less concentrated solution and 20 x's in the more concentrated solution.*

13.3.   *Gasoline is a nonpolar liquid that has only dispersion forces holding its molecules together. Water molecules are tightly held together by hydrogen bonding. Water molecules have greater attractions for each other than they do for molecules in gasoline and so they exclude the gasoline molecules.*

13.4.   *Soda is a solution of carbon dioxide dissolved in water. A sealed soda bottle contains an equilibrium vapor pressure of carbon dioxide above the liquid. When the cap is removed, the CO_2 above the liquid escapes to the environment lowering the partial pressure. Gases are less soluble at lower partial pressures above the solution and bubbles form and begin to escape the solution. Nonpolar carbon dioxide is not very soluble in polar water at lower pressure because the dispersion forces that hold CO_2 in solution are small compared to the hydrogen bonding that holds water molecules together.*

13.5.   *One solution is darker because it is more concentrated than the other. At the molecular level, the more concentrated solution has more copper(II) ions so they collectively absorb more light making the solution darker.*

13.6.   *Only the short-chain alcohols are completely miscible in water because as the chains get longer, the dominant forces are dispersion forces, typical of nonpolar molecules. In increasingly long-chain alcohols, the -OH groups become less dominant and the molecules behave as nonpolar substances. This is evident by the fact that the table shows that the longer chain alcohols are completely miscible with nonpolar hexane where dispersion forces dominate.*

CHEMICAL KINETICS

The content in this topic is the basis for mastering all the Learning Objectives in Big Idea 4: 4.1–4.9 as found in the Curriculum Framework.

Chemical kinetics provides answers to the question, how and why do chemical reactions occur? Kinetics provides both qualitative and quantitative models to examine how molecular collisions between reactants lead to formation of products.

When you finish reviewing this topic, be sure you are able to:

- Define rate of reaction and list common ways to express the rate of reaction
- Design an experiment or interpret experimental data that measure rate
- Explain the factors that affect the rate of reaction
- Use the collision model to justify how concentration, pressure, temperature, and the phase of the reactants affect reaction rates
- Rationalize how the frequency and success of molecular collisions and their orientations affect reaction rate
- Examine concentration versus reaction rate data using the method of initial rates to determine the rate law and the order of a reaction
- Describe a rate constant and explain how it characterizes a reaction
- Connect the half-life of a first-order reaction to its rate constant
- Infer reaction order from plots of concentration versus time data
- Justify how temperature affects a rate constant
- Interpret Maxwell–Boltzmann plots that describe distributions of particle energies
- Use energy profiles to make qualitative predictions about the relative rates of reactions
- Evaluate reaction mechanisms and determine which are consistent with rate data
- Interpret data that infer the presence of reaction intermediates
- Explain how catalysts work, including acid–base catalysts, surface catalysts, and enzymes

Reaction Rates   Section 14.2

Reaction rate is a measure of the speed of a chemical reaction. Rate of reaction is expressed as the change in the amount of reactants or products per unit time. Most often the unit for reaction rate is molarity per second (M/s).

Concentrations of reactants and products and the rate of reaction change with time.

Figure 14.1 illustrates how the concentration of reactant A changes with time in the hypothetical reaction A → B. Chemical reactions usually start fast and begin to slow down with time. Consequently, the concentration of A usually decreases in a nonlinear fashion.

The **instantaneous rate** of a reaction is the slope of the tangent line at any point $(t, [A])$. The rate is:

$$Rate = -\Delta[A]/\Delta t$$

Rates are always expressed as positive quantities. Because the slope in the graph in Figure 14.1a is negative, a negative sign is used to express rate as a positive quantity. A typical reaction rate starts fast and becomes slower as time goes on. The initial rate at $t = 0$ is usually the largest rate.

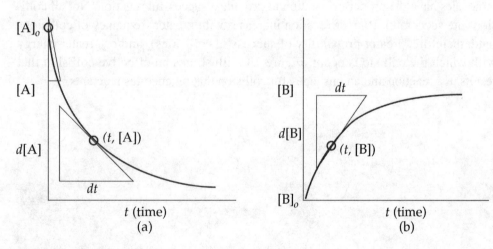

Figure 14.1 a. Graph of a typical reaction A → B showing how [A] decreases with time. b. Graph of a typical reaction A → B showing how [B] increases with time.

Figure 14.1b illustrates how [B] changes with time. As time increases, the concentration of B increases. The slope of the tangent line at any point $(t, [B])$ represents the instantaneous rate of the reaction. The rate is:

$$Rate = +\Delta[B]/\Delta t$$

Notice that the slope of the line is positive, so a positive sign in the expression denotes a positive rate.

Common misconception: Molarity per second is often expressed as mol $L^{-1} \cdot s^{-1}$.

$$M/s = mol/L \cdot s = mol \, L^{-1} \cdot s^{-1}$$

Reaction rate can also be expressed in pressure units per time (atm/s or torr/s) or sometimes in absorbance units per time. (For more on how absorbance can be used to monitor the changing concentration of a reactant or product, see A Closer Look: Using Spectroscopic Methods to Measure Reaction Rates in Section 14.2 of *Chemistry: The Central Science*.)

Section 14.1   Factors That Affect Reaction Rates

The **collision model** is a model that explains reaction rates and is based on the idea that molecules must collide to react. The collision model is based on kinetic-molecular theory and accounts for the factors that affect the rate of a reaction.

On a molecular level, reaction rates depend on the frequency of collisions between molecules, the energy with which the molecules collide, and whether the colliding molecules have the proper orientation to provide a successful reaction. Not all collisions are successful. Rate of reaction increases with greater frequency of collisions (and, therefore, greater probability of successful collisions), and/or greater energy with which the collisions occur. Figure 14.2 illustrates an effective collision that results in a reaction and an unsuccessful collision that regenerates reactants.

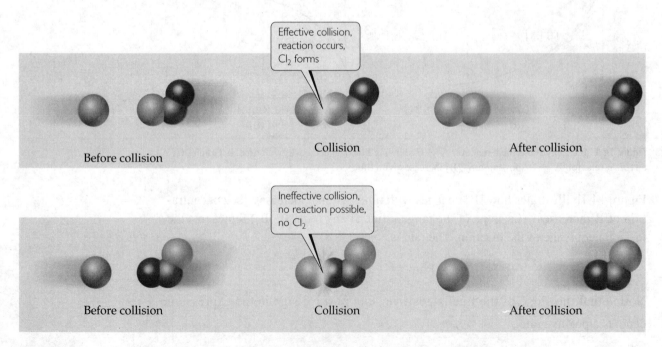

Figure 14.2 Molecular collisions may or may not lead to a chemical reaction between Cl and NOCl: $Cl + NOCl \rightarrow Cl_2 + NO$.

Your Turn 14.1

Use Figure 14.2 and energy considerations to explain why some molecular collisions lead to reaction and others do not. Write your answer in the space provided.

_____

The major factors that affect reaction rate are the following:

1. **Concentrations of reactants.** Higher concentrations of reactants usually produce a faster reaction. As concentration increases, the frequency of collisions increases, thus increasing reaction rate because more molecules collide with the proper orientation. Figure 14.3 shows a molecular view of two different systems, one with a high concentration of molecules and one with a low concentration. If the molecules are in rapid, random motion, the ones in higher concentration would collide more often giving a faster rate of reaction.

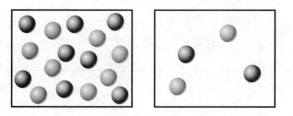

Figure 14.3 A higher concentration of molecules yields more frequent collisions and thus a higher rate of reaction.

2. **Temperature.** Increasing temperature increases reaction rate. Figure 14.4 illustrates the effect of temperature on the Maxwell–Boltzmann distribution of the kinetic energies of a sample of molecules. Higher temperatures provide increased kinetic energies of molecules, so the molecules move more rapidly. At higher temperatures, there is a higher fraction of molecules with the required energy for reaction. Thus, more collisions result in a reaction.

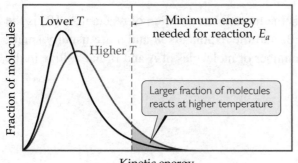

Figure 14.4 The effect of temperature on the distribution of kinetic energies of molecules in a sample.

3. **Physical state of the reactants**. Usually, homogeneous mixtures of either liquids or gases react faster than heterogeneous mixtures. A solid, for example, tends to react more slowly with either a liquid or a gas because molecular collisions are limited to the **surface area** of the solid. Increasing the surface area will increase the frequency of collisions, and thus increase the rate of reaction.

4. **The presence of a catalyst.** A catalyst increases the rate of reaction by affecting the kinds of collisions that lead to a reaction. (See Section 14.7.) A catalyst acts by lowering the energy the molecules need to react and/or by changing the pathway of the reaction. A **reaction mechanism**, discussed in Section 14.6, is a step-by-step process or pathway by which reactants become products.

Your Turn 14.2

←——————————————————————————————

Mine explosions from the ignition of powdered coal dust are relatively common, yet lumps of coal burn without exploding. Explain. Write your answer in the space provided.

Section 14.3

Concentration and Rate Laws

A **rate law** is a mathematical relationship that shows how rate of reaction depends on the concentrations of reactants. For any general reaction where:

$$a\,A + b\,B \rightarrow \text{products}$$

the rate law takes the form:

$$\text{Rate} = k[A]^m[B]^n$$

where k is the rate constant, $[A]$ is the molar concentration of reactant A, $[B]$ is the molar concentration of reactant B, and the exponents m and n are usually small, whole numbers that relate to the number of molecules of A and B that collide in the step-by-step mechanism.

Common misconception: The coefficients that balance the equation, a and b, are not necessarily the same as the exponents, m and n, in the rate law. The exponents n and m must be determined by experiment, not by the balanced equation.

Reaction order is the sum of the exponents m and n in a rate law. For example, consider the rate law:

$$\text{Rate} = k[A]^1[B]^2$$

The reaction is said to be "first order in A" and "second order in B." The **overall order** of the reaction is the sum of m and n. In this example, $1+2=3$, so the reaction is "third order" overall.

The rate law for any chemical reaction must be determined experimentally, often by observing the effect of changing the initial concentrations of the reactants on the initial rate of the reaction.

Consider the reaction:

$$A + 2B \rightarrow 2C + D$$

The rate law always takes the form:

$$\text{Rate} = k[A]^m[B]^n$$

A series of experiments measuring initial rate at various concentrations of reactants might give the data in Table 14.1.

Table 14.1   The effect of changing concentrations on the initial rate of a reaction.

Experiment	[A] (M)	[B] (M)	Rate $= -d[A]/dt$ (M/s)
1	0.10	0.10	0.04
2	0.10	0.20	0.08
3	0.20	0.20	0.32

Experiments 1 and 2 show that the rate is doubled when [B] is doubled while [A] is constant. This means that the exponent of [B] is 1 ($2^1 = 2$ so $n = 1$).

Experiments 2 and 3 show that the rate is quadrupled when [A] is doubled while [B] is constant. This means that the exponent of [A] is 2 ($2^2 = 4$ so $m = 2$). The data in The data in Table 14.1 show that the rate law is:

$$\text{Rate} = k[A]^2[B]^1$$

The reaction is second order in A, first order in B, and third order overall.

The data in Table 14.1 can be used to calculate the value of the rate constant.

Example:

What is the numerical value of the rate constant for the reaction described in Table 14.1. Specify its units.

Solution:

$Rate = k[A]^2[B]^1$

$0.04 \, M/s = k[0.10 \, M]^2[0.10 \, M]^1$

$k = (0.04 \, M/s)/(0.01 \, M^2 \times 0.1 \, M)$

$\quad = 40/M^{-2}s^{-1}$

Your Turn 14.3

What are the units for each rate constant for the following rate laws? Assume each rate is expressed in M/s. a. Rate $= k[A]$; b. Rate $= k[A]^2$; c. Rate $= k[A]^3$. Write your answers in the space provided.

Your Turn 14.4

Consider the single-step reaction $A + B \rightarrow AB$. a. If the reaction is first order in A and first order in B, what is the rate law? b. If the rate constant for this reaction is large, discuss the relative frequency and success of the collisions. Write your answers in the space provided.

The coefficients that balance a chemical equation are proportional to the rates of appearance or disappearance of reactants and products. Reaction rate relates directly to stoichiometry.

Example:

Consider the reaction between gaseous hydrogen and gaseous nitrogen to produce ammonia gas.

$$3H_2(g) + N_2(g) \rightarrow 2NH_3(g)$$

At a particular time during the reaction, $H_2(g)$ disappears at the rate of 3.0 M/s.
a. What is the rate of disappearance of $N_2(g)$?
b. What is the rate of appearance of $NH_3(g)$?

Solution:

a. In the balanced equation, $N_2(g)$ has a coefficient of 1, whereas $H_2(g)$ has a coefficient of 3. $N_2(g)$ disappears at one-third the rate of $H_2(g)$.

$$1/3(3.0\ M/s) = 1.0\ M/s$$

b. $NH_3(g)$ appears at two-thirds the rate of $H_2(g)$.

$$2/3(3.0\ M/s) = 2.0\ M/s$$

Your Turn 14.5

If ammonia appears at 2.6 M/s, how fast does hydrogen disappear? Write your answer in the space provided.

The following equation applies to the reaction in the example:

$$-\Delta H_2(g)/\Delta t = -3\ \Delta N_2(g)/\Delta t = +3/2\ \Delta NH_3(g)/\Delta t$$

Notice the use and placement of signs and the coefficients that balance the chemical equation. If they seem counterintuitive, translate the mathematical expression into words: "The rate of disappearance of hydrogen gas is three times the rate of the disappearance of nitrogen gas and three-halves the rate of appearance of ammonia gas."

The application of stoichiometry to the data in Table 14.1 can be used to calculate various rates.

Example:

From the data for Experiment 1 in Table 14.1, calculate the rate of appearance of C.

Solution:

The initial rate of disappearance of A in Experiment 1 is 0.04 M/s. The balanced equation shows that C has a coefficient twice that of A, so the rate of appearance of C is twice that of A.

$$+\Delta C/\Delta t = -2\Delta A/\Delta t = 2(0.040\ M/s) = 0.080\ M/s$$

Section 14.4   The Change of Concentration with Time

A **first-order reaction** (a **unimolecular reaction**) is a reaction whose rate depends on the concentration of a single reactant raised to the first power.

The rate of a first-order reaction is expressed both by the rate law and by the slope of the tangent line at any point $(t,[A])$ on the graph in Figure 14.5a.

$$\text{Rate} = k[A] = -\Delta[A]/\Delta t \quad \text{differential rate law}$$

Using calculus, this equation is transformed into the equation of the curved line in Figure 14.5a. The equation of the line is:

$$\ln[A]_t = -kt + \ln[A]_0 \quad \text{integrated rate law}$$

Notice that the equation takes the form of the simple linear equation, $y = mx + b$, where $y = \ln[A]_t$, $b = \ln[A]_0$, and the slope of the line $= -k$, the rate constant.

For a first-order reaction, a plot of $\ln[A]$ versus time will yield a straight line with a slope of $-k$ as shown in Figure 14.5b. This is a useful graphical method for determining rate constants for first-order reactions.

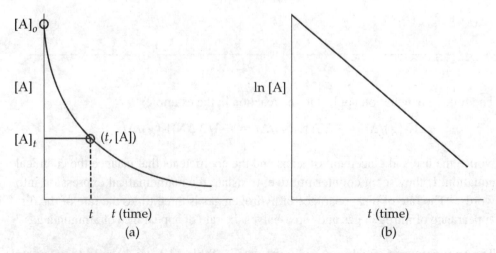

Figure 14.5 a. Plot of [A] versus time for a first-order reaction. b. Plot of ln[A] versus time for a first-order reaction. The negative slope of the line equals the rate constant.

Often the equation of the line for a first-order reaction is written in the more familiar expression:

$$\ln([A]_0/[A]_t) = +kt$$

A first-order reaction is a **unimolecular process**. That is, it depends only on the concentration of **one reactant**. In a unimolecular process, collisions with other molecules, either reactant molecules or solvent molecules, activate the reactant in a way that it is converted to products. Figure 14.6 illustrates how a single molecule might be activated to produce a reaction. Imagine collisions of solvent molecules with methyl isonitrile in such a way that the C—N bond breaks and a C—C bond forms instead.

Methyl isonitrile

Figure 14.6 The first-order reaction of CH_3NC conversion to CH_3CN.

Acetonitrile

For a first-order reaction, the **exponent of one** in the rate equation,

$$\text{Rate} = k[A]^1,$$

is interpreted to mean that only **one molecule** of A is involved in the reaction.

Radioactive decay is another example of first-order kinetics. For example, the nucleus of a uranium-238 atom spontaneously decomposes into a thorium-234 nucleus and a helium nucleus:

$$^{238}_{92}U \rightarrow ^{234}_{90}Th + ^{4}_{2}He$$

A simple **second-order reaction** (a bimolecular reaction) is one whose rate depends on the concentration of one reactant raised to the second power as in this hypothetical chemical equation: $A \rightarrow B$.

The characteristic equations are:

$$\text{Rate} = k[A]^2 = -\Delta A/\Delta t \quad \text{differential rate law}$$

and

$$1/[A]_t = kt + 1/[A]_0 \quad \text{integrated rate law}$$

Note that the integrated rate law is a linear equation of the form:

$$y = mx + b$$

A plot of $1/[A]$ versus time will yield a straight line whose slope is the rate constant k as shown in Figure 14.7b.

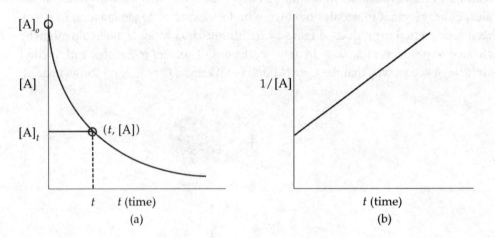

Figure 14.7 a. Plot of [A] versus time for a second-order reaction. b. Plot of $1/[A]$ versus time for a second-order reaction. The slope of the line equals the rate constant.

A second-order reaction is a **bimolecular process**. That is, it depends on the collision of two molecules of reactant to produce a product. In a bimolecular process, collisions between reactant molecules change reactants to products. The **exponent of two** in the rate equation for a second-order reaction,

$$\text{Rate} = k[A]^2,$$

is interpreted to mean that **two molecules** of A collide to produce a reaction.

A **zero-order reaction** is one in which the rate of disappearance of A is independent of the concentration of A: Rate $= k[A]^0 = k$. A plot of [A] versus time for a zero-order reaction is a straight line as illustrated in Figure 14.8.

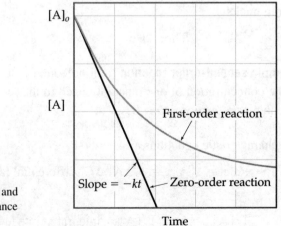

Figure 14.8 Comparison of first-order and zero-order reactions for the disappearance of reactant A with time.

A gas that undergoes decomposition on the surface of a solid is the most common type of zero-order reaction. For example, a catalytic converter in an automobile converts carbon monoxide to carbon dioxide. Diatomic oxygen molecules are absorbed onto the metal catalyst and then converted into monatomic oxygen atoms by a zero-order reaction.

$$O_2 \rightarrow O + O$$

The oxygen atoms then react with carbon monoxide to produce carbon dioxide:

$$O + CO \rightarrow CO_2$$

The **half-life** of a reaction, $t_{1/2}$, is the time required for the initial concentration of a reactant to fall to half its value.

For a first-order reaction: $t_{1/2} = 0.693/k$.

For a second-order reaction: $t_{1/2} = 1/k[A]_0$.

Notice that for a first-order reaction, the half-life is independent of the concentration of the reactant A. The half-life is inversely proportional to the rate constant.

Table 14.2 summarizes the mathematical relationships of zero-, first- and second-order reactions.

Table 14.2 Mathematical relationships of first-, second-, and zero-order kinetics.

Order of Reaction	First	Second	Zero
Differential rate law	Rate $= k[A] = -\Delta[A]/\Delta t$	Rate $= k[A]^2 = -\Delta[A]/\Delta t$	Rate $= k = -\Delta[A]/\Delta t$
Integrated rate law	$\ln[A]_t = -kt + \ln[A]_0$ or $\ln([A]_0/[A]_t) = +kt$	$1/[A]_t = kt + 1/[A]_0$	$[A]_t = -kt + [A]_0$ or $[A]_0 = +kt + [A]_t$
Half-life	$t_{1/2} = 0.693/k$	$t_{1/2} = 1/k[A]_0$	$t_{1/2} = [A]_0/2k$
Straight line plot	$\ln[A]$ versus time	$1/[A]$ versus time	$[A]$ versus time
Slope $=$	$-k$	k	$-kt$

Temperature and Rate   Section 14.5

Generally, increasing temperature increases reaction rate. The collision model, based on kinetic-molecular theory, says that for molecules to react they must collide. Temperature increases the speed of molecules, and as molecules move faster, they collide more frequently and with more energy, increasing the fraction of molecules that have sufficient energy to react. Thus, the probability for reaction increases and so does the rate. Figure 14.4 shows that at a higher temperature, a higher fraction of molecules have sufficient energy to react than at a lower temperature.

Figure 14.9 shows how the rate constant for a chemical reaction varies with temperature. Generally, the rate constant increases with increasing temperature.

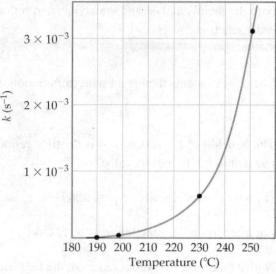

Figure 14.9 The rate constant, k, varies with temperature, T.

The algebraic equation that describes the line in Figure 14.9 relates activation energy, E_a, to the rate constant, k, at various temperatures, T.

$$\ln(k_1/k_2) = (E_a/R)(1/T_2 - 1/T_1)$$

k_1 = the rate constant at temperature T_1

k_2 = the rate constant at temperature T_2

E_a is the activation energy

(All temperatures must be expressed in Kelvin.)

$R = 8.314\,\text{J/K mol}$

Figure 14.10 shows the **energy profile** of a typical exothermic reaction. The y-axis represents relative energies of the molecules in the system. The x-axis represents the progress of the reaction as successful molecular collisions of reactants produce products.

Activation energy, E_a, is the minimum amount of energy required to initiate a chemical reaction. The activation energy can be considered to be an energy barrier that molecules must overcome before they react. On the energy profile in Figure 14.10, the activation energy is the energy difference between the reactants and the highest point of the profile.

The **enthalpy of the reaction,** ΔH, on the reaction profile is the difference between the energy of reactants and energy of products.

The **activated complex** (also called the **transition state**) is the highest energy arrangement of molecules as they change from reactants to products. The very top of the energy profile represents the energy of the activated complex.

A **catalyst** acts to lower the activation energy of a chemical reaction and thus increases the rate of reaction.

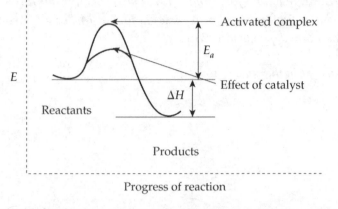

Figure 14.10 Energy profile for a typical exothermic reaction showing activation energy, E_a, change in enthalpy, ΔH, and the effect of a catalyst.

For any reaction, the higher the activation energy, the slower the rate. Very fast reactions have low activation energies and slow reactions have high activation energies. At any given temperature, only a fraction of reactant molecules have sufficient energy to react. If a reaction profile has a relatively high activation energy, relatively few molecular collisions will result in a reaction. If the activation energy is low, more collisions will produce products. Increasing the temperature of a reaction increases the fraction of molecules having sufficient activation energies to react, so the rate of the reaction increases with increasing temperature.

Figure 14.11 illustrates the relationship of activation energy to reaction rate. Profile 1 describes a reaction with the fastest rate because it has the lowest activation energy, the lowest difference between reactants and the transition state. The reaction for Profile 2 has the slowest rate because it has the highest activation energy.

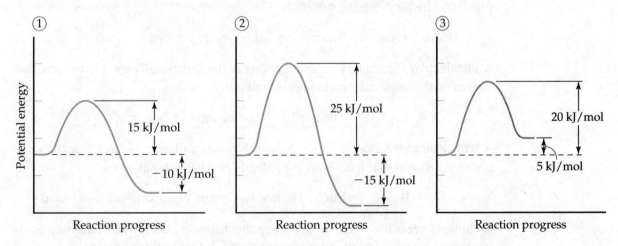

Figure 14.11 Energy profiles of two exothermic reactions and one endothermic reaction showing the activation energies. The higher the activation energy, the higher the rate of reaction.

Your Turn 14.6

      a.   *Explain using collision theory why temperature affects the rate of reaction.*

      b.   *Consider the reactions shown in Figure 14.11. Rank the relative rates of the REVERSE reactions for Profiles 1, 2, and 3. Justify your answer.*

      c.   *Which reaction (forward or reverse) in Figure 14.11 will have the highest temperature dependence? Why?*

Write your answer in the space provided.

Section 14.6

Reaction Mechanisms

A **reaction mechanism** is the step-by-step process by which a chemical reaction occurs.

An **elementary reaction** is each single event or single step in a mechanism.

The **molecularity** of a reaction is the number of molecules that participate as reactants in an elementary reaction.

A **unimolecular** elementary reaction involves one reactant molecule. It is first order, meaning that only one reactant molecule participates. That molecule is likely activated by collisions with the solvent.

$$AB \rightarrow A + B \quad \text{The rate law is first order:} \quad \text{rate} = k[AB]$$

A **bimolecular** elementary reaction involves the direct collision of two reactant molecules. A bimolecular process is second order.

$$A + B \rightarrow AB \quad \text{The rate law is second order:} \quad \text{rate} = k[A][B]$$

A **termolecular** reaction involves the simultaneous collision of three reactant molecules. A termolecular reaction is exceedingly rare but not impossible.

$$A + B + C \rightarrow ABC \quad \text{The rate law is third order:} \quad \text{rate} = k[A][B][C]$$

Commonly reactions occur in multistep mechanisms. Each individual step is an elementary reaction and the sum of the individual steps gives the balanced chemical equation for the overall process. Usually, we write each elementary step in a mechanism to be a unimolecular or bimolecular process because termolecular processes are rare.

Example:

Consider the following overall process and write a mechanism that can explain how reactants A and B become the product A_2B_2. Write the rate law for each elementary step.

$$2A + 2B \rightarrow A_2B_2$$

Solution:

By invoking only unimolecular and bimolecular elementary steps, a possible mechanism is:

Elementary step	Rate law for each elementary step
1. $A + A \rightarrow A_2$	$Rate = k[A]^2$
2. $A_2 + B \rightarrow A_2B$	$Rate = k[A_2][B]$
3. $\underline{A_2B + B \rightarrow A_2B_2}$	$Rate = k[A_2B][B]$
$2A + 2B \rightarrow A_2B_2$	

Notice that the sum of the elementary steps of a mechanism gives the chemical equation for the overall process.

An **intermediate** is a chemical species that is formed in one elementary step of a multistep mechanism and consumed in another. In the above mechanism, A_2 and A_2B are intermediates. An intermediate is neither a reactant nor a product of the overall reaction. Intermediates never appear in the rate law for the overall reaction.

Chemists often seek to detect intermediates in a reaction mixture to obtain clues about the mechanism of the reaction.

The **rate-determining step** is the slowest step of a multistep mechanism and governs the rate of the overall reaction.

The slowest step in a multistep mechanism is reflected in the rate law. The rate law includes only those reactant molecules that react during and before the rate-determining step. Therefore, the rate law must be determined experimentally and cannot be determined from the overall balanced equation.

For example, if Step 1 in the above mechanism is the slowest step, the rate law is rate $= k[A]^2$, because two molecules of A and zero molecules of B have taken part in the mechanism up to this step.

If Step 2 is slowest, the rate law will be rate $= k[A]^2[B]$, because two molecules of A and one molecule of B have taken part through Step 2 of the mechanism.

If Step 3 is slowest, the rate law will include two molecules of A and two molecules of B, because they all have taken part through Step 3 of the mechanism: rate $= k[A]^2[B]^2$.

Common misconception: A rate law that is third order or higher does not mean that the mechanism involves a three-molecule collision of reactants. Most often it involves a series of unimolecular and bimolecular elementary steps, the sum of which add to the overall balanced equation as shown in the example above.

Your Turn 14.7

Propose an alternate mechanism for the overall reaction: $2A + 2B \rightarrow A_2B_2$. Identify any intermediates involved. Write your answer in the space provided.

Section 14.7

Catalysis

A **catalyst** is a substance that increases the rate of a chemical reaction without undergoing a permanent change in the process. Generally, catalysts act by changing the mechanism of a reaction, so that the slowest step in the uncatalyzed reaction does not exist in the catalyzed process. The effect of a catalyst is to lower the activation energy of the overall process by replacing the slowest step with one or more faster steps having activation energies lower than that of the uncatalyzed rate-determining step.

To illustrate the action of a catalyst that changes the reaction mechanism, consider the ozone cycle, the process that cycles diatomic oxygen to ozone and back to diatomic oxygen in the upper atmosphere. In its simplest form, the mechanism might look something like this:

Step 1 $O_2(g) + h\nu \rightarrow O(g) + O(g)$

Step 2 $O(g) + O_2(g) \rightarrow O_3(g)$

Step 3 $O_3(g) + h\nu \rightarrow O_2(g) + O(g)$

Step 4 $\underline{O(g) + O(g) \rightarrow O_2(g)}$

Overall: $O_3(g) + O_2(g) \rightarrow O_2(g) + O_3(g)$

Steps 1–4 continually repeat, producing and destroying ozone at the same rate while absorbing harmful ultraviolet radiation ($h\nu$) from the sun.

It has been shown that chlorine atoms from chlorofluorocarbons released to the atmosphere catalyze the $O_3 \rightarrow O_2$ reaction. The net result is that ozone is depleted faster than it is generated by the natural cycle. Thus, chlorine atoms from chlorofluorocarbons catalytically deplete ozone in the stratosphere. In its simplest form, the mechanism that catalyzes O_3 to O_2 is:

Step 1 $2Cl(g) + 2O_3(g) \rightarrow 2ClO(g) + 2O_2(g)$

Step 2 $\underline{ClO(g) + ClO(g) \rightarrow O_2(g) + 2Cl(g)}$

Overall: $2O_3(g) \rightarrow 3O_2(g)$

Notice that $ClO(g)$ is an intermediate. $ClO(g)$ is generated as a product in one elementary step and is consumed as a reactant in another later elementary step. Experimental detection of intermediates is an important means to study reaction mechanisms.

By contrast, Cl is a catalyst. It is consumed as a reactant in one elementary step and is regenerated as a product in a later step. A catalyst increases the rate of a chemical reaction without undergoing a permanent change. A catalyst acts by providing a different mechanism for the reaction, one that has a lower activation energy.

A catalyst is present at the start of a reaction, whereas an intermediate is formed as the reaction progresses.

(For more detailed information about the natural ozone cycle and its catalytic depletion by chlorofluorocarbons, see Section 18.2 of *Chemistry: The Central Science*.)

A catalyst can act by stabilizing the transition state, therefore lowering the activation energy. For example, the uncatalyzed reaction of hydrogen gas with ethene to produce ethane is not likely to occur by way of simple bimolecular collisions because the activation energy to break the H—H bonds is too high.

$H_2(g) + C_2H_4(g) \rightarrow C_2H_6(g)$

However, Figure 14.12 shows that at the surface of a metal catalyst, the H—H bonds readily break and the hydrogen atoms attach easily to the ethene molecule.

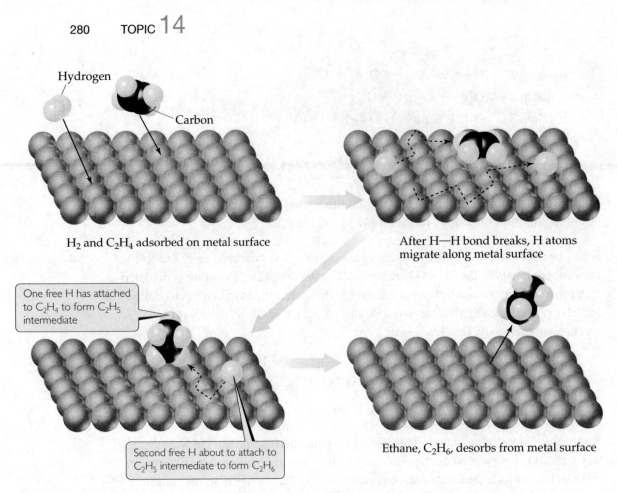

Figure 14.12 Heterogeneous catalysis. Mechanism for reaction of ethylene with hydrogen on a catalytic surface.

An **enzyme** is a large biomolecule called a protein that acts to catalyze specific biochemical reactions. Figure 14.13 shows the oversimplified lock-and-key model for enzyme catalysis. A smaller molecule called a **substrate** fits neatly into and binds with a geometric active site on the enzyme. The binding of this **enzyme–substrate complex** is accomplished by hydrogen bonding, dipole–dipole interactions, and dispersion forces. Upon binding, the electronic environment of the substrate molecule is changed causing it to break apart to form products. The enzyme acts to greatly lower the activation energy of an improbable reaction.

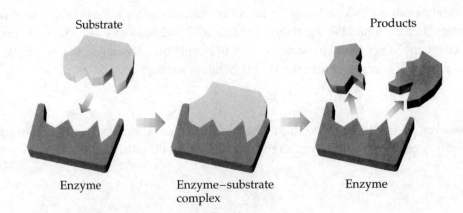

Figure 14.13 Lock-and-key model for enzyme action.

Multiple Choice Questions

1. Which of these change with time for a first-order reaction?

   I.   rate of reaction

   II. rate constant

   III. half-life

   IV. concentration of reactant

   A) I only

   B) III only

   C) I and II only

   D) I and IV only

2. Under certain conditions, the average rate of appearance of oxygen gas in the reaction:

   $$2O_3(g) \rightarrow 3O_2(g)$$

   is 6.0 torr s^{-1}. What is the average rate expressed in units of torr s^{-1} for the disappearance of O_3?

   A) 9.0

   B) 6.0

   C) 4.0

   D) 3.0

3. For irreversible chemical reactions, the rate will be affected by changes in all of these factors EXCEPT

   A) temperature.

   B) concentration of reactants.

   C) presence of a catalyst.

   D) concentration of products.

4. The rate expression for a third-order reaction could be:

   A) rate $= k[X]$

   B) rate $= k[X]^2[Y]$

   C) rate $= k[X][Y]$

   D) rate $= k[X]^2[Y]^2$

5. The slowest step of a reaction mechanism is called the

   A) elementary step.

   B) inhibitor.

   C) rate law.

   D) rate-determining step.

6. The dissociation of XY molecules, as shown below, occurs at a temperature of 800 K. The rate constant $k = 6.0 \times 10^{-3} s^{-1}$.

$$2XY(g) \rightarrow X_2(g) + Y_2(g)$$

What is the reaction order?

A) 0

B) 1

C) 2

D) 3

7. The rate law of a certain reaction is rate $= k[X][Y]$. The units of k, with time measured in seconds, is

A) s^{-1}.

B) $M^{-1}s^{-1}$.

C) $M^{-2}s^{-1}$.

D) M^{-1}.

8. For a first-order reaction of half-life 75 min, what is the rate constant in min^{-1}?

A) (0.693)/75

B) (0.693)/1.25

C) (0.693)(75)

D) 75/(0.693)

9. The half-life of ^{14}C is 5730 years. Approximately how many years will it take for 94% of a sample to decay?

A) 5730

B) 2 × 5730

C) 3 × 5730

D) 4 × 5730

10. A reaction between X_2 and Y was found to be described by the rate equation: rate $= k[X_2][Y]^2$. What can be said about the process?

A) The balanced chemical equation for the reaction is $X_2 + 2Y \rightarrow X_2Y_2$.

B) The rate-determining step must be a three-atom collision.

C) The rate-determining step must be the first step of a multistep mechanism.

D) The mechanism is most likely to be multistep.

11. *Strontium-90 undergoes radioactive decay with a half-life of about 30 years. Approximately how many years will have elapsed before 97% of the ^{90}Sr in a sample will have decayed?*

A) *30*

B) *60*

C) *120*

D) *150*

12. *The rate constants for a forward reaction and its corresponding reverse reaction are generally expected to*

A) *be independent of temperature.*

B) *decrease with increasing temperature.*

C) *increase with increasing temperature.*

D) *increase with increasing temperature, only for the endothermic reaction.*

13. *The rate expression for a first-order reaction could be*

A) *rate = $k[A]$*

B) *rate = $k[A]^2[B]$*

C) *rate = $k[A][B]$*

D) *rate = $k[A]^2[B]^2$*

14. *An endothermic reaction at equilibrium will proceed at higher temperatures*

A) *at a faster rate while its K_c increases.*

B) *at a faster rate while its K_c decreases.*

C) *at a slower rate while its K_c increases.*

D) *at a slower rate while its K_c decreases.*

15. *What can be correctly said about the energy diagram for a reversible endothermic reaction?*

A) *The energy of activation is greater for the reverse reaction than for the forward reaction.*

B) *The energy of activation is greater for the forward reaction than for the reverse reaction.*

C) *The energy of activation is the same for the reaction in both directions.*

D) *The forward reaction is faster than the reverse reaction.*

Free Response Questions

1. The overall chemical equation for the reaction of nitrogen oxide, NO, with chlorine, Cl_2, is:

$$2\,NO + Cl_2 \rightarrow 2\,NOCl$$

The initial rates of reaction for various concentrations of the reactants were measured and recorded at constant temperature as follows:

Experiment	$[NO](M)$	$[Cl_2](M)$	$-\Delta[Cl_2]/\Delta t\ (M/h)$
1	0.25	0.50	0.75
2	0.25	1.00	3.02
3	0.50	2.00	24.10

a. Determine the rate law for this reaction.

b. Calculate the numerical value for the rate constant and specify the units.

c. What is the order of this reaction with respect to each reactant and what is the overall order of the reaction?

d. What is the rate of disappearance of Cl_2 when the initial concentrations of the reactants are $[NO] = 0.50\,M$ and $[Cl_2] = 0.10\,M$?

e. When Cl_2 is disappearing at 4.5 M/h, what is the rate of appearance of NOCl?

f. What is the rate of appearance of NOCl when the initial concentrations of the reactants are $[NO] = 0.20\,M$ and $[Cl_2] = 0.30\,M$?

2. Consider the proposed mechanism for the reaction between nitrogen monoxide and hydrogen gas. Assume the mechanism is correct.
   Step 1: $2NO \rightarrow N_2O_2$
   Step 2: $N_2O_2 + H_2 \rightarrow N_2O + H_2O$
   Step 3: $N_2O + H_2 \rightarrow N_2 + H_2O$

a. Use the steps in the mechanism to determine the overall balanced equation for the reaction. Clearly show your method.

b. If Step 2 is the rate-determining step, write the rate law for the reaction. Explain your answer.

c. If the observed rate law is rate $= k[NO]^2[H_2]^2$, which step is rate determining? Explain your reasoning.

d. Identify all the intermediates in the mechanism.

e. If the first step is the rate-determining step, what is the order of the reaction with respect to each reactant?

3. Consider the exothermic reaction between nitrogen monoxide and ozone to form nitrogen dioxide and diatomic oxygen.

   a. Write and balance a chemical equation.

   b. Convert the chemical equation into a particle view of the molecules.

   c. Sketch an energy profile for the reaction and use particle views to label the reactants and products. Show the effect a catalyst might have on the energy profile.

   d. Draw a possible transition state for the bimolecular reaction. Use dashed lines to represent the bonds that break and those that form.

Multiple Choice Answers and Explanations

1. D. Rate decreases with time because the concentrations of reactants decrease. The half-life of a first-order reaction remains constant as does the rate constant at constant temperature.

2. C. Relative rates of disappearance of reactants and appearance of products are proportional to the stoichiometry of the reactants. Using the coefficients of the balanced equation, O_2 appears $3/2$ as fast as O_3 disappears. Thus, the rate at which O_3 disappears $= 2/3 \times 6.0$ torr $s^{-1} = 4.0$ torr s^{-1}.

3. D. The frequency of collisions of reactant molecules largely determines reaction rate. Any factor that changes the frequency of collisions will affect the rate. Concentrations of products of an irreversible reaction do not affect the rate of a reaction because collisions of product molecules do not aid the forward reaction. Changing temperature, reactant concentrations, and the surface area of a solid reactant all change the frequency of collisions. A catalyst increases the rate of reaction by changing the reaction mechanism, eliminating the slowest step, and lowering the activation energy of the overall process.

4. B. The overall order of a reaction is the sum of the exponents of the rate law.

5. D. An elementary step is each individual step in a mechanism. The rate law is a mathematical equation that relates rate to concentrations of reactants. A catalyst is a substance that increases the speed of a chemical reaction by changing the mechanism. An inhibitor is a substance that decreases the rate of a chemical reaction.

6. B. The units of the rate constant conveniently reveal the order of the reaction. The rate constant for a first-order reaction contains one unit, reciprocal time, s^{-1}. Second-order rate constants contain two units: $M^{-1}s^{-1}$. Third-order rate constants contain three units: $M^{-2}s^{-1}$; and so on. Notice that if units of a third-order reaction are given as L^2 mol^{-2} s^{-1}, this relationship is often obscured. Be sure to change L^2 mol^{-2} s^{-1} to the more familiar $M^{-2}s^{-1}$.

7. B. The sum of the exponents of the rate law is 2, so this is a second-order reaction. Second-order reactions are identified by one concentration unit and one time unit for a total of two units. (See the explanation to Question 6.)

8. A. The equation for the half-life of a first-order reaction is $t_{1/2} = 0.693/k$. Substituting, $75\ min = 0.693/k$ or $k = (0.693)/(75)\ min^{-1}$.

9. D. Half-life is the time it takes for the amount of a reactant to lose half its value. One half-life would leave 50% of the original amount, two would leave 25%, three would leave 12.5%, and four would leave 6.25%. An amount of 6.25% left means that about 94% has been consumed in four half-lives. The total time elapsed is approximately 4×5730 years.

10. D. The rate equation does not necessarily relate to the balanced chemical equation in a multistep mechanism, nor does it suggest the nature of the products. Three-atom collisions are highly unlikely, so a single elementary step is not highly probable; therefore, while the rate-determining step can be a three-atom collision, it is not required. The best that can be said is that the mechanism takes place in two or more steps, and the first step is not the rate-determining step.

11. D. If 97% is decayed, 3% of the original sample remains. 3% represents the amount left after about five half-lives: $100\% \times \frac{1}{2} \times \frac{1}{2} \times \frac{1}{2} \times \frac{1}{2} \times \frac{1}{2} = 3.1\%$. Five half-lives $= 5 \times 30$ years $= 150$ years.

12. C. Rate constants for all reactions generally increase with temperature because increasing temperature imparts greater speed to the reactant molecules resulting in more frequent collisions at higher energies.

13. A. The order of a reaction is the sum of the exponents of the rate law.

14. A. Temperature changes the equilibrium constant. Increasing temperature increases the rates of both the forward and reverse reactions and will favor products in an endothermic reaction. The equilibrium constant will increase due to higher concentrations of products in the K_c expression. $K_c = [Products]/[Reactants]$

15. B. The energy of activation on an energy profile is the difference in energy between the reactants and the activated complex (the highest point on the profile).

Free Response Answers

1. a. The rate law will always take the form:
   Rate $= k[Reactant\ 1]^m[Reactant\ 2]^n$, where, in this case, Reactant 1 is NO and Reactant 2 is Cl_2. The object is to use the data in the given table to determine the exponents, m and n.

   Experiments 1 and 2 show that the rate quadruples (apparently within experimental error) when $[Cl_2]$ doubles while $[NO]$ remains constant. Replacing Cl_2 with 2 and the rate with 4, while ignoring the remainder of the equation because nothing else changes, we get $4 = 2^n$. So, $n = 2$.

   Experiments 2 and 3 show that the rate increases by a factor of 8 when both $[NO]$ and $[Cl_2]$ double. Replacing Cl_2 with 2, NO with 2, and the rate with 8, while ignoring the rest because nothing else changes, we get $8 = 2^m \times 2^2$. So, $m = 1$.

   The answer is rate $= k[NO]^1[Cl_2]^2$.

b. *Substitute the data from Experiment 1 (you can use any of the three experiments!) into the rate law and solve for k.*

$$Rate = k[NO]^1[Cl_2]^2$$

$$0.75 \, M/h = k(0.25 \, M)(0.50 \, M)^2$$

$$k = (0.75 \, M/h)/(0.25 \, M)(0.25 \, M^2)$$

$$k = 12/M^2h = 12 \, L^2 \, mol^{-2} \, h^{-1}$$

c. *The order with respect to each reactant is the exponent of that reactant, and the overall order is the sum of the exponents.*

The reaction is first order in NO, second order in Cl_2, and third order overall. (Notice that the units for the rate constant, k, are consistent with a third-order overall reaction. That is, they contain two units of M, and one unit of time, or a total of three units for a third-order reaction.)

d. *Substitute the given values and the calculated rate constant (with all units!) into the rate law and solve for rate.*

$$Rate = k[NO]^1[Cl_2]^2$$

$$Rate = 12/M^2 \, h(0.50 \, M)(0.10 \, M)^2$$

$$Rate = 12/M^2 \, h(0.50 \, M)(0.01 \, M^2)$$

$$Rate = 0.060 \, M/h$$

e. *The rate of one reactant or product compared to the rate of another reactant or product is always proportional to the balanced overall equation for the reaction. The balanced equation shows that two moles of NOCl appear when one mole of Cl_2 disappears. So, if the rate of disappearance of Cl_2 is 4.5 M/h, then the rate of appearance of NOCl is twice that or $2 \times 4.5 \, M/h = 9.0 \, M/h$.*

f. *The table and the rate law are good only for the disappearance of Cl_2. Neither is valid for the appearance of NOCl. The best you can do is substitute the given data and the calculated rate constant into the rate law and solve for the rate of disappearance of Cl_2. Then, multiply your answer by 2 to take into account that the rate of appearance of NOCl is twice the rate of disappearance of Cl_2. (Notice how the solution to Part e gives you a clue to the solution to Part f!)*

$$Rate = k[NO]^1[Cl_2]^2$$

$$Rate = 12/M^2h(0.20 \, M)(0.30 \, M)^2$$

$$Rate = 12/M^2h(0.20 \, M)(0.09 \, M^2)$$

$$Rate = 0.22 \, M/h$$

This calculated rate is for the disappearance of Cl_2, because that is what the rate law calculates. To find the rate of appearance of NOCl, multiply by 2 to take into account the stoichiometry of the reaction!

$$0.22 \, M/h \times 2 = 0.44 \, M/h$$

2. a. *To determine the overall reaction, add the individual steps and cancel the like terms that appear on both sides of the equations:*

Step 1: $2NO \rightarrow N_2O_2$

Step 2: $N_2O_2 + H_2 \rightarrow N_2O + H_2O$

Step 3: $\dfrac{N_2O + H_2 \rightarrow N_2 + H_2O}{2NO + 2H_2 \rightarrow N_2 + 2H_2O}$

b. *Through Step 2, two molecules of NO and one molecule of H_2 have reacted. So, if Step 2 is limiting, the rate law would be:*

$$Rate = k[NO]^2[H_2]$$

c. *The given rate law tells us that through the rate-determining step, two molecules of NO and two molecules of H_2 have reacted. This condition applies only if Step 3 is the rate-determining step.*

d. *An intermediate is a substance that is produced in one elementary step and consumed in a later step. Notice that each strikethrough in the solution to Part a identifies an intermediate: N_2O_2 and N_2O.*

e. *The order of the reaction with respect to an individual reactant is the exponent of that reactant in the rate law. If Step 1 is rate determining, the rate law is rate = $k[NO]^2$. The reaction is second order in NO, and zero order in H_2.*

3. a. $NO + O_3 \rightarrow NO_2 + O_2$

b.

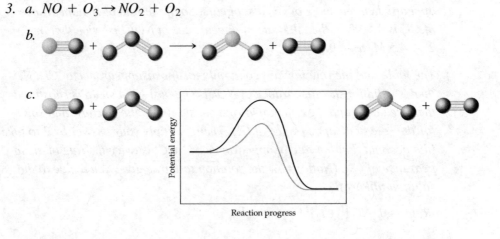

c.

d. $N{=}O\text{---}O\text{---}O{=}O$

Your Turn Answers

14.1.   *Some collisions are successful because the orientation of the molecules is such that new chemical bonds leading to products can form. For example, in Figure 14.2, a collision of a free chlorine atom with a bonded chlorine atom on an NOCl molecule is of the proper orientation to form a Cl—Cl bond. However, if the free chlorine atom collides with an oxygen atom or a nitrogen atom, no Cl—Cl bond will form. Also, the collision must be of sufficient energy to cause a reaction to occur.*

14.2.   *The surface area of powdered coal is much greater than the surface area of lumps of coal, causing powdered coal to burn at a much more rapid rate than coal lumps. The small particle size of coal dust allows for more efficient mixing with gaseous oxygen from the air.*

14.3.   a. *Rate $= k[A], k = s^{-1}$;*

b. *Rate $= k[A]^2, k = M^{-1}s^{-1}$;*

c. *Rate $= k[A]^3, k = M^{-2}s^{-1}$.*

14.4.   a. *Rate $= k[A][B]$.*

b. *A relatively large rate constant means that even at low concentrations of reactants, the rate is relatively large. Thus, the frequency of collisions is relatively large and so is the success of those collisions.*

14.5.   *Hydrogen disappears 3/2 as fast as ammonia appears. $3/2(2.6) = 3.9\,M/s$*

14.6.   a. *Increasing temperature increases the kinetic energy of atoms and molecules. The particles move faster and collide more often with greater energy, resulting in more frequent collisions with sufficient energy for reaction.*

b. *The relative rates of the reverse reactions are $3 > 1 > 2$. Generally, reaction rate increases with increasing activation energy. The reverse reaction represented by Profile 3 has an activation energy of 15 kJ/mol, so it has the fastest rate. The reverse reaction of Profile 1 shows an activation energy of 25 kJ/mol and the activation energy of Profile 2's reverse reaction is 40 kJ/mol.*

c. *The forward and reverse reactions represented by Profile 2 will be the most temperature dependent because they have the highest activation energies (25 and 40 kJ/mol). As temperature increases, the kinetic energy of molecules increases and the fraction of molecules with sufficient energy to get over the activation barrier increases (see Figure 14.4). Reactions with high activation energies have the most molecules with insufficient energy to react. Increasing the temperature activates these molecules so they can react.*

14.7. *Possible mechanisms*   *Intermediates*

    1. $B + B \rightarrow B_2$

    2. $B_2 + A \rightarrow AB_2$ B_2, AB_2

    3. $AB_2 + A \rightarrow A_2B_2$

or

    1. $A + B \rightarrow AB$

    2. $AB + AB \rightarrow A_2B_2$ AB

or

    1. $A + B \rightarrow AB$

    2. $AB + A \rightarrow A_2B$ AB, A_2B

    3. $A_2B + B \rightarrow A_2B_2$

Other mechanisms are possible.

CHEMICAL EQUILIBRIUM

The content in this topic is the basis for mastering Learning Objectives 6.1–6.10 as found in the Curriculum Framework.

When you finish reviewing this topic, be sure you are able to:

- Write equilibrium and nonequilibrium expressions for K and Q
- Explain observations in terms of the reversibility of a chemical or physical system under a specified set of conditions.
- Predict how Q and K change when conditions change
- Calculate equilibrium constants using numerical or graphical data
- Use stoichiometry and the law of mass action to calculate equilibrium concentrations and partial pressures
- Predict the relative concentrations of reactants and products from the magnitudes of equilibrium constants
- Use Le Châtelier's principle and kinetics to predict the relative rates of forward and reverse reactions
- Use Le Châtelier's principle to predict the direction a reaction will proceed as a result of a given change
- Use Le Châtelier's principle to explain the effect a change will have on Q or K
- Use Le Châtelier's principle to design a set of conditions that will optimize a desired result

The Concept of Equilibrium   Section 15.1

Chemical equilibrium occurs when two opposite reactions occur at the same rate. A chemical equilibrium is dynamic. That is, even though no macroscopic changes are observable, on the submicroscopic level, atoms, ions, and molecules continue to change as both a forward and a reverse reaction occur at the same rate.

Consider the reaction of the colorless gas dinitrogen tetroxide to form brown nitrogen dioxide gas in a clear container:

$$N_2O_4(g) \rightarrow 2NO_2(g)$$
colorless   brown

At the beginning of the reaction, only N_2O_4 is present so the contents of the container are colorless. Soon a brown color appears, which gets darker and darker with time. Finally, no further change of color is observed. At this point, spectroscopic evidence shows that the flask contains both N_2O_4 and NO_2 and the concentration of both gases remains constant. The system is at equilibrium:

$$N_2O_4(g) \rightleftharpoons 2NO_2(g)$$
colorless   brown

The " $\rightleftharpoons$ " denotes the equilibrium condition. That is, the forward and reverse reactions occur at the same rate. At equilibrium, there is no observable change in concentration, temperature, pressure, color, or any other property. Even so, the molecules continue to interconvert as forward and reverse reactions occur at the same rate.

Figure 15.1a shows what happens to the concentration of each gas as a function of time. Notice that at equilibrium, although not equal, the concentration of each gas remains constant.

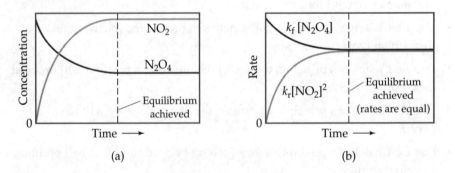

Figure 15.1 Achieving chemical equilibrium in the $N_2O_4(g) \rightleftharpoons 2NO_2(g)$ reaction. Equilibrium occurs when the rate of the forward reaction equals the rate of the reverse reaction.

Figure 15.1b illustrates the change in the rates of the forward and reverse reactions as the system approaches equilibrium. Notice that at equilibrium, the rates are equal.

For the forward reaction,

$$N_2O_4(g) \rightarrow 2NO_2(g) \quad \text{rate}_f = k_f[N_2O_4]$$

For the reverse reaction,

$$2NO_2(g) \rightarrow N_2O_4(g) \quad \text{rate}_r = k_r[NO_2]^2$$

At equilibrium, the rates are equal, so $k_f[N_2O_4] = k_r[NO_2]^2$.

Rearranging: $[NO_2]^2/[N_2O_4] = k_f/k_r$.

The constant k_f/k_r is called the equilibrium constant, K.

Your Turn 15.1

A drop of water is placed in the center of a plastic petri dish in a dry environment and the mass of the system is determined. The mass of the lid is determined and then placed on the petri dish. An ice chip is placed on top of the lid. Momentarily, a fog appears on the underside of the lid just below the ice chip. The ice chip is removed and the outside top of the lid is dried and weighed. The bottom of the petri dish is weighed. Answer the following questions about this system.

a. What happens to the drop of water in the petri dish as time elapses?

b. What is the fog on the underside of the lid?

c. Write an equation describing what happens to the water in the system.

d. What observation might support the supposition that equilibrium is eventually established?

e. What observation might support the supposition that the process represented by the equation in Answer c is reversible?

Write your answers in the space provided.

The Equilibrium Constant   Section 15.2

The **equilibrium-constant expression**, also called the **law of mass action**, for any reaction takes the form of a ratio of the molar concentrations of products divided by those of reactants.

For example, for the reaction:

$$N_2O_4(g) \rightleftharpoons 2NO_2(g)$$

the equilibrium-constant expression is:

$$K_c = [NO_2]^2/[N_2O_4]$$

Each molar concentration is raised to the power of the respective coefficient in the balanced chemical equation.

The "c" in K_c denotes that the amounts of reactants and products are expressed in the molar concentration unit, M, moles per liter.

If the reactants and products are expressed in partial pressures in a gaseous reaction, the equilibrium-constant expression is written:

$$K_p = P_{NO_2}^2/P_{N_2O_4}$$

The "p" in K_p denotes that all the reactants and products are expressed as partial pressures, in atmospheres. The exponents are the coefficients in the balanced equation.

The relationship between K_c and K_p is given:

$$K_p = K_c(RT)^{\Delta n}$$

where R, the universal gas constant $= 0.0821$ L atm/mol K

T is the absolute temperature in K

Δn is the change in number of moles of gas (gaseous products minus gaseous reactants)

In the example, $N_2O_4(g) \rightleftharpoons 2NO_2(g)$, $\Delta n = +1$ because one mole of gaseous reactants becomes two moles of gaseous products, which is a net gain of one mole.

Whenever a pure solid and/or a pure liquid appears in the equilibrium reaction, its concentration is not included in the equilibrium expression.

For example, the equilibrium expression for the reaction:

$$AgCl(s) \rightleftharpoons Ag^+(aq) + Cl^-(aq)$$

does not include the solid $AgCl(s)$.

$$K_c = [Ag^+][Cl^-]$$

Similarly, for $2H_2O(l) \rightleftharpoons H_3O^+(aq) + OH^-(aq)$, the equilibrium expression is:

$$K_c = [H_3O^+][OH^-]$$

Write the equilibrium-constant expressions, K_c and K_p, for the following reaction:

$$CaCO_3(s) \rightleftharpoons CaO(s) + CO_2(g)$$

Write your answer in the space provided.

Understanding and Working with Equilibrium Constants   Section 15.3

The magnitude of the equilibrium constant for a given reaction roughly reflects the ratio of products to reactants and suggests whether products or reactants predominate at equilibrium.

A very large value for an equilibrium constant means that products predominate, and the equilibrium reaction is said to "lie to the right." For example:

$$2NO(g) + O_2(g) \rightleftharpoons 2NO_2(g), \quad K_c = 5.0 \times 10^{12}$$

A very small value for an equilibrium constant means that reactants predominate, and the reaction "lies to the left." For example:

$$2HBr(g) \rightleftharpoons H_2(g) + Br_2(g), \quad K_c = 5.8 \times 10^{-18}$$

When a reaction is written in reverse, the equilibrium expression for the reverse reaction is the reciprocal of that of the forward reaction.

Example:

K_c *for* $AgCl(s) \rightleftharpoons Ag^+(aq) + Cl^-(aq)$ *is* 1.8×10^{-10}.
What is K_c *for* $Ag^+(aq) + Cl^-(aq) \rightleftharpoons AgCl(s)$?

Solution:

For the first reaction, $K_c = 1.8 \times 10^{-10} = [Ag^+][Cl^-]$

For the reaction in question, $K_c = 1/[Ag^+][Cl^-] = 1/1.8 \times 10^{-10}$
$$= 5.6 \times 10^{+9}$$

Your Turn 15.3 ◄─────────────────────────────────

For which reaction in the above example do products predominate? Which reaction lies to the left? Explain. Write your answer in the space provided.

─────────────────────────────────

When a reaction is balanced by doubling the coefficients, then the equilibrium constant for the reaction balanced with the doubled coefficients is the square of the equilibrium constant of the original reaction.

Example:

At 1000 K for $SO_2(g) + \frac{1}{2}O_2(g) \rightleftharpoons SO_3(g)$, $K_p = 1.85$.
What is K_p at 1000 K for $2SO_2(g) + O_2(g) \rightleftharpoons 2SO_3(g)$?

Solution:

For $SO_2(g) + \frac{1}{2}O_2(g) \rightleftharpoons SO_3(g)$,

$K_p = P_{SO_3}/(P_{O_2})^{1/2}(P_{SO_2}) = 1.85$

For $2SO_2(g) + O_2(g) \rightleftharpoons 2SO_3(g)$, $K_p = (P_{SO_3})^2/(P_{O_2})(P_{SO_2})^2$
$= (1.85)^2 = 3.42$

Your Turn 15.4 ◄─────────────────────────────────

The equilibrium constant at 25 °C for the reaction, $N_2(g) + O_2(g) \rightleftharpoons 2NO(g)$ is 1×10^{-30}. Calculate the equilibrium constants for the following reactions:

a. $\frac{1}{2}N_2(g) + \frac{1}{2}O_2(g) \rightleftharpoons NO(g)$

b. $2NO(g) \rightleftharpoons N_2(g) + O_2(g)$

Justify your answers. Write your answers in the space provided.

─────────────────────────────────

Calculating Equilibrium Constants   Section 15.5

Calculations of equilibrium constants from initial and equilibrium concentrations and/or pressures are important calculations required for mastery of the Advanced Placement exam in chemistry. Often an ICE table is used to analyze and manipulate the data. ICE stands for "initial," "change," and "equilibrium."

Example:

Initially, 0.40 mol of nitrogen and 0.96 mol of hydrogen are placed in a 2.0 L container at constant temperature. The mixture is allowed to react, and at equilibrium, the molar concentration of ammonia is found to be 0.14 M. Calculate the equilibrium constant, K_c, for the reaction:

$$N_2(g) + 3H_2(g) \rightleftharpoons 2NH_3(g)$$

Solution:

First, calculate the initial concentrations of the reactants from the initial amounts and the volume of the container.

$[N_2] = 0.40 \, mol/2.0 \, L = 0.20 \, M = $ *"I" (initial concentration) for N_2.*
$[H_2] = 0.96 \, mol/2.0 \, L = 0.48 \, M = $ *"I" (initial concentration) for H_2.*

Assume the molar concentration of nitrogen that reacts is "x." Then, the molar concentration of hydrogen that reacts is 3x, because the balanced chemical equation tells us that for each 1 mol of nitrogen that reacts, 3 mol of hydrogen react. By similar reasoning, the molar concentration of ammonia formed is 2x. Therefore,

"C" (change) for nitrogen $= -x$

"C" (change) for hydrogen $= -3x$

"C" (change) for ammonia $= +2x$

Next, set up an ICE table as follows, and add "I" + "C" for each quantity to obtain "E," the corresponding equilibrium quantity:

	$N_2(g)$	$+3H_2(g)$	$\rightleftharpoons$	$2NH_3(g)$
I	0.20 M	0.48 M		0 M
C	$-x$	$-3x$		$+2x$
E	$0.20 - x$	$0.48 - 3x$		$2x$

The equilibrium concentration of ammonia is given in the problem as 0.14 M NH_3.
So, 2x = 0.14 M and x = 0.070 M.
At equilibrium, $[N_2] = 0.20 - x = 0.20 - 0.070 = 0.13 \, M$.
At equilibrium, $[H_2] = 0.48 - 3x = 0.48 - 3(0.070) = 0.27 \, M$.

Substituting into the equilibrium-constant expression for the reaction:
$K_c = [NH_3]^2/[N_2][H_2]^3 = (0.140 \, M)^2/(0.13 \, M)(0.27 \, M)^3 = 7.66$

(Note: The units for equilibrium constants are rarely included.)

Section 15.6   # Applications of Equilibrium Constants

The **reaction quotient expression**, Q, for any chemical reaction is defined in the same way as the equilibrium-constant expression. However, unlike the equilibrium-constant expression, nonequilibrium values for concentrations or partial pressures may be substituted into the reaction quotient expression.

The reaction quotient, Q, is useful in determining the direction (forward or reverse) a chemical reaction will go to achieve equilibrium.

To determine the direction the reaction will go toward equilibrium, compare the value of Q to the value of K_c (or K_p).

If $K_c = Q$, the system is already at equilibrium.

If $K_c < Q$, the system will go to the left to achieve equilibrium.

If $K_c > Q$, the system will go to the right to achieve equilibrium.

(Notice that if K_c and Q are placed in alphabetical order, the $=$, $<$, and $>$ signs point the direction the reaction will go toward equilibrium.)

Examples:

Consider the interaction of dinitrogen tetroxide and nitrogen dioxide:

$$N_2O_4(g) \rightleftharpoons 2NO_2(g) \text{ at } 100\,°C, \quad K_c = 0.211$$

Which direction will the reaction go if $[N_2O_4] = 1.0\ M$ *and* $[NO_2] = 0.5\ M$?

Solution:

Substitute the given initial concentrations into the expression for Q, which is the same as the expression for K_c.

$$Q = [NO_2]^2/[N_2O_4] = (0.50)^2/(1.0) = 0.25$$

$$K_c = 0.211 < 0.25 = Q$$

The reaction goes from right to left toward reactants to establish equilibrium. Notice that at the given concentrations, there is too much $NO_2(g)$, *and not enough* $N_2O_4(g)$. *The reaction goes toward* $N_2O_4(g)$ *to achieve equilibrium. Notice that if Q is greater than K, there are more products present than there will be at equilibrium. More molecules of product will cause higher molecular collisions between product molecules and increase the rate of the reverse reaction. This will drive the net reaction toward more reactants (to the left) until equilibrium is reestablished.*

Le Châtelier's Principle   Section 15.7

Le Châtelier's principle summarizes the behavior of a chemical reaction at equilibrium when a stress is imposed on the reaction. It states that if a change is applied to a system at equilibrium, the system will move in a direction that minimizes the change.

To understand Le Châtelier's principle and why changes affect equilibria, it is important to remember that the equilibrium condition is when the rates of the forward and reverse reactions of a chemical system are equal. By a change to a system at equilibrium, we mean a change that alters the rate of either the forward or reverse reaction so the system is no longer at equilibrium. The system responds to move in a direction that reestablishes equilibrium. The system is said to "shift right" (toward products) or "shift left" (toward reactants) depending on the change that disturbs the equilibrium.

Changes that affect equilibria are the following:

1. Change in concentrations of reactants or products.

Adding a reactant shifts the equilibrium toward products. The increased concentration of the reactant makes the forward reaction faster than the reverse reaction, causing the reaction to shift toward products. (Recall that increasing the concentration of a reactant increases the rate of the forward reaction because, at higher concentrations, collisions are more frequent.)

Removing a reactant shifts the equilibrium toward reactants. A decreased concentration of a reactant decreases the molecular collisions between reactants. This slows the forward reaction, making it slower than the reverse reaction, causing the reaction to shift toward reactants.

Adding a product shifts the equilibrium toward reactants. An increased concentration of product speeds the reverse reaction by increasing molecular collisions and shifting the reaction toward reactants.

Removing a product shifts the equilibrium toward products. Decreased product concentration slows the reverse reaction, causing the reaction to favor products.

Figure 15.2 summarizes the effect of changing the concentrations of reactants or products on a system at equilibrium.

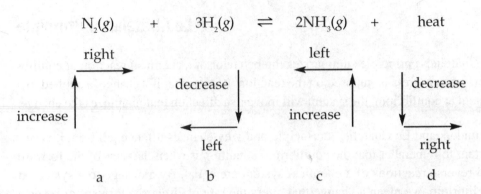

Figure 15.2 The effect of adding or removing reactants or products on a system at equilibrium.

a. Adding reactants shifts equilibrium toward products because increased molecular collisions between reactants speed the forward reaction.
b. Removing reactants shifts equilibrium toward reactants because fewer molecular collisions slow the forward reaction.
c. Adding products increases the collisions between product molecules, increases the reverse reaction, and shifts equilibrium toward reactants.
d. Removing products slows the reverse reaction and shifts equilibrium toward products.

Common misconception: Figure 15.2 tells *what direction* a system at equilibrium will shift under a given set of conditions. However, questions on the Advanced Placement exam often ask *why* a system behaves as it does. Be sure to study the discussion of why the rate of the forward or reverse reaction changes (the frequency of molecular collisions changes) and how that change affects the equilibrium position.

Your Turn 15.5

How will decreasing the concentration of hydrogen gas affect the amount of hydrogen iodide present at equilibrium? Explain. Write your answer in the space provided.

$$H_2(g) + I_2(g) \rightleftharpoons 2HI(g) + heat$$

2. Change in volume (affects gaseous equilibria only).

Decreasing volume shifts the reaction in the direction of the least number of moles of gas in the balanced equation. Decreasing the volume for a gaseous system at equilibrium increases the pressures (and, therefore, concentrations) of both the gaseous reactants and products.

For example, decreasing the container volume of the reaction:

$$N_2(g) + 3H_2(g) \rightleftharpoons 2NH_3(g) + \text{heat}$$

causes the equilibrium to move toward products because the formation of a lesser number of moles will decrease the pressure.

Decreasing the volume increases the total pressure. The system responds by moving in a direction that will reduce the total pressure. In this case, the reaction shifts toward NH_3, because the number of moles in the system will decrease and the pressure will decrease. Another way to say this is that when the total pressure increases, the equilibrium shifts in a direction that reduces the number of moles of gas, in this case, to the right.

For example, if the volume of the container is halved, the pressures of each gas will double. However, the equilibrium constant, K_p, is defined in terms of the stoichiometry of the reaction and doubling all pressures increases the numerator (a squared term) less than the denominator (the combination of terms raised to the third and first powers). Thus, the equilibrium is out of balance and adjusts to the right to rebalance the mixture keeping K_p a constant.

$$K_p = P_{NH_3}^2 / P_{N_2} P_{H_2}^3$$

On a molecular level, consider that an increase in pressure increases the rates of both the forward and reverse reactions because the number of collisions for both reactants and products are more frequent. However, the rates of the forward and reverse reactions are not increased equally. The rate of the forward reaction, because it has more moles of gas, increases more than the rate of the reverse reaction. The reaction shifts right consuming enough reactants to again make the rates equal.

Your Turn 15.6

What is the effect on the equilibrium between ozone, O_3, and oxygen, O_2, when the volume of the container is increased? Explain your answer discussing changes in the relative rates of reaction. Write your answer in the space provided.

$$2O_3(g) \rightleftharpoons 3O_2(g)$$

3. Change in temperature.

Increasing temperature favors the endothermic reaction. The rate of both the forward and reverse reactions is increased because of faster moving particles, more frequent collisions, and more effective collisions. However, the rate of the endothermic reaction increases more than does the rate of the exothermic reaction. This is because the activation energy of the endothermic reaction is always greater than that of the exothermic reaction. At low temperatures, enough exothermic reactants already have sufficient energy to overcome the relatively low activation barrier. At low temperature, very few endothermic reactants have the requisite energy to go over the relatively high activation barrier. Increasing temperature increases the energy of both reactants and products. However, high temperature aids the lower-energy endothermic reactants more than the higher-energy exothermic reactants. Thus, increasing temperature increases the rate of the endothermic reaction more than it increases the rate of the exothermic reaction.

Decreasing temperature favors the exothermic reaction. A lower temperature slows the rate of both forward and reverse reactions. However, at low temperatures, enough exothermic reactants still have sufficient energy to surmount the energy barrier and react.

Changing temperature changes the equilibrium constant. In contrast, changes in concentration, volume, or pressure change the position of an equilibrium without changing the equilibrium constant. Figure 15.2 shows that you can deduce the effect of temperature on the direction of change of an equilibrium system if you treat temperature as a reactant (in an endothermic reaction) or a product (in an exothermic reaction).

The Effect of a Catalyst

A catalyst does not affect the position of the equilibrium, but it does increase the rate at which equilibrium is established. A catalyst increases the rate of a reaction by lowering the activation energy. However, a catalyst lowers the activation energies of both the forward and reverse reactions by equal amounts (see Figure 15.3).

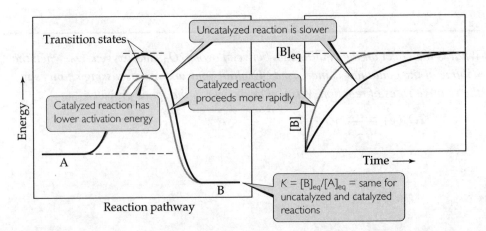

Figure 15.3 A catalyst works by providing a different pathway from reactants to products. The activation energy of both the forward and reverse reactions is low. A catalyst does not affect the position of the equilibrium.

Multiple Choice Questions

1. $3H_2(g) + N_2(g) \rightleftharpoons 2NH_3(g)$ $\Delta H = -92.2\,kJ$

    The number of moles of $H_2(g)$ are decreased by

    A) decreasing the container size.

    B) adding NH_3.

    C) increasing the temperature.

    D) removing N_2.

2. Consider a reaction: $3A(g) + B(s) \rightleftharpoons 2C(g)$. If 2.0 mol A, 3.0 mol B, and 2.0 mol C are present in a 1.0 L flask at equilibrium, what is the value of K_c?

    A) 4.0

    B) 1.0

    C) 2.0

    D) 0.50

3. Consider the following reaction:

    $2SO_2(g) + O_2(g) \rightleftharpoons 2SO_3(g)$ $K_p = 9.0$ at a certain temperature.

    At the same temperature, what is K_p for $SO_2(g) + \frac{1}{2}O_2(g) \rightleftharpoons SO_3(g)$?

    A) 9.0

    B) 4.5

    C) 3.0

    D) 18

4. For the chemical reaction, $PCl_3(g) + Cl_2(g) \rightleftharpoons PCl_5(g)$, $\Delta H^\circ_{rxn} = -92.6\,kJ$, which conditions favor maximum conversion of the reactants to product?

    A) high pressure and high temperature

    B) high pressure and low temperature

    C) low pressure and low temperature

    D) low pressure and high temperature

5. Which of the following equilibrium constants indicates that its corresponding reaction goes nearly to completion?

    A) $K_c = 1.0 \times 10^{-2}$

    B) $K_c = 1.0 \times 10^{-8}$

    C) $K_c = 1.0$

    D) $K_c = 1.0 \times 10^{+8}$

6. Identify the equilibrium expression for the decomposition of ammonium carbonate, $(NH_4)_2CO_3$, according to the following equation.

$$(NH_4)_2CO_3(s) \rightleftharpoons 2NH_3(g) + CO_2(g) + H_2O(g)$$

A) $K_c = [NH_3][CO_2][H_2O]$

B) $K_c = [NH_3]^2[CO_2][H_2O]$

C) $K_c = [NH_3]^2[CO_2][H_2O]/[(NH_4)_2CO_3]$

D) $K_c = [(NH_3)_2CO_3]/[NH_3]^2[CO_2][H_2O]$

7. In the presence of a catalyst, sulfur dioxide reacts with oxygen to form sulfur trioxide.

$$2SO_2(g) + O_2(g) \rightleftharpoons 2SO_3(g)$$

When 2.00 mol of O_2 and 2.00 mol of SO_2 are placed in a 1 L container, and allowed to come to equilibrium at a certain temperature, the mixture is found to contain 1.00 mol of SO_3. What is the amount of O_2 at equilibrium?

A) 0.00 mol

B) 1.00 mol

C) 1.50 mol

D) 0.50 mol

8. Ammonia is placed in a flask and allowed to come to equilibrium at a specified temperature according to the equation:

$$3H_2(g) + N_2(g) \rightleftharpoons 2NH_3(g)$$

Analysis of the equilibrium mixture shows that it contains 3.00 atm NH_3 and 1.00 atm N_2. What is the value of the equilibrium constant, K_p?

A) 0.333

B) 27

C) 3.00

D) 0.25

Questions 9–12 refer to the following system at equilibrium:

$$CaO(s) + CO_2(g) \rightleftharpoons CaCO_3(s) + heat$$

9. Which factor will affect both the value of the equilibrium constant AND the position of equilibrium for the formation of calcium carbonate?

A) increasing the volume of the container

B) adding CO_2

C) removing $CaO(s)$

D) raising the temperature

10. The most convenient way to measure the equilibrium constant for the system is to measure

   A) the temperature of the reaction.

   B) the pressure of the CO_2 gas.

   C) the molar concentrations of all the reactants.

   D) the forward and reverse rate constants.

11. For the reaction at a certain temperature, $K_p = 2.5$. If the partial pressure of CO_2 at that temperature is 1.5 atm, what are the relative values of Q and K and which direction will the reaction go to reestablish equilibrium?

   A) $K < Q$. The reaction goes to the right.

   B) $K > Q$. The reaction goes to the right.

   C) $K < Q$. The reaction goes to the left.

   D) $K > Q$. The reaction goes to the left.

12. What changes and corresponding observations would you be able to make to this system that might explain the reversibility of this reaction?

   A) If the volume of the container were doubled, the pressure would half.

   B) If the volume of the container were halved, the pressure would change, but not double.

   C) If $CaCO_3(s)$ were added to the container under the same conditions, no change in pressure would be observed.

   D) If $CaO(s)$ were added to the container under the same conditions, the pressure would decrease.

Refer to the following information to answer Questions 13–16.

The diagrams below represent three systems at equilibrium, all in the same-size containers.

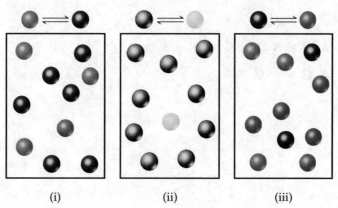

   (i)   (ii)   (iii)

13. *Rank the equilibrium constants in order of increasing magnitudes, lowest to highest.*

   A) *i < ii < iii*

   B) *iii < i < ii*

   C) *ii < i < iii*

   D) *i < iii < ii*

14. *Assume each container is 100 L and each molecule represents 0.1 mol. What is the value of the equilibrium constant for System ii?*

   A) *9*

   B) *1/9*

   C) *0.09*

   D) *0.009*

15. *If more reactant were added to System i under the same conditions, what would be the result when equilibrium is reestablished?*

   A) *There would be no change in the amounts of reactants or products.*

   B) *More product would be produced because, until equilibrium is reestablished, the forward rate would exceed the reverse rate.*

   C) *Less product would be produced because, until equilibrium is reestablished, the forward rate would exceed the reverse rate.*

   D) *More product would be produced because, until equilibrium is reestablished, the reverse rate would exceed the forward rate.*

16. *If product molecules were added to System iii under the same conditions at equilibrium, what would happen to the relative values of Q and K, before the addition, immediately after the addition, and upon the return to equilibrium?*

   A) *Q = K, throughout the process*

   B) *Q = K, Q > K, Q = K*

   C) *Q < K, Q = K Q > K*

   D) *Q = K, Q < K, Q = K*

Free Response Questions

1. A 40.0 g sample of solid ammonium carbonate is placed in a closed, evacuated 3.00 L flask and heated to 400°C. It decomposes to produce ammonia, water, and carbon dioxide according to the equation:

$$(NH_4)_2CO_3(s) \rightleftharpoons 2NH_3(g) + H_2O(g) + CO_2(g)$$

The equilibrium constant, K_p, for the reaction is 0.295 at 400 °C.

a. Write the K_p equilibrium-constant expression for the reaction.

b. Calculate K_c at 400 °C.

c. Calculate the partial pressure of $NH_3(g)$ at equilibrium at 400 °C.

d. Calculate the total pressure inside the flask at equilibrium.

e. Calculate the number of grams of solid ammonium carbonate in the flask at equilibrium.

f. What is the minimum amount in grams of solid $(NH_4)_2CO_3$ that is necessary to be placed in the flask in order for the system to come to equilibrium?

2. Hydrogen gas reacts with solid sulfur to produce hydrogen sulfide gas.

$$H_2(g) + S(s) \rightleftharpoons H_2S(g) \quad \Delta H_{rxn} = -20.17 \, kJ/mol$$

An amount of solid S and an amount of gaseous H_2 are placed in an evacuated container at 25 °C. At equilibrium, some solid S remains in the container.

Predict and explain each of the following. In each case, predict what the stated change will have on the relative values of K and Q.

a. the effect on the equilibrium partial pressure of H_2S gas when additional solid sulfur is introduced into the container

b. the effect on the equilibrium partial pressure of H_2 gas when additional H_2S gas is introduced into the container

c. the effect on the mass of solid sulfur present when the volume of the container is increased

d. the effect on the mass of solid sulfur present when the temperature is decreased

e. the effect of adding a catalyst to initial amounts of reactants

Multiple Choice Answers and Explanations

1. A. According to Boyle's law, decreasing the container size will increase the partial pressures of all three gases and hence the total pressure. Because there are more moles of gaseous reactants (4), than gaseous products (2), reactant molecules will tend to collide more frequently than product molecules. The forward reaction rate will increase more than the reverse reaction rate. The system will shift toward products, decreasing the number of moles of $H_2(g)$.

2. D. $K_c = [C]^2/[A]^3 = (2.0\,M)^2/(2.0\,M)^3 = 0.50$.

   (*Note that calculators are not allowed on the multiple choice section, so complex numeric problems such as this one require relatively simple arithmetic.*)

3. C. The reaction in question is the same as the given reaction except that it is balanced with coefficients half the value of the given reaction. Since coefficients are exponents in equilibrium-constant expressions, K_p for the second reaction is the square root of K_p for the given reaction: $(9.0)^{1/2} = 3.0$.

4. B. The reaction is exothermic so low temperature will favor products. Additionally, high pressure will shift the reaction toward products because compressing the gases will cause the forward reaction to become faster than the reverse reaction. At higher pressures, more molecular collisions are likely to take place. The two moles of gas on the left react to form one mole of gas on the right, lowering the pressure.

5. D. "Nearly to completion" means that by the time the system reaches equilibrium, most of the reactants have become products. K_c is the ratio of products to reactants, so the larger the K_c, the larger the quantity of products at equilibrium.

6. B. The equilibrium constant, K_c, equals the ratio of the concentrations of products to reactants, each raised to the power of the coefficient that balances the equation. Equilibrium constants do not include reactants or products that are pure solids or liquids.

7. C. An ICE table would look like this:

	$2SO_2(g)$	$+O_2(g)$	$\rightleftharpoons$	$2SO_3(g)$
I	2.00	2.00		0
C	$-2x$	$-x$		$+2x$
E	$2.00-2x$	$2.00-x$		$2x$

   $2x = 1.00\,mol/L$, $x = 0.50\,mol/L$, $2.00-x = 1.50\,mol/L$
   $1.50\,mol/L \times 1L = 1.50\,mol$

8. A. An ICE table would look like this:

	$3H_2(g)$	$+N_2(g)$	$\rightleftharpoons$	$2NH_3(g)$
I	0	0		
C	$+3x$	$+x$		$-2x$
E	$3x$	x		3.00

   $x = 1.00$, $3x = 3.00$
   $K_p = (P_{NH_3})^2/(P_{H_2})^3(P_{N_2}) = (3.00)^2/(3.00)^3(1.00) = 0.333$

9. D. Temperature is the only variable that will change the equilibrium constant. Increasing the temperature will favor the endothermic (in this case, the reverse) reaction, causing the equilibrium to shift to the left increasing the partial pressure of CO_2 and decreasing K_p.

10. B. $K_p = 1/P_{CO_2}$. The partial pressure of CO_2 at equilibrium is equal to the reciprocal of the equilibrium constant, K_p. Equilibrium constants do not include reactants or products that are pure solids or liquids.

11. B. Because all chemical species participating in the reaction, other than CO_2, are solids, $K_p = 1/P_{CO_2}$. So, $K_p > Q$ under the given set of conditions. The reaction will go in a direction so that Q eventually equals K at equilibrium, so the reaction will go to the right, decreasing the partial pressure of CO_2 and increasing Q.

12. B. If the system were not a reversible reaction at equilibrium, halving the volume would double the pressure according to Boyle's law. However, if the system is at equilibrium, it has two opposite reversible reactions occurring at the same rate. Thus, halving the volume would increase the pressure causing the reaction to consume some carbon dioxide and produce more calcium carbonate until equilibrium is again established. The net effect would be that the pressure would increase but not as much as predicted by Boyle's law.

13. C. The equilibrium constant is a ratio of products over reactants. The more products relative to reactants, the larger the magnitude of the equilibrium constant. All the systems contain a total of 10 molecules of reactants and products. System ii shows only one product molecule. System i shows six product molecules and System iii shows eight molecules of product.

14. B. The equilibrium-constant expression for System ii is
$K_c = [products]/[reactants]$
$= (1)(0.1\ mol)/(100\ L)/(9)(0.1\ mol)/(100\ L) = 1/9$.

15. B. Adding more reactants would cause more molecular collisions between reactant molecules, thereby increasing the rate of the forward reaction. As reactants are converted to products, the forward rate slows while the reverse rate increases. Eventually equilibrium is reestablished with more products present.

16. B. The equilibrium constant is $K = [products/reactants]$. At equilibrium, $Q = K$. When $Q > K$, products will be converted to reactants until equilibrium is reestablished. When $Q < K$, reactants will be converted to products until equilibrium is reestablished.

Free Response Answers

1. a. $K_p = P_{NH_3}^2 P_{H_2O} P_{CO_2}$. The K_p expression is the product of the partial pressures of products raised to the power of the coefficients that balance the equation. Pure solids and liquids are excluded from any equilibrium expression.

b. $K_c = K_p/(RT)^{\Delta n}$, where $R = 0.0821$ L atm/mol K, T is the absolute temperature in Kelvin, and Δn is the change in number of moles of gas as the reaction proceeds left to right. In this case, $\Delta n = +4$, because four moles of gas are produced from zero moles of gas.

$$K_c = K_p/(RT)^{\Delta n} = 0.295/[(0.0821)(400+273)]^4 = 3.17 \times 10^{-8}$$

c. If x equals the partial pressure of H_2O formed in the reaction, an ICE table will look like this:

$$(NH_4)_2CO_3(s) \rightleftharpoons 2NH_3(g) + H_2O(g) + CO_2(g)$$

I	0	0	0
C	$+2x$	$+x$	$+x$
E	$2x$	x	x

(Note: It is not important to know how much solid is present initially or at equilibrium.)

$$K_p = P^2_{NH_3}P_{H_2O}P_{CO_2} = 0.295 = (2x)^2(x)(x) = 4x^4$$

$$x = 0.521$$

$$P_{NH_3} = 2x = 2\,(0.521) = 1.04 \text{ atm}$$

d. $x = P_{CO_2} = 0.521$ atm $= P_{H_2O}$ and $2x = P_{NH_3} = 2 \times 0.521 = 1.04$ atm

$$P_{total} = P_{CO_2} + P_{H_2O} + P_{NH_3} = 0.521 + 0.521 + 1.04 = 2.08 \text{ atm}$$

e. To calculate the number of grams of ammonium carbonate remaining at equilibrium, we must calculate the number of grams that reacted and subtract from the original 40.0 g. From the stoichiometry of the reaction, the moles of ammonium carbonate that reacted are equal to the number of moles of water found in the flask at equilibrium. The moles of water can be calculated from the partial pressure of water using the ideal-gas equation.

Moles of water at equilibrium $= PV/RT = (0.521 \text{ atm})(3.00 \text{ L})/$ $(0.0821 \text{ L atm/mol K})(400+273) = 0.0283 \text{ mol } H_2O$.

$0.0238 \text{ mol } H_2O = 0.0283 \text{ mol of } (NH_4)_2CO_3(s)$ that reacted.

The molar mass of ammonium carbonate is 96.0 g/mol.

The number of grams of $(NH_4)_2CO_3(s)$ that reacted is $0.0283 \text{ mol} \times 96.0 \text{ g/mol} = 2.72g$.

The number of grams that remain is $40.0 \text{ g} - 2.72 \text{ g} = 37.3 \text{ g}$.

f. If 2.72 g react to establish equilibrium, then just slightly more than 2.72 g of $(NH_4)_2CO_3(s)$ must be present initially for equilibrium to be established because at equilibrium, some solid must remain.

2. a. Increasing or decreasing the amount of solid in an equilibrium mixture has no effect on the position of the equilibrium. S(s) does not appear in the equilibrium expression, so Q and K will remain the same.

b. *The partial pressure of $H_2(g)$ will increase. Additional $H_2S(g)$ added to the container increases the rate of the reverse reaction, causing more reactants to form as the equilibrium system rebalances. At first, Q will be greater than K until equilibrium is reestablished when Q = K.*

c. *The mass of the solid sulfur remains the same. Increasing the volume of the container decreases the partial pressures of both gasses, but because there is one mole of gas on each side of the equilibrium equation, the equilibrium system does not change. If more moles of gas were on one side than the other, the equilibrium would shift toward the side with the greater number of moles of gas. The values of Q and K will remain the same.*

d. *The mass of the solid sulfur will increase. Heating a reaction increases the rate of both forward and reverse reactions because increasing temperature increases the speed with which the molecules move and the kinetic energy they have. Thus, at a higher temperature, the collisions between molecules become more frequent. However, increasing temperature always increases the rate of the endothermic reaction more than the rate of the exothermic reaction, because the higher temperature gives more molecules on the endothermic side sufficient energy required to surmount the energy barrier. The value of K will decrease so at first, it will be less than Q. Because the reaction is written as exothermic, upon heating, more reactants will form making the ratio of the products to reactants less. As the equilibrium is reestablished toward the left, Q will decrease until it equals K at a new equilibrium.*

Notice that this question can be tricky. Because pure solids are not included in the equilibrium expression, their relative amounts do not affect the position of the equilibrium. But their amounts are affected by changes in the equilibrium. Be sure to read each question carefully and answer the question directly.

e. *The final equilibrium position will not be affected even though the system will reach equilibrium faster. Catalysts increase the rates of both the forward and reverse reactions equally by lowering the activation energy. Q and K will not change.*

Your Turn Answers

15.1. a. *The water evaporates.*

 b. *Condensed water vapor*

 c. $H_2O(l) \rightarrow H_2O(g)$

 d. *The lid has gained mass equal to the mass that the bottom has lost. Repeated weighings over time would yield no further change in masses.*

 e. *The loss of water in the bottom of the petri dish indicates that some of it evaporated. The gain of water on the lid, which is equal to the loss on the bottom, indicates that water vapor condensed. Evaporation and condensation are opposite and reversible processes.*

15.2. $K_c = [CO_2]. K_p = P_{CO_2}.$

15.3.   In the reaction, $Ag^+(aq) + Cl^-(aq) \rightleftharpoons AgCl(s)$, products predominate because the equilibrium constant, $K_c = 5.6 \times 10^{+9}$, is very large.

   The reaction, $AgCl(s) \rightleftharpoons Ag^+(aq) + Cl^-(aq)$, lies to the left where reactants predominate because the equilibrium constant, $K_c = 1.8 \times 10^{-10}$, is very small.

15.4. a. 1×10^{-15}. Reaction a is balanced using coefficients that are half the value of the given reaction. Therefore, the equilibrium constant is the square root of the given value.

   b. 1×10^{30}. Reaction b is the reverse of the given reaction, so the equilibrium constant is the reciprocal of the given value.

15.5.   Decreasing $[H_2]$ will decrease the amount of HI present. The equilibrium will shift left consuming HI, because more infrequent collisions will decrease the rate of reaction. The rate of the reverse reaction will then be faster than that of the forward reaction, producing more reactants until equilibrium is again established toward the left.

15.6.   Increasing the volume of the container decreases the pressure of both of the gases present. The equilibrium will shift in a direction to increase the pressure (to the right, toward oxygen). Decreasing the pressure of both of the gases decreases their concentrations and decreases the rates of both the forward and reverse reactions. The rate of the forward reaction will decrease less than the rate of the reverse reaction, causing the equilibrium to shift toward products.

ACID–BASE EQUILIBRIA

The content in this topic is the basis for mastering Learning Objectives 2.2, 3.7, 6.11, 6.12, 6.14, 6.15, and 6.16 as found in the Curriculum Framework.

When you finish reviewing this topic, be sure you are able to:

- Predict strong and weak acids and bases from their formulas
- Estimate and calculate quantities such as pH, molar concentrations of various species, and percentage ionization of solutions of strong and weak acids and bases
- Write chemical equations that illustrate the Brønsted–Lowry definition of acids and bases
- Identify acid–base conjugate pairs
- Interconvert K_a and K_b expressions for conjugate pairs
- Construct particle representations for the reactions of acids with bases
- Write and explain equations for acid–base hydrolysis of salt solutions
- Justify with examples why chemical structure affects acid–base behavior

Acids and Bases: A Brief Review   Section 16.1

The **Arrhenius** idea of acids and bases states that acids ionize in water solution to produce hydrogen ions. **Acids are substances that increase the hydrogen ion, H$^+$, concentration when dissolved in water.** For example:

$$HCl(g) \rightarrow H^+(aq) + Cl^-(aq)$$
$$HNO_3(aq) \rightarrow H^+(aq) + NO_3^-(aq)$$

Bases are substances that increase the concentration of hydroxide ion, OH$^-$, when dissolved in water. A base dissociates to produce hydroxide ions in water. Notice in the examples on the next page that sodium hydroxide is "monobasic" and barium hydroxide is "dibasic." The prefixes mono- and di- refer to the number of available hydroxides in each formula.

Sodium hydroxide is monobasic: $NaOH(s) \rightarrow Na^+(aq) + OH^-(aq)$

Barium hydroxide is dibasic: $Ba(OH)_2(s) \rightarrow Ba^{2+}(aq) + 2OH^-(aq)$

Section 16.2

Brønsted–Lowry Acids and Bases

The **Brønsted–Lowry** theory states:

Acids are proton (H^+) donors.

Bases are proton acceptors.

Consider the interaction of hydrogen chloride gas with water. Figure 16.1 shows the same reaction using three different representations: (a) the symbolic chemical equation; (b) Lewis structures representing the species; and (c) a particle model view.

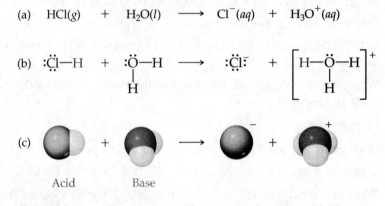

Figure 16.1 Three representations of the reaction of hydrogen chloride with water.

The reaction in Figure 16.1 shows HCl as an acid because it donates a proton to water. H_2O is a base because it accepts a proton.

Hydronium ion, $H_3O^+(aq)$, is a hydrated proton. When water accepts a proton from an acid, the product is a hydronium ion.

Notice that when water accepts a proton from HCl, it becomes H_3O^+. $H_3O^+(aq)$ is a hydrated proton called the hydronium ion.

Common misconception: Chemists use $H^+(aq)$ and $H_3O^+(aq)$ interchangeably to represent a hydrated proton, the ion responsible for the acidic properties of an aqueous solution. Both of the following equations are chemically equivalent. Notice how one emphasizes the Brønsted–Lowry model and the other represents the Arrhenius model.

$$HCl(g) + H_2O(l) \rightarrow H_3O^+(aq) + Cl^-(aq) \qquad \text{Brønsted–Lowry model}$$
$$\underset{\text{acid}}{} \quad \underset{\text{base}}{}$$

$$HCl(g) \rightarrow H^+(aq) + Cl^-(aq) \qquad\qquad \text{Arrhenius model}$$

Sodium carbonate, Na_2CO_3, is a Brønsted–Lowry base because the carbonate ion accepts a proton from water. Water is an acid because it donates a proton to carbonate ion. Since the sodium ion is a neutral ion, we ignore it in the equation:

$$\underset{\text{base}}{CO_3^{2-}(aq)} + \underset{\text{acid}}{H_2O(l)} \rightleftharpoons HCO_3^-(aq) + OH^-(aq)$$

Conjugate acid–base pairs are two substances in aqueous solution whose formulas differ by an H^+. The acid is the more positive species having the extra H (see Table 16.1).

Table 16.1   Examples of acid–base conjugate pairs.

Acid	Base	Equations Involving Acid–Base Conjugate Pairs
NH_4^+ H_2O	NH_3 OH^-	$\underset{\text{base}}{NH_3(g)} + \underset{\text{acid}}{H_2O(l)} \rightleftharpoons \underset{\text{acid}}{NH_4^+(aq)} + \underset{\text{base}}{OH^-(aq)}$
H_2SO_3 H_3O^+	HSO_3^- H_2O	$\underset{\text{acid}}{H_2SO_3(aq)} + \underset{\text{base}}{H_2O(l)} \rightleftharpoons \underset{\text{base}}{HSO_3^-(aq)} + \underset{\text{acid}}{H_3O^+(aq)}$

Acid–base reactions are reversible reactions. The reversible equations in Table 16.1 illustrate the focus on the transfer of protons according to the Brønsted–Lowry model. In each reaction, there are two sets of acid–base conjugate pairs.

Common misconception: HF is a weak acid, so F⁻ is the conjugate base of HF. The reaction of HF with water is expressed as a reversible equilibrium:

$$HF(aq) + H_2O(l) \rightleftharpoons F^-(aq) + H_3O^+(aq)$$

However, HCl is a strong acid, so Cl⁻ is *not* a conjugate base of HCl. The reaction of HCl with water is expressed as an irreversible reaction:

$$HCl(aq) + H_2O(l) \rightarrow Cl^-(aq) + H_3O^+(aq)$$

Because the HCl reaction is not reversible, Cl⁻ does not accept a proton, and is not a base. The same is true of all anions of strong monoprotic acids.

An **amphoteric** (also called **amphiprotic**) substance is one that can act as either an acid or a base. Notice in Table 16.1 that water acts as an acid when it transfers a proton to ammonia. Water acts as a base when accepting a proton from sulfurous acid. Water is amphoteric because it can act as an acid or a base.

Section 16.3

The Autoionization of Water

The **autoionization of water** is a reversible equilibrium where a water molecule transfers a proton to another water molecule.

$$H_2O(l) \; + \; H_2O(l) \; \rightleftharpoons \; OH^-(aq) \; + \; H_3O^+(aq)$$

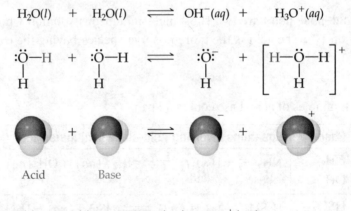

$$\underset{\text{acid}}{H_2O(l)} + \underset{\text{base}}{H_2O(l)} \rightleftharpoons \underset{\text{base}}{OH^-(aq)} + \underset{\text{acid}}{H_3O^+(aq)}$$

Water is both a weak acid and a weak base. It is amphoteric. It can act as a proton donor (an acid) or a proton acceptor (a base).

The **ion product constant** for water, K_w, is the equilibrium constant for the autoionization of water. K_w is a special case of K_c.

$$K_c = K_w = [OH^-][H_3O^+] = 1.0 \times 10^{-14} \text{ at 25 °C.}$$

The pH Scale   Section 16.4

Molar concentrations of $H^+(aq)$ are often expressed as pH, approximated for most solutions as the negative logarithm (base 10) of $[H^+]$.

$$pH = -\log[H^+] \quad \text{or} \quad pH = -\log[H_3O^+]$$

This mathematical model is accurate for pH values ranging from 2 to 12 and is often used as an approximation for pH values ranging from 0 to 14. Table 16.2 shows the relationships among $[H^+]$, $[OH^-]$, pH, and pOH for various solutions.

Table 16.2   The pH scale: Relationships among $[H^+]$, $[OH^-]$, pH, and pOH.

$[H^+]$	pH		pOH	$[OH^-]$
1×10^{-14}	14		0	1×10^{-0}
1×10^{-13}	13		1	1×10^{-1}
1×10^{-12}	12		2	1×10^{-2}
1×10^{-11}	11		3	1×10^{-3}
1×10^{-10}	10		4	1×10^{-4}
1×10^{-9}	9		5	1×10^{-5}
1×10^{-8}	8	basic	6	1×10^{-6}
1×10^{-7}	7	neutral	7	1×10^{-7}
1×10^{-6}	6	acidic	8	1×10^{-8}
1×10^{-5}	5		9	1×10^{-9}
1×10^{-4}	4		10	1×10^{-10}
1×10^{-3}	3		11	1×10^{-11}
1×10^{-2}	2		12	1×10^{-12}
1×10^{-1}	1		13	1×10^{-13}
1×10^{-0}	0		14	1×10^{-14}

Common misconception: It is common to see pH scales ranging from 0 to 14 as illustrated in Table 16.2. However, the assumption that $pH = -\log[H^+]$ is valid only for pH values ranging from about 2 through 12. At higher and lower pH values, which represent higher concentrations of acid or base, ion–ion pairing is common and $pH = -\log[H^+]$ is invalid.

Table 16.3 shows the mathematical relationships involving pH. Notice that the equations in the left-hand column of Table 16.3 are the logarithmic forms of the equations in the right-hand column.

Table 16.3   Mathematical relationships for interconverting $[H^+]$, $[OH^-]$, pH, and pOH.

$pH = -\log[H^+]$	$[H^+] = 10^{-pH}$
$pOH = -\log[OH^-]$	$[OH^-] = 10^{-pOH}$
$pH + pOH = 14$	$[H^+][OH^-] = 1 \times 10^{-14}$

Your Turn 16.1

At 0 °C, the ion product constant for water, K_w, is 1.2×10^{-15}.

a. Is the autoionization of water an exothermic or endothermic reaction? Explain using a thermochemical equation.

b. Calculate the pH of a neutral solution at 0 °C.

c. At the human body temperature of 37 °C, will the pH of water be greater or less than 7? Justify your answer.

Section 16.5

Strong Acids and Bases

Strong acids and strong bases are strong electrolytes. Strong acids and strong bases ionize completely in dilute aqueous solution. There are seven common strong acids and eight common strong bases. It is useful to refer to their names and formulas given in Table 16.4. Notice that the strong bases are the hydroxides of the Group 1 alkali metals and the hydroxides of the Group 2 alkaline earth metals. Strong acids and bases are generally, but not always, associated with the Arrhenius model for acids and bases.

Table 16.4   The names and formulas of strong acids and strong bases.

Strong Acids		Strong Bases	
sulfuric acid*	H_2SO_4	lithium hydroxide	LiOH
nitric acid	HNO_3	sodium hydroxide	NaOH
perchloric acid	$HClO_4$	potassium hydroxide	KOH
chloric acid	$HClO_3$	rubidium hydroxide	RbOH
hydrochloric acid	HCl	cesium hydroxide	CsOH
hydrobromic acid	HBr	calcium hydroxide**	$Ca(OH)_2$
hydroiodic acid	HI	strontium hydroxide**	$Sr(OH)_2$
		barium hydroxide**	$Ba(OH)_2$

*Sulfuric acid is a diprotic acid and only the first proton ionizes completely.
**$Ca(OH)_2$, $Sr(OH)_2$, and $Ba(OH)_2$ are dibasic, which means that two moles of hydroxide ions are produced per formula unit of base that ionizes.

Neutral ions are generally the aqueous anions of strong acids and the aqueous cations of strong bases. Table 16.5 lists the common cations and anions that are neutral in aqueous solution. Generally, most of all other anions are slightly basic and most of all other cations are slightly acidic.

Common misconception: The strong diprotic acid, sulfuric acid, H_2SO_4, does not dissociate completely. Therefore, in an aqueous solution of sulfuric acid, the concentration of the H^+ ions is not double the concentration of the acid. The same is not true of strong dibasic bases such as calcium hydroxide, which ionize completely in solution. In a solution of calcium hydroxide, $Ca(OH)_2$, the concentration of the OH^- ion is double that of the calcium hydroxide.

Table 16.5   Neutral ions are the aqueous anions of strong acids and the aqueous cations of strong bases.

Neutral Aqueous Anions		Neutral Aqueous Cations	
nitrate	NO_3^-	lithium ion	Li^+
perchlorate	ClO_4^-	sodium ion	Na^+
chlorate	ClO_3^-	potassium ion	K^+
chloride	Cl^-	rubidium ion	Rb^+
bromide	Br^-	cesium ion	Cs^+
iodide	I^-	calcium ion	Ca^{2+}
sulfate*	SO_4^{2-}	strontium ion	Sr^{2+}
		barium ion	Ba^{2+}

*Sulfate ion, SO_4^{2-}, is weakly basic.

 **Common misconception:** Although aqueous calcium ion, Ca^{2+}, is the cation of a strong base and is generally considered to be neutral, it does show slightly acidic properties consistent with Lewis acid character and ion pairing.

Your Turn 16.2

Explain why aqueous solutions of each of the following salts are neutral: NaCl, KNO_3, $LiClO_4$, $BaBr_2$, CsI. Write your answer in the space provided.

Sections 16.6 and 16.7

Weak Acids and Weak Bases

Weak acids are acidic substances that only partially ionize in aqueous solution, usually about 1% or less. Weak acids are weak electrolytes. For example, hydrofluoric acid, acetic acid, and nitrous acid are all weak acids. (Each ionizes only partially to establish an equilibrium between the acid and its conjugate base.)

Table 16.6 shows the ionization of some weak acids in water. A comprehensive listing of the ionization constants of weak acids can be found in Appendix D, Table D-1 of *Chemistry: The Central Science.*

Table 16.6   Ionization of some weak acids in water.

Weak Acid Conjugate Base	Equilibrium Expression, K_a	Value of K_a
$HF(aq) + H_2O(l) \rightleftharpoons H_3O^+(aq) + F^-(aq)$	$K_a = [H_3O^+][F^-]/[HF]$	6.8×10^{-4}
$HClO(aq) + H_2O(l) \rightleftharpoons H_3O^+(aq) + ClO^-(aq)$	$K_a = [H_3O^+][ClO^-]/[HClO]$	3.0×10^{-8}
$HIO(aq) + H_2O(l) \rightleftharpoons H_3O^+(aq) + IO^-(aq)$	$K_a = [H_3O^+][IO^-]/[HIO]$	2.3×10^{-11}
$H_2CO_3(aq) + H_2O(l) \rightleftharpoons H_3O^+(aq) + HCO_3^-(aq)$	$K_{a_1} = [H_3O^+][HCO_3^-]/[H_2CO_3]$	4.3×10^{-7}
$HCO_3^-(aq) + H_2O(l) \rightleftharpoons H_3O^+(aq) + CO_3^{2-}(aq)$	$K_{a_2} = [H_3O^+][CO_3^{2-}]/[HCO_3^-]$	5.6×10^{-11}

Your Turn 16.3

a. *Examine the figure below and identify which acid, HX or HY, is the stronger acid. Justify your answer.*

b. *Is either HX or HY a strong acid? Explain your reasoning.*

c. *Make a similar sketch to show how the system might look if HCl were the acid. Explain your drawing.*

Write your answers in the space provided.

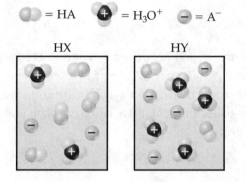

Weak bases are also weak electrolytes. Weak bases only partially ionize in solution.

Table 16.7 shows the ionization of some weak bases in water. A comprehensive listing of the ionization constants of weak bases can be found in Appendix D, Table D-2 of *Chemistry: The Central Science.*

Table 16.7   Ionization of some weak bases in water.

Weak Base	Conjugate Acid	Equilibrium Expression, K_b	Value of K_b
$NH_3(aq) + H_2O(l) \rightleftharpoons OH^-(aq) + NH_4^+(aq)$		$K_b = [OH^-][NH_4^+]/[NH_3]$	1.8×10^{-5}
$C_5H_5N(aq) + H_2O(l) \rightleftharpoons OH^-(aq) + C_5H_5NH^+(aq)$		$K_b = [OH^-][C_5H_5NH^+]/[C_5H_5N]$	1.7×10^{-9}
$HCO_3^-(aq) + H_2O(l) \rightleftharpoons OH^-(aq) + H_2CO_3(aq)$		$K_b = [OH^-][H_2CO_3]/[HCO_3^-]$	2.3×10^{-8}
$F^-(aq) + H_2O(l) \rightleftharpoons OH^-(aq) + HF(aq)$		$K_b = [OH^-][HF]/[F^-]$	1.5×10^{-11}

Weak bases tend to be **anions** other than anions of strong acids. Neutral nitrogen compounds called **amines** are also weak bases. Amines have a pair of electrons that can attract protons. Anions have negative charges that can also attract protons.

The **acid ionization constant**, K_a, is the equilibrium constant for the ionization of a weak acid in water.

The **base ionization constant**, K_b, is the ionization constant for a weak base.

Common misconception: K_a and K_b are not new ideas. The respective subscripts "a" and "b" denote that K_a is a special case of K_c used to specify the ionization of a weak acid in water and that K_b is a special case for a weak base. Also, K_a and K_b are sometimes called the acid dissociation constant and the base dissociation constant, respectively.

The value of K_a or K_b indicates the relative extent to which a weak acid or weak base ionizes. For example, the larger the K_a, the greater the extent to which the acid ionizes. When comparing two weak acids, the one with the larger K_a is said to be the "stronger" weak acid. It ionizes to a larger extent. Of the acids listed in Table 16.6, hydrofluoric acid, HF, has the largest K_a, so it ionizes to the greatest extent. HF is said to be the strongest of the weak acids listed. Similarly, of the bases listed in Table 16.7, ammonia, NH_3, has the largest K_b, so it is the strongest weak base of those listed.

Your Turn 16.4 ←——————————————————————————

Which acid listed in Table 16.6 is the weakest? Which base listed in Table 16.7 is the weakest? Justify your choices. Write your answers in the space provided.

——————————————————————————————————————

Carbonic acid, H_2CO_3, is an example of a weak diprotic acid. Table 16.6 shows two ionization constants for carbonic acid. K_{a_1} is the equilibrium constant for the ionization of the first proton. K_{a_2} represents the equilibrium constant for the ionization of the second proton. For all polyprotic acids, the first proton to ionize is always the most readily ionized. The K_a value becomes successively smaller as successive protons are removed, so $K_{a_1} > K_{a_2} > K_{a_3} \cdots$.

Each of two 50 mL solutions has a pH of 5. One contains hydrochloric acid and the other contains acetic acid. Which solution has the higher

a. *concentration of acid?*

b. *percentage ionization of acid?*

c. *amount of 0.1 M NaOH needed to neutralize the acid?*

d. *conductivity?*

Explain your answers. Write your answers in the space provided.

Relationship Between K_a and K_b Section 16.8

For any conjugate acid–base pair, $K_w = K_a \times K_b$.

Consider, for example, the reaction of carbonic acid with water:

$$H_2CO_3(aq) + H_2O(l) \rightleftharpoons H_3O^+(aq) + HCO_3^-(aq)$$
$$K_a = [H_3O^+][HCO_3^-]/[H_2CO_3] = 4.3 \times 10^{-7}$$

Hydrogen carbonate ion, HCO_3^-, is the conjugate base of the weak acid, H_2CO_3. Hydrogen carbonate ion reacts with water according to the following equation:

$$HCO_3^-(aq) + H_2O(l) \rightleftharpoons OH^-(aq) + H_2CO_3(aq)$$
$$K_b = [OH^-][H_2CO_3]/[HCO_3^-] = 2.3 \times 10^{-8}$$

K_b for any conjugate base is the ratio of K_w to K_a of the acid:

$$K_b = K_w/K_a = ([OH^-][H_3O^+])/([H_3O^+][HCO_3^-]/[H_2CO_3])$$
$$= [OH^-][H_2CO_3]/[HCO_3^-]$$
$$K_b = K_w/K_a = 1.0 \times 10^{-14}/4.3 \times 10^{-7} = 2.3 \times 10^{-8}$$

Common misconception: It is customary to tabulate only K_a or K_b for a conjugate pair because, using the relationship, $K_w = K_a \times K_b$, one can be conveniently converted to the other. Typically, only the equilibrium constants for nonionic species appear in a table. For example, the K_b for ammonia, NH_3, is reported in Appendix D of *Chemistry: The Central Science*, but not the K_a for the conjugate acid ammonium ion, NH_4^+. Similarly, the K_a for acetic acid, CH_3COOH, appears in Appendix D, but not the K_b for the conjugate base acetate ion, CH_3COO^-. It is important to be able to recognize the conjugate of any given acid or base and to know how to calculate its corresponding K_a or K_b.

Recall that water and protonated anions (HCO_3^-, HSO_3^-, $H_2PO_4^-$, etc.) tend to be amphoteric. That is, they can act as either acids or bases. To tell whether a protonated anion is acidic or basic in water, we can do one of three things: measure the pH of an aqueous solution containing the anion, use an acid–base indicator, or calculate and compare the K_a and K_b of the anion. If the K_a of the anion is larger than its corresponding K_b, the anion forms an aqueous solution that is acidic. If its K_b is larger than its K_a, the solution is basic.

Consider the triprotic acid, phosphoric acid, H_3PO_4. The sequential ionization of its three protons and the corresponding K_a values are illustrated by the equations in Table 16.8. Notice that two species involved in the equations are amphoteric protonated anions, $H_2PO_4^-$ and HPO_4^{2-}. Their reactions as bases are also illustrated in Table 16.8.

Table 16.8   The ionization of phosphoric acid.

	Acid Ionization	Acid Ionization Constant
1	$H_3PO_4(aq) + H_2O(l) \rightleftharpoons H_3O^+(aq) + H_2PO_4^-(aq)$	$K_{a_1} = 7.5 \times 10^{-3}$
2	$H_2PO_4^-(aq) + H_2O(l) \rightleftharpoons H_3O^+(aq) + HPO_4^{2-}(aq)$	$K_{a_2} = 6.2 \times 10^{-8}$
3	$HPO_4^{2-}(aq) + H_2O(l) \rightleftharpoons H_3O^+(aq) + PO_4^{3-}(aq)$	$K_{a_3} = 4.2 \times 10^{-13}$
	Base Ionization	**Base Ionization Constant**
4	$H_2PO_4^-(aq) + H_2O(l) \rightleftharpoons OH^-(aq) + H_3PO_4(aq)$	$K_b = K_w/K_{a_1}$
5	$HPO_4^{2-}(aq) + H_2O(l) \rightleftharpoons OH^-(aq) + H_2PO_4^-(aq)$	$K_b = K_w/K_{a_2}$
6	$PO_4^{3-}(aq) + H_2O(l) \rightleftharpoons OH^-(aq) + HPO_4^{2-}(aq)$	$K_b = K_w/K_{a_3}$

Example:

Is an aqueous solution of Na_2HPO_4 acidic or basic?

Solution:

First, write the reaction: $HPO_4^{2-}(aq) + H_2O(l) \rightarrow OH^-(aq) + H_2PO_4^-(aq)$

Calculate the value of K_b for HPO_4^{2-} and compare it to the value of K_{a_3} for HPO_4^{2-}. (Keep in mind that the aqueous sodium ion, $Na^+(aq)$, is neutral.) The larger ionization constant will predict the acid–base characteristic of its aqueous solution.

For Equation 5, $K_b = K_w/K_{a_2} = 1.0 \times 10^{-14}/6.2 \times 10^{-8} = 1.6 \times 10^{-7}$.

(We use K_{a_2} to calculate the K_b for Equation 5 because Equation 5 includes the same conjugate pair as Equation 2.)

$$K_a = 4.2 \times 10^{-13} < K_b = 1.6 \times 10^{-7}$$

Because its K_b is larger than its K_a, HPO_4^{2-} forms a basic solution.

The Arrhenius and Brønsted–Lowry theories are two different ways of visualizing the same concept. The different classifications lead to different insights in understanding acid–base reactions.

The Arrhenius model focuses on the ions (H^+ for acids and OH^- for bases) produced in solution. The Brønsted–Lowry model demonstrates acids and bases as proton transfer agents in chemical reactions.

Consider the reaction of ammonia with water:

$$NH_3(g) + H_2O \rightarrow NH_4^+(aq) + OH^-(aq)$$

Ammonia is clearly an Arrhenius base because it increases the hydroxide ions in solution. It is also a Brønsted–Lowry base because it accepts a proton. Table 16.9 summarizes the major points of the two acid–base theories.

Table 16.9 Comparing acid–base models with definitions and examples.

Model	Definition	Example Equation
Arrhenius acid	Increases H^+ in solution	$HCl(g) \rightarrow H^+(aq) + Cl^-(aq)$
Arrhenius base	Increases OH^- in solution	$NaOH(s) \rightarrow Na^+(aq) + OH^-(aq)$
Brønsted acid	Proton donor	$HNO_2(aq) + H_2O(l) \rightleftharpoons H_3O^+(aq) + NO_2^-(aq)$
Brønsted base	Proton acceptor	$NH_3(aq) + H_2O(l) \rightleftharpoons NH_4^+(aq) + OH^-(aq)$

Calculations Involving Strong Acids and Strong Bases

Table 16.10 shows the mathematical relationships for calculating concentrations of ions in strong and weak acid and base solutions. Although these relationships are useful, understand that they are simply mathematical models for the chemistry that takes place in solutions.

Table 16.10 Mathematical relationships for calculating $[H^+]$ and $[OH^-]$ in strong and weak acid and base solutions.

	Acid	Base
Strong	$x = I$	$y = I$ (monobasic)
		$y = 2 \times I$ (dibasic)
Weak	$K_a = x^2/I$ if $I > 100\,K_a$ $K_a \times K_b = K_w = 1 \times 10^{-14}$	$K_b = y^2/I$ if $I > 100\,K_b$

I = initial molar concentration of acid or base
x = the moles per liter of acid that ionizes
y = the moles per liter of base that ionizes

Common misconception: The most difficult part of performing calculations involving strong and weak acids and bases is recognizing the chemistry. Does the problem involve an acid or a base? Is the acid or base strong or weak? If you can first answer these questions based on the chemistry, then the calculations are less complicated.

Strong acids ionize completely. Therefore, no equilibrium is established because all the initial concentration of the reactant acid is converted to products. For all strong acids, the ICE tables are the same. For example, the ICE table for the ionization of 0.20 M nitric acid is:

$$HNO_3(aq) \rightarrow H^+(aq) + NO_3^-(aq)$$

I	0.20	0	0
C	−0.20	+0.20	+0.20
E	0	0.20	0.20

All the strong acid ionizes, so the initial concentration of the acid is the same as the final concentration of H^+ ion or $x = I$.

Example:

Calculate the $[H^+]$ and pH in a solution of 0.015 M nitric acid, HNO_3.

Solution:

$I = x$
$[HNO_3] = [H^+] = 0.015\,M$
$pH = -log\,(0.015) = 1.82$

By similar reasoning, the $[OH^-]$ of a strong base solution is the same as the concentration of a monobasic strong base and double the concentration of a dibasic strong base.

$I = y$ for monobasic and

$I = 2y$ for dibasic, where $y =$ the moles per liter of base that ionize

Example:

Calculate the $[OH^-]$ and the pH in a 0.025 M KOH solution and the $[OH^-]$ and the pH in a 0.025 M Ba(OH)$_2$ solution.

Solution:

For the KOH solution,
$[KOH] = [OH^-] = 0.025\ M$
$pOH = -log(0.025) = 1.60$
$pH = 14 - pOH = 14 - 1.60 = 12.40$

For the Ba(OH)$_2$ solution,
$[OH^-] = 2 \times [Ba(OH)_2] = 2 \times 0.025\ M = 0.050\ M$
$pOH = -log\ (0.050) = 1.30$
$pH = 14 - pOH = 14 - 1.30 = 12.70$

Calculations Involving Weak Acids

The ionization of a weak acid in water is a reversible equilibrium, and each weak acid ionization produces the same ICE table.

Example:

Calculate the pH of a 0.15 M solution of acetic acid, CH$_3$COOH.

Solution:

First, set up an ICE table for the ionization of an initial concentration of acetic acid, CH$_3$COOH. Let x equal the number of moles per liter of weak acid that ionizes.

$$CH_3COOH(aq) + H_2O(l) \rightleftharpoons H_3O^+(aq) + CH_3COO^-(aq)$$
$K_a = 1.8 \times 10^{-5}$

I	I	0	0
C	$-x$	$+x$	$+x$
E	$I-x$	x	x

$$K_a = [H_3O^+][CH_3COO^-]/[CH_3COOH] = (x)(x)/(I-x)$$

In general, if $I > 100\ K_a$, then the assumption $I - x = I$ is a good approximation. Most weak acids have a K_a that is less than 10^{-3}, so I is usually greater than $100\ K_a$.

The equation used for calculations involving the ionization of weak acids simplifies to:

$$K_a = x^2/I$$

where K_a is the ionization constant for the weak acid, x is the number of moles per liter of weak acid that ionizes, and I is the initial molar concentration of weak acid.

$$K_a = x^2/I$$

$$1.8 \times 10^{-5} = x^2/0.15$$

$$x = [H^+] = 1.6 \times 10^{-3} M$$

$$pH = -log[H^+] = -log(1.6 \times 10^{-3}) = 2.78$$

Calculations Involving Weak Bases

Like weak acids, all weak bases have the same ICE table. Even better, the ICE table for weak bases is the same as that for weak acids, except that base ionization produces hydroxide ion rather than hydrogen ion.

Example:

Calculate the pH of a 0.75 M solution of aqueous ammonia.

Solution:

Set up an ICE table for the reaction of ammonia with water.

$$NH_3(aq) + H_2O(l) \rightleftharpoons NH_4^+(aq) + OH^-(aq) \quad K_b = 1.8 \times 10^{-5}$$

I	I	0	0
C	$-y$	$+y$	$+y$
E	$I-y$	y	y

For clarity, "y" is used instead of "x" to represent the number of moles per liter of base that ionizes.

$$K_b = [OH^-][NH_4^+]/[NH_3] = (y)(y)/(I-y)$$

If $I > 100\, K_b$, then y is very small compared to I, so the generic equation for calculations involving weak base ionizations is:

$$K_b = y^2/I$$

where K_b is the ionization constant for the weak base, y is the number of moles per liter of weak base that ionizes, and I is the initial molar concentration of weak base.

$$K_b = y^2/I$$

$$1.8 \times 10^{-5} = y^2/0.75$$

$$y = [OH^-] = 3.7 \times 10^{-3} M$$

$$pOH = -log[OH^-] = -log(3.7 \times 10^{-3}) = 2.43$$

$$pH = 14 - pOH = 14 - 2.43 = 11.57$$

Your Turn 16.6

Classify the following 0.10 M solutions as strong or weak acids or bases: hydro-chloric acid, ammonium chloride, calcium hydroxide, ethylamine, and sodium cyanide. Estimate the approximate pH for each solution. Justify your answers. Write your answers in the space provided.

Once the identity of a strong or weak acid or base solution is established, the calculations fall into a predictable pattern.

Example:

Measurements show that the pH of a 0.10 M solution of acetic acid is 2.87. Calculate K_b for potassium acetate, CH_3COOK.

Solution:

The question provides information for a solution of a weak acid but asks for the K_b of its conjugate weak base. First, calculate K_a for the weak acid and then convert it to K_b for the conjugate base.

$$CH_3COOH(aq) + H_2O(l) \rightleftharpoons H_3O^+(aq) + CH_3COO^-(aq)$$

$$K_a = x^2/I$$

If the pH is 2.87, the $[H^+] = 10^{-2.87} = 1.3 \times 10^{-3} M$.

$$[H^+] = [CH_3COO^-] = x = 1.3 \times 10^{-3} M$$

Substituting:

$$K_a = x^2/(0.10 - x)$$
$$K_a = (1.3 \times 10^{-3})(1.3 \times 10^{-3})/(0.10 - 1.3 \times 10^{-3} M)$$
$$K_a = 1.7 \times 10^{-5}$$
$$K_b = K_w/K_a = 1.0 \times 10^{-14}/1.7 \times 10^{-5} = 5.9 \times 10^{-10}$$

Acid–Base Properties of Salt Solutions   Section 16.9

Hydrolysis of salts refers to the reactions of salt ions with water. Recall that, except for the anions of strong acids, anions tend to be weak bases. Their negative charges tend to attract protons from water. Similarly, except for the cations of strong bases, cations are weakly acidic, either by attracting a pair of electrons from water, as with Lewis acids, or by donating an available proton to water.

To classify a salt solution as acidic, basic, or neutral, disregard any neutral cations or anions listed in Table 16.2. If what is left is an anion, the salt is basic. If a cation remains, the salt is acidic. If both the cation and anion are listed in Table 16.2, the salt is neutral. If neither the cation nor anion is neutral, the acid or base character of the salt cannot be determined by examining its formula.

Example:

Classify the salt, sodium nitrite, $NaNO_2$, as acid, base, or neutral. Explain your reasoning. Write a chemical equation for its reaction with water.

Solution:

Sodium nitrite is a base. The sodium ion is a cation of a strong base, so it is neutral. Nitrite is the conjugate base of the weak acid, nitrous acid, HNO_2. A solution of sodium nitrite in water will be basic because of the hydrolysis reaction of the nitrite ion with water. (We ignore the sodium ion because it is neutral.) The K_b of the nitrite ion can be calculated from the K_a of nitrous acid.

$$NO_2^-(aq) + H_2O(l) \rightleftharpoons HNO_2(aq) + OH^-(aq)$$

Example:

Classify an aqueous solution of methylammonium chloride, CH_3NH_3Cl, as acidic, basic, or neutral. Explain your reasoning. Write an equation to illustrate your answer.

Solution:

Methylammonium chloride is acidic because the chloride ion is neutral and the methylammonium ion is the conjugate weak acid of the base, methylamine, CH_3NH_2. The K_a of methylammonium ion can be calculated from the K_b of methylamine.

$$CH_3NH_3^+(aq) + H_2O(l) \rightleftharpoons CH_3NH_2(aq) + H_3O^+(aq)$$

Section 16.10   **Acid–Base Behavior and Chemical Structure**

Acidity of a substance is directly related to the strength of attraction for a pair of electrons to a central atom. Generally, acidity increases with stronger attractions for electrons.

Three factors affect attraction for electrons:

1. **Ionic charge:** When comparing similar ions, the more positive ions are stronger acids. (The more negative ions are more strongly basic.) For example:

Relative acid strengths: $Na^+ < Ca^{2+} < Cu^{2+} < Al^{3+}$

Metal cations of higher charge act as Lewis acids in water. The higher the charge, the greater the attraction for electrons and the stronger the acid. If the charges are equal, the smaller ion displays the stronger attraction for electrons.

Relative acid strengths: $PO_4^{3-} < HPO_4^{2-} < H_2PO_4^- < H_3PO_4$

Note that, in this example, PO_4^{3-} is clearly a base because it has a negative charge, and H_3PO_4 is clearly an oxyacid. However, HPO_4^{2-} and $H_2PO_4^-$ are recognized as amphoteric, because they are protonated anions. The ionic charge generalization cannot predict whether a substance will be an acid (more acidic than water) or a base (less acidic than water) relative to water. It can predict only the acidity of substances relative to each other.

2. **Oxidation number:** When comparing similar formulas with the same central atom, the greater the oxidation number of the central atom, the stronger the acid. A greater number of electronegative oxygen atoms withdraws more electrons from the O—H bond, making the bond weaker. For example:

Relative strengths: $HClO < HClO_2 < HClO_3 < HClO_4$

Relative strengths: $H_2SO_3 < H_2SO_4$

3. **Electronegativity:** When comparing similar formulas with different central atoms, generally, the greater the electronegativity of the central atom, the stronger the acid.

Relative strengths: $H_3BO_3 < H_2CO_3 < H_2SO_3 < HNO_3$

(Recall that the electronegativity of elements generally increases from the lower left to the upper right of the periodic table.)

Some Common Acid–Base Reactions

Strong bases also include oxides of Groups 1 and 2 such as Li_2O, MgO, and CaO. These "base anhydrides" react with water to give hydroxides:

$$Li_2O(s) + H_2O(l) \rightarrow 2\,Li^+(aq) + 2OH^-(aq)$$
$$CaO(s) + H_2O(l) \rightarrow Ca^{2+}(aq) + 2OH^-(aq)$$

Similarly, nonmetal oxides, called acid anhydrides, give solutions of acids in water.

$$SO_2(g) + H_2O(l) \rightleftharpoons H_2SO_3(aq)$$

$$SO_3(g) + H_2O(l) \rightarrow H^+(aq) + HSO_4^-(aq)$$

$$CO_2(g) + H_2O(l) \rightleftharpoons H_2CO_3(aq)$$

$$Cl_2O(g) + H_2O(l) \rightleftharpoons 2HClO(aq)$$

$$Cl_2O_7(g) + H_2O(l) \rightarrow 2H^+(aq) + 2ClO_4^-(aq)$$

$$P_2O_5(s) + 3H_2O(l) \rightleftharpoons 2H_3PO_4(aq)$$

Notice that the nonmetal tends to retain its oxidation number when going from the oxide to the acid. One notable exception is the reaction of nitrogen dioxide with water to form nitric acid and nitrous acid.

$$2NO_2(g) + H_2O(l) \rightarrow H^+(aq) + NO_3^-(aq) + HNO_2(aq)$$

Notice that in all the equations, whenever a strong acid is formed, it is written in its ionized form to reflect its strong electrolytic character.

Multiple Choice Questions

Questions 1–5 refer to the following 0.2 M solutions: NaCl, NaHSO$_4$, NaHCO$_3$, Na$_2$CO$_3$, NH$_4$Cl.

1. Which solution will have the lowest $[OH^-]$?

    A) Na$_2$CO$_3$

    B) NaHCO$_3$

    C) NaCl

    D) NaHSO$_4$

2. Which solution will be the strongest base?

    A) Na$_2$CO$_3$

    B) NaHCO$_3$

    C) NaCl

    D) NH$_4$Cl

3. Which aqueous solutions are acidic?

    A) Na$_2$CO$_3$ and NaHCO$_3$

    B) NaCl and NH$_4$Cl

    C) NaHSO$_4$ and NH$_4$Cl

    D) NaHSO$_4$ and NaHCO$_3$

4. What is the order of increasing pH (lowest pH first) of the solutions?

    A) Na$_2$CO$_3$ < NaHCO$_3$ < NaCl < NH$_4$Cl

    B) NaCl < Na$_2$CO$_3$ < NaHCO$_3$ < NH$_4$Cl

    C) NH$_4$Cl < NaHCO$_3$ < NaCl < Na$_2$CO$_3$

    D) NH$_4$Cl < NaCl < NaHCO$_3$ < Na$_2$CO$_3$

5. Which solution will have the highest concentration of Na$^+$ ions?

    A) Na$_2$CO$_3$

    B) NaHCO$_3$

    C) NaCl

    D) NaHSO$_4$

6. According to the Brønsted–Lowry definition, an acid is a substance that

    A) increases the hydrogen ion concentration in water.

    B) can react with water to form H$^+$ ions.

    C) can accept an electron pair to form a covalent bond.

    D) can donate a proton to a base.

7. Which pair of chemical species is NOT a conjugate acid–base pair?

A) H_2CO_3 and CO_3^{2-}

B) OH^- and H_2O

C) HPO_4^{2-} and PO_4^{3-}

D) CH_3NH_2 and CH_3NH^-

8. When equal molar amounts of these oxides are each mixed in the same volume of water, which forms a solution with the lowest pH?

A) CaO

B) CO_2

C) SO_2

D) SO_3

9. Aqueous solutions of equal molar concentrations of these salts are listed in order of increasing pH.
$NaBr < NaIO_3 < NaF < NaC_2H_3O_2 < Na_2SO_3$

Which acid is the weakest?

A) HBr

B) HIO_3

C) HF

D) $NaHSO_3$

10. The net ionic equation for the addition of 10.0 mL of 0.10 M sulfurous acid to 10.0 mL of 0.10 M aqueous sodium hydroxide is

A) $H_2SO_3 + 2OH^- \rightleftharpoons 2H_2O + SO_3^{2-}$

B) $H_2SO_4 + OH^- \rightleftharpoons H_2O + HSO_4^-$

C) $H_2SO_3 + OH^- \rightleftharpoons H_2O + HSO_3^-$

D) $H^+ + OH^- \rightleftharpoons H_2O$

11. Identify the acid anhydride of chlorous acid, $HClO_2$.

A) Cl_2O

B) ClO

C) ClO_2

D) Cl_2O_3

12. The acid dissociation constants for the diprotic acid, malonic acid, $H_2C_3H_2O_4$, are $K_{a_1} = 1.5 \times 10^{-3}$ and $K_{a_2} = 2.0 \times 10^{-6}$.

Which of the following represents the K_b for $HC_3H_2O_4^-$?

A) $K_w \times K_{a_1}$

B) $K_w \times K_{a_2}$

C) K_w / K_{a_1}

D) K_w / K_{a_2}

13. Percentage ionization is defined as the number of moles of weak acid that ionizes expressed as a percentage of the original concentration: % ionization $= (x/I)(100)$. Calculate the percentage ionization of a 0.10 M solution of hydrazoic acid, HN_3. $K_a = 1.9 \times 10^{-5}$.

A) 1.9×10^{-3}

B) 1.9

C) 0.19

D) 1.4

14. Each of the following is amphoteric except

A) HSO_3^-

B) HPO_4^{2-}

C) NH_4^+

D) H_2O

15. Which oxide dissolves in water to give the strongest acid?

A) SO_3

B) CaO

C) P_4O_{10}

D) CO_2

Free Response Questions

1. Sulfurous acid, H_2SO_3, is a diprotic acid. $K_{a_1} = 1.7 \times 10^{-2}$; $K_{a_2} = 6.4 \times 10^{-8}$

   a. Write an ionic equation for the aqueous ionization that corresponds to K_{a_1}.

   Write an ionic equation for the aqueous ionization that corresponds to K_{a_2}.

   Identify the conjugate acid–base pairs in each of your two equations.

   b. Identify any amphoteric species, other than water, in your equations.

   c. Assume the amphoteric species you identified in Part b is a base. Write an ionic equation for its aqueous ionization and calculate the corresponding K_b.

   d. Is an aqueous solution of $NaHSO_3$ acidic or basic? Explain your reasoning.

   e. Calculate the pH of a 0.50 M solution of Na_2SO_3.

2. *It is found that 0.30 M solutions of the three salts Na$_3$X, Na$_2$Y, and NaZ have pH values of 8.5, 7.0, and 10.5, not necessarily in order. (X, Y, and Z are anions. Na is sodium ion.)*

   a. *Explain how anions can act as bases in aqueous solution. Write a chemical equation to explain your answer.*

   b. *Which pH most likely goes with which salt? Explain.*

   c. *What is the approximate pH of a 0.010 M solution of HZ? Explain your reasoning.*

   d. *Calculate the acid dissociation constants, K$_a$, for each of the acids, HX^{2-}, HY$^-$, and HZ, and rank them in order of increasing strength, the weakest first. Justify your reasoning.*

3. *Two solutions, one a strong acid and one a weak acid, each have a pH of 4.0.*

   a. *When solution A is mixed with an equal volume of 0.50 M sodium carbonate solution, significant effervescence is observed. When the experiment is repeated with solution B, only slight bubbling is observed. Identify which solution is the strong acid and which is the weak acid. Justify your answer comparing the concentrations and percentage ionization of the two solutions.*

   b. *Compare the amounts of sodium hydroxide that would be required to neutralize each solution. Explain your answer.*

   c. *Draw particle representations of the neutralizations of the weak acid and of the strong acid with sodium hydroxide. Explain the differences.*

Multiple Choice Answers and Explanations

1. *D. Sulfate ion is a neutral ion of the strong acid, sulfuric acid. Sodium hydrogen sulfate contains the second ionizable proton of sulfuric acid, so it is also relatively strong.*

2. *A. Carbonate ion has a 2– charge, the greatest negative-charged anion represented. It will have the greatest tendency to attract a positive proton.*

3. *C. Sodium ion and chloride ion are both neutral species in solution. Hydrogen sulfate ion and ammonium ion are both acids in solution.*

4. *D. A lower pH implies a stronger acid. In general, cations (except for the cations of strong bases) tend to be acidic and anions (except for the anions of strong acids) tend to be basic. The more positive the charge, the more acidic the cation, and the more negative the charge, the more basic the anion. Sodium ion is the neutral ion of the strong base, NaOH, and chloride ion is the neutral ion of the strong acid, HCl, so sodium chloride is neutral. Ammonium ion is slightly acidic, and hydrogen carbonate is the ion found in baking soda. Carbonate ion, because of its 2– charge, is a stronger base than is hydrogen carbonate.*

5. *A. All are strong electrolytes, but sodium carbonate provides two moles of sodium ion per mole. The others provide only one each.*

6. D. A Brønsted–Lowry acid is a proton donor. An Arrhenius acid increases $[H^+]$ when dissolved in water.

7. A. An acid–base conjugate pair consists of two chemical species that differ in formula by an H^+. The species of the pair with the more positive charge (and hence the extra H) is the acid.

8. D. A lower pH implies a stronger acid. Nonmetal oxides tend to be acidic (acid anhydrides) while metal oxides tend to be basic (base anhydrides). When comparing oxides having different central atoms, the more electronegative atom forms the strongest acid. Sulfur is the most electronegative atom represented. When comparing oxides having the same central atom, the one with the greater number of oxygen atoms is more acidic.

9. D. A higher pH implies a stronger base. The strongest base, Na_2SO_3, has the weakest conjugate acid, $NaHSO_3$. The sodium ions are neutral because Na^+ is the cation of the strong base, NaOH.

10. C. Sulfurous acid, H_2SO_3, is a weak acid and should not be confused with sulfuric acid, H_2SO_4, a strong acid. Sodium hydroxide is a strong electrolyte, so the sodium ion is a spectator ion. Only one millimole each of the acid and base is present, so only one of the two ionizable protons on sulfurous acid will react.

11. D. The oxidation number of chlorine in $HClO_2$ is $+3$. The acid anhydride of an acid is generally the nonmetal oxide with the same oxidation number of the nonmetal.

12. C. The chemical reactions are:

1. $H_2C_3H_2O_4 + H_2O \rightleftharpoons HC_3H_2O_4^- + H_3O^+$

   $K_{a_1} = [HC_3H_2O_4^-][H_3O^+]/[H_2C_3H_2O_4]$

2. $HC_3H_2O_4^- + H_2O \rightleftharpoons C_3H_2O_4^{2-} + H_3O^+$

   $K_{a_2} = [C_3H_2O_4^{2-}][H_3O^+]/[HC_3H_2O_4^-]$

3. $HC_3H_2O_4^- + H_2O \rightleftharpoons H_2C_3H_2O_4 + OH^-$

   $K_b = [H_2C_3H_2O_4][OH^-]/[HC_3H_2O_4^-]$

4. $H_2O + H_2O \rightleftharpoons H_3O^+ + OH^-$

   $k_w = [H_3O^+][OH^-]$

The relationship between K_a and K_b is $K_b = K_w/K_a$. Which K_a is the correct one to use in this case?

Substituting $K_b = K_w/K_{a_1}$, we get the correct solution:

$[H_2C_3H_2O_4][OH^-]/[HC_3H_2O_4^-] = \cancel{[H_3O^+]}[OH^-]/$

$([HC_3H_2O_4^-]\cancel{[H_3O^+]}/[H_2C_3H_2O_4])$

Alternatively, Reaction 3 includes the same conjugate pair as Reaction 1, so $K_b = K_w/K_{a_1}$ is correct.

13. D. $K_a = x^2/I$ and % ionization $= (x/I)(100)$, where x is the moles per liter ionized and I is the initial concentration.

$1.9 \times 10^{-5} = x^2/0.10$

$x = 1.4 \times 10^{-3}$

% ionization $= (1.4 \times 10^{-3}/0.10)(100) = 1.4$

14. C. Generally, protonated anions and water are amphoteric. Amphoteric substances can both donate and accept a proton. Protonated anions have protons to donate and negative charges that will attract them. NH_4^+ can donate a proton, but because like charges repel, it's unlikely to accept a positively charged proton.

15. A. Nonmetal oxides react with water to yield acids. The nonmetal usually retains its oxidation number as it changes from oxide to oxyacid. Sulfur trioxide in water yields the strong acid, sulfuric acid.

$$SO_3(g) + H_2O(l) \longrightarrow H^+(aq) + HSO_4^-(aq)$$

Free Response Answers

1. a. $H_2SO_3(aq) + H_2O(l) \rightleftharpoons H_3O^+(aq) + HSO_3^-(aq)$
       acid   base   acid   base

   $HSO_3^-(aq) + H_2O(l) \rightleftharpoons H_3O^+(aq) + SO_3^{2-}(aq)$
       acid   base   acid   base

   b. $HSO_3^-(aq)$

   c. $HSO_3^-(aq) + H_2O(l) \rightleftharpoons OH^-(aq) + H_2SO_3(aq)$

   $K_b = K_w/K_{a_1} = 1.0 \times 10^{-14}/1.7 \times 10^{-2} = 5.9 \times 10^{-13}$

   d. $HSO_3^-(aq)$ forms an acidic solution because its K_a is much greater than its K_b.

   $K_{a_2} = 6.4 \times 10^{-8} > K_b = 5.9 \times 10^{-13}$

   e. $K_b = K_w/K_{a_2} = 1.00 \times 10^{-14}/6.4 \times 10^{-8} = 1.56 \times 10^{-7}$

   $K_b = y^2/I$

   $1.56 \times 10^{-7} = y^2/0.50$

   $y = 2.8 \times 10^{-4} = [OH^-]$

   $pOH = -\log[OH^-] = -\log(2.8 \times 10^{-4}) = 3.55$

   $pH = 14.00 - pOH = 14.00 - 3.55 = 10.45$

2. a. Most anions, except those of strong acids, act as weak bases because their negative charges attract protons from water molecules, leaving hydroxide ions in solution.

   $X^{3-} + H_2O \rightarrow HX^{2-} + OH^-$

b. $Na_3X = pH\ 10.5;\ Na_2Y = pH\ 8.5;\ and\ NaZ = pH\ 7.0.$
   Generally, the anion with the most negative charge will be the most basic because it has the greatest tendency to attract a proton from a water molecule.

c. *Because HZ has a neutral anion, it is most likely a strong acid that ionizes completely in water:*

$$HZ \rightarrow H^+ + Z^-$$

A 0.01 M solution of HZ will produce a 0.01 M solution of H^+.
$pH = -\log[H^+] = -\log(0.01) = 2.0.$

d. *For HZ, K_a is undefined because it is a strong acid.*

For HX^{2-},

$K_a = K_w/K_b$, *where K_b is the base dissociation constant for*
$X^{3-} + H_2O \rightarrow HX^{2-} + OH^-$

$K_b = [HX^{2-}][OH^-]/[X^{3-}]\ pH = 10.5,\ so\ pOH = 14.0 - 10.5 = 3.5$

$[HX^{2-}] = [OH^-] = 10^{-pH} = 10^{-3.5}$

$K_b = (10^{-3.5})(10^{-3.5})/0.30 = 3.3 \times 10^{-7}$

$K_a = 1.0 \times 10^{-14}/3.3 \times 10^{-7} = 3.0 \times 10^{-8}$

For HY^-,

$K_a = K_w/K_b$, *where K_b is the base dissociation constant for*
$Y^{2-} + H_2O \rightarrow HY^- + OH^-$

$K_b = [HY^-][OH^-]/[Y^{2-}]\ pH = 8.5,\ so\ pOH = 14.0 - 8.5 = 5.5$

$[HY^-] = [OH^-] = 10^{-pH} = 10^{-5.5}$

$K_b = (10^{-5.5})(10^{-5.5})/0.30 = 3.3 \times 10^{-11}$

$K_a = 1.0 \times 10^{-14}/3.3 \times 10^{-11} = 3.0 \times 10^{-4}$

Order of acid strength: $HX^{2-} < HY^- < HZ$

The larger the value of K_a, the stronger the acid.

3. a. *Solution A is a weak acid and solution B is a strong acid. A weak acid solution of pH 4 will be much more concentrated and, therefore, much more reactive toward sodium carbonate. The weak acid might be approximately the same concentration as the sodium carbonate, whereas the strong acid will have a concentration of only about 0.0001 M. The weak acid, while much more concentrated, ionizes only 1% or less. The strong acid ionizes 100%, but its concentration is so low that there is little acid available to react with the sodium carbonate.*

b. *The weak acid will require much more sodium hydroxide than the strong acid to neutralize it because the weak acid is much more concentrated.*

c. Weak acid:

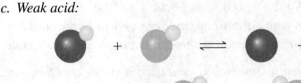

Very few weak acid molecules ionize in solution. Therefore, the particle representation shows the undissociated weak acid molecule as a reactant and the weak acid anion as a product. In contrast, the strong acid is completely ionized in solution, so its anion is a spectator ion and is not shown in the particle representation.

Your Turn Answers

16.1. a. *Because K_w at 0 °C is less than K_w at 25 °C, the autoionization of water is endothermic. If heat is a "reactant" in the thermochemical equation, a decrease in temperature will drive the reaction to the left, decreasing the equilibrium constant.*

$$Heat + H_2O(l) + H_2O(l) \rightleftharpoons OH^-(aq) + H_3O^+(aq)$$

b. $K_w = [OH^-][H_3O^+] = 1.2 \times 10^{-15}$ *at* $0°C$
   $[OH^-] = [H_3O^+]$ *in pure water*
   $1.2 \times 10^{-15} = [H_3O^+]^2$
   $[H_3O^+]^2 = 1.2 \times 10^{-15}$ *or* $[H_3O^+] = (1.2 \times 10^{-15})^{1/2} = 3.5 \times 10^{-7}$
   $pH = -\log(3.5 \times 10^{-7}) = 7.46$

c. *The pH of water at 37 °C will be less than 7 because at higher temperatures, K_w increases, so both $[H_3O^+]$ and $[OH^-]$ increase.*

16.2. *Aqueous solutions of the salts $NaCl$, KNO_3, $LiClO_4$, $BaBr_2$, and CsI are neutral because they contain neutral cations and neutral anions. The cations are all cations of strong bases, and the anions are all anions of strong acids.*

16.3. a. *HY is stronger than HX as evidenced by the fact that four of the six molecules of HY have ionized, whereas only two of the six HX molecules have ionized. The greater the ionization, the stronger the acid.*

b. *Neither HX nor HY is a strong acid because, in each case, some of the unionized acid remains in solution. Strong acids ionize 100%, meaning that no unionized acid is left.*

c.

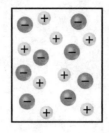

The sketch depicts the reaction: $HCl(g) \rightarrow H^+(aq) + Cl^-(aq)$, where all the HCl molecule have ionized. (Alternatively, H_3O^+ ions can be shown instead of H^+ ions.)

16.4. Of the acids listed in Table 16.6, HIO is the weakest because it has the smallest K_a value. In Table 16.7, fluoride ion is the weakest base listed because it has the smallest value of K_b.

16.5. a. Acetic acid, a weak acid, requires a greater concentration of acid to achieve the same pH as the strong acid, HCl, because weak acids ionize only about 1% or less, whereas strong acids ionize 100%.

b. Acetic acid ionizes less than 1%. HCl ionizes 100%.

c. Because acetic acid is more concentrated, an equal volume requires more base to neutralize all the acid present.

d. Both solutions will have equal conductivity because the ion concentrations are equal. Although HCl ionizes completely and acetic acid ionizes only about 1%, the same pH requires the hydrogen ion concentrations to be equal so the chloride and acetate ion concentrations are also equal.

16.6. Hydrochloric acid is listed in Table 16.4 as a strong acid and its pH is about 1. Chloride is listed as a neutral ion in Table 16.5.

Ammonium ion, NH_4^+, is the conjugate acid of the weak base ammonia, NH_3, so its pH is about 5, less than 7 but more than 1.

Calcium hydroxide is listed in Table 16.4 as a dibasic strong base. Its pH would be very high, perhaps 12–13.

Ethylamine is a neutral nitrogen compound and a weak base, so its pH is higher than 7, perhaps about 9.

Cyanide ion, CN^-, is the weak conjugate base of hydrocyanic acid, HCN, so its pH is greater than 7, perhaps about 9. Sodium ion is listed in Table 16.5 as a neutral ion.

ADDITIONAL ASPECTS OF AQUEOUS EQUILIBRIA

The content in this topic is the basis for mastering Learning Objectives 6.13 and 6.17–6.23 as found in the Curriculum Framework.

When you finish reviewing this topic, be sure you are able to:

- Given a mixture of strong and weak acids and bases, predict the reaction that will occur, write a net ionic equation, and identify what chemical species will be present at equilibrium
- Calculate the pH of a buffer, given the concentrations of its components
- Calculate the concentrations needed to obtain a desired pH and buffer capacity
- Tell whether the conjugate acid or the conjugate base will predominate in solution at a given pH, given the pK_a of an acid
- Identify a buffer from its components or its behavior in solution
- Explain how a buffer works to resist a change in pH
- Interpret weak acid–strong base titration data to determine the equivalence point, the pH at the equivalence point, the concentration of the weak acid, and the pK_a of the weak acid
- Predict and rank the solubilities of various salts, given their solubility product constants
- Explain and justify the factors that influence the solubility of salts

Understanding the reactions of acids with bases is central to mastering many of the qualitative and quantitative ideas in this topic. Consider the reactions of equal molar amounts of the following acids and bases. Notice that in all cases both strong acids and strong bases react completely.

1. A **strong acid** reacts completely with a **strong base** to yield a neutral solution.

   Complete equation: $HCl(aq) + NaOH(aq) \rightarrow H_2O(l) + NaCl(aq)$

   Net ionic equation: $H^+(aq) + OH^-(aq) \rightleftharpoons H_2O(l)$

   The **solution is neutral** because both the sodium and chloride ions are neutral ions.

2. A **strong acid** reacts completely with a **weak base** to yield a weak acid.

   Complete equation:

   $HCl(aq) + CH_3COONa(aq) \rightleftharpoons NaCl(aq) + CH_3COOH(aq)$

   Net ionic equation: $H^+(aq) + CH_3COO^-(aq) \rightleftharpoons CH_3COOH(aq)$

   The **solution is weakly acidic** because a weak acid is a product of the reaction.

   Various sources use two different forms of the chemical formula for acetic acid: CH_3COOH and $HC_2H_3O_2$. Similarly, you may see the formula for acetate ion written as CH_3COO^- or $C_2H_3O_2^-$.

3. A **strong base** reacts completely with a **weak acid** to yield a weak base.

   Complete equation:

   $NaOH(aq) + CH_3COOH(aq) \rightleftharpoons CH_3COONa(aq) + H_2O(l)$

   Net ionic equation:

   $OH^-(aq) + CH_3COOH(aq) \rightleftharpoons CH_3COO^-(aq) + H_2O(l)$

   The **solution is weakly basic** because a weak base is a product of the reaction.

4. A **weak acid** does not react appreciably with a conjugate **weak base**.

   $CH_3COOH(aq) + CH_3COO^-(aq) \rightleftharpoons CH_3COO^-(aq)$
   $+ CH_3COOH(aq)$ (no net reaction)

   The **solution is a buffer** (described below) because a weak base exists simultaneously with a weak acid, both in significant concentrations.

The Common-Ion Effect   Section 17.1

The **common-ion effect** decreases the ionization of a weak electrolyte when a common ion is added to the solution.

Consider the ionization of 1 L of 0.2 M acetic acid in water. The acetic acid ionizes about 1%, so there is very little weak base present.

$$CH_3COOH(aq) + H_2O(l) \rightleftharpoons CH_3COO^-(aq) + H_3O^+(aq)$$
$$\sim 99\% \qquad\qquad \sim 1\% \qquad \sim 1\%$$

Now add 0.2 mol of sodium acetate, CH_3COONa, to this solution to increase the concentration of acetate ion, $CH_3COO^-(aq)$.

$$CH_3COOH(aq) + H_2O(l) \rightleftharpoons CH_3COO^-(aq) + H_3O^+(aq)$$
$$\sim 100\% \qquad\qquad \sim 100\% \qquad \sim 0.001\%$$

The equilibrium shifts to the left according to Le Châtelier's principle, decreasing the ionization of acetic acid. The resulting solution is a **buffered solution** containing significant amounts of both a weak acid and a conjugate weak base.

Your Turn 17.1

Write net ionic equations for the reactions of equal volumes of the following 0.1 M pairs of solutions. In each case, tell which reactions go almost to completion and which species will be present in large concentrations at equilibrium. Write your answers in the space provided.

    a.   ammonia + nitric acid

    b.   potassium hydroxide + hydrochloric acid

    c.   acetic acid + sodium hydroxide

    d.   phosphoric acid + potassium hydroxide

    e.   ammonium chloride + ammonia

Section 17.2   Buffered Solutions

A **buffered solution** is a solution that resists appreciable changes in pH upon addition of small amounts of strong acid or base. A mixture of a weak acid and its conjugate base, both existing in significant quantities in the same solution, constitutes an effective buffer.

Figure 17.1 is a schematic that shows the buffer action of a solution made from equal moles of hydrofluoric acid and sodium fluoride. The solution's resistance to pH change arises because the hydrofluoric acid can react with and neutralize small quantities of strong base, and the fluoride ion can react with small quantities of strong acid.

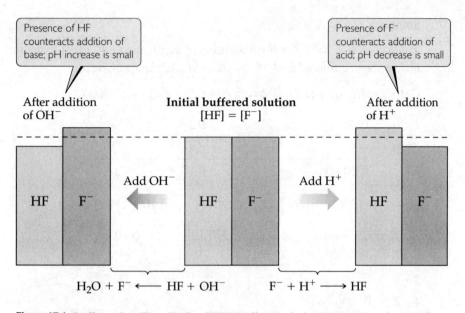

Figure 17.1 Buffer action. The pH of an HF/F⁻ buffered solution changes by only a small amount in response to addition of an acid or a base.

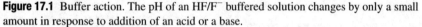

Your Turn 17.2

When equal volumes of the following solutions are mixed, which would act as an effective buffer? Explain what a buffer is and why the pH of a buffer solution does not change appreciably when a small amount of acid or base is added to the buffer. Write net ionic equations to support your claim.

0.10 *M CH₃COOH* + 0.10 *M HCl*

0.10 *M CH₃COONa* + 0.10 *M NaOH*

0.10 *M CH₃COOH* + 0.10 *M CH₃COONa*

Write your answers in the space provided.

Calculating the pH of a Buffer

The pH of a buffered solution is calculated just like the pH of a weak acid solution.

Example:

What is the pH of an aqueous mixture containing 0.20 M acetic acid and 0.10 M sodium acetate?

Solution:

Employ an ICE table for the ionization of acetic acid and include the initial concentrations of both the weak acid and the weak base:

$$CH_3COOH(aq) + H_2O(l) \rightleftharpoons CH_3COO^-(aq) + H^+(aq)$$

I	0.20	0.10	0
C	−x	+x	+x
E	0.20−x	0.10+x	x

$K_a = [CH_3COO^-][H^+]/[CH_3COOH] = (0.10+x)\,(x)/(0.20-x)$

If x is small compared to 0.10, then $0.10+x \cong 0.10$ *and* $0.20-x \cong 0.20$

So,
$K_a = 0.10x/0.20$
$1.8 \times 10^{-5} = 0.10x/0.20$
$x = [H_3O^+] = 3.6 \times 10^{-5}$
$pH = -log[H_3O^+] = -log(3.6 \times 10^{-5}) = 4.44$

Because the ICE tables for all buffered solutions are the same, the equation used in all buffer calculations can be generalized as:

$$K_a = x[\text{base}]/[\text{acid}]$$

or its logarithmic form, the Henderson–Hasselbalch equation:

$$pH = pK_a + log([\text{base}]/[\text{acid}])$$

where K_a is the ionization constant of the weak acid,
x is the molar concentration of hydrogen ion, $[H^+]$,
[base] is the initial molar concentration of the weak base, and
[acid] is the initial molar concentration of the weak acid.

Notice that using the logarithmic form of the equation to solve this problem shows that the pH of a buffered solution is usually very near the pK_a of the weak acid:

$$pH = pK_a + log([\text{base}]/[\text{acid}])$$
$$pH = 4.74 + log(0.10/0.20) = 4.74 + log(0.50) = 4.74 - 0.30 = 4.44$$

Common misconception: Although calculations involving acid–base equilibria can be reduced to a few simple equations, the key to solving acid–base equilibria problems lies in understanding the chemistry and how the equations apply to the chemical reactions involved. Although the math may seem simple, the chemistry can be complex.

Table 17.1 reviews the equations used in solving quantitative acid–base problems.

Table 17.1   Common equations useful in solving acid–base equilibria problems.

Strong acid	$x = I$	$x = [H^+]$ = initial acid concentration
Strong base	$y = I$ $(y = 2I$ for dibasic$)$	$y = [OH^-]$ = initial base concentration
Weak acid	$K_a = x^2/I$	K_a = weak acid ionization constant
Weak base	$K_b = y^2/I$	K_b = weak base ionization constant
Buffer	$K_a = x[\text{base}]/[\text{acid}]$ or $\text{pH} = pK_a + \log([\text{base}]/[\text{acid}])$	$[\text{base}]$ = initial base concentration $[\text{acid}]$ = initial acid concentration $pK_a = -\log K_a$

Buffer capacity is the amount of strong acid or base a buffer can neutralize before the pH changes appreciably. Generally, the higher the concentrations of the weak acid and base, the higher the buffer capacity.

Your Turn 17.3

Calculate and compare the pH's of two buffer solutions, one containing 0.40 M HF and 0.40 M NaF, and the other containing 0.040 M HF and 0.040 M NaF. Which has the greater buffer capacity? Why? Write your answer in the space provided.

The **pH range** refers to the range of pH over which a buffer will act effectively. Generally, a buffer will be effective at or within one-half a pH unit of the pK_a of the acid from which it is made.

Your Turn 17.4

Refer to Appendix D of Chemistry: The Central Science. *At what pH range will each buffer made from the following acid–base pairs operate effectively? Acetic acid and sodium acetate; hydrofluoric acid and sodium fluoride, hydrocyanic acid and sodium cyanide, ammonia and ammonium chloride. Explain your answers. Write your answers in the space provided.*

The chemistry of each acid–base solution must be understood in order to apply the equations in Table 17.1. Table 17.2 summarizes what happens when an acid and a base are mixed.

Table 17.2   Solutions resulting from various acid–base reactions.

If the Solution Contains	And the Base Is in Excess, the Resulting Solution Is a	And the Acid Is in Excess, the Resulting Solution Is a	And Neither the Acid nor the Base Is in Excess, the Resulting Solution Is a
strong acid + strong base	strong base pH $\gg$ 7	strong acid pH $\ll$ 7	neutral solution pH = 7
strong acid + weak base	buffer* pH ~ pK_a	strong acid pH $\ll$ 7	weak acid pH < 7
weak acid + strong base	strong base pH $\gg$ 7	buffer* pH ~ pK_a	weak base pH > 7
weak acid + weak base	buffer* pH ~ pK_a	buffer* pH ~ pK_a	buffer* pH ~ pK_a

*Whenever a buffer solution results, the volume change need not be considered when calculating pH.

Common misconception: A buffer can be prepared from more than just a weak acid and the salt of the acid or a weak base and the salt of the base. A buffer is formed whenever a limiting amount of strong base is added to an excess amount of weak acid because the strong base reacts completely, converting some of the weak acid, but not all of it, to its conjugate base. Similarly, a limiting amount of strong acid added to an excess amount of weak base forms a buffer solution.

Your Turn 17.5

Explain how nitric acid and sodium acetate can be used to make a buffer solution. Illustrate your answer using a chemical equation. What is the predominant form of the acetate ion in the buffer? Write your answers in the space provided.

Examples:

a. Calculate the pH of a solution made by mixing 1.0 L of 0.10 M HCl with 2.0 L of 0.060 M NaOH.

1. Write the net ionic equation.

$$H^+(aq) + OH^-(aq) \rightarrow H_2O(l)$$

2. Calculate the amount of moles of acid and base.

$mol\ HCl = 1.0\ L \times 0.10\ mol/L = 0.10\ mol\ HCl$
$mol\ NaOH = 2.0\ L \times 0.06\ mol/L = 0.12\ mol\ NaOH$

3. Subtract the limiting reactant from the excess reactant to obtain the amount of excess reactant that remains. (A strong acid and a strong base will react completely to the extent of the limiting reactant.)

$0.12\ mol\ NaOH - 0.10\ mol\ HCl = 0.02\ mol\ NaOH$

4. Calculate the total volume of the solution and the concentration(s) of the acid or base in solution.

$Volume = 1.0\ L + 2.0\ L = 3.0\ L$
$[OH^-] = 0.02\ mol/3.0\ L = 0.0067\ M$

5. Calculate the pH.

$pOH = -log[OH^-] = -log(.0067) = 2.17$
$pH = 14 - pOH = 14 - 2.18 = 11.82$

6. Is the answer reasonable? Yes. This pH is consistent for a solution containing an excess of strong base.

b. Calculate the pH of a solution made by mixing 1.0 L of 0.11 M HCl with 3.0 L of 0.080 M NaF.

1. Write the net ionic equation.

$$H^+(aq) + F^-(aq) \rightarrow HF(aq)$$

2. *Calculate the amount of moles of acid and base.*

mol HCl = $1.0\,L \times 0.11\,mol/L = 0.11\,mol\,HCl$
mol NaF = $3.0\,L \times 0.080\,mol/L = 0.24\,mol\,NaF$

3. *All the limiting strong acid will react with the base to form an amount of conjugate acid equal to the amount of limiting acid. Additionally, there is some weak base left over.*

$0.24\,mol\,NaF - 0.11\,mol\,HCl = 0.13\,mol\,NaF + 0.11\,mol\,HF$

4. *This is a buffer because it contains weak acid and weak base and the volume change is not important.*

5. *Calculate the pH.*

$pH = pK_a + log\,[base]/[acid]$. K_a *for HF* = 6.8×10^{-4}
(*from Table D-1 of* Chemistry: The Central Science)

$pK_a = -log\,K_a = -log\,6.8 \times 10^{-4} = 3.17$
$pH = 3.17 + log(0.13/0.11) = 3.24$

6. *Is the answer reasonable? Yes. This pH is consistent for a buffer solution containing slightly more weak base than weak acid and whose weak acid has a $pK_a = 3.17$.*

c. *Calculate the pH of a solution made by mixing 1.0 L of 0.20 M HNO_3 with 2.0 L of 0.10 M NaCN.*

1. *Write the net ionic equation.*

$H^+(aq) + CN^-(aq) \rightleftharpoons HCN(aq)$

2. *Calculate the amount of moles of acid and base.*

mol HNO_3 = $1.0\,L \times 0.20\,mol/L = 0.20\,mol\,HNO_3$
mol NaCN = $2.0\,L \times 0.10\,mol/L = 0.20\,mol\,NaCN$

3. *Neither strong acid nor weak base is in excess. The strong acid will convert all the weak base into 0.20 mol of HCN.*

4. *Calculate the total volume of the solution and the concentration(s) of the species in solution.*

Volume = $1.0\,L + 2.0\,L = 3.0\,L$
$[HCN] = 0.20\,mol/3.0\,L = 0.067\,M$

5. *Calculate the pH.*
This is a 0.067 M solution of the weak acid HCN.

$K_a = x^2/I$
$4.9 \times 10^{-10} = x^2/0.067$
$x = 5.7 \times 10^{-6} = [H^+]$
$pH = -log[H^+] = -log(5.7 \times 10^{-6}) = 5.24$

6. *Is the answer reasonable? Yes. A pH of 5.24 is consistent for a solution containing a weak acid.*

d. *Calculate the pH of a solution made by mixing 2.5 L of 0.20 M CH₃COOH with 1.0 L of 0.30 M CH₃COOK.*

Because this is a mixture of a weak acid and its conjugate weak base, no reaction will occur. This is a buffer solution.

1. *Calculate the moles of acid and base.*

$$mol\ CH_3COOH = 2.5\ L \times 0.20\ mol/L = 0.50\ mol\ CH_3COOH$$
$$mol\ CH_3COOK = 1.0\ L \times 0.30\ mol/L = 0.30\ mol\ CH_3COOK$$

Because a weak acid does not react appreciably with a weak base, skip to Step 5.

5. *Calculate the pH.*

$$pH = pK_a + log[base]/[acid]$$
$$pK_a\ of\ CH_3COOH = -log\ K_a = -log(1.8 \times 10^{-5}) = 4.74$$
$$pH = 4.74 + log(0.30/0.50) = 4.74 - 0.22 = 4.52$$

6. *Is the answer reasonable? Yes. A pH of 4.52 is consistent with a buffer whose weak acid has a K_a of 4.74. Because the buffer contains more weak acid than weak base, the pH is slightly lower than the pK_a.*

Acid–Base Titrations   Section 17.3

An **acid–base titration** is a method to determine an unknown concentration of an acid or a base. A titration determines the volume of a standard solution of base of known concentration that is required to completely react with the acid sample. Similarly, a standard solution of an acid is used to measure an unknown concentration of base.

An **acid–base indicator** changes color at the **end point** of the titration.

The indicator signals the **equivalence point**, the point at which there are equal molar amounts of acid and base.

Alternatively, a pH meter can be used to monitor a titration from beginning to end.

A **titration curve** is a graph of pH versus mL of titrant. Various acid–base titrations produce distinctive titration curves.

Figure 17.2 shows a typical titration curve for a strong acid and a strong base. A strong acid–strong base titration curve is typified by the following properties:

A. The pH before the titration begins is that of a strong acid.
B. As strong base is added, the pH rises slightly because the concentration of the strong acid decreases as it becomes neutralized by strong base.

C. Near the equivalence point, the pH rises dramatically. The pH at the equivalence point is always 7 for a strong acid–strong base titration.

D. After the equivalence point, the pH is that of a strong base. It rises slightly because of the increasing amount of strong base.

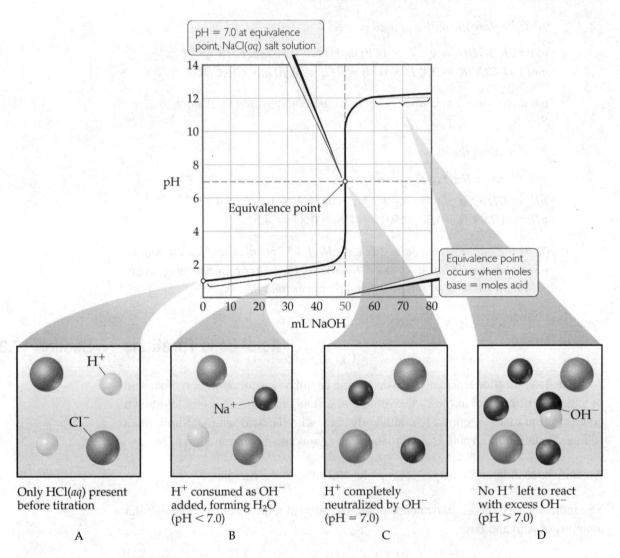

Figure 17.2 Typical acid–base titration curve for a strong acid and a strong base.

Assume that Figure 17.2 represents the titration of 40.0 mL of a nitric acid solution with a 0.20 M sodium hydroxide solution. Calculate the concentration of the nitric acid solution. Why does the pH = 7 at the equivalence point? Illustrate your answer with a net ionic equation. Write your answers in the space provided.

Figure 17.3 shows a titration curve of a weak acid and a strong base. Although a weak acid–strong base titration curve looks similar to a titration curve for a strong acid and strong base, there are significant differences:

A. The pH before the titration begins is higher because it is that of a weak acid in water.

B. The "buffered region" of the titration curve shows that the pH changes slightly as more and more strong base is added, which replaces some, but not all, of the weak acid with conjugate base.

$$HA(aq) + OH^-(aq) \rightleftharpoons A^-(aq) + H_2O(l)$$
$$pH = pK_a + \log([\text{base}]/[\text{acid}])$$

B'. The pH where the amount of titrant is equal to half the amount required to reach the equivalence point defines the pK_a of the weak acid because when [base] = [acid] in the equation,

$$pH = pK_a + \log([\text{base}]/[\text{acid}]),$$
$$\text{then } pH = pK_a.$$

C. At the equivalence point, the rise in pH is not as significant for a weak acid–strong base titration. The equivalence point of a weak acid–strong base always has a pH greater than 7. At this point, only conjugate weak base is in solution.

D. Beyond the equivalence point, only the concentration of strong base needs to be considered to calculate the pH of the solution.

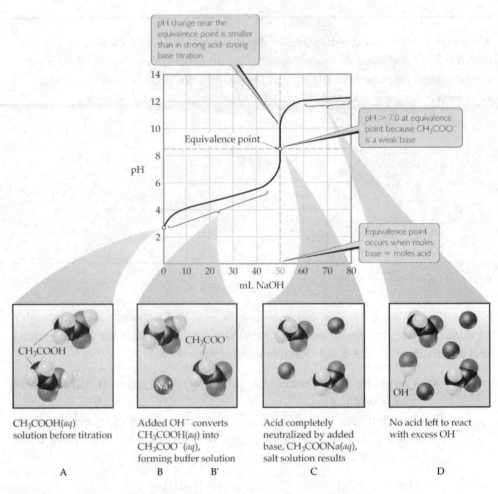

Figure 17.3. A weak acid titrated with a strong base.

Your Turn 17.7

Assume that Figure 17.3 represents the titration of a 0.25 M acetic acid solution with a 0.15 M sodium hydroxide solution.

   a.   Calculate the volume of the acetic acid solution used in the titration.
   b.   Estimate the pH at the equivalence point. Why is the pH greater than 7? Support your claim with a net ionic equation.
   c.   Use the graph to estimate the pKₐ of acetic acid. Justify your answer.

Write your answers in the space provided.

In order for an indicator to accurately signal the equivalence point of a titration, the pH at which it changes color must match the pH of the equivalence point. Table 17.3 shows the pK_a values and pH ranges in which common indicators change color.

Table 17.3   Color changes of acid–base indicators and their pK_a values.

Indicator	Color Change	pH Range	pK_a
Bromphenol blue	Yellow to blue	3–4.5	4
Bromcresol green	Yellow to blue	4–5	4.5
Methyl red	Red to yellow	4.5–6	5
Bromthymol blue	Yellow to blue	6–7.5	7
Phenol red	Yellow to red	7–8	7.5
Phenolphthalein	Colorless to pink	8–10	9
Alizarin yellow R	Yellow to red	10–12	11

Solubility Equilibria   Section 17.4

All salts containing sodium, potassium, ammonium, or nitrate ions are soluble in water. Many other salts form precipitates in water.

When a precipitate forms from the mixing of two solutions, an equilibrium is established between the solid precipitate and its dissolved ions. For example, consider the slightly soluble salt, silver chloride, AgCl. In a saturated solution, one that has dissolved the maximum amount of solute, the ions are in equilibrium with the solid:

$$AgCl(s) \rightleftharpoons Ag^+(aq) + Cl^-(aq)$$

The equilibrium expression for this reaction is:

$$K_{sp} = [Ag^+][Cl^-]$$

The equilibrium constant, K_{sp}, is another special case of K_c and is called the **solubility product constant**.

For silver chloride, $K_{sp} = 1.8 \times 10^{-10}$ (from Appendix D, Table D-3 of *Chemistry: The Central Science*).

The ICE table is:

	AgCl(s) $\rightleftharpoons$	$Ag^+(aq) +$	$Cl^-(aq)$
I	I	0	0
C	$-x$	$+x$	$+x$
E	$I-x$	x	x

The **molar solubility** of silver chloride is the number of moles of silver chloride that dissolve in a liter of water. That is, the molar solubility $= x$. For every mole of AgCl that dissolves, 1 mol of Ag^+ and 1 mol of Cl^- are formed, so:

$$x = [Ag^+] = [Cl^-] \quad \text{and}$$
$$K_{sp} = [Ag^+][Cl^-]$$

Substituting:

$$K_{sp} = x^2$$
$$1.8 \times 10^{-10} = x^2$$
$$x = 1.3 \times 10^{-5} \, M = \text{the molar solubility of silver chloride}$$

Consider the slightly soluble salt, lead(II) chloride, $PbCl_2$. In a saturated solution, the ions are in equilibrium with the solid:

$$PbCl_2(s) \rightleftharpoons Pb^{2+}(aq) + 2\,Cl^-(aq)$$

The equilibrium expression for this reaction is:

$$K_{sp} = [Pb^{2+}][Cl^-]^2$$

For lead(II) chloride, $K_{sp} = 1.6 \times 10^{-5}$.

For every mole of $PbCl_2$ that dissolves, 1 mol of Pb^{2+} and 2 mol of Cl^- are formed, so:

$$x = [Pb^{2+}] \quad \text{and} \quad [Cl^-] = 2x$$

Substituting:

$$K_{sp} = (x)(2x)^2 = 4x^3$$
$$(1.6 \times 10^{-5})/4 = x^3$$
$$x = 0.016 \, M = \text{the molar solubility of lead(II) chloride}$$

When a solid precipitate establishes an equilibrium with its ions in solution, the resulting K_{sp} expression and its relationship to the molar solubility, x, is derived from the ICE table. It is dependent on the stoichiometry of the dissolution reaction. Table 17.4 shows the relationship of the K_{sp} expression and the molar solubility in water expression for various reactions.

Table 17.4   The K_{sp} expressions and molar solubility in water expressions for various solubility equilibria reactions.

Dissolution Equilibrium	K_{sp} Expression	Molar Solubility, x
$AgCl(s) \rightleftharpoons Ag^+(aq) + Cl^-(aq)$	$K_{sp} = [Ag^+][Cl^-]$	$K_{sp} = (x)(x) = x^2$
$PbCl_2(s) \rightleftharpoons Pb^{2+}(aq) + 2Cl^-(aq)$	$K_{sp} = [Pb^{2+}][Cl^-]^2$	$K_{sp} = (x)(2x)^2 = 4x^3$
$LaF_3(s) \rightleftharpoons La^{3+}(aq) + 3F^-(aq)$	$K_{sp} = [La^{3+}][F^-]^3$	$K_{sp} = (x)(3x)^3 = 27x^4$
$Ca_3(PO_4)_2(s) \rightleftharpoons 3Ca^{2+}(aq) + 2PO_4^{3-}(aq)$	$K_{sp} = [Ca^{2+}]^3[PO_4^{3-}]^2$	$K_{sp} = (3x)^3(2x)^2 = 108x^5$

Factors That Affect Solubility   Section 17.5

The molar solubility of a slightly soluble salt is always greater in pure water than in an aqueous solution containing a common ion. For example, consider the following solubility equilibrium reaction:

$$CeF_3(s) \rightleftharpoons Ce^{3+}(aq) + 3F^-(aq)$$

If sodium fluoride, NaF, is added to the mixture, the common ion, fluoride, drives the equilibrium to the left according to Le Châtelier's principle, making cerium fluoride less soluble in a solution of sodium fluoride than in pure water.

Common misconception: The molar solubility expression in water does not apply to solutions containing common ions. For common ions, the molar solubility must be derived from an ICE table.

Example:

Calculate the molar solubility of cerium fluoride, CeF_3, in
a. pure water.
b. a solution containing 0.2 M $CeCl_3$.
c. a solution containing 0.2 M NaF.

$$K_{sp} = 8 \times 10^{-16}$$

Solution:

a. *The reaction is $CeF_3(s) \rightleftharpoons Ce^{3+}(aq) + 3F^-(aq)$.*
    The K_{sp} expression is

$$K_{sp} = [Ce^{3+}][F^-]^3$$

$$K_{sp} = (x)(3x)^3 = 27x^4$$

$$K_{sp} = 8 \times 10^{-16} = 27x^4$$

$$x = 7 \times 10^{-5}\,M$$

b. *The molar solubility expression in water does not apply to solutions containing common ions. It must be derived from the ICE table. Cerium ion is the common ion. (Chloride is a spectator ion because $CeCl_3$ is soluble in water.)*

	$CeF_3(s) \rightleftharpoons$	$Ce^{3+}(aq) +$	$3F^-(aq)$
I	I	0.2	0
C	$-x$	$+x$	$+3x$
E	$I - x$	$0.2 + x$	$3x$

$$K_{sp} = [Ce^{3+}][F^-]^3$$

$$K_{sp} = 8 \times 10^{-16} = (0.2+x)(3x)^3$$

If $x <<<< 0.2$, then $0.2 + x \cong 0.2$

$$8 \times 10^{-16} = (0.2)(3x)^3$$

$$x = 5 \times 10^{-6} M$$

c. The ICE table is similar to Part b except that here, fluoride ion is the common ion. (Sodium ion is a soluble spectator ion.)

$$CeF_3(s) \rightleftharpoons Ce^{3+}(aq) + 3F^-(aq)$$

		Ce^{3+}	F^-
I	I	0	0.2
C	$-x$	$+x$	$+3x$
E	$I-x$	x	$0.2+3x$

$$K_{sp} = [Ce^{3+}][F^-]^3$$

$$K_{sp} = 8 \times 10^{-16} = (x)(0.2+3x)^3$$

If $3x <<<< 0.2$, then $0.2 + 3x \cong 0.2$

$$8 \times 10^{-16} = (x)(0.2)^3$$

$$x = 1 \times 10^{-13} M$$

Notice that in Parts b and c where a common ion is involved, the molar solubility of cerium fluoride is less than in pure water.

The **reaction quotient**, Q, is used to predict whether a precipitate will form under a set of given conditions.

Example:

Consider a solution made by adding 175 mL of 0.10 M $BaCl_2$ to 40 mL of 0.50 M NaOH. Assume the volumes are additive. K_{sp} for barium hydroxide is 5.0×10^{-3}.

a. *Write the net ionic equation for the dissolution of barium hydroxide.*
b. *What is the value of Q?*
c. *K_{sp} for $Ba(OH)_2$ is 5.0×10^{-3}. Will a precipitate form?*
d. *What must be the concentration of OH^- for a precipitate to form in 0.10 M $BaCl_2$?*

Solution:

a. $Ba(OH)_2(s) \rightleftharpoons Ba^{2+}(aq) + 2OH(aq)$
b. $Q = [Ba^{2+}][OH^-]^2$

$$Q = (0.10\,M)(175/215)[(0.50)(40/215)]^2 = 7.0 \times 10^{-4}$$

c. $K_{sp} > Q$. No precipitate will form because the concentrations of the ions are too small. Q must be at least as large as K_{sp}.
d. $K_{sp} = [Ba^{2+}][OH^-]^2$

$$5.0 \times 10^{-3} = [0.10][OH^-]^2$$

$$[OH^-] = 0.22\,M$$

The solubility of an acid or a base is dependent on the pH. For example, cadmium hydroxide is much more soluble in acid than in pure water because cadmium hydroxide is a base and readily reacts with acid:

$$Cd(OH)_2(s) \rightleftharpoons Cd^{2+}(aq) + 2OH^-(aq)$$
$$H^+(aq) + OH^-(aq) \rightleftharpoons H_2O(l)$$

The second reaction consumes hydroxide ions from the first reaction. Le Châtelier's principle states that the first reaction will go toward the right, making cadmium hydroxide more soluble.

Addition of the two reactions provides a net reaction where cadmium hydroxide dissolves:

$$Cd(OH)_2(s) + 2H^+(aq) \rightleftharpoons Cd^{2+}(aq) + 2H_2O(l)$$

Multiple Choice Questions

1. When dissolved in aqueous solution, which pair would behave as a buffer?

   A) HCl and NaCl

   B) KOH and KCl

   C) HNO_2 and $NaNO_2$

   D) HNO_3 and NH_4NO_3

2. The K_{sp} of CaF_2 is 4.3×10^{-11} in pure water. In acidic solution, the solubility of CaF_2 is expected to

   A) increase because Ca^{2+} ion is acidic.

   B) decrease because Ca^{2+} ion is acidic.

   C) increase because F^- ion is basic.

   D) decrease because F^- ion is basic.

3. Which has the greatest molar solubility in water at 25 °C?

   A) ammonium nitrate

   B) barium sulfate

   C) iron(II) sulfide

   D) lead(II) carbonate

4. When mixed, which pair of aqueous solutions will most likely form a precipitate?

   A) KNO_3 and $CaBr_2$

   B) $NaNO_3$ and $(NH_4)_2CO_3$

   C) $CaCl_2$ and K_2CO_3

   D) K_2SO_4 and $(NH_4)_2S$

5. Which of these slightly soluble salts shows an increased solubility in a 1.0 M aqueous solution of HCl?

   I. $PbCl_2$

   II. $CuCO_3$

   III. $Ba_3(PO_4)_2$

   A) I only

   B) II only

   C) I and II only

   D) II and III only

6. If equal volumes of the following pairs are mixed, which of the resulting solutions will NOT make a buffer solution?

A) 0.20 M NaCN and 0.40 M HCN

B) 0.20 M HF and 0.10 M KOH

C) 0.20 M KF and 0.05 M HCl

D) 0.15 M NaCN and 0.20M HCl

Questions 7–12 refer to the following system:

A total of 30.0 mL of a 0.10 M solution of a monoprotic acid ($K_a = 1.0 \times 10^{-5}$) is titrated with 0.20 M sodium hydroxide solution.

7. Before the titration begins, the pH of the solution is about

A) 2.

B) 3.

C) 7.

D) 9.

8. At the equivalence point, the pH of the solution is about

A) 2.

B) 5.

C) 7.

D) 9.

9. The amount of NaOH required to reach the equivalence point is

A) 15.0 mL.

B) 30.0 mL.

C) 45.0 mL.

D) 60.0 mL.

10. The approximate pH of the solution when the weak acid is half neutralized is

A) 2.

B) 5.

C) 7.

D) 9.

11. *What is true of a buffer made from the weak acid that has a pH of 4.0?*

    A) $[HA] = [A^-]$

    B) $[HA] = 10[A^-]$

    C) $10[HA] = [A^-]$

    D) $2[HA] = [A^-]$

12. *Which indicator is the most appropriate for signaling the endpoint of the titration? The approximate pH range for the color change of each indicator is given.*

    A) *bromphenyl blue* $pH = 3-4.5$

    B) *phenolphthalein* $pH = 8-10$

    C) *thymol blue* $pH = 1.5-2.5$

    D) *alizarin yellow R* $pH = 11-12$

Questions 13–16 refer to the following acids and bases.

A) *hydrazoic acid*	HN_3	$K_a = 1.9 \times 10^{-5}$
B) *hydrofluoric acid*	HF	$K_a = 6.8 \times 10^{-4}$
C) *nitrous acid*	HNO_2	$K_a = 4.5 \times 10^{-4}$
D) *phenol*	C_6H_5OH	$K_a = 1.3 \times 10^{-10}$

13. *Which compound is best when preparing a buffer of pH = 9.5?*

14. *Which 0.20 M solution will have the lowest pH?*

15. *Which 0.10 molar solution will have the lowest percentage ionization?*

16. *Rank the compounds in order of increasing acid strength, lowest to highest.*

    A) $D < A < C < B$

    B) $D < A < C < B$

    C) $D < A < B < C$

    D) $B < C < A < D$

Free Response Questions

1. *Solid NaCl is added slowly to a solution containing 0.10 M $AgNO_3$ and 0.20 M $Pb(NO_3)_2$. K_{sp} for AgCl is 1.8×10^{-10}. K_{sp} for $PbCl_2$ is 1.6×10^{-5}.*

   a. *Write a net ionic equation and corresponding K_{sp} expression for the dissolution of the following solids:*
      i.   *silver chloride*
      ii. *lead(II) chloride*

   b. *Calculate the $[Cl^-]$ required to form each precipitate.*

   c. *Which precipitate forms first? Explain your answer.*

   d. *What is the concentration of the first metal ion to precipitate when the second one just begins to precipitate?*

   e. *If 100 mL of 0.05 M NaCl is added to 200 mL of solution containing 0.005 M $AgNO_3$ and 0.10 M $Pb(NO_3)_2$, does a precipitate form? If so, which one(s) form? Explain.*

2. *A total of 0.450 mol of hydrazoic acid, HN_3 ($K_a = 1.9 \times 10^{-5}$), is added to enough water to make 1.55 L of solution.*

   a. *Write a chemical equation for the reaction of hydrazoic acid with water and write the corresponding equilibrium expression.*

   b. *Calculate the pH of the solution.*

   c. *Calculate the number of moles of added sodium azide or hydrozoic acid (indicate which) required to make the pH = 5.00. Assume no volume change.*

   d. *Calculate the pH of the solution made by adding 0.10 mol of sodium azide to 0.20 mol of hydrazoic acid to make the solution volume 1.00 L. Compare the buffer capacity of this solution to that of the solution prepared in Part c.*

   e. *What is the pH of a 0.350 M solution of NaN_3?*

Multiple Choice Answers and Explanations

1. *C. A buffer consists of a weak acid and its conjugate weak base. The only conjugate pair listed is nitrous acid and sodium nitrite.*

2. *C. Most anions are basic. Their negative charges attract protons. The only neutral anions are those anions of strong acids. HF is a weak acid.*

3. *A. All common salts of ammonium, sodium, and potassium ions are soluble in water.*

4. *C. All sodium, potassium, ammonium, and nitrate salts are soluble. The only possible product that does not contain one of these ions is $CaCO_3$.*

5. **D.** *The anions of weak acids are basic and will show increased solubility in acids. The anions of strong acids are neutral and the solubility of neutral salts will not be affected.*

6. **D.** *A buffer consists of a weak acid and a conjugate weak base. It can be formed by mixing the conjugates directly or, in this case, by mixing an excess of weak base with a limiting strong acid or by mixing excess weak acid by limiting strong base. Excess strong or weak acid will not result in a buffer solution.*

7. **B.** *Only the weak acid is present in the solution before the titration. The hydrogen ion concentration, x, is estimated by the equation:*

    $$K_a = [H^+][A^-]/HA = x^2/I$$
    $$1.0 \times 10^{-5} = x^2/0.10$$
    $$x = (1.0 \times 10^{-6})^{1/2} = 0.0010 \, pH = -log(0.0010) = 3$$

8. **D.** *At the equivalence point, all the weak acid is neutralized and converted to the conjugate weak base. Thus, the solution will have a weakly basic pH.*

    $$HA + OH^- \rightarrow HOH + A^-$$

9. **A.** *Because the NaOH is twice the concentration of the weak acid, the base will require half the volume of the acid to neutralize it. The volume of the NaOH required to neutralize the acid is given by the equation:* $M_aV_a = M_bV_b$.

    $$V_b = M_aV_a/M_b = (0.10 \, M)(30.0 \, mL)/(0.20 \, M) = 15 \, mL$$

10. **B.** *When the weak acid is half neutralized, the concentration of the acid equals the concentration of the conjugate weak base,*
    $$[HA] = [A^-].$$
    $$pH = pK_a + log[A^-]/[HA]$$
    $$pH = pK_a + 0$$
    $$pK_a = -logK_a = -log\,10^{-5} = 5$$

11. **B.** *A buffer containing equal concentrations of the acid–base conjugate pair would have a pH = pK_a = 5. Every pH unit change represents a 10-fold difference in concentration of the two species. A pH of 4 means that there is 10 times as much weak acid as weak base.*

12. **B.** *For an indicator to correctly signal the endpoint of the titration, the color change must closely match the pH of the equivalence point of the titration. A titration of a weak acid with a strong base will produce only a weak base at the equivalence point. Therefore, the pH of the equivalence point will be higher than 7, but not in the strong base range (pH > 11).*

13. **D.** *The pH of a buffer will be close to the pK_a of the weak acid from which it is made.*
    $$pH = pK_a + log[base]/[acid]$$
    The pK_a of phenol = $-log \, K_a = -log(1.3 \times 10^{-10}) = 9.9$

14. **B.** HF has the largest K_a value, so it is the strongest acid. It will produce more hydrogen ions in solution, resulting in the lowest pH.

15. **D.** Phenol has the smallest equilibrium constant, so it will ionize to the least extent.

16. **B.** Acid strength increases with increasing K_a. Because aniline is a base, it is the least acidic.

Free Response Answers

1. a. i. $AgCl(s) \rightleftharpoons Ag^+(aq) + Cl^-(aq)$ $K_{sp} = [Ag^+][Cl^-]$

   ii. $PbCl_2(s) \rightleftharpoons Pb^{2+}(aq) + 2Cl^-(aq)$ $K_{sp} = [Pb^{2+}][Cl^-]^2$

   b. $K_{sp} = [Ag^+][Cl^-]$

   $1.8 \times 10^{-10} = (0.10)[Cl^-]$

   $[Cl^-] = 1.8 \times 10^{-9}\,M$ required to precipitate AgCl.

   $K_{sp} = [Pb^{2+}][Cl^-]^2$

   $1.6 \times 10^{-5} = [(0.20)][Cl^-]^2$

   $[Cl^-] = 8.9 \times 10^{-3}\,M$ required to precipitate $PbCl_2$.

   c. AgCl precipitates first because it requires less $[Cl^-]$ to form a precipitate.

   d. The second metal ion, Pb^{2+}, just begins to precipitate when $[Cl^-]$ reaches $8.9 \times 10^{-3}\,M$. At this chloride ion concentration, the silver ion can be calculated from:

   $K_{sp} = [Ag^+][Cl^-]$

   $1.8 \times 10^{-10} = [Ag^+](8.9 \times 10^{-3}\,M)$

   $[Ag^+] = 2.0 \times 10^{-8}\,M$

   e. Calculate Q for each equilibrium in Part a and compare each Q to the corresponding K_{sp}. In each case, if $K_{sp} < Q$, a precipitate will form.

   $Q = [Ag^+][Cl^-] = [(0.005\,M)(200/300)][(0.05)(100/300)]$

   $ = 5.6 \times 10^{-5}$

   $K_{sp} < Q$ for AgCl, so a precipitate forms.

   $Q = [Pb^{2+}][Cl^-]^2$

   $1.6 \times 10^{-5} = (0.10\,M)(200/300)[(0.05)(100/300)]^2 = 1.9 \times 10^{-5}$

   $K_{sp} < Q$ for $PbCl_2$, so a precipitate forms.

2. a. $HN_3 + H_2O\,(l) \rightleftharpoons N_3^-(aq) + H_3O^+(aq)$

   $K_a = [N_3^-][H_3O^+]/[HN_3]$

   b. $K_a = [N_3^-][H_3O^+]/[HN_3]$

   $[HN_3] = 0.450\,mol/1.55\,L = 0.290\,M$

   $x = [N_3^-] = [H_3O^+]$

   $1.9 \times 10^{-5} = (x)(x)/(0.290\,M)$

   $x = [H_3O^+] = 2.35 \times 10^{-3}\,M$

   $pH = -log[H_3O^+] = -log(2.35 \times 10^{-3}) = 2.63$

c. $pK_a = -\log K_a = -\log(1.9 \times 10^{-5}) = 4.72$. *To make the pH = 5.00, conjugate base, sodium azide, must be added.*

$$pH = pK_a + \log([N_3^-]/[HN_3])$$

$$5.00 = 4.72 + \log([N_3^-]/0.450 \, mol)$$

$$0.28 = \log([N_3^-]/0.450 \, mol)$$

$$10^{0.28} = [N_3^-]/0.450 \, mol$$

$$1.91 = [N_3^-]/0.450 \, mol$$

$$[N_3^-] = 0.857 \, mol$$

d. $pH = pK_a + \log([N_3^-]/[HN_3])$

$pH = 4.72 + \log(0.10)/(0.20)$

$pH = 4.72 - 0.30 = 4.42$

Solution c contains 0.857 mol of N_3^- and 0.450 mol of HN_3.

Solution d contains 0.10 mol of N_3^- and 0.20 mol of HN_3.

Solution c will have the greater buffer capacity. It will be able to neutralize more added strong or weak acid or base because of its higher amounts of weak acid and base.

e. $K_b = K_w/K_a = (y)(y)/0.350 = 1 \times 10^{-14}/1.9 \times 10^{-5} = y^2/0.350$

$y = [OH^-] = 1.36 \times 10^{-5} \, M$

$pOH = -\log(1.36 \times 10^{-5}) = 4.87$

$pH = 14 = pOH = 14 - 4.87 = 9.13$

Your Turn Answers

17.1.a. $NH_3 + H^+ \rightleftharpoons NH_4^+$

Because a strong acid reacts completely, the solution will consist mainly of ammonium ions and nitrate ions. (Nitrate ions are spectator ions.)

b. $OH^- + H^+ \rightleftharpoons H_2O$

The reaction goes to completion, so only the spectator ions, K^+ and Cl^-, will exist in solution in large concentrations.

c. $CH_3COOH + OH^- \rightleftharpoons CH_3COO^- + H_2O$

The solution will consist mainly of sodium ions and acetate ions because the reaction goes to completion.

d. $H_3PO_4 + OH^- \rightarrow H_2PO_4^- + H_2O$

Because there are equal moles of weak acid and strong base, only one ionizable proton from the triprotic acid will be neutralized. The solution will consist mainly of potassium ions and dihydrogen phosphate ions. The reaction goes to completion.

e. *Ammonium chloride, a weak acid but strong electrolyte, and ammonia, the weak base, will not react appreciably. The solution will consist mainly of ammonium ions, chloride ions, and ammonia molecules.*

17.2. The acetic acid + sodium acetate solution will act as an effective buffer. A buffer consists of a solution of weak acid and its conjugate weak base, both in significant concentrations. A buffered solution resists change in pH because the weak acid present will neutralize any added strong base and an added strong acid will react completely with the conjugate weak base of the buffer.

$$CH_3COOH + OH^- \rightarrow H_2O + CH_3COO^-$$

$$CH_3COO^- + H^+ \rightarrow CH_3COOH$$

17.3. The K_a for HF is 6.8×10^{-4}. $pK_a = -log(6.8 \times 10^{-4}) = 3.17$

$$pH = pK_a + log([base]/[acid]) = 3.17 + log(0.40/0.40) = 3.17$$

$$pH = pK_a + log([base]/[acid]) = 3.17 + log(0.040/0.040) = 3.17$$

While the two buffers have the same pH, the more concentrated buffer has the greater buffer capacity because there is more weak acid and weak base available to neutralize any added strong base or acid.

17.4. A buffer effectively operates within one-half pH unit of the pK_a of the weak acid that composes it.

Acetic acid and sodium acetate: The pK_a of acetic acid is $-log(1.8 \times 10^{-5}) = 4.74$. The buffer will operate effectively at $pH = 4.74 \pm 0.5$.

Hydrofluoric acid and sodium fluoride:
$pK_a = -log(6.8 \times 10^{-4}) = 3.17$. Buffer range $= pH\, 3.17 \pm 0.5$.

Hydrocyanic acid and sodium cyanide:
$pK_a = -log(4.9 \times 10^{-10}) = 9.31$. Buffer range $= pH\, 9.31 \pm 0.5$.

Ammonia and ammonium chloride: K_a for NH_4^+ ion $= K_w/K_b$
for $NH_3 = 1.0 \times 10^{-14}/1.8 \times 10^{-5} = 5.56 \times 10^{-10}$
$pK_a = -log(5.56 \times 10^{-10}) = 9.31$. Buffer range $= pH\, 9.26 \pm 0.5$.

17.5. A limiting amount of nitric acid added to an excess of sodium acetate will form a buffer because the strong acid will convert some, but not all, of the weak base to acetic acid, a weak acid. The resulting solution will contain both a weak acid and its conjugate weak base.

$H^+(aq) + CH_3COO^-(aq) \rightleftharpoons CH_3COOH(aq)$ (the reaction goes nearly to completion)

Two predominant forms exist in significant concentration of the buffer: acetic acid, CH_3COOH, produced by the partial neutralization of acetate ion by nitric acid and excess acetate ion, CH_3COO^-, that is left unreacted.

17.6. At the equivalence point of any acid–base titration, the moles of acid equal the moles of base. Reading the graph, the equivalence point occurs when 50.0 mL of NaOH is added.

mol HNO_3 = mol NaOH or

mol/L HNO_3 × L HNO_3 = mol/L NaOH × L NaOH

(M HNO_3)(40.0 mL HNO_3) = (0.20 M NaOH)(50.0 mL NaOH) or

M_{acid} × V_{acid} = M_{base} × V_{base}

M_{acid} = (M_{base} × V_{base})/V_{acid} = (0.20 M)(50.0 mL)/(40.0 mL)
= 0.25 M HNO_3

The pH equals 7 at the equivalence point of a strong acid–strong base titration because water is the only product and sodium ion and nitrate ion are spectator ions.

$H^+(aq) + OH^-(aq) \rightleftharpoons H_2O(l)$

17.7. a. From the graph, it takes 50.0 mL of NaOH to reach the equivalence point: M_{acid} × V_{acid} = M_{base} × V_{base}.

V_{acid} = (M_{base} × V_{base})/M_{acid} = (0.15 M)(50.0 mL)/(0.25 M)
= 30.0 mL

or

mol CH_3COOH = mol NaOH

mol/L CH_3COOH × L CH_3COOH = mol/L NaOH × L NaOH

(0.25 M CH_3COOH)(mL CH_3COOH) = (0.15 M NaOH)(50.0 mL NaOH)

mL CH_3COOH = 30.0 mL

b. pH = 8.5. The pH at the equivalence point is greater than 7 because acetate ion, CH_3COO^-, the conjugate weak base of acetic acid is a major product of the reaction. $OH^-(aq) + CH_3COOH(aq) \rightleftharpoons CH_3COO^-(aq) + H_2O(l)$

c. The pK_a of acetic acid is approximately 4.8. As the titration proceeds toward the equivalence point, the above reaction creates a buffer whose pH can be calculated by the equation:
pH = pK_a + log([CH_3COO^-]/[CH_3COOH]).

Exactly halfway to the equivalence point, at 25.0 mL of NaOH, half of the acetic acid has been converted to acetate ion, leaving half of the acetic acid unreacted. At this point, [CH_3COO^-] = [CH_3COOH], so pH = pK_a. Reading the graph, the pH halfway through the titration is approximately 4.8.

CHEMISTRY OF THE ENVIRONMENT

TOPIC 18

Chapter 18 of *Chemistry: The Central Science* is perhaps the most interesting chapter even though very little of its content is found on the Advanced Placement Chemistry exam. Expect no more than one or two general knowledge multiple choice questions from this chapter. In preparation for the exam, do little more than read this summary.

The four major gases that make up the composition of dry air (in mole fraction) are the following:

Nitrogen, N_2, 0.781

Oxygen, O_2, 0.209

Argon, Ar, 0.00934

Carbon dioxide, CO_2, 0.000375

Water and carbon dioxide are the gases principally responsible for the natural greenhouse effect, the trapping of heat in the earth's atmosphere.

The combustion of fossil fuels such as coal and petroleum contributes to the increasing amount of carbon dioxide in the atmosphere.

$$2C_8H_{18}(l) + 25O_2(g) \rightarrow 16CO_2(g) + 18H_2O(g)$$

Sulfur dioxide, SO_2, is a principal air pollutant resulting from the combustion of various forms of sulfur in coal and oil.

$$S(s) + O_2(g) \rightarrow SO_2(g)$$

Acid rain is formed when sulfur dioxide is oxidized to sulfur trioxide in the atmosphere and then combines with water.

$$SO_3(g) + H_2O(l) \rightarrow H_2SO_4(aq)$$

Powdered limestone ($CaCO_3$) injected into the furnace of a power plant decomposes to lime (CaO) and carbon dioxide.

$$CaCO_3(s) + heat \rightarrow CaO(s) + CO_2(g)$$

The lime prevents the escape of sulfur dioxide by reacting to form calcium sulfite.

$$CaO(s) + SO_2(g) \rightarrow CaSO_3(s)$$

The high heats generated by internal combustion engines cause the chief components of air to react to form nitrogen monoxide.

$$N_2(g) + O_2(g) + heat \rightarrow 2NO(g)$$

Nitrogen monoxide oxidizes in air to form nitrogen dioxide.

$$2NO(g) + O_2(g) \rightarrow 2NO_2(g)$$

Nitrogen dioxide undergoes photodissociation in sunlight to form atomic oxygen.

$$NO_2(g) + h\nu \rightarrow NO(g) + O(g)$$

Atomic oxygen produces ozone as well as other products, collectively referred to as photochemical smog.

$$O(g) + O_2(g) \rightarrow O_3(g)$$

Municipalities treat water by adding lime, CaO, and alum, $Al_2(SO_4)_3$. Lime in water forms calcium hydroxide.

$$CaO(s) + H_2O(l) \rightarrow Ca^{2+}(aq) + 2OH^-(aq)$$

Aluminum ions react with hydroxide ions to produce a spongy, gelatinous precipitate that absorbs suspended particles and bacteria as it settles, removing them from the water.

$$Al^{3+}(aq) + 3OH^-(aq) \rightarrow Al(OH)_3(s)$$

Chlorine added to water produces hydrochloric acid, a strong acid, and hypochlorous acid, a weak acid, which is deadly to any remaining bacteria.

$$Cl_2(g) + H_2O(l) \rightarrow H^+(aq) + Cl^-(aq) + HClO(aq)$$

Notice that, in the above disproportionation, chlorine atoms are both oxidized and reduced. Also the strong acid is written in ionic form and the weak acid is written in molecular form.

CHEMICAL THERMODYNAMICS

The content in this topic is the basis for mastering Learning Objectives 5.12–5.15 and 6.25 as found in the Curriculum Framework.

When you finish reviewing this topic, be sure you are able to:

- Distinguish between exothermic and endothermic changes and understand the direction of energy flow for each

- Explain using the kinetic-molecular theory the concept of entropy in a chemical system

- Explain the direction and relative magnitudes of changes in entropy when phase changes occur in solids, liquids, or gases

- Use models and representations to explain how molecular complexity affects entropy

- Calculate entropy changes from thermodynamic data

- Use $\Delta G° = \Delta H° - T\Delta S°$ to predict the thermodynamic favorability of a chemical or physical change

- Calculate $\Delta G°$ to determine the thermodynamic favorability of a chemical change

- Use the relationship between $\Delta G°$ and K ($\Delta G° = -RT \ln K$) to estimate the magnitude of K and the thermodynamic favorability of a process

Chemical thermodynamics answers a fundamental question. Why does change occur?

The driving influences for any chemical and physical change are:

1. **Change in enthalpy**, ΔH (heat transferred between the system and the surroundings).

2. **Change in entropy**, ΔS (randomness or disorder of the system).

Generally, chemical and physical systems tend to change in a direction that moves toward lower enthalpy (they release heat to the environment) and higher entropy (they become more random or disordered).

Sometimes, these two influences are in direct conflict with each other and the reaction seeks a balance between moving toward lower enthalpy and higher entropy. Systems reach this balance at **equilibrium**.

Section 19.1

Spontaneous Processes

A **spontaneous process** is one that is thermodynamically favored. It continues on its own without outside assistance. A thermodynamically favored change occurs in a definite direction. Processes that are thermodynamically favored in one direction are not favored in the opposite direction. For example, a rock falls to the ground spontaneously. The opposite process, a rock rising from the ground, is not thermodynamically favored. Similarly, a burning campfire is thermodynamically favored. The "unburning" of a campfire is not thermodynamically favored.

Review Section 5.3

Enthalpy

Recall from Topic 5 that **enthalpy** is the heat transferred between a chemical or physical system and its surroundings during a constant-pressure process.

The **change in enthalpy**, ΔH, is the **heat absorbed** by a system at constant pressure.

An **endothermic process** is one that absorbs heat from the environment. ΔH is positive.

An **exothermic process** is one that releases heat to the environment. ΔH is negative.

The **first law of thermodynamics**, also called the law of conservation of energy, states that, in all cases, energy is conserved. Energy can be neither created nor destroyed. This means that the amount of energy gained by a system must equal the amount of energy lost by the environment and vice versa.

A major driving influence for any chemical or physical change is the tendency for systems to move toward lower enthalpy by releasing energy to the environment. Thus, exothermic processes, those that release energy to the environment, usually but not always, are thermodynamically favored. They occur on their own without any outside assistance.

Recall from Section 5.7 of *Chemistry: The Central Science* that the enthalpy change for a given reaction can be calculated from the enthalpies of formation for products minus the enthalpies of formation for reactants:

$$\Delta H^{\circ}_{rxn} = \Sigma\, H^{\circ}_{products} - \Sigma\, H^{\circ}_{reactants}$$

Entropy and the Second Law of Thermodynamics

Entropy for qualitative purposes can be considered to be the extent of randomness or disorder in a chemical or physical system. Entropy increases when matter or energy is dispersed. For example, gases are more random than are liquids because the molecules are more dispersed. A gas at a higher temperature is more dispersed than a gas at a lower temperature because the distribution of kinetic energy among the gas particles increases at higher temperatures.

Kinetic-molecular theory states that gases consist of a large number of atoms and/or molecules having a high kinetic energy, so they are in continuous, random motion. The attractive forces between gas particles are negligible compared to their kinetic energy (see Section 10.1). In contrast, liquids have low kinetic energy and the attractive forces between the particles are sufficiently significant to hold the molecules together but still allow them to freely move past one another. Solids have relatively low kinetic energy and the attractive forces work to lock the molecules into place, often in a very ordered crystal lattice (see Section 11.1). Gases, because of their relative disorder, have higher entropy than do liquids. Solids generally have lower entropy than either liquids or gases.

The **change in entropy**, ΔS, for any process is a measure of the change in randomness or disorder of the system. Generally, as the phase of a given system changes from solid to liquid to gas, the entropy of the system increases and ΔS is positive for such changes. Phase changes from gas to liquid, gas to solid, or liquid to solid all happen with a decrease in entropy and ΔS is negative. Table 19.1 illustrates examples of entropy changes for various physical and chemical processes.

Table 19.1   Changes that increase entropy: ΔS is positive.

Generally, Entropy Increases When	Example
solids change to liquids or gases	$CO_2(s) \rightarrow CO_2(g)$
liquids change to gases	$H_2O(l) \rightarrow H_2O(g)$
solids dissolve in liquid solutions	$NaCl(s) \rightarrow Na^+(aq) + Cl^-(aq)$
the number of gas molecules increase	$2NH_3(g) \rightarrow N_2(g) + 3H_2(g)$
temperature increases	Water increases in temperature
volume increases	A gas expands
the number of particles increase	A rock is crushed
two or more pure substances are mixed	Sugar dissolves in water

Your Turn 19.1

---

a. *When helium is released from a toy balloon, does the entropy of the system increase or decrease? Explain your answer.*

b. *Draw a distribution plot of the number of gas molecules versus their kinetic energies in a sealed rigid container at two different temperatures and explain how entropy changes. Write your answers in the space provided.*

Section 19.3   Molecular Interpretation of Entropy

Entropy also increases for substances with increasing molecular complexity. For example, under the same conditions, O_3 has a higher entropy than O_2 because it is more complex. Figure 19.1 shows three hydrocarbons and the entropy associated with each.

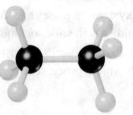
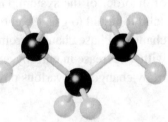

Methane, CH_4
$S° = 186.3$ J/mol-K

Ethane, C_2H_6
$S° = 229.6$ J/mol-K

Propane, C_3H_8
$S° = 270.3$ J/mol-K

Figure 19.1   Entropy increases with increasing molecular complexity.

Your Turn 19.2

Under the same conditions of pressure and temperature, which has greater entropy, gaseous propane or gaseous butane? Explain. Which has greater entropy, steam or ice? Explain. Write your answers in the space provided.

The **second law of thermodynamics** states that any thermodynamically favored change is always accompanied by an overall increase in entropy in the universe.

The **third law of thermodynamics** states that the entropy of a pure crystalline substance at absolute zero is zero. Upon heating, the entropy of a pure crystalline substance gradually increases. Continued heating brings upon a sharp increase in entropy upon melting and another marked increase upon boiling as illustrated in Figure 19.2.

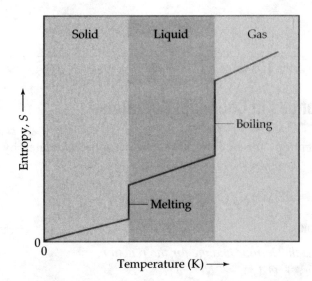

Figure 19.2   As the temperature of a substance increases, its entropy increases. Large changes in entropy are associated with phase changes.

Standard molar entropies, $S°$, are values for pure substances at 1 atm pressure and 298 K. The unit most often used for $S°$ is J/mol-K. Table 19.2 lists some examples. Notice that $S°$ is comparatively larger for gases than for liquids or solids. Also, substances having the same phase but having higher molar mass and/or higher molecular complexity have higher entropy values. A more detailed list of standard entropy values is given in Appendix C of *Chemistry: The Central Science*.

Table 19.2   Standard molar entropies of selected substances at 298 K.

Substance	S°, J/mol-K	Substance	S°, J/mol-K
$I_2(s)$	116.73	$NO(g)$	210.62
$I_2(l)$	180.66	$NO_2(g)$	240.45
$I_2(g)$	260.57	$N_2O_4(g)$	304.30
$O(g)$	161.0	$H_2O(l)$	69.91
$O_2(g)$	205.0	$H_2O(g)$	188.83
$O_3(g)$	237.6		

Your Turn 19.3   ←───

Rationalize the difference in the standard molar entropy values of solid, liquid, and gaseous iodine as listed in Table 19.2. Write your answer in the space provided.

Section 19.4

Entropy Changes in Chemical Reactions

The change in entropy for a chemical reaction can be calculated by the following equation:

$$\Delta S°_{rxn} = \Sigma\, S°_{products} - \Sigma\, S°_{reactants}$$

Example:

What is the entropy change for the reaction,
$2NO(g) + O_2(g) \rightarrow 2NO_2(g)?$

Solution:

Substitute the entropy values listed in Table 19.2 into the equation. Do not forget to use the coefficients that balance the equation!

$\Delta S°_{rxn} = \Sigma\, S°_{products} - \Sigma\, S°_{reactants}$
$\Delta S°_{rxn} = 2(240.45\,J/mol\text{-}K) - 205.0\,J/mol\text{-}K - 2(210.62\,J/mol\text{-}K)$
$\Delta S°_{rxn} = -145.34\,J/mol\text{-}K$

The answer is negative and makes sense because the system moves from three moles of gas to two moles of gas with a decrease in entropy.

Section 19.5

Gibbs Free Energy

Free energy (or **change in free energy, ΔG**) represents the amount of useful work that can be obtained from a process at constant temperature and pressure. Free energy, enthalpy, and entropy are related by the equation:

$$\Delta G = \Delta H - T\Delta S$$

ΔG is change in free energy measured in kJ/mol.

ΔH is change in enthalpy measured in kJ/mol.

ΔS is change in entropy measured in J/mol-K.

T is absolute temperature in K.

The sign of ΔG tells if any given process is thermodynamically favored as illustrated by Table 19.3.

Table 19.3   The sign of ΔG and its thermodynamic meaning.

If ΔG Is	The Process Is
negative ($-$)	thermodynamically favored (spontaneous)
positive ($+$)	not thermodynamically favored (nonspontaneous) (the reverse reaction is spontaneous)
zero (0)	at equilibrium

The change in free energy of a reaction can be calculated by the following equation:

$$\Delta G°_{rxn} = \Sigma \Delta G°_{f\,products} - \Sigma \Delta G°_{f\,reactants}$$

The standard free energies of formation, $\Delta G°_f$, of various substances are listed in Appendix C of *Chemistry: The Central Science*.

Example:

What is the standard free energy change for the reaction,
$$2NO(g) + O_2(g) \rightarrow 2NO_2(g)?$$

Solution:

Obtain the values of standard free energy of formation for each of the re-actants and products from Appendix C of Chemistry: The Central Science *and substitute them into the equation. Do not forget to take into account the number of moles of each substance as defined by the coefficients of the balanced equation.*

$$\Delta G°_{rxn} = \Sigma G°_{products} - \Sigma G°_{reactants}$$
$$\Delta G°_{rxn} = 2(+51.58\,kJ/mol) - 0 - 2(+86.71\,kJ/mol)$$
$$= -70.26\,kJ/mol$$

The sign of $\Delta G°$ for the reaction is negative, indicating that this is a ther-modynamically favored process at 298 K.

Free Energy and Temperature   Section 19.6

What causes a process to be thermodynamically favored? What influences chemi-cal and physical change? Every process involves the two thermodynamic proper-ties, enthalpy and entropy. Often a balance exists between enthalpy and entropy, and temperature determines in which direction a reversible reaction will continue spontaneously.

Phase change provides a good example of the role that temperature plays in deter-mining thermodynamic favorability. Consider the melting of ice and freezing of liquid water. Ice melts spontaneously at temperatures above 0 °C and liquid water freezes spontaneously at temperatures below 0 °C. Whether ice melts spontaneously or liquid water freezes spontaneously depends on the temperature.

Ice melts spontaneously at temperatures higher than 0 °C because liquid water is more random than is solid water. The increase in entropy (the positive ΔS), as ice melts, is the driving influence for the change from solid to liquid.

Liquid water freezes spontaneously at temperatures lower than 0 °C because freezing is exothermic (ΔH is negative) and the move to lower enthalpy as liquid changes to solid influences the change.

$$H_2O(l) \rightarrow H_2O(s) + \text{heat}$$

At exactly 0 °C, an equilibrium is established. At 0 °C, ice changes to liquid water at the same rate that liquid water changes to ice. At equilibrium, the drive toward lower enthalpy exactly balances the drive toward higher entropy.

The equation, $\Delta G = \Delta H - T\Delta S$, and the signs of ΔH and ΔS are useful to predict qualitatively the spontaneity of any given reaction. It provides a model to guide our thinking in determining whether a reaction will be thermodynamically favored or not (see Table 19.4).

Table 19.4 The effect of temperature on the spontaneity of reactions.

ΔH	ΔS	$-T\Delta S$	ΔG	**The Reaction Is Thermodynamically**
−	+	−	−	favored at all temperatures
+	−	+	+	not favored at all temperatures
−	−	+	+/−	favored only at low temperatures
+	+	−	+/−	favored only at high temperatures

If ΔH is negative and ΔS is positive, ΔG is always negative and the reaction is thermodynamically favored at all temperatures because the reaction goes toward lower enthalpy and higher entropy.

If ΔH is positive and ΔS is negative, ΔG is always positive and the reaction is not thermodynamically favored at any temperature. (However, the reverse reaction is favored at all temperatures.)

Table 19.5 illustrates that often the change in free energy represents a balance between systems tending toward decreasing enthalpy and increasing entropy. If ΔH and ΔS both are positive, ΔG is negative only when the temperature is high enough for the entropy term to outweigh the enthalpy term. On the other hand, if ΔH and ΔS both are negative, ΔG is negative only when the temperature is low enough for the enthalpy term to outweigh the entropy term.

Table 19.5 A summary of important thermodynamic quantities.

Quantity	Change in Enthalpy	Change in Entropy	Change in Free Energy
Symbol	ΔH	ΔS	ΔG
Unit	kJ/mol	J/mol-K	kJ/mol
Definition	Heat gained by a system	Change in randomness of a system	Available useful work
Comments	+ for endothermic − for exothermic	+ for increasing randomness − for decreasing randomness	+ for nonfavored reactions − for thermodynamically favored reactions $\Delta G = 0$ at equilibrium

---

Your Turn 19.4

Is ΔG for a burning campfire positive or negative? Explain citing the positive or negative signs of ΔH and ΔS for the process. Is there a temperature at which ΔG for a burning campfire will change signs? Explain. Write your answers in the space provided.

Free Energy and the Equilibrium Constant   Section 19.7

The free energy change for any reaction under nonstandard conditions, ΔG, can be calculated from the standard free energy change, $\Delta G°$, by the following equation:

$$\Delta G = \Delta G° + RT \ln Q$$

ΔG = the free energy change under nonstandard conditions

$\Delta G°$ = the free energy change under standard conditions: 25 °C and

1 atm partial pressure of all gases and 1 M concentration for all solutes

R = 8.314 J/mol-K, the ideal-gas constant

T = the absolute temperature in K

Q = the reaction quotient

Example:

Using standard free energies of formation for the reaction,

$$2H_2S(g) + 3O_2(g) \rightarrow 2H_2O(g) + 2SO_2(g),$$

calculate $\Delta G°$ and ΔG for a mixture at 25 °C with the composition below.

$$P_{H_2S} = 1.00 \; atm \quad P_{H_2O} = 0.500 \; atm \quad P_{O_2} = 2.00 \; atm$$

$$P_{SO_2} = 0.750 \; atm$$

Solution:

Using the standard free energies of formation from Appendix C of Chemistry: The Central Science, calculate $\Delta G°$ for the reaction.

$$\Delta G°_{rxn} = \Sigma \; \Delta G°_{products} - \Sigma \; \Delta G°_{reactants}$$

$$\Delta G°_{rxn} = 2(-300.4) + 2(-228.57) - 2(-33.01) - 0$$

$$\Delta G°_{rxn} = -991.9 \; kJ$$

Evaluate Q and use the equation, $\Delta G = \Delta G° + RT \ln Q$, to calculate ΔG.

$$Q = P^2_{SO_2} P^2_{H_2O} / P^2_{H_2S} P^3_{O_2} = (0.750)^2(0.500)^2/(1.00)^2(2.0)^3$$

$$= 0.0176$$

$$\Delta G = \Delta G° + RT \ln Q$$

$$= -991.9 \; kJ + (8.314 \; J/mol\text{-}K)(298 \; K)(1 \; kJ/1000 \; J) \ln (0.0176)$$

$$= -1002 \; kJ$$

Common misconception: When using the equation $\Delta G = \Delta G° + RT \ln Q$, keep in mind that $\Delta G°$ is usually given in kJ/mol, whereas R is in units of J/mol-K. Be sure to convert J to kJ using 1 kJ = 1000 J.

The standard free energy for any reaction is related to the equilibrium constant. At equilibrium, $\Delta G = 0$ and $Q = K$, the equilibrium constant. At equilibrium,

$$\Delta G° = -RT \ln K$$

Example:

The standard free energy change for the following reaction at 25 °C is $-118.4 \; kJ/mol$:

$$KClO_3(s) \rightarrow KCl(s) + 3/2 \; O_2(g)$$

Calculate K_p for the reaction at 25 °C and the equilibrium pressure of O_2 gas.

Solution:

$\Delta G° = -RT \ln K$

$-118.4 \, kJ/mol = -(8.314 \, J/mol\text{-}K)(298 \, K)(1 \, kJ/1000 \, J) \ln K_p$

$\ln K_p = 47.8$

$K_p = e^{47.8} = 5.68 \times 10^{20}$

$K_p = P_{O_2}^{3/2}$

$P_{O_2} = K_p^{2/3} = (5.68 \times 10^{20})^{2/3} = 6.9 \times 10^{13} \, atm$

Multiple Choice Questions

1. The standard free energy of formation, $\Delta G°_f$, for sodium chloride is the free energy change for which of the following reactions?

   A) $Na^+(g) + Cl^-(g) \rightarrow NaCl(g)$

   B) $Na^+(g) + Cl^-(g) \rightarrow NaCl(s)$

   C) $2Na(s) + Cl_2(g) \rightarrow 2NaCl(s)$

   D) $Na(s) + 1/2Cl_2(g) \rightarrow NaCl(s)$

2. For which of these processes is the value of ΔS expected to be negative?

   I.   NaCl is dissolved in water.

   II. Steam condenses to liquid water.

   III. $MgCO_3$ is decomposed into MgO and CO_2.

   A) I only

   B) I and III only

   C) II only

   D) II and III only

3. What are the signs of the enthalpy change and entropy change for the melting of ice?

   $H_2O(s) \rightarrow H_2O(l)$

	$\Delta H°$	$\Delta S°$
A)	+	+
B)	−	−
C)	−	+
D)	+	−

4. Under which set of conditions does a temperature exist at which equilibrium can be established with all reactants and products in standard states?

   I. ΔS is + , ΔH is +

   II. ΔS is − , ΔH is −

   III. ΔS is + , ΔH is −

   A) I only

   B) II only

   C) III only

   D) I and II only

5. Which of the following substances is expected to have the largest standard molar entropy?

   A) $H_2O(l)$

   B) $H_2O(g)$

   C) $H_2O_2(l)$

   D) $H_2O_2(g)$

6. In which process would ΔG be expected to be positive?

   A) melting ice at $-10\,°C$ and 1.0 atm pressure

   B) water evaporating at $25\,°C$ into dry air

   C) cooling hot water to room temperature

   D) sublimation of dry ice (solid carbon dioxide) at $25\,°C$

7. Which is not expected to have a value of zero?

   A) $\Delta H°_f$ for $O_2(g)$

   B) $\Delta G°_f$ for $K(s)$

   C) S for $Ca(s)$ at 0 K

   D) $\Delta G°_f$ for $O(g)$

8. Which process is exothermic and occurs with a decrease in entropy?

   A) $H_2O(l) \rightarrow H_2O(s)$

   B) $H_2O(l) \rightarrow H_2O(g)$

   C) $H_2O(s) \rightarrow H_2O(g)$

   D) $2H_2O(l) \rightarrow 2H_2(g) + O_2(g)$

9. To calculate the entropy change for the following reaction at $25\,°C$ and 1 atm, what thermodynamic information is needed?

   $C(solid\ graphite) + O_2(g) \rightarrow CO_2(g)$

   A) $\Delta H°_f$ for $CO_2(g)$

   B) $\Delta G°_f$ for $CO_2(g)$

   C) $\Delta H°_f$ and $\Delta G°_f$ for $CO_2(g)$

   D) $S°$ for $CO_2(g)$

10. For a certain reaction, $\Delta H° = -150\ kJ/mol$ and $\Delta S° = -50\ J/mol\text{-}K$. Which of the following statements is true about the reaction?

    A) It is thermodynamically favored at high temperatures only.

    B) It is thermodynamically favored at low temperatures only.

    C) It is thermodynamically favored at all temperatures.

    D) It is NOT thermodynamically favored at any temperature.

11. What can be correctly said about the energy diagram for a reversible endothermic reaction?

A) The energy of activation is greater for the reverse reaction than for the forward reaction.

B) The energy of activation is greater for the forward reaction than for the reverse reaction.

C) The energy of activation is the same for the reaction in both directions.

D) The enthalpy of reactants is greater than the enthalpy of products.

12. Which condition describes a reaction at equilibrium?

A) $\Delta G > 0$

B) $\Delta G < 0$

C) $\Delta G = 0$

D) $K = 0$

13. Which substance has the largest standard molar entropy at 25 °C?

A) butane gas

B) ethane gas

C) methane gas

D) pentane gas

14. Which substance has a nonzero standard free energy of formation?

A) $Pb(s)$

B) $Hg(l)$

C) $Cl_2(g)$

D) $O_3(g)$

15. Carbon monoxide reacts with oxygen according to the following thermodynamic equation at 25 °C and 1 atmosphere pressure:

$$2CO(g) + O_2(g) \rightarrow 2CO_2(g) \quad \Delta H = -566 \, kJ$$

Which statement(s) is (are) true?

I.   The reaction is endothermic

II.   The heat of combustion of gaseous carbon monoxide is -283 kJ/mol

III. The standard heat of formation for $CO_2(g)$ is -283 kJ/mol

A) I only

B) II only

C) III only

D) II and III only

Free Response Questions

1. At 25 °C, the equilibrium constant, K_p, for the reaction below is 0.281 atm.

   $$Br_2(l) \rightarrow Br_2(g)$$

   a. Calculate $\Delta G°$ for this reaction.

   b. It takes 193 J to vaporize 1.00 g of $Br_2(l)$ at 25 °C and 1.00 atm pressure. Calculate $\Delta H°$ at 298 K.

   c. Calculate $\Delta S°$ at 298 K for this reaction.

   d. The normal boiling point of a liquid is the temperature at which the liquid and its vapor are at equilibrium at 1 atm pressure. Calculate the normal boiling point of bromine. Assume that $\Delta H°$ and $\Delta S°$ remain constant as the temperature is changed.

   e. What is the equilibrium vapor pressure of bromine in torr at 25 °C?

2. In principle, ethanol can be prepared by the following reaction.

   $$2C(s) + 2H_2(g) + H_2O(l) \rightarrow C_2H_5OH(l)$$

$\Delta H°_f =$	0	0	−285.85	−277.69	kJ/mol
$S° =$	5.740	130.6	69.91	160.7	J/mol-K

   a. Calculate the standard enthalpy change, $\Delta H°$, for the reaction above.

   b. Calculate the standard entropy change, $\Delta S°$, for the reaction above.

   c. Calculate the standard free energy change, $\Delta G°$, for the reaction above at 298 K.

   d. Calculate the value of the equilibrium constant, K_p, at 25 °C for the reaction above.

   e. Calculate the partial pressure of $H_2(g)$ at equilibrium.

3. Calcium chloride dissolves in water with an increase in temperature.

   a. Draw a representation of a hydrated calcium ion and discuss the forces that are involved.

   b. Compare these forces with those of a hydrated sodium ion. Use Coulomb's law to predict which hydrated ion, calcium or sodium, will have the larger intermolecular forces. Justify your answer.

   c. Is the dissolving of calcium chloride an exothermic or endothermic process? Use your answer to predict relative strengths of the ion–ion forces in solid calcium chloride and the ion–dipole forces in the solution.

   d. Predict the sign of ΔG for the dissolving of calcium chloride. Is the process thermodynamically favored? Justify your answer.

Multiple Choice Answers and Explanations

1. D. The standard free energy of formation is the free energy change of a formation reaction, one that forms one mole of a substance from its component elements in their most stable forms. Solid sodium and gaseous diatomic chlorine are the most stable forms of those elements.

2. C. A negative ΔS denotes a change from a more random state to one of more order. In general, solids are more ordered than liquids, which are more ordered than gases. Liquid water is more ordered than steam. When solid NaCl dissolves in liquid water, it dissociates into more random aqueous ions in the liquid phase. Carbon dioxide gas is more random than solid magnesium carbonate.

3. A. All solids melt endothermically (where $\Delta H°$ is positive) because solids must absorb energy to overcome the strong attractive forces that hold the particles together. All solids melt with an increase in entropy (where $\Delta S°$ is positive) because liquids are more random than solids.

4. D. The fundamental thermodynamic condition at equilibrium is when ΔG is zero. At equilibrium, the equation $\Delta G = \Delta H - T\Delta S$ becomes $\Delta H = T\Delta S$. Because T is the absolute temperature in Kelvin, it must be positive. A positive temperature can only exist when the signs of ΔH and ΔS are both negative or both positive.

5. D. Entropy is the degree of randomness or disorder of a system. Gases have higher entropies than liquids, which have higher entropies than solids. Additionally, when comparing substances having the same phase, the more complex the substance, the higher its entropy because complex substances have more possible rotational and vibrational modes of motion.

6. A. ΔG is positive for nonthermodynamically favored processes. When determining qualitatively the sign of ΔG, pose the question: left on its own, does it happen? If the answer is yes, the process is thermodynamically favored and the sign of ΔG is negative. If the answer is no, the process is not favored thermodynamically and the sign of ΔG is positive. Ice will not melt spontaneously at $-10\,°C$ unless it is under pressure. ΔG is negative for all the other processes listed because left on their own, they will happen spontaneously.

7. D. $O(g)$ is not the most stable form of oxygen, so its standard free energy is nonzero. Standard heats of formation, $\Delta H°_f$, and standard free energies of formation, $\Delta G°_f$, are zero for elements in their most stable form at 25 °C. The most stable forms of oxygen, potassium, and bromine are $O_2(g)$, $K(s)$, and $Br_2(l)$, respectively. The third law of thermodynamics states that the entropy, S, of a pure crystalline substance at absolute zero is zero. $Ca(s)$ at 0 K has $S = 0$.

8. A. In general, gases have more entropy than liquids and liquids have more entropy than solids. Phase changes from gas to liquid, gas to solid, and liquid to solid all are exothermic (release heat to the environment) and occur with a decrease in entropy (result in less random, more ordered products). The decomposition of liquid water to form gaseous products is endothermic and takes place with a large increase in entropy.

9. **C.** The given reaction is the formation reaction for $CO_2(g)$. Therefore, the values for $\Delta H°_f$ and $\Delta G°_f$ for $CO_2(g)$ are the same as the values for $\Delta H°_{rxn}$ and $\Delta G°_{rxn}$ for $CO_2(g)$. ΔS_{rxn} can be calculated using the equation, $\Delta G°_{rxn} = \Delta H°_{rxn} - T\,\Delta S°_{rxn}$. The given Celsius temperature must be converted to Kelvin. $\Delta H°_f$ and $\Delta G°_f$ for neither C(solid graphite) nor $O_2(g)$ are necessary because both are elements in their most stable forms, so their values are each, by definition, zero.

10. **B.** Use the equation, $\Delta G = \Delta H - T\Delta S$, to guide your thinking. To be thermodynamically favored requires a negative ΔG and that can only be achieved if the absolute value of the negative ΔH term is larger than the absolute value of the $T\Delta S$ term. At low temperatures, ΔG will be negative. At high temperatures, it will be positive. There is a temperature at which ΔG will be zero and the system will reach equilibrium.

11. **B.** An endothermic reaction has a higher activation energy for the forward reaction than for the reverse reaction and the rate of reaction decreases with increasing activation energy. The enthalpy of products for an endothermic reaction is higher than the enthalpy of reactants.

12. **C.** The equilibrium condition is when $\Delta G = 0$. When $\Delta G = 0$ in the equation, $\Delta G = \Delta H - T\Delta S$, then $\Delta H = T\,\Delta S$. This means that the change in enthalpy of the system exactly balances the change in entropy.

13. **D.** Entropy increases with increasing molecular complexity. Methane, ethane, butane, and pentane have 1, 2, 4, and 5 carbon atoms, respectively. Pentane having 5 carbon atoms and 12 hydrogen atoms is more complex than the others.

14. **D.** The standard free energy of formation is $\Delta G°_f$ for the formation of one mole of a substance from its elements in their most stable thermodynamic form at 25 °C. That means that the $\Delta G°_f$ for all elements in their most stable form is zero. Ozone is not the most stable form of oxygen so its standard free energy of formation is nonzero.

15. **B.** The reaction is exothermic because ΔH is negative. When two moles of carbon monoxide are combusted, -566 kJ is released so $1/2\,(-566) = -283$ kJ/mol is released upon the combustion of one mole of carbon monoxide. The heat of formation of carbon dioxide is the heat of the formation reaction: $C(s) + O_2(g) \rightarrow CO_2(g)$.

Free Response Answers

1. a. $\Delta G° = -RT \ln K = -(8.314\ J/mol\text{-}K)(25 + 273\ K) \ln (0.281)$
   $= 3145\ J/mol = 3.15\ kJ/mol$

   b. $x\ kJ/mol = (193\ J/g)(160\ g/mol)(1\ kJ/1000\ J) = 30.9\ kJ/mol$

   c. $\Delta G° = \Delta H° - T\Delta S°$
   $\Delta S° = (\Delta H° - \Delta G°)/T = (30.9 - 3.15)/298\ K$
   $= .0931\ kJ/mol\text{-}K = 93.1\ J/mol\text{-}K$

d. *The boiling point is the temperature at which the equilibrium vapor pressure of bromine equals the external pressure. Because the system is at equilibrium, $\Delta G = 0$.*

$$\Delta G = \Delta H - T\Delta S$$
$$0 = 30.9\ kJ/mol - T(.0931\ kJ/mol\text{-}K)$$
$$T = 30.9/.0931 = 332\ K$$

e. $K_p = P_{Br_2}(g)$
   $K_p = (0.281\ atm)(760\ torr/atm) = 214\ torr$

2. a. $\Delta H°_{rxn} = \Sigma\ \Delta H°_{f\,products} - \Sigma\ \Delta H°_{f\,reactants}$
      $= -(-285.85) + (-277.69) = +8.16\ kJ/mol$

   b. $\Delta S°rxn = \Sigma S°_{products} - \Sigma S°_{reactants}$
      $= +160.7 - 69.91 - 2(130.6) - 2(5.740) = -181.9\ J/mol\text{-}K$

   c. $\Delta G°_{rxn} = \Delta H°_{rxn} - T\Delta S°_{rxn}$
      $\Delta G°_{rxn} = +8.16\ kJ/mol - (298K)(-181.9\ J/mol\text{-}K)$
      $(1\ kJ/1000\ J) = +62.4\ kJ/mol$
      $\Delta G° = -RT\ ln\ K$

   d. $ln\ K = -(+62.4\ kJ/mol)/\left[(8.314\ J/mol\text{-}K)(1\ kJ/1000\ J)(298\ K)\right]$
      $= -25.2$
      $K = e^{-25.2} = 1.14 \times 10^{-11}$

   e. $K_p = P_{H_2}^{-2}$
      $P_{H_2} = K_p^{-1/2} = (1.14 \times 10^{-11})^{-1/2} = 2.96 \times 10^5\ atm$

3. *This question reviews the concepts learned in Topic 13 and connects them to the material in this topic.*

   a. *The drawing will look much like the far-right depiction in Figure 13.1, except Ca^{2+} replaces Na^+. Relatively strong ion–dipole attractions occur between the positive calcium ion and the negative ends of the water molecules.*

   b. *The ion–dipole force between calcium ion and water is stronger than that between sodium ion and water because calcium carries a 2+ charge, whereas sodium's charge is 1+. Coulomb's law states that the force of attraction between two particles is directly proportional to their charges.*

   c. *Calcium chloride dissolves exothermically as evidenced by the observation that the temperature of the solution increases. Because heat is released, the ion–dipole forces in the solution must be stronger than the ion–ion forces of the solid ionic compound.*

   d. *The sign of ΔG is negative because the dissolving process happens spontaneously. That is, it is thermodynamically favored.*

Your Turn Answers

19.1. a. *Entropy of the system increases when helium is released from a toy balloon because the gas from the balloon mixes with the gases in the atmosphere, causing an increase in randomness or disorder.*

b.

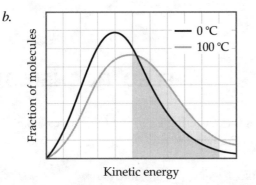

Entropy increases with increasing temperature because the distribution of kinetic energies of the molecules increases.

19.2. *Butane, $CH_3CH_2CH_2CH_3$, has greater entropy than propane, $CH_3CH_2CH_3$, because the molecules of propane are more complex than the molecules of methane.*

Steam has more entropy than ice because gases are more random and disordered than are solids.

19.3. *Gaseous iodine has a higher standard molar entropy than either liquid or solid iodine because gases are more random than liquids or solids. Liquid iodine has a higher value than solid iodine because liquids are more random than solids.*

19.4. *A burning campfire is a thermodynamically favored process where ΔG is negative. For the process, ΔH is negative and ΔS is positive, so ΔG is negative at all temperatures. Thus, a burning campfire will never reach equilibrium nor become thermodynamically unfavored.*

ELECTROCHEMISTRY

The content in this topic is the basis for mastering Learning Objectives 3.8, 3.9, 3.12, and 3.13 as found in the Curriculum Framework.

When you finish reviewing this topic, be sure you are able to:

- Identify redox reactions by the electrons transferred from the oxidized reactant to the reduced reactant
- Assign an oxidation number to each atom in a chemical formula
- Balance a redox reaction using the half-reaction method
- Calculate quantities involved in a redox titration
- Identify important redox reactions related to energy production such as the combustion of fossil fuels and the metabolism of food
- Interpret diagrams of voltaic and electrolytic cells
- Identify oxidation at the anode and reduction at the cathode of an electrochemical cell.
- Calculate cell potential (voltage, EMF) under standard conditions using a table of standard reduction potentials
- Compare qualitatively, using Le Châtelier's principle, the voltage and electron flow in a cell at nonstandard conditions to that of a cell at standard conditions
- Predict spontaneity (thermodynamic favorability) from the cell potential of a redox reaction and its standard free energy, $\Delta G°$
- Calculate quantities such as mass, current, time, charge, and number of moles of electrons using Faraday's constant and the stoichiometry of a redox reaction

Section 20.1   **Oxidation States and Oxidation–Reduction Reactions**

Electrochemistry refers to the interchange of electrical and chemical energy. In electrochemical processes, chemical energy is transformed to electrical energy or electricity is used to cause chemical change.

An **oxidation number**, also called **oxidation state**, is a positive or negative number assigned to an element in a molecule or ion according to a set of rules.

Common misconception: Oxidation state or oxidation number is often incorrectly confused with charge. Oxidation number is not charge. Oxidation number and charge are equivalent only when considering a monatomic ion.

Oxidation numbers are a way to keep track of electrons in redox reactions. Table 20.1 lists a set of simplified rules for determining oxidation numbers. For a more complete list of rules, see Section 4.4 of *Chemistry: The Central Science*.

Table 20.1   Simplified rules for determining oxidation numbers.

1. The oxidation number of combined oxygen is usually $2-$, except in the peroxide ion, O_2^{2-}, where the oxidation number of oxygen is $1-$. Examples: In H_2O_2 and BaO_2, O is $1-$.
2. The oxidation number of combined hydrogen is usually $1+$, except in the hydride ion, H^-, where it is $1-$. Examples: In NaH and CaH_2, H is $1-$.
3. The oxidation numbers of all individual atoms of a formula add to the charge on that formula. When in doubt, separate ionic compounds into common cation–anion pairs. Examples:

Na	K^+	O_2	Ca^{2+}	H_2SO_4	NO_3^-	$Mg_3(PO_4)_2 =$	Mg^{2+}	PO_4^{3-}
0	$1+$	0	$2+$	$1+6+2-$	$5+2-$	$2+$ $5+2-$	$2+$	$5+2-$

Your Turn 20.1

What is the oxidation number of sulfur in each of the following atoms, molecules, and ions: sulfate, thiosulfate, sulfide, sulfite, thiocyanate, sulfur, sulfur dioxide, sulfur trioxide? In which case(s) is(are) oxidation number equal to charge?

Write your answer in the space provided.

An **oxidation–reduction reaction**, also called a **redox reaction**, is a reaction where electrons are transferred between reactants. The oxidation numbers of some of the elements change as they become products.

Oxidation is the loss of electrons. Substances that lose electrons are said to be oxidized.

Reduction is the gain of electrons. Substances that gain electrons are reduced. Both an oxidation and a reduction occur in all redox reactions.

In a redox reaction, one substance loses electrons and another gains electrons. For example, the chemical reaction in a common alkaline flashlight cell is complex, but it can be approximately represented by the equation below. The oxidation numbers of each element are assigned according to the rules given in Table 20.1.

$$2MnO_2(s) + Zn(s) + 2H_2O(l) \rightarrow 2MnO(OH)(s) + Zn(OH)_2(s)$$
$$4+\ 2-\quad\ 0\quad\ \ 1+\ 2-\quad\ \ 3+\ 2-\ 2-\ 1+\quad\ 2+\ 2-\ 1+$$

Notice that Mn changes oxidation numbers from 4+ to 3+ as it goes from MnO_2 to $MnO(OH)$. Also Zn changes from 0 to 2+. MnO_2 is reduced because it has gained electrons. (The oxidation number of Mn has been reduced.) Zn is oxidized because it has lost electrons. (The oxidation number of Zn has increased.)

In the alkaline cell reaction, there is a transfer of electrons from Zn to MnO_2. The cell is designed to take advantage of this transfer of electrons by allowing the electrons to flow as electricity through an external circuit.

Common misconception: Although you will see the terms *reducing agent* and *oxidizing agent* in many texts, these terms are not used on the AP exam. *In the reaction above, Zn is called the reducing agent because it is the agent that provides electrons for MnO_2 to be reduced. MnO_2 is the oxidizing agent because it is the agent that takes electrons away from Zn, causing Zn to be oxidized. The substance oxidized is the reducing agent and the substance reduced is the oxidizing agent.*

Your Turn 20.2

How can you tell that the following reaction is a redox reaction? Explain your reasoning. Assign oxidation numbers and identify the reactant that is oxidized and the reduced reactant.

$N_2(g) + 3H_2(g) \rightarrow 2NH_3(g)$. *Write your answers in the space provided.*

Balancing Redox Equations   Section 20.2

A **half-reaction** is an equation that shows either a reduction or an oxidation. Aqueous redox equations are conveniently balanced by the method of half-reactions. For example, we can represent the alkaline cell reaction shown above as separate oxidation and reduction half-reactions.

The **reduction half-reaction** shows electrons as reactants. The **oxidation half-reaction** shows electrons as products. The sum of the half-reactions yields the complete equation.

Table 20.2 illustrates some simplified rules for balancing half-reactions. For a detailed set of rules, see Section 20.2 of *Chemistry: The Central Science*.

Table 20.2   Simplified rules for balancing half-reactions.

If the reaction is in acidic solution, stop at Step 4:
1. Balance all elements other than H or O.
2. Balance O by adding H_2O as required.
3. Balance H by adding H^+ as required.
4. Balance charge by adding e^- to the more positive side.
If the reaction is in basic solution, continue through Step 7:
5. Count H^+ and add equal numbers of OH^- to both sides.
6. Combine each H^+ and OH^- on one side to yield water. ($H^+ + OH^- \rightarrow H_2O$).
7. Combine or cancel water molecules as needed.

Example:

Balance the following equation in acidic solution.

$$HOCl(aq) + NO(g) \rightarrow Cl_2(g) + NO_3^-(aq)$$

Solution:

First, separate the reactants and products into two half-reactions. HOCl and Cl_2 go together because they both contain Cl. Also, NO and NO_3^- are a pair because they both have N. Once the reactants and products are separated, just follow the rules.

$$HOCl(aq) \rightarrow Cl_2(g) \qquad NO(g) \rightarrow NO_3^-(aq)$$

1. $2HOCl(aq) \rightarrow Cl_2(g)$
2. $2HOCl(aq) \rightarrow Cl_2(g) + 2H_2O$
3. $2H^+ + 2HOCl(aq) \rightarrow Cl_2(g) + 2H_2O$
4. $2e^- + 2H^+ + 2HOCl(aq) \rightarrow Cl_2(g) + 2H_2O$

$NO(g) \rightarrow NO_3^-(aq)$

1. $NO(g) \rightarrow NO_3^-(aq)$
2. $2H_2O + NO(g) \rightarrow NO_3^-(aq)$
3. $2H_2O + NO(g) \rightarrow NO_3^-(aq) + 4H^+$
4. $2H_2O + NO(g) \rightarrow NO_3^-(aq) + 4H^+ + 3e^-$

Now, equalize the number of electrons transferred in the half-reactions by multiplying the Cl reaction by 3 and the N reaction by 2 and add the half-reactions. The goal is to cancel all the electrons in the final balanced equation.

$3(2e^- + 2H^+ + 2HOCl(aq) \rightarrow Cl_2(g) + 2H_2O) =$
$\quad 6e^- + 6H^+ + 6HOCl(aq) \rightarrow 3Cl_2(g) + 6H_2O$
$2(2H_2O + NO(g) \rightarrow NO_3^-(aq) + 4H^+ + 3e^-) =$
$\quad \underline{4H_2O + 2NO(g) \rightarrow 2NO_3^-(aq) + 8H^+ + 6e^-}$
$6HOCl(aq) + 2NO(g) \rightarrow 3Cl_2(g) + 2NO_3^-(aq) + 2H_2O + 2H^+$

Example:

Balance the above reaction assuming it also happens in basic solution.

Solution:

First, apply Rules 1–4 as if the reaction were in acidic solution. Then, continue with Rules 5–7 to balance it in basic solution:

$6HOCl(aq) + 2NO(g) \rightarrow 3Cl_2(g) + 2NO_3^-(aq) + 2H_2O + 2H^+$

5. $2OH^- + 6HOCl(aq) + 2NO(g) \rightarrow 3Cl_2(g) + 2NO_3^-(aq) + 2H_2O +$
$\quad 2H^+ + 2OH^-$
6. $2OH^- + 6HOCl(aq) + 2NO(g) \rightarrow 3Cl_2(g) + 2NO_3^-(aq) + 2H_2O + 2H_2O$
7. $2OH^- + 6HOCl(aq) + 2NO(g) \rightarrow 3Cl_2(g) + 2NO_3^-(aq) + 4H_2O$

The percentage of hydrogen peroxide can be determined by a redox titration of the unknown solution into a standard solution of potassium permanganate. The endpoint of the titration is visualized by the abrupt disappearance of the deep purple permanganate ion to yield a colorless solution. The standard solution is prepared by dissolving 20.65 g of $KMnO_4$ in enough water to make 500 mL of solution. Exactly 25.00 mL of this solution is titrated with an unknown solution of hydrogen peroxide. The endpoint is reached upon addition of 34.05 mL of H_2O_2. The density of the H_2O_2 solution is 1.05 g/mL. The half-reactions are given:

$$H_2O_2 \rightarrow 2H^+ + O_2 + 2e^-$$
$$5e^- + 8H^+ + MnO_4^- \rightarrow 4H_2O + Mn^{2+}$$

a. *Calculate the molar concentration of the standard $KMnO_4$ solution.*
b. *Write a balanced chemical equation for the reaction.*
c. *Determine the molar concentration of the H_2O_2 solution.*
d. *Calculate the grams of H_2O_2 used in the experiment.*
e. *Determine the percent of hydrogen peroxide in the solution.*

Write your answers in the space provided.

The production of energy by burning fossil fuels or metabolizing food is a practical application of redox reactions. For example, methane in natural gas and propane in a barbecue grill burn exothermically in air to produce carbon dioxide, water, and significant amounts of heat:

$$CH_4(g) + 2\,O_2(g) \rightarrow CO_2(g) + 2\,H_2O(g) \quad \Delta H = -802\,kJ$$
$$2\,C_3H_8(l) + 5\,O_2(g) \rightarrow 3\,CO_2(g) + 4\,H_2O(g) \quad \Delta H = -2132\,kJ$$

Your Turn 20.4

Glucose, $C_6H_{12}O_6$, is a typical carbohydrate that has a heat of combustion of $-2803\ kJ/mol$. The fat tristearin, $C_{57}H_{110}O_6$, has a food value of about 9.00 Cal/g.

    a. Write and balance thermochemical equations for the combustion of each of these foods.

    b. Calculate the food value in Calories per gram for glucose.

    c. Calculate the molar heat of combustion of tristearin.

Write your answers in the space provided.

Section 20.3

Voltaic Cells

A **voltaic cell** (also called a galvanic cell) is a device that spontaneously transforms chemical energy into electrical energy. The transfer of electrons of a redox reaction takes place through an external pathway.

Figure 20.1 illustrates a typical voltaic cell. Two compartments, called half-cells, physically separate the reactants. Each half-cell consists of a metal electrode immersed in an aqueous solution.

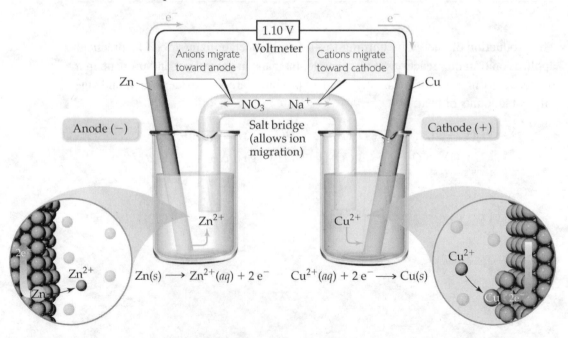

Figure 20.1 A voltaic cell uses a redox reaction to spontaneously generate an electric current. Electrons flow from the anode to the cathode. Anions migrate toward the anode and cations migrate toward the cathode.

The **anode** compartment is where **oxidation**, the loss of electrons, takes place. In Figure 20.1, the anode compartment contains a zinc metal anode and a zinc nitrate solution.

In the **cathode** compartment, **reduction**, the gain of electrons, takes place. The cathode compartment in Figure 20.1 contains a copper metal cathode and a copper(II) nitrate solution.

Because the reactants are separated, the reaction can occur only when the transfer of electrons takes place through an external circuit. Electrons always flow spontaneously from the anode to the cathode.

The voltaic cell uses a **salt bridge** to complete the electrical circuit. As oxidation and reduction take place, ions from the half-cell compartments migrate through the salt bridge to maintain the electrical neutrality of the respective solutions. Cations always move toward the cathode and anions move toward the anode.

Anode compartment oxidation half-reaction: $Zn(s) \rightarrow Zn^{2+}(aq) + 2e^-$

Cathode compartment reduction half-reaction: $Cu^{2+}(aq) + 2e^- \rightarrow Cu(s)$

Overall reaction: $Zn(s) + Cu^{2+}(aq) \rightarrow Zn^{2+}(aq) + Cu(s)$

Cell Potentials Under Standard Conditions   Section 20.4

Cell potential, E_{cell} (also called electromotive force, EMF), is the potential difference that exists between the anode and the cathode of a voltaic cell. As a redox reaction takes place in a voltaic cell, the cell potential pushes electrons through the external circuit. Cell potential is measured in volts.

One **volt** is the potential difference required to impart one joule of energy to one coulomb of charge (1 volt = 1 joule per coulomb, 1 V = 1 J/C).

Cell voltage, E_{cell}, is positive for a spontaneous (thermodynamically favored) reaction.

A **standard reduction potential**, $E°_{cell}$, for a given half-reaction is the electric potential when that half-cell is coupled with a reference half-cell. The standard conditions are 25 °C, 1 atm pressure, and 1 M solutions. The reference half-cell is the standard hydrogen electrode whose potential is assigned 0.000 V. The reduction half-reaction of the hydrogen electrode is:

$$2H^+(aq) + 2e^- \rightarrow H_2(g) \qquad E°_{red} = 0.000 \text{ V}$$

Common misconception: Do not confuse E_{cell} with $E°_{cell}$. E_{cell} refers to a cell potential under any nonstandard conditions. $E°_{cell}$ denotes a cell voltage under the standard conditions of 25 °C, 1 atm pressure, and 1 M solutions.

Table 20.3 lists the standard reduction potentials of several half-cells. (Appendix E of *Chemistry: The Central Science* has a more detailed list of standard reduction potentials.) For convenience, all half-reactions are written as reductions. The reverse reactions (oxidations) have the same cell voltage but with the opposite sign.

Table 20.3   Selected standard reduction potentials.

Oxidized/Reduced Substances	Half-Reaction	$E°_{red}$(volts) Forward Reaction	$E°_{ox}$ (volts) Reverse Reaction
F_2/F^-	$F_2(g) + 2e^- \rightarrow 2F^-(aq)$	+2.87	−2.87
Cl_2/Cl^-	$Cl_2(g) + 2e^- \rightarrow 2Cl^-(aq)$	+1.359	−1.359
Ag^+/Ag	$Ag^+(aq) + 1e^- \rightarrow Ag(s)$	+0.799	−0.799
Cu^{2+}/Cu	$Cu^{2+}(aq) + 2e^- \rightarrow Cu(s)$	+0.337	−0.337
H^+/H_2	$2H^+(aq) + 2e^- \rightarrow H_2(g)$	0.000	0.000
Zn^{2+}/Zn	$Zn^{2+}(aq) + 2e^- \rightarrow Zn(s)$	−0.762	+0.762
Al^{3+}/Al	$Al^{3+}(aq) + 3e^- \rightarrow Al(s)$	−1.66	+1.66

Reactants that lose electrons are oxidized. A table of standard reduction potentials lists the relative tendency for a substance to be reduced. Easily reduced reactants have relatively high positive values of $E°_{red}$. The more positive the $E°_{red}$ value for a substance, the more easily the species is reduced. For example, $F_2(g)$ is the most easily reduced substance listed in Table 20.3. Al^{3+} is the least easily reduced substance in Table 20.3 because it has the most negative $E°_{red}$.

Reactants that are oxidized lose electrons. If all the half-reactions in a table of standard reduction potentials are reversed, the signs of the accompanying $E°$ values are reversed as well. Such a "reverse table" is a table of oxidation potentials. The more positive the $E°_{ox}$ value, the more readily the substance is oxidized. For example, $Al(s)$ is the most easily oxidized substance listed in Table 20.3.

A table of standard reduction potentials is useful in determining the thermodynamically favored reaction that will take place in a voltaic cell and what its voltage will be. When comparing two reduction potentials, a more positive voltage signifies a greater tendency for reduction. Therefore, when coupling two half-reactions, the one with the more positive voltage will be the reduction and it will force the other half-reaction to occur in reverse and become the oxidation.

All modern references employ tables of standard reduction potentials only. An oxidation potential has the same value as a corresponding reduction potential with an opposite sign.

To determine the thermodynamically favored reaction for any cell made up of two half-cells, reverse the half-reaction with the less positive $E°_{red}$, and add it to the half-reaction with the more positive voltage.

To determine the cell potential of any two coupled half-reactions, use the equation:

$$E°_{cell} = E°_{red} + E°_{ox}$$

Example:

What is the reaction that occurs when a Ag half-cell is coupled with a Cu half-cell? Calculate the cell potential.

Solution:

From Table 20.3, the half-reactions are:

	Half-reaction	$E°_{red}(V)$	$E°_{ox}(V)$
Ag^+/Ag	$Ag^+(aq) + 1e^- \rightarrow Ag(s)$	$+0.799$	-0.799
Cu^{2+}/Cu	$Cu^{2+}(aq) + 2e^- \rightarrow Cu(s)$	$+0.337$	-0.337

The Ag half-reaction has the more positive voltage. Reverse the Cu half-reaction and add it to the Ag half-reaction. (Notice that to cancel the electrons, the Ag half-reaction is multiplied by a factor of 2! This factor does not change the value of $E°_{red}$!)

$$2Ag^+(aq) + 2e^- \rightarrow 2Ag(s) \qquad E°_{red} = +0.799$$

$$Cu(s) \rightarrow Cu^{2+}(aq) + 2e^- \qquad E°_{ox} = -0.337$$

$$\overline{2Ag^+(aq) + Cu(s) \rightarrow 2Ag(s) + Cu^{2+} \qquad E°_{cell} = +0.462}$$

To determine the voltage, $E°_{cell}$, for the cell, add the voltages of the half-reactions. (Remember to change the sign of the reduction potential for the oxidation half-reaction.)

$$E°_{cell} = E°_{red} + E°_{ox} = 0.799 + (-0.337) = +0.462 \text{ V}$$

Common misconception: Changing the coefficient in a balanced half-reaction does not affect the value of the standard reduction potential. Although, in the example, the Ag half-reaction is multiplied by a factor of 2 to make the electrons balance, the value of $E°$ is not proportional to the balanced equation and should not be multiplied by 2!

Table 20.4 summarizes how to determine a cell potential from a table of standard reduction potentials.

Table 20.4 Simplified rules for using a table of standard reduction potentials to determine the overall reaction and the voltage, $E°_{cell}$, for a cell consisting of any two half-cells.

1. Select the half-reaction with the more positive voltage as the reduction.
2. Reverse the half-reaction with the less positive voltage and add it to the reduction half-reaction.
3. Calculate the cell voltage, $E°_{cell}$, by adding $E°_{red}$ for the reduction half-reaction to $-E°_{red}$ for the oxidation half-reaction.
$E°_{cell} = E°_{red} + E°_{ox}$ ($E°_{ox} = -E°_{red}$ for the reversed reaction.)

Your Turn 20.5

Using the data in Table 20.3, choose the half-cells that, when coupled, will give the most positive voltage. Write the balanced equation for the reaction and calculate the voltage. Explain your answer. Write your answer in the space provided.

Section 20.5

Free Energy and Redox Reactions

A **thermodynamically favored (spontaneous) process** is one that happens on its own without any outside assistance. A thermodynamically favored reaction has a negative value for free energy, ΔG, and a positive value for cell potential, E_{cell}.

Free energy and cell potential are related by the following equation:

$$\Delta G° = -nFE°$$

where ΔG is free energy in kJ/mol

n is the number of moles of electrons transferred

F is Faraday's constant. One Faraday is the electrical charge carried by one mole of electrons. $1\ F = 96{,}485$ coulombs/mol e^- = 96,485 J/V-mol e^-.

$E°$ is the cell potential

Example:

Assume that aluminum and zinc half-cells are suitably connected at 298 K and that both aqueous solutions are 1.00 M concentrations (standard conditions).

a. *Write the half-reaction for the cathode.*
b. *Write the half-reaction for the anode.*
c. *Write the overall cell reaction.*
d. *Calculate the $E°$ for the voltaic cell.*
e. *Calculate the free energy change for the cell. Is the reaction thermodynamically favored? Explain.*
f. *Calculate the equilibrium constant for this reaction.*

Solution:

a. *From Table 20.3, the reduction half-reactions and their corresponding $E°$ values are:*

$Zn^{2+}/Zn \quad Zn^{2+}(aq) + 2e^- \rightarrow Zn(s) \quad -0.762$

$Al^{3+}/Al \quad Al^{3+}(aq) + 3e^- \rightarrow Al(s) \quad -1.66$

The reduction half-reaction is the Zn^{2+}/Zn half-reaction because it has the more positive $E°_{red}$.

$Zn^{2+}(aq) + 2e^- \rightarrow Zn(s) \; E°_{red} = -0.762 \; V$

b. *The oxidation half-reaction is the reverse of the listed Al^{3+}/Al half-reaction:*

$Al(s) \rightarrow Al^{3+}(aq) + 3e^- \quad E°_{ox} = +1.66 \; V$

c. *Multiply each half-reaction by coefficients that balance the electrons and add the half-reactions.*

$3(Zn^{2+}(aq) + 2e^- \rightarrow Zn(s)) \quad = 3Zn^{2+}(aq) + 6e^- \rightarrow 3Zn(s)$

$2(Al(s) \rightarrow Al^{3+}(aq) + 3e^-) \quad = 2Al(s) \rightarrow 2Al^{3+}(aq) + 6e^-$

$3Zn^{2+}(aq) + 2Al(s) \rightarrow 3Zn(s) + 2Al^{3+}(aq)$

d. *Add the cell potentials of the two half-reactions. Do not multiply the cell voltages by the coefficients that balance the equation.*

$E°_{cell} = E°_{red} + E°_{ox} = -0.762 \; V + 1.66 \; V = +0.90 \; V$

e. *In the equation, $\Delta G° = -nFE°$, the number of moles of electrons transferred is 6, as evidenced by the balanced half-reactions.*

$\Delta G° = -nFE°$

$\Delta G° = -(6 \; mol \; e^-)(96{,}485 \; J/V\text{-}mol \; e^-)(+0.90 \; V) = -520{,}000 \; J$

$= -520 \; kJ$

The positive value of $E°$ and the corresponding negative value of $\Delta G°$ both indicate that the reaction is thermodynamically favored, which we would expect in a voltaic cell.

f. *From Topic 19, $\Delta G = -RT \ln K$*

where $R = 8.314 \; J/K \; mol$

T = absolute temperature

K = the equilibrium constant

$\Delta G° = -RT \ln K$

$-520{,}000 \; J/mol = -(8.314 \; J/K \; mol)(298 \; K) \ln K$

$\ln K = 210$

$K = e^{210} = 1.6 \times 10^{91}$

The equilibrium constant is very large, which means that the reaction goes nearly to completion. This is consistent with the very large negative free energy, indicating a thermodynamically favored reaction.

Section 20.6

Cell Potentials Under Nonstandard Conditions

As a voltaic cell discharges, reactants are consumed and products are generated. The concentrations of reactants decrease while those of products increase. As the cell operates, the conditions become nonstandard and the voltage drops. Some useful predictions can be made by considering the value of Q in the thermodynamic equation, $\Delta G = \Delta G° + RT \ln Q$.

Consider the cell reaction in the previous example.

$$3Zn^{2+}(aq) + 2Al(s) \rightarrow 3Zn(s) + 2Al^{3+}(aq) \quad E°_{cell} = +0.90 \text{ V}$$

The voltage of the cell is dependent on the concentrations of reactants and products. As the cell operates, $[Zn^{2+}]$ decreases and $[Al^{3+}]$ increases. As the value of Q becomes greater, the value of ΔG becomes more positive and the reaction is less thermodynamically favored in the forward direction. A less thermodynamically favored reaction will experience a drop in voltage from the standard 0.90 V. As time goes on, the reaction eventually reaches equilibrium and the cell voltage becomes zero.

Your Turn 20.6

←───

Under what conditions might the reaction in the above example have a cell voltage that is greater than 0.90 V? Justify your answer by considering the value of Q. Write your answer in the space provided.

Common misconception: Remember that E_{cell} is the voltage of a cell at nonstandard conditions and that $E°_{cell}$ is the voltage at standard conditions.

Section 20.9

Electrolysis

Electrolysis is the application of an electric current to a chemical system.

An **electrolytic cell** is a device that uses electrical energy to cause a nonthermodynamically favored (nonspontaneous) chemical reaction to occur. An electrolytic cell converts electrical energy into chemical energy. Figure 20.2 illustrates an electrolytic cell.

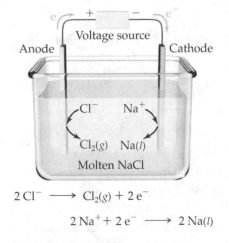

$$2\,Cl^- \longrightarrow Cl_2(g) + 2\,e^-$$

$$2\,Na^+ + 2\,e^- \longrightarrow 2\,Na(l)$$

Figure 20.2 Diagram of an electrolytic cell for the electrolysis of molten NaCl.

Solid sodium chloride does not conduct electricity and cannot be electrolyzed because the ions are locked in place in a strong three-dimensional ionic lattice.

However, molten sodium chloride does conduct electricity. The energy required to melt the solid overcomes the attractive forces that hold the ions in the lattice. The ions are free to migrate to the electrodes. Negative chloride ions migrate to the anode and give up their electrons to become chlorine gas. Positive sodium ions move to the cathode, collect electrons, and become liquid sodium. The half-reactions, the overall equation, and the corresponding voltages of the electrolytic cell are:

Anode reduction: $Cl^- \rightarrow 1/2\,Cl_2(g) + 1\,e^-$ $E°_{ox} = -1.359\ V$

Cathode oxidation: $Na^+ + 1\,e^- \rightarrow Na(l)$ $E°_{red} = -2.71\ V$

Overall reaction: $Na^+ + Cl^- \rightarrow Na(l) + 1/2\,Cl_2(g)$ $E°_{red} = -4.07\ V$

Notice that the overall reaction has a negative voltage, so it is not thermodynamically favored. It required just over 4 V to electrolyze molten sodium chloride. All electrolysis reactions are not thermodynamically favored.

The Electrolysis of Water Using an Inert Electrolyte

Water, in the presence of an inert electrolyte such as sodium sulfate, will undergo electrolysis. While pure water does not conduct electricity, inert ions in water can migrate toward the electrodes and carry an electric current sufficient to electrolyze water. Because water is a polar molecule, the partially positive hydrogen end of a molecule will migrate toward the negative cathode and pick up electrons to become hydrogen gas. The oxygen end of a water molecule will migrate toward the anode and give up electrons to become oxygen gas. The half-reactions and the overall reaction are:

Cathode reduction:

$$2H_2O(l) + 2e^- \rightarrow H_2(g) + 2OH^-(aq) \qquad E°_{red} = -0.83 \text{ V}$$

Anode oxidation:

$$H_2O(l) \rightarrow 1/2\,O_2(g) + 2H^+(aq) + 2e^- \qquad E°_{ox} = -1.23 \text{ V}$$

Overall reaction: $3H_2O(l) \rightarrow H_2(g) + 2OH^-(aq) + 1/2\,O_2(g) + 2H^+(aq)$

$$E°_{cell} = -2.06 \text{ V}$$

Or $H_2O(l) \rightarrow H_2(g) + 1/2\,O_2(g) \qquad E°_{cell} = -2.06 \text{ V}$

The electrolysis of water with an inert electrolyte requires just over 2 V.

The Electrolysis of an Aqueous Sodium Chloride Solution

Electrolysis of an aqueous solution of sodium chloride produces hydrogen gas at the cathode and chlorine gas at the anode. The half-reactions and the overall process are given below.

$$2H_2O(l) + 2\,e^- \rightarrow H_2(g) + 2OH^-(aq) \qquad E°_{red} = -0.83 \text{ V}$$
$$2Cl^- \rightarrow Cl_2(g) + 2\,e^- \qquad E°_{ox} = -1.359 \text{ V}$$
$$2H_2O(l) + 2Cl^- \rightarrow H_2(g) + 2OH^-(aq) + Cl_2(g) \qquad E°_{cell} = -2.19 \text{ V}$$

In the case of the electrolysis of aqueous sodium chloride, there are two possible reductions that can take place at the cathode. Either water will gain electrons and produce hydrogen gas or sodium ions pick up electrons to become sodium metal.

Possible cathode reductions:

$$Na^+(aq) + 1\,e^- \rightarrow Na(l) \qquad E°_{red} = -2.71 \text{ V}$$
$$2H_2O(l) + 2\,e^- \rightarrow H_2(g) + 2OH^-(aq) \qquad E°_{red} = -0.83 \text{ V}$$

It is usually possible to predict which of the possible half-reactions will occur when solutions are electrolyzed on the basis of their relative $E°_{red}$ values. The reduction potential for water is more favorable than the reduction potential for sodium ion, because water has the more positive value for $E°_{red}$. Therefore, the water reduction, not the sodium ion reduction, will occur at the cathode.

The same analysis can be made for the possible oxidation reactions. Generally, the oxidation with the more positive $E°_{ox}$ value will predominate.

The Chloride Ion Is an Uncommon Exception

The oxidation potential for chloride ion is less positive than the oxidation potential for water, so from a thermodynamic argument, water should oxidize in the presence of aqueous chloride ion. And, indeed, it does. However, the oxidation of water is kinetically very slow. By comparison, the oxidation of chloride ion is rapid. Additionally, both half-reactions require similar voltages to carry out. Usually, in most electrolytic cells, there is sufficient voltage to drive both reactions. Because of the relative rates of reaction, chlorine gas, not oxygen gas, is produced at the anode.

Possible anode oxidations:

$$Cl^-(aq) \rightarrow 1/2\,Cl_2(g) + 1\,e^- \qquad\qquad E^\circ_{ox} = -1.359\text{ V}$$

$$H_2O(l) \rightarrow 1/2\,O_2(g) + 2H^+(aq) + 2e^- \qquad E^\circ_{ox} = -1.23\text{ V}$$

Electroplating

Electrolysis is commonly used in electroplating, the process of depositing a thin coating of one metal onto another metal for ornamental purposes or for corrosion resistance. For example, steel is commonly plated with nickel or chromium and eating utensils are often plated with silver or gold.

To plate nickel on a steel surface, for example, an electrolysis apparatus illustrated in Figure 20.3 consisting of a nickel anode and a steel cathode is used. Both electrodes are immersed in an aqueous solution of nickel nitrate. Voltage applied to the cell forces electrons from the anode to the cathode. Reduction of Ni^{2+} ions occurs at the cathode where nickel metal plates the steel. The nickel anode oxidizes to nickel ions that replace the ions in solution.

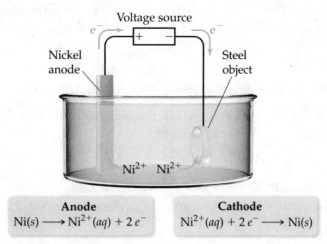

Figure 20.3 Electrolysis device for plating nickel onto a piece of steel.

The half-reactions are:

Reduction at the cathode: $Ni^{2+}(aq) + 2e^- \rightarrow Ni(s) \qquad E^\circ_{red} = -0.28\text{ V}$

Oxidation at the anode: $Ni(s) \rightarrow Ni^{2+}(aq) + 2e^- \qquad E^\circ_{ox} = +0.28\text{ V}$

The other possible anode and cathode reactions are the oxidation and reduction of water, both of which have less favorable potentials than do the nickel reactions.

Cathode reduction: $H_2O(l) + 2\,e^- \rightarrow H_2(g) + 2OH^-(aq) \qquad E^\circ_{red} = -0.83\text{ V}$

Anode oxidation: $H_2O(l) \rightarrow 1/2\,O_2(g) + 2H^+(aq) + 2e^- \qquad E^\circ_{ox} = -1.23\text{ V}$

The nickel reactions predominate and the net effect is to move nickel atoms from the anode to the surface of the steel cathode.

Quantitative Aspects of Electrolysis

A balanced half-reaction tells how many moles of electrons are involved in a redox reaction. For example, when silver ion is reduced to silver metal, one mole of electrons is transferred. When water is reduced to hydrogen gas and hydroxide ion, two moles of electrons are involved.

$$Ag^+(aq) + 1\,e^- \rightarrow Ag(s)$$
$$2H_2O(l) + 2\,e^- \rightarrow H_2(g) + 2OH^-(aq)$$

The amount of a substance that is oxidized or reduced in an electrolytic cell is directly proportional to the number of electrons passed through the cell. The balanced half-reaction is a way to convert electrical quantities into moles of chemical quantities and vice versa.

Example:

How many liters of dry hydrogen gas at 30 °C and 720 torr can be obtained by the electrolysis of water for 1 h at 2.50 A?

Solution:

The key ideas in this quantitative electrolysis problem are:

The balanced half-reaction relates moles of electrons transferred to moles of chemical reactants or products:

$2\ mol\ e^- = 1\ mol\ H_2(g)$

The ampere is the measure of electric current. One ampere is one coulomb of electric charge passing a point in an electrical circuit in 1 s:

$2.50\ A = 2.50\ Coulombs\ per\ second = 2.50\ C/s$

Faraday's constant tells the quantity of electric charge carried by a mole of electrons:

$1\ mol\ e^- = 96{,}485\ C\ (Faraday's\ constant)$

The ideal-gas equation calculates volume in liters from number of moles, n, absolute temperature, T, pressure in atmospheres, P, and the universal gas constant, R. $R = 0.0821\ L\text{-}atm/mol\text{-}K$.

$V = nRT/P$

$x\ mol\ H_2(g) = 1\ h(60\ min/h)(60\ s/min)(2.50\ C/s)(1\ mole\ e^-/96{,}485\ C)$
$(1\ mol\ H_2/(2\ mol\ e^-) = 0.0466\ mol\ H_2$

$V = nRT/P = (0.0466\ mol)(0.0821\ L\text{-}atm/mol\text{-}K)(303\ K)/$
$(720/760)\ atm = 1.22\ L$

Multiple Choice Questions

1. When the following compounds are listed in order of increasing oxidation number of the sulfur atoms (most negative to most positive oxidation number), the correct order is

   A) CuS, $K_2S_2O_3$, SO_2, Na_2SO_4.

   B) CuS, SO_2, $K_2S_2O_3$, Na_2SO_4.

   C) CuS, SO_2, Na_2SO_4, $K_2S_2O_3$.

   D) Na_2SO_4, CuS, $K_2S_2O_3$, SO_2.

2. Use the reduction potentials in the table to determine which one of the reactions below is thermodynamically favored.

Half-Reaction	$E°$
$Cd^{2+} + 2e^- \rightarrow Cd$	-0.403 V
$Mn^{2+} + 2e^- \rightarrow Mn$	-1.18 V
$Cu^+ + 1e^- \rightarrow Cu$	$+0.521$ V
$Fe^{3+} + 1e^- \rightarrow Fe^{2+}$	$+0.771$ V

   A) $Cd^{2+} + 2Cu \rightarrow Cd + 2Cu^+$

   B) $Mn^{2+} + 2Cu \rightarrow Mn + 2Cu^+$

   C) $Cd^{2+} + Mn \rightarrow Cd + Mn^{2+}$

   D) $Cu^+ + Fe^{2+} \rightarrow Cu + Fe^{3+}$

3. What is the coefficient for MnO_4^- when the following redox equation is balanced in acidic solution using the smallest whole-number coefficients?
   $$H^+ + Cr_2O_7^{2-} + Mn^{2+} \rightarrow H_2O + Cr^{3+} + MnO_4^-$$

   A) 1

   B) 2

   C) 5

   D) 6

4. Which element can have the highest positive oxidation number?

   A) Cr

   B) C

   C) Cl

   D) N

5. Magnesium reacts with dilute hydrochloric acid to produce hydrogen gas. Silver does not react in dilute hydrochloric acid. Based on this information, which of the following reactions will occur as written?

A) $H_2(g) + Mg^{2+}(aq) \rightarrow 2H^+(aq) + Mg(s)$

B) $2Ag(s) + Mg^{2+}(aq) \rightarrow 2Ag^+(aq) + Mg(s)$

C) $2Ag^+(aq) + Mg(s) \rightarrow 2Ag(s) + Mg^{2+}(aq)$

D) $2Ag + 2H^+(aq) \rightarrow H_2(g) + 2Ag^+(aq)$

Use the following information to answer Questions 6–8.
A cell is set up using the following half-reactions under standard conditions.

$$Mg^{2+} + 2e^- \rightarrow Mg \qquad E° = -2.37 \text{ V}$$
$$Ag^+ + 1e^- \rightarrow Ag \qquad E° = +0.80 \text{ V}$$

6. What is the voltage of the cell?

A) $+1.57$ V

B) $+3.17$ V

C) $+3.97$ V

D) -0.77 V

7. What are the products of the reaction?

A) $Mg^{2+} + Ag^+$

B) $Mg^{2+} + Ag$

C) $Ag^+ + Mg$

D) $Ag^+ + Mg^{2+}$

8. If the $[Mg^{2+}]$ is changed to 0.50 M, what will initially happen to the voltage?

A) no change

B) increase

C) decrease to a nonzero value

D) drop to zero

9. When the following reaction in aqueous solution is balanced using whole number coefficients, what is the coefficient of H^+?
$$MnO_4^- + NO_2 \rightarrow MnO_2 + NO_3^-$$

A) 2

B) 4

C) 5

D) 6

10. Which is most easily oxidized?

    A) fluorine

    B) fluoride ion

    C) aluminum

    D) aluminum ion

Oxidized/reduced substances	Half-reaction	$E°$ (volts)
F_2/F^-	$F_2(g) + 2e^- \rightarrow 2F^-(aq)$	+2.87
Cl_2/Cl^-	$Cl_2(g) + 2e^- \rightarrow 2Cl^-(aq)$	+1.359
Ag^+/Ag	$Ag^+(aq) + 1e^- \rightarrow Ag(s)$	+0.799
Zn^{2+}/Zn	$Zn^{2+}(aq) + 2e^- \rightarrow Zn(s)$	−0.762
Al^{3+}/Al	$Al^{3+}(aq) + 3e^- \rightarrow Al(s)$	−1.66

11. Calculate the voltage for a cell consisting of the following half-cells suitably connected.

    $Cu^{2+}(aq) + 2e^- \rightarrow Cu(s)$ $E° = 0.337\ V$

    $Al^{3+}(aq) + 3e^- \rightarrow Al(s)$ $E° = -1.66\ V$

    A) 1.32 V

    B) 2.00 V

    C) 2.30 V

    D) −2.30 V

Use the following equation to answer Questions 12 and 13.

$ClO_3^-(aq) + 5Cl^-(aq) + 6H^+(aq) \rightarrow 3Cl_2(g) + 3H_2O(l)$

12. The oxidized and reduced substances are, respectively,

    A) $Cl^-(aq)$ and $ClO_3^-(aq)$

    B) $ClO_3^-(aq)$ and $Cl^-(aq)$

    C) $ClO_3^-(aq)$ and $H^+(aq)$

    D) $Cl^-(aq)$ and $H^+(aq)$

13. The number of electrons transferred in the balanced equation are

    A) 5

    B) 6

    C) 10

    D) 12

14. What is a product formed at the anode of the electrolysis of an aqueous sodium sulfate solution?

    A) $H_2(g)$

    B) $O_2(g)$

    C) $Na(s)$

    D) $SO_2(g)$

15. What is a product formed at the cathode of the electrolysis of an aqueous copper nitrate solution?

    A) $H_2(g)$

    B) $O_2(g)$

    C) $Cu(s)$

    D) $NO(g)$

Free Response Questions

1. Suppose that gold and silver half-cells are suitably connected.

   $$Au^{3+} + 3e^- \rightarrow Au(s) \quad E° = +1.50 \text{ V}$$

   $$Ag^+ + 1e^- \rightarrow Ag(s) \quad E° = +0.80 \text{ V}$$

   a. i. Identify the cathode and anode half-reactions.

      ii. Write the overall cell reaction.

      iii. Calculate $E°$ for the cell.

   b. Calculate $\Delta G°$ for the cell.

   c. Calculate the equilibrium constant for the cell reaction at 25°C.

   d. If $[Ag^+]$ is increased to 1.50 M, will the reaction be more spontaneous or less spontaneous? Will the cell voltage increase, decrease, or remain the same? Justify your answer.

   e. In a separate experiment, how many grams of gold can be plated onto a piece of jewelry if a 1.00 M solution of gold(III) nitrate is suitably electrolyzed for 45 min at 2.50 A?

   f. In yet another experiment, how many minutes are required to plate 1.00 g of silver onto an inert electrode at 1.25 A?

2. Consider the following half-reactions and their standard reduction potentials at 25 °C.

   $$PbO_2(s) + H_2O(l) + 2e^- \rightarrow PbO(s) + 2OH^-(aq) \qquad E° = +0.28 \text{ V}$$

   $$IO_3^- + 2\,H_2O + 4\,e^- \rightarrow IO^- + 4OH^- \qquad E° = +0.56 \text{ V}$$

   $$PO_4^{3-} + 2\,H_2O + 1/2\,O_2 + 2e^- \rightarrow HPO_4^{2-} + 3OH^- \qquad E° = -1.05 \text{ V}$$

a. i. Which two half-reactions when combined will give the voltaic cell with the largest $E°$ for the cell?

   ii. Write the overall cell reaction that would take place.

   iii. Calculate $E°$ for the cell.

b. Indicate how the E_{cell} will be affected by the following changes. Justify your answers.

   i. If the pH of both the anode and cathode compartments is decreased.

   ii. If $[OH^-]$ is fixed at 1.0 M, $O_2(g)$ is fixed at 1 atm, and all other ion concentrations are changed to 0.10 M.

   iii. If the temperature is increased while all concentrations remain at 1.0 M.

Multiple Choice Answers and Explanations

1. A. The oxidation numbers of sulfur in CuS, $K_2S_2O_3$, SO_2, and Na_2SO_4 are -2, $+2$, $+4$, and $+6$, respectively. As a monatomic ion in CuS, sulfur has a -2 charge, so its oxidation number is equal to its charge. The oxidation number of each sulfur adds to the oxidation number of each oxygen to equal the charge in the polyatomic ion, $S_2O_3^{2-}$. $(3 \times 2-$ for each oxygen$) + (2 \times 2+$ for each sulfur$) = 2-$. (Note: In $S_2O_3^{2-}$, one sulfur carries a $4+$ oxidation number, whereas the other sulfur is zero, an average of $2+$ for each sulfur.) The oxidation number of sulfur in SO_2 is $4+$ because it adds to the oxidation numbers of each oxygen to equal the zero charge on SO_2. $4 + 2(2-) = 0$. A $6+$ oxidation number for sulfur in SO_4^{2-} adds to the four $2-$ oxidation numbers of oxygen to give a charge of $2-$. $6 + 4(2-) = 2-$.

2. C. For an overall reaction to be thermodynamically favored, the $E°_{cell}$ for the reaction must be positive. Half-reaction 1 adds to the reverse of half-reaction 2 to give a positive $E°_{cell}$.

1:	$Cd^{2+} + 2e^- \rightarrow Cd$	-0.403 V
plus reverse of 2:	$Mn \rightarrow 2e^- + Mn^{2+}$	$+1.18$ V
yields	$Cd^{2+} + Mn \rightarrow Cd + Mn^{2+}$	$+0.78$ V

The other combinations listed all yield a negative $E°_{cell}$.

3. D. Taking apart the unbalanced equation provides two skeletal half-reactions and each is balanced according to the rules given in Table 20.2:

   1. Balance all elements other than H or O.

   2. Balance O by adding H_2O as required.

   3. Balance H by adding H^+ as required.

   4. Balance charge by adding e^- to more positive side.

1. $Mn^{2+} \rightarrow MnO_4^-$

2. $4H_2O(l) + Mn^{2+} \rightarrow MnO_4^-$

3. $4H_2O(l) + Mn^{2+} \rightarrow MnO_4^- + 8H^+(aq)$

4. $4H_2O(l) + Mn^{2+} \rightarrow MnO_4^- + 8H^+(aq) + 5e^-$

1. $Cr_2O_7^{2-} \rightarrow 2Cr^{3+}$

2. $Cr_2O_7^{2-} \rightarrow 2Cr^{3+} + 7H_2O(l)$

3. $14H^+(aq) + Cr_2O_7^{2-} \rightarrow 2Cr^{3+} + 7H_2O(l)$

4. $6e^- + 14H^+(aq) + Cr_2O_7^{2-} \rightarrow 2Cr^{3+} + 7H_2O(l)$

Multiplication of the Mn and Cr half-reactions to make the electrons equal requires factors of 6 and 5, respectively. The resulting balanced equation will have a coefficient of 6 for MnO_4^-.

An alternate way to arrive at the answer is to assign oxidation numbers to all the elements and note that Mn changes by five electrons (from 2+ to 7+) and that Cr changes by three electrons (from 6+ to 3+) twice for a total of six electrons. The lowest common multiple of 5 and 6 is 30, so the Mn half-reaction must be multiplied by 6, giving the MnO_4^- a coefficient of 6.

4. **C.** *Cl displays a 7+ oxidation number in the perchlorate ion, ClO_4^-. Cr is 6+ in CrO_4^{2-}. C is 4+ in CO_2. Nitrogen is 5+ in NO_3^-.*

5. **C.** *On the basis of their behavior in the presence of hydrochloric acid, Mg is a more active metal than Ag. Thus, Mg will react with Ag^+ ions, but Ag will not react with Mg^{2+}. Also Ag, because it does not react with HCl, does not react with H^+.*

6. **B.** *The Ag half-reaction has the more positive voltage, so it is the reduction. The Mg half-cell is the oxidation and its voltage changes to $+2.37$ V.*

$E°_{cell} = E°_{red} + E°_{ox} = 0.80 + 2.37 = 3.17$ V

(Note: The stoichiometry is not taken into account because voltage is independent of the number of electrons transferred.)

7. **B.** *Reversing the half-reaction with the most negative voltage and adding it to the other yields: $Mg + Ag^+ \rightarrow Mg^{2+} + Ag$*

8. **B.** *If the $[Mg^{2+}]$ decreases from its standard concentration of 1.0 M to 0.50 M, Q becomes smaller and the voltage will increase.*

9. **A.** *The balanced equation is: $H_2O + MnO_4^- + 3NO_2 \rightarrow MnO_2 + 3NO_3^- + 2H^+$*

A quick way to estimate the coefficient of H^+ is to recognize that the oxidation number of Mn changes from +7 to +4 and nitrogen changes from +4 to +5. This means the coefficients for the nitrogen species are both 3 whereas the coefficients for the Mn species are both 1. Those coefficients yield 11 O on the right so 1 H_2O must be added to the 10 O on the left. One H_2O has two H so the coefficient of H^+ is 2.

10. C. An easily reduced substance has a large positive standard reduction potential, $E°$, and the most easily oxidized substance has the highest oxidation potential. Only reduction potentials are shown in the table and fluorine has the largest standard reduction potential so it is most easily reduced. Aluminum is easily oxidized because the reverse reaction of the reduction shown in the table has the highest oxidation potential at $+1.66$ V.

11. B. Reduction of copper(II) ions is more favorable than the reduction of aluminum ions because the voltage of the copper reduction half-reaction is more positive. Therefore the aluminum reaction will be the oxidation and the sign of its voltage will change from – to +.

$$Cu^{2+}(aq) + 2e^- \rightarrow Cu(s) \qquad E°_{red} = 0.337 \text{ V}$$

$$Al(s) \rightarrow Al^{3+}(aq) + 3e^- \qquad E°_{ox} = +1.66 \text{ V}$$

$$E°_{cell} = E°_{ox} + E°_{red} = 0.337 + 1.66 = 2.00 \text{ V}$$

12. A. An oxidized substance loses electrons and its oxidation number becomes more positive. Chlorine's oxidation number changes from -1 to 0 as Cl^- becomes Cl_2: $2Cl^- \rightarrow Cl_2 + 2e^-$ A reduced substance gains electrons and its oxidation number becomes less positive. Chlorine's oxidation number changes from $+5$ to 0 as ClO_3^- becomes Cl_2: $2ClO_3^- + 10e^- \rightarrow Cl_2$

13. A. In the balanced equation, five chloride ions gain five electrons and one chlorate ion loses the same five electrons.

14. B. The anode and cathode reactions are:

Anode: $H_2O(l) \rightarrow 2H^+(aq) + 1/2\ O_2(g) + 2e^-$

Cathode: $2H_2O(l) + 2e^- \rightarrow H_2(g) + 2OH^-(aq)$

Sodium sulfate is an inert electrolyte.

15. A. The anode and cathode reactions are:

Anode: $Cu(s) \rightarrow Cu^{2+}(aq) + 2e^-$

Cathode: $2H_2O(l) + 2e^- \rightarrow H_2(g) + 2OH^-(aq)$

Nitrate is an inert anion in this electrolysis.

Free Response Answers

1. a. i. Cathode half-cell reaction:

$$Au^{3+} + 3e^- \rightarrow Au(s) \qquad E° = +1.500 \text{ V}$$

Anode half-cell reaction: $Ag(s) \rightarrow Ag^+ + 1e^-$ $E° = -0.800 \text{ V}$

ii. Overall cell reaction:

$$Au^{3+} + 3Ag(s) \rightarrow Au(s) \rightarrow +3Ag^+$$

iii. $E°_{cell} = E°_{ox} + E°_{red} = +1.50 \text{ V} - 0.800 \text{ V} = 0.700 \text{ V}$

b. $\Delta G^{\circ} = -nFE^{\circ} = -(3\ mol\ e^{-})(96{,}500\ C/mol\ e^{-})$

$(0.700\ J/C) = -203\ kJ\ (1\ V = 1\ J/C)$

c. $\Delta G^{\circ} = -RT\ ln\ K$

$-203\ kJ = -(8.314\ J/mol\text{-}K)(1\ kJ/1000\ J)(298\ K)\ ln\ K$

$ln\ K = +81.9$

$K = e^{+81.9} = 3.7 \times 10^{35}$

d. Because $[Ag^{+}]$ is a product of the cell reaction, an increase in $[Ag^{+}]$ will decrease the voltage because Q becomes smaller as the reaction becomes less thermodynamically favored.

e. $x\ g\ Au = 45\ min\ (60\ s/min)(2.50\ C/s)(1\ mol\ e^{-}/96{,}500\ C)$

$(1\ mol\ Au/3\ mol\ e^{-})(197\ g/mol) = 4.59\ g$

f. $x\ min = 1.00\ g\ Ag\ (1\ mol/108\ g)(1\ mol\ e^{-}/1\ mol\ Ag)$

$(96{,}500\ C/mole\ e^{-})(1\ s/1.25\ C)(1\ min/60\ s) = 11.9\ min$

2. a. i. $IO_3^{-} + 2H_2O + 4\ e^{-} \rightarrow IO^{-} + 4OH^{-}$ $E^{\circ}_{red} = +0.56\ V$

   $HPO_4^{2-} + 3OH^{-} \rightarrow PO_4^{3-} + 2\ H_2O + 1/2\ O_2 + 2e^{-}$ $E^{\circ}_{ox} = +1.05\ V$

   ii. $2HPO_4^{2-} + 2OH^{-} + IO_3^{-} \rightarrow 2PO_4^{3-} + 2H_2O + IO^{-} + O_2$

   iii. $E^{\circ} = E^{\circ}_{ox} + E^{\circ}_{red} = +1.05\ V + 0.56\ V = +1.61\ V$

b. i. If the pH of both the anode and cathode compartments is decreased, the net effect will be to decrease $[OH^{-}]$. The voltage will also decrease because Q will increase making ΔG more positive.

   ii. If $[OH^{-}]$ is fixed at 1.0 M and all other ion concentrations are changed to 0.10 M, the voltage will remain the same because, other than hydroxide, there are three moles of ions on both sides of the balanced equation.

   iii. If the temperature is increased while all concentrations remain at 1.0 M, the voltage will drop because the exothermic reaction will become less thermodynamically favorable. The reaction is exothermic because the voltage is positive.

Your Turn Answers

20.1. SO_4^{2-}, 6+; $S_2O_3^{2-}$, 4+ and 0 (The average oxidation number for each S is 2+ .); S^{2-}, 2−; SO_3^{2-}, 4+; SCN^{-}, 2−; S, 0; SO_2, 4+; SO_3, 6+. Oxidation number and charge are equivalent only in sulfide, S^{2-}, and sulfur, S.

20.2. A redox reaction is one in which one reactant transfers electrons to another reactant. As a result, the oxidation numbers of some of the atoms in the reactants change as they become products. The reactant that gains electrons is reduced. N_2 is the substance reduced because it gains electrons. The oxidation number of N changes from 0 to 3− as N_2 becomes NH_3. The reactant that loses electrons is oxidized. H_2 is oxidized because the oxidation number of H changes from 0 to 1+ as it changes from H_2 to NH_3.

20.3. a. *Molarity of $KMnO_4$ solution $=$ moles $KMnO_4$/liters solution*
       $= (20.65\ g/158.0\ g/mol)/0.500\ L = 0.2614\ M\ KMnO_4$

   b. $5H_2O_2(aq) + 2MnO_4^-(aq) + 6H^+(aq) \rightarrow 5O_2(g) + 2Mn^{2+}(aq)$
      $+ 8H_2O(l)$

   c. *Follow the mole road from 25.00 mL of $KMnO_4$ solution to molarity of H_2O_2 solution:*

$$5H_2O_2(aq) + 2MnO_4^-(aq) + 6H^+(aq) \longrightarrow 5O_2(g) + 2Mn^{2+}(aq) + 8H_2O(l)$$

Molarity of $H_2O_2 = (25.00\ mL/1000\ mL/L)(0.2614\ mol/L)$
$(5\ mol\ H_2O_2/2\ mol\ MnO_4^-)/(0.03405\ L) = 0.4798\ M$

   d. *On the road map, go from moles of H_2O_2 to grams of*
      $H_2O_2(25.00/1000)(0.2614)(5/2)\ mol\ H_2O_2\ (34.0\ g/mol) = 0.555\ g\ H_2O_2$

   e. *% $H_2O_2 = (g\ H_2O_2/g\ solution)(100)$*
      g solution $= 34.05\ mL \times 1.05\ g/mL = 35.8\ g$ solution
      % $H_2O_2 = (0.555g\ H_2O_2/35.8\ g\ solution)(100) = 1.55\%$

20.4. a. $C_6H_{12}O_6 + 6\ O_2(g) \rightarrow 6\ CO_2(g) + 6\ H_2O(l)\quad \Delta H = -2803\ kJ$
       $2C_{57}H_{110}O_6 + 163\ O_2(g) \rightarrow 114\ CO_2(g) + 110\ H_2O(l)\quad \Delta H = -75,520\ kJ$

   b. $x\ Cal/g = -2803\ kJ/mol(1\ mol/180\ g)(1\ Cal/4.184\ kJ) = 3.72\ Cal/g$

   c. $x\ kJ/mol = 9.0\ Cal/g(890\ g/mol)(4.184\ kJ/Cal) = 33,500\ kJ/mol$

20.5. *When coupled, the two half-reactions with the largest difference in $E°$ value will give the most thermodynamically favored reaction, the one with the largest positive cell voltage. Reverse the half-reaction with the most negative voltage and add it to the half-reaction with the most positive voltage. Use coefficients to balance the electrons. Change the sign of the $E°$ for the reversed reaction and add it to the $E°$ of the forward reaction.*

$3F_2(g) + 6e^- \rightarrow 6F^-(aq)$	+2.87 V
$2Al(s) \rightarrow 2Al^{3+}(aq) + 6e^-$	+1.66 V
$3F_2(g) + 2Al(s) \rightarrow 6F^-(aq) + 2Al^{3+}(aq)$	+4.53 V

20.6. *The cell voltage will be greater than the voltage at standard conditions when either $[Zn^{2+}]$ is greater than 1 M or $[Al^{3+}]$ is less than 1 M. The cell voltage increases whenever the ΔG becomes less positive or more negative (more thermodynamically favored). Use the equation, $\Delta G = \Delta G° + RT \ln Q$, where $Q = [Al^{3+}]/[Zn^{2+}]$. Whenever Q becomes smaller, ΔG becomes more negative and the reaction is more thermodynamically favored with a higher voltage.*

CHEMISTRY PRACTICE TEST 1

A few weeks before the Advanced Placement exam, you should approach the finish of your review of all the topics in this book. You should also be approaching the end of your coursework leading up to the AP exam. When you are ready, take Practice Test 1 within the suggested time limits. When you are finished, look up the answers and calculate your score. The following scoring system is simplified and informal. Although it cannot predict what you will score on the real AP exam, it serves as a measure of your strengths and weaknesses a few weeks before the exam.

Self-score your practice exam this way:

Multiple Choice Questions   Section I

Number right: _____ × 0.833   = _____ A

Free Response Questions   Section II

For Questions 1–7, divide the maximum number of points for each question outlined below by the number of subquestions contained in that question. Award yourself a corresponding number of points for each correct response for each subquestion but no more than the maximum number of points listed for each.

Question 1: maximum of 10 points   = _____ B
Question 2: maximum of 10 points   = _____ C
Question 3: maximum of 10 points   = _____ D
Question 4: maximum of 5 points   = _____ E
Question 5: maximum of 5 points   = _____ F
Question 6: maximum of 5 points   = _____ G
Question 7: maximum of 5 points   = _____ H

Total points (add lines A–H):   = _____ = total score

A minimum score of about 76–80 might correspond to a 5.

A minimum score of about 63–67 might correspond to a 4.

A minimum score of about 50–54 might correspond to a 3.

When you finish Practice Test 1 and have analyzed your results and corrected your mistakes, repeat the process with Practice Test 2.

CHEMISTRY PRACTICE TEST 1

Multiple Choice Questions

90 minutes

You may not use a calculator on this section.

Directions: For each of the following questions or incomplete statements, select the best answer or completion from the choices given.

Questions 1–3 refer to the following data table that lists the solubilities, in grams of solute per 100 grams of H_2O, of various salts at two different temperatures.

	Salt	20°C	60°C
I	$Ce_2(SO_4)_3 \cdot 9H_2O$	9.16	3.73
II	KNO_3	31.6	110.0
III	$NaCl$	36.0	37.3
IV	$K_2Cr_2O_7$	13.1	50.5

1. For which of these salts will the solution process have a ΔH closest to zero?

    A) I

    B) II

    C) III

    D) IV

2. Which of these salts dissolve(s) exothermically?

    A) I only

    B) II only

    C) II, III and IV only

    D) III and IV only

3. For which of these salts is entropy but not enthalpy the driving force for dissolution?

    A) I

    B) II

    C) III

    D) II, III, and IV

4. Complete combustion of a compound containing only carbon, hydrogen, and oxygen yields data that allow for elemental analysis. The analysis of the combustion products relies upon which of these assumptions?

    I.   The quantity of carbon dioxide formed relates directly to the amount of carbon present in the sample.

    II. The quantity of water formed relates directly to the amount of hydrogen present in the sample.

III. The quantity of water formed is limited by the amount of oxygen present in the sample.

IV. The quantity of carbon dioxide formed is limited by the amount of air present.

A) I only

B) II only

C) I, II, and III only

D) I and II only

5. Atom Y has 3 valence electrons and atom Z has 6 valence electrons. What is the simplest formula expected for the binary ionic compound composed of Y and Z?

A) Y_2Z

B) YZ_2

C) Y_2Z_3

D) Y_3Z_2

6. The table shows various bond dissociation energies in kJ/mol to two significant figures. Estimate the molar heat of formation of gaseous ammonia.

H—H	N—H	N≡N
450	400	950

A) $-50\,\text{kJ/mol}$

B) $-100\,\text{kJ/mol}$

C) $-550\,\text{kJ/mol}$

D) $-1100\,\text{kJ/mol}$

7. One liter of oxygen gas, O_2, and 3 L of sulfur dioxide gas, SO_2, react to form gaseous sulfur trioxide, SO_3, at a given temperature and pressure. How many liters of $SO_3(g)$ can be produced at the same temperature and pressure?

A) 1

B) 2

C) 3

D) 4

8. Considering effective nuclear charge, predict which element will have the smallest atomic radius.

A) H

B) He

C) Li

D) Be

9. Which molecules are polar?

I. H_2O

II. CO_2

III. NO_2

IV. SO_2

A) I and III only

B) I, II, and III only

C) I, II, III, and IV only

D) I, III, and IV only

10. Which of the following species is in the greatest concentration in an aqueous 0.100 molar solution of H_3PO_4?

A) H_3O^+

B) H_3PO_4

C) $H_2PO_4^-$

D) HPO_4^{2-}

Questions 11–15 relate to the following information.

Consider the pictured gas samples at the same temperature and under conditions where they all behave as ideal gases.

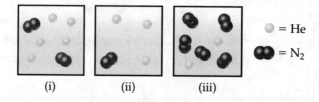

11. Which gas sample has the highest density?

A) i

B) ii

C) iii

D) All are the same

12. Which gas sample has the highest average kinetic energy of particles?

A) i

B) ii

C) iii

D) All are the same

13. Which gas sample has the highest average velocity of particles?

A) i

B) ii

C) iii

D) All are the same

14. Which gas sample has the highest energy collisions per time with the walls of the container?

A) ii only

B) iii only

C) i and iii only

D) All are the same

15. Assume that conditions change such that all the gas samples behave as real gases. Which gas sample deviates the most from ideal behavior?

A) i

B) ii

C) iii

D) All are the same

16. The electronegativity values are shown for two of four elements.

O	F
---	4.0
S	Cl
2.5	---

Select the true statement about the relative values of electronegativity for oxygen and chlorine.

A) O > Cl because coulombic forces are higher for the smaller O.

B) O > Cl because the effective nuclear charge is higher for O.

C) Cl > O because the effective nuclear charge is higher for Cl.

D) Cl and O are about equal because difference in effective nuclear charge roughly offsets size difference.

17. For 0.1 M solutions:

$KHSO_3$	$NaHCO_3$
pH = 5	pH = 9

Which of the following explains these observations?

A) Potassium ions are more acidic than sodium ions.

B) Sulfur is more electronegative than carbon.

C) The HSO_3^- ion is a better proton acceptor than the HCO_3^- ion.

D) Carbon is smaller than sulfur.

18. A drop of HCl is added to a drop of sodium hydrogen carbonate and the mixture effervesces. A drop of NaOH is added to a drop of ammonium nitrate. No bubbles are evident but a piece of filter paper wetted with phenolphthalein and held above the drop, turns bright pink. All the aqueous reagent solutions are 1.0 M.

All the following statements are true. What statement best explains why bubbles form in the HCl experiment but not in the NaOH experiment.

A) Ammonia is polar and CO_2 is nonpolar.

B) Ammonia is basic and CO_2 is acidic.

C) CO_2 has a much larger molar mass than ammonia.

D) Ammonia gas deviates from ideality more than CO_2 gas.

19. The pH of a freshly made 1.0 M solution of sodium hydrogen carbonate is monitored for several hours while constantly stirred. The results are shown in the graph. What best explains the data?

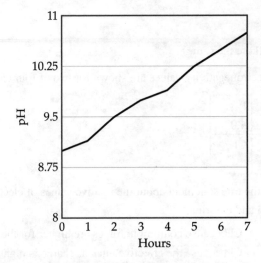

A) The solution slowly absorbed oxygen from the air.

B) The solution slowly absorbed carbon dioxide from the air.

C) The solution slowly lost water through evaporation.

D) Hydrogen carbonate ion slowly reacted to form carbonate ion.

20. The diagram represents a collection of reactant molecules. The dark spheres represent N and the light spheres represent O.

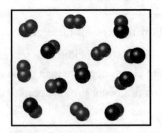

Nitrogen monoxide reacts with oxygen to form nitrogen dioxide. How many nitrogen dioxide molecules would you draw as products if the reaction had a 75% yield?

A) 4

B) 6

C) 7

D) 8

21. Which intermolecular forces shown in the diagram are the strongest?

A) v and z only

B) w only

C) x and y only

D) All are equally strong.

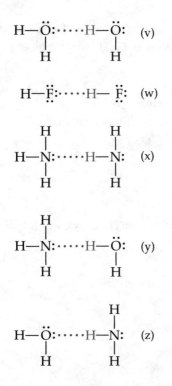

22. The experimental data from the reaction A → products gives these three graphs. What is the most likely order for this reaction?

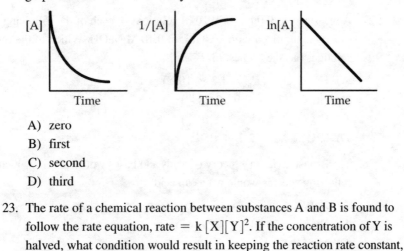

A) zero
B) first
C) second
D) third

23. The rate of a chemical reaction between substances A and B is found to follow the rate equation, rate $= k\,[X][Y]^2$. If the concentration of Y is halved, what condition would result in keeping the reaction rate constant, assuming no temperature change?

A) If [X] is quadrupled.
B) If [X] is doubled.
C) If [X] is halved.
D) If [X] is tripled.

24. A mixture of 1.00 mole of $H_2(g)$ and 1.00 mole of $I_2(g)$ is placed in a 1.00 L flask at a constant temperature and is allowed to come to equilibrium according to the equation

    $H_2(g) + I_2(g) \rightleftharpoons 2\,HI(g)$.

    If the equilibrium constant at this temperature is $K_c = 36.0$, what is the molar concentration of $H_2(g)$ in the equilibrium mixture?

    A) 0.500 M
    B) 1.00 M
    C) 0.750 M
    D) 0.250 M

25. Which substance in aqueous solution is an electrolyte and is basic?

    A) NH_4NO_3
    B) CH_3COOH
    C) CH_3OH
    D) KOH

26. The solubility of which compound is pH dependent?

    A) CaF_2
    B) KNO_3
    C) NaCl
    D) CH_3OH

27. A measure of 20.0 mL of 0.10 M solutions of each of the following acids are exactly neutralized with 20.0 mL of 0.10 M NaOH. Which of the resulting solutions has the highest pH?

    A) $HC_2H_3O_2$ $(K_a = 1.8 \times 10^{-5})$
    B) HCN $(K_a = 4.9 \times 10^{-10})$
    C) HBrO $(K_a = 2.5 \times 10^{-9})$
    D) HIO $(K_a = 2.3 \times 10^{-11})$

28. The Brønsted–Lowry theory of acids and bases would predict which of the following species would act as an acid?

    A) NaH
    B) NH_4^+
    C) Mg_3N_2
    D) NH_2^-

Use the data for the synthesis of ammonia below to answer Questions 29–31.

Temperature (°C)	K_p
300	4.34×10^{-3}
400	1.64×10^{-4}
450	4.51×10^{-5}
500	1.45×10^{-5}
550	5.38×10^{-6}
600	2.25×10^{-6}

Variation in K_p with temperature for $N_2(g) + 3H_2(g) \rightarrow 2NH_3(g)$

$\Delta S°_f$ for ammonia gas $= -198.2$ J/mol-K

29. The reaction for the synthesis of ammonia is

    A) endothermic with an increase in entropy.

    B) endothermic with a decrease in entropy.

    C) exothermic with an increase in entropy.

    D) exothermic with a decrease in entropy.

30. Which conditions would be the best to enhance the amount of ammonia formed?

    A) high temperature and high pressure

    B) low temperature and high pressure

    C) high temperature and low pressure

    D) low temperature and low pressure

31. Would the use of a catalyst be of practical help in increasing the amount of ammonia formed in the reaction?

    A) No. A catalyst does not change the position of the equilibrium.

    B) No. A catalyst increases the speed of both forward and reverse reactions.

    C) Yes. A catalyst will increase the rate of reaction at lower temperatures.

    D) Yes. A catalyst will increase the rate of reaction and produce more products at all temperatures.

32. What is the value of the equilibrium constant for the following reaction when the equilibrium concentrations are

$[N_2] = 2.0\,M\,[H_2] = 2.0\,M\,[NH_3] = 2.0\,M$

$N_2(g) + 3H_2(g) \rightleftharpoons 2\,NH_3(g)$

    A) 0.25

    B) 0.50

    C) 0.75

    D) 1.00

33. What is the molar solubility of silver chloride ($K_{sp} = 1.8 \times 10^{-10}$) in 0.050 M sodium chloride?

    A) $(1.8/0.050) \times 10^{-10}\,M$

    B) $(1.8/0.050)^{1/2} \times 10^{-5}\,M$

    C) $(0.050/1.8)^{1/2} \times 10^{-5}\,M$

    D) $(0.050/1.8) \times 10^{-10}\,M$

34. What would be the expected result when 100 mL of a solution that is 0.0020 M $Ca(NO_3)_2$ and 0.0020 M $Pb(NO_3)_2$ is mixed with 100 mL of 0.002 M Na_2SO_4? The K_{sp} of $CaSO_4$ is 2.4×10^{-5} and the K_{sp} of $PbSO_4$ is 6.3×10^{-7}.

    A) Both $CaSO_4$ and $PbSO_4$ will precipitate.

    B) Only $CaSO_4$ will precipitate.

    C) Only $PbSO_4$ will precipitate.

    D) Neither $CaSO_4$ nor $PbSO_4$ will precipitate.

Use the figure showing the titration curve for 20.0 mL of analyte titrated with 0.2 M titrant to answer Questions 35–40.

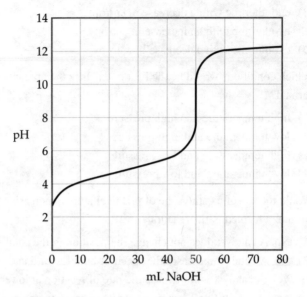

35. The figure shows data for the titration of which analyte/titrant pair?

    A) weak acid/weak base
    B) weak acid/strong base
    C) weak base/strong acid
    D) weak base/weak acid

36. Estimate the molar concentration of analyte.

    A) 0.1 M
    B) 0.2 M
    C) 0.25 M
    D) 0.5 M

37. Estimate the approximate K_a or K_b for the analyte.

    A) 10^{-3}
    B) 10^{-5}
    C) 10^{-9}
    D) 10^{-12}

38. Estimate the approximate pH of the equivalence point.

    A) 3
    B) 5
    C) 9
    D) 12

39. Estimate the pH range at which the solution acts as a buffer

    A) 3–4
    B) 4–6
    C) 11–12
    D) 10–40

40. Estimate the approximate K_a required of a colored indicator to detect a meaningful end-point of the titration.

   A) 10^{-3}

   B) 10^{-5}

   C) 10^{-9}

   D) 10^{-12}

41. If the process illustrated in the figure happens spontaneously, indicate the signs for ΔH, ΔS, and ΔG, respectively.

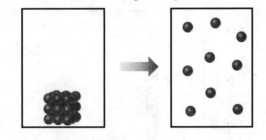

   A) $\Delta H = +, \Delta S = +, \Delta G = -$

   B) $\Delta H = -, \Delta S = -, \Delta G$ depends on temperature

   C) $\Delta H = -, \Delta S = +, \Delta G = -$

   D) $\Delta H = +, \Delta S = -, \Delta G$ depends on temperature

42. All of the structures pictured below are stable. Which of them could carry a charge and still have an octet Lewis structure?

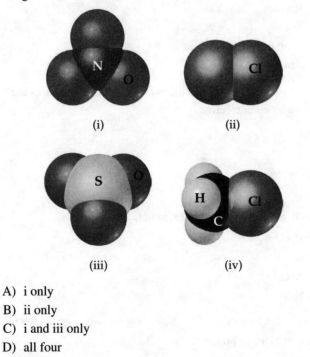

(i)   (ii)

(iii)   (iv)

   A) i only

   B) ii only

   C) i and iii only

   D) all four

43. Which element can be expected to have the most positive enthalpy for loss of an electron in the gas phase?

   A) Al

   B) Si

   C) P

   D) S

44. Which element can be expected to have the most negative enthalpy upon attracting an electron in the gas phase?

    A) B

    B) C

    C) N

    D) O

45. The mass spectrum shown is most likely that of

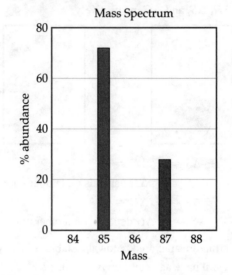

Mass Spectrum

    A) Rb only

    B) Sr only

    C) a mixture of Rb and Sr

    D) a mixture of At and Fr

46. For the isoelectronic series below, which species requires the least energy to remove an outer electron?

    A) O^{2-}

    B) F^-

    C) Ne

    D) Na^+

47. Which species below does not violate the octet rule?

    A) BrF_3

    B) BF_3

    C) N_2O

    D) NO_2

48. How do the properties of the following reaction vary as the reaction goes from reactants to products? A → B

    A) Rate remains the same and half-life decreases.

    B) Rate decreases and half-life remains the same.

    C) Rate and half-life both decrease.

    D) Rate and half-life both increase.

49. The data in the table of initial rates show that the rate law for the reaction
    A → B is:

Experiment	[A], M	[B], M	Rate, M/s
1	0.10	0.10	1
2	0.10	0.20	2
3	0.20	0.40	16

A) Rate $= k[A][B]$

B) Rate $= k[A][B]^2$

C) Rate $= k[A]^2[B]$

D) Rate $= k[A]^2[B]^2$

50. The photoelectron spectrum was carried out using 12 kJ photons. The spectrum is most likely a partial spectrum of which element?

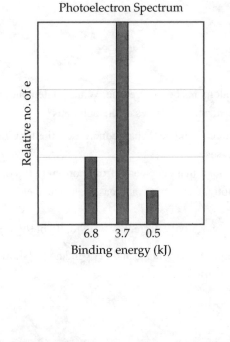

Photoelectron Spectrum

A) Na

B) Mg

C) Al

D) F

Element	Electron Configuration	Melting Point (°C)	Density	Atomic Radius (A°)	I_1 (kJ/mol)
Fluorine	$[He]2s^2 2p^5$	−220	1.69 g/L	0.57	1681
Chlorine	$[Ne]3s^2 3p^5$	−102		1.02	1251
Bromine	$[Ar]4s^2 3d^{10} 4p^5$		3.12 g/cm³	1.20	1140
Iodine	$[Kr]5s^2 4d^{10} 5p^5$	114	4.94 g/cm³	1.39	1008

The table above shows some properties of halogens with some data missing. Use the information in the table to answer Questions 51–54.

51. Predict the approximate melting point of bromine.

    A) −50 °C

    B) 0 °C

    C) 50 °C

    D) 100 °C

52. Which halogen is most likely a liquid at room temperature?

    A) Fluorine

    B) Chlorine

    C) Bromine

    D) Iodine

53. Estimate the approximate density of chlorine at room temperature and pressure.

    A) 1 g/L

    B) 2 g/L

    C) 3 g/L

    D) 4 g/L

54. All the statements below are true. Which statement best explains the trend in the first ionization energies of the halogens?

    A) As effective nuclear charge increases, the first ionization energy increases.

    B) The molar mass decreases from bottom to top of a group.

    C) Coulombic attractions increase as valence electrons get closer to the nucleus.

    D) Electronegativity decreases from top to bottom of a group.

55. The formulas for n-pentane and neopentane are shown below. Which statement is true?

n-Pentane (C_5H_{12})   Neopentane (C_5H_{12})

    A) Neopentane has the higher boiling point because its electrons are more polarizable.

    B) Neopentane has the lower boiling point because it has a greater molar mass.

    C) The n-pentane molecule has the higher boiling point because its electrons are more polarizable.

    D) Neopentane has the lower boiling point because it has a lower surface area.

Questions 56–60 relate to the following information.

A voltaic cell is constructed using the following half-reactions.

Half-reaction	$E°$
$Cr^{3+}(aq) + 3\,e^- \rightarrow Cr(s)$	-0.41 V
$PbSO_4(s) + H^+(aq) + 2e^- \rightarrow Pb(s) + HSO_4^-(aq)$	$+1.69$ V

56. The cell voltage is

    A) 1.28
    B) 2.10
    C) 2.15
    D) 4.61

57. The number of electrons transferred in the balanced equation for the cell are

    A) 2
    B) 3
    C) 5
    D) 6

58. As the voltaic cell operates, the oxidized and reduced substances are, respectively,

    A) $Cr(s)$ and $PbSO_4(s)$
    B) Cr^{3+} and $Cr(s)$
    C) $H^+(aq)$ and $HSO_4^-(aq)$
    D) $PbSO_4(s)$ and $Cr^{3+}(aq)$

59. Which change will increase the voltage of the cell?

    A) Increasing the size of the Cr electrode.
    B) Increasing the amount of $PbSO_4(s)$
    C) Decreasing the pH
    D) Increasing the $[Cr^{3+}]$

60. Approximately how many grams of metal will be plated at the anode in 100 s at 10 amps?

    A) 1/4
    B) 1/3
    C) 1
    D) 3/2

CHEMISTRY PRACTICE TEST 1

Section II

105 minutes

You may use a calculator for this section.

Directions: Answer each of the following questions, clearly showing the methods you use and the steps involved at arriving at the answers. Partial credit will be given for work shown and little or no credit will be given for not showing numerical work, even if the answers are correct.

Question 1

a. The acid ionization constants for the triprotic acid, phosphoric acid, are

$$K_{a_1} = 7.5 \times 10^{-3}, K_{a_2} = 6.2 \times 10^{-8}, \text{ and } K_{a_3} = 4.2 \times 10^{-13}.$$

  i. Write three ionic equations, one for each of the successive ionizations of the three protons of phosphoric acid. Clearly indicate which equilibrium constant corresponds to each ionic equation.

  ii. Calculate the number of grams of sodium dihydrogen phosphate dihydrate needed to prepare 1.00 L of a 0.250 molar solution.

  iii. Write a net ionic equation for the hydrolysis of aqueous sodium phosphate and calculate the value of the corresponding equilibrium constant for the reaction.

b. The acid ionization constant, K_a, for acetic acid is 1.8×10^{-5}. Exactly 41.00 g of sodium acetate is added to water to make 1.00 L of solution. Calculate:

  i. the pH of the solution.

  ii. the percent ionization of the acetate in the solution.

c. Calculate the pH of a solution resulting from mixing 200.0 mL of the solution prepared in Part b with 200.0 mL of 0.200 M hydrochloric acid.

d. Calculate the number of milliliters of 1.00 M hydrochloric acid or 1.00 M sodium hydroxide (specify which and justify your answer) that needs to be added to 82.00 g of sodium acetate to obtain a buffer having a pH of 4.44.

Question 2

Mercury(II) chloride reacts with oxalate ion according to the following equation:

$$2HgCl_2(aq) + C_2O_4^{2-}(aq) \rightarrow 2Cl^-(aq) + 2CO_2(g) + Hg_2Cl_2(s)$$

The initial rate of the reaction was determined for several concentrations of the reactants and the following rate data were obtained for the appearance of chloride ion:

Experiment	$[HgCl_2](mol\ L^{-1})$	$[C_2O_4^{2-}](mol\ L^{-1})$	Rate $(mol\ L^{-1}s^{-1})$
1	0.144	0.132	5.63×10^{-5}
2	0.144	0.396	5.10×10^{-4}
3	0.072	0.396	2.51×10^{-4}
4	0.288	0.132	1.13×10^{-4}

a. Write the rate law for this reaction.
b. Calculate the rate constant and specify its units.
c. What is the reaction rate when the concentration of both reactants is 0.150 M?
d. What is the rate of disappearance of oxalate ion when $[C_2O_4^{2-}] = 0.10$ M and $[HgCl_2] = 0.20$ M?
e. Is the overall equation likely to be an elementary step? Explain.
f. Which species is oxidized in the reaction and which is reduced?

Question 3

The empirical and molecular formulas of a hydrocarbon are determined by combustion analysis.

a. Combustion of a 1.214 g sample of a hydrocarbon results in 4.059 g of carbon dioxide and 0.9494 g of water.

  i.   How many moles of carbon are contained in the sample?
  ii. How many moles of H are contained in the sample?
  iii. What is the empirical formula of the hydrocarbon?

b. The mass spectrum of the hydrocarbon shows a parent peak at 184 mass units.

  i.   Predict the molar mass of the hydrocarbon.
  ii. What is the molecular formula of the hydrocarbon?
  iii. Write and balance a chemical equation for the complete combustion of the hydrocarbon.

Question 4

In an experiment, a hydrocarbon and carbon tetrachloride were each found not to dissolve in water.

a. Draw the Lewis structure and a line-angle representation for carbon tetrachloride and make a sketch of a space-filling model.
b. What is the molecular geometry of carbon tetrachloride and what are the bond angles in the molecule?
c. Does the molecule have any polar bonds? Explain. Is the molecule polar? Explain.

d. Explain the fact that carbon tetrachloride does not dissolve in water.

e. What principal intermolecular force(s) is(are) acting in the carbon tetrachloride solution of the hydrocarbon?

Question 5

Consider the following equilibrium system:

$$NH_4Cl(s) \rightleftharpoons NH_3(g) + HCl(g) \quad \Delta H = +176 \text{ kJ/mol}$$

State the effect on the number of grams of solid ammonium chloride present at equilibrium (increase, decrease, or stay the same) and, in each case, explain your reasoning, when:

a. the partial pressure of ammonia is increased.

b. the temperature is increased.

c. the products are passed through liquid water.

d. the volume of the container is decreased.

Question 6

The first ionization energy of potassium is $+419 \text{ kJ/mol}$. The electron affinity of chlorine is -349 kJ/mol. Electron affinity is the energy change that occurs when an electron is added to a gaseous atom.

a. Define first ionization energy and write a thermochemical equation that represents the first ionization energy of potassium.

b. Write a thermochemical equation that represents the electron affinity of chlorine.

c. Write the sum of the reactions you wrote in Parts a and b and calculate the heat of the reaction in the gas phase. Specify if the reaction is endothermic or exothermic.

d. The reaction between potassium metal and chlorine gas to produce solid potassium chloride is highly exothermic ($\Delta H = -435 \text{ kJ/mol}$).

   i. Write the formation reaction of potassium chloride.

   ii. Besides the ionization of potassium, what forces must be overcome in the formation of potassium chloride?

   iii. Explain why this reaction releases so much energy.

e. Predict whether the formation of calcium chloride would be more or less exothermic than the formation of potassium chloride. Explain the basis of your prediction.

Question 7

A 5.0 g sample of sodium chloride is added to 10.0 mL of water at 20 °C. Upon mixing, the salt dissolves and the temperature of the mixture is measured. The experiment is repeated with ammonium chloride and again with calcium chloride. The data in the table summarize the results:

Experiment	Salt	T_1	T_2
1	NaCl	20 °C	20 °C
2	NH_4Cl	20 °C	5 °C
3	$CaCl_2$	20 °C	35 °C

a. Predict the signs of ΔG, ΔS, and ΔH for each of the three experiments. Explain your reasoning.

b. Consider the dissolution of ammonium chloride in water.

   i. Write a thermochemical equation, including the heat term, for the dissolution of ammonium chloride.

   ii. Discuss the nature and relative magnitudes of the bonds and intermolecular forces that break and those that form when ammonium chloride dissolves in water.

   iii. What is the driving force for the change? Use the equation, $\Delta G = \Delta H - T\Delta S$, to explain your reasoning.

c. Is there a temperature at which an equilibrium will be established for the dissolution of ammonium chloride? Justify your answer.

MULTIPLE CHOICE ANSWERS AND EXPLANATIONS TO PRACTICE TEST 1

1. C. The change in solubility of NaCl with temperature is minimal compared to the others indicating that solid NaCl dissolves in water with little or no heat change.

2. A. As temperature increases, the solubility of cerium sulfate decreases indicating that cerium sulfate dissolves exothermically. Heating an exothermic process will cause the reaction to shift toward reactants, in this case decreasing solubility.

3. D. The two driving forces that influence chemical and physical change are a decrease in enthalpy and an increase in entropy. Most salts dissolve endothermically but the accompanying increase in entropy (randomness of the system) overcomes the increase in enthalpy associated with an endothermic reaction. All salts that dissolve endothermically fit into this category.

4. D. The only products obtained from the complete combustion are carbon dioxide and water. The assumptions are that all the carbon in the sample is converted to carbon dioxide and all the hydrogen in the sample is converted to water. The amounts of carbon and hydrogen can be determined by measuring the masses of carbon dioxide and water produced.

5. C. Atom Y loses three valence electrons to form a Y^{3+} ion. Atom Z gains two electrons to form a Z^{2-} ion. The two ions combine to form Y_2Z_3.

6. A. The formation reaction for one mole of gaseous ammonia is one-half of this balanced equation:

   $3H_2(g) + N_2(g) \rightleftharpoons 2NH_3(g)$

   Heat of formation $= +\dfrac{1}{2}[3(H{-}H) + (N{\equiv}N) - 3(N{-}H)]$

   $= \dfrac{1}{2}[3(450) + (950) - 6(400)] = -50\,\text{kJ/mol}$

7. B. The balanced equation is: $O_2(g) + 2SO_2(g) \rightarrow 2SO_3(g)$. Oxygen is the limiting reactant so twice as many moles of SO_3 can be formed from the available moles of oxygen. At the same conditions of temperature and pressure, liters are proportional to moles.

   $x\,\text{L SO}_3 = 1\,\text{L O}_2(2\,\text{L SO}_3/1\,\text{L O}_2) = 2\,\text{L SO}_3$.

8. B. Effective nuclear charge increases from left to right along any period. Neither electron is screened from the charge of the two protons on He making helium's effective nuclear charge double that of hydrogen. Consequently, helium is smaller than hydrogen.

9. D. Carbon dioxide has two polar bonds but its linear geometry causes the dipoles to cancel. All the others have polar bonds and have nonlinear geometry.

10. B. Phosphoric acid is a weak polyprotic acid, which ionizes only slightly. While all five of the listed species exist in solution, H_3PO_4 exists to the greatest extent.

11. C. Nitrogen molecules have a higher molar mass than helium atoms.

12. D. Temperature is a measure of the average kinetic energy of molecules. At the same temperature all three systems have the same average kinetic energy.

13. B. On average, lighter molecules move faster than heavier ones at the same temperature. In System i, 5/7 (20/28) of the molecules are light. In System ii, 3/4 (21/28) of the molecules are light. In System iii, only 2/7 (8/28) of the molecules are light.

14. D. The volumes and temperatures are the same so the pressures are equal, which means that, on average, the energy with which the particles hit the walls of the container are equal.

15. C. Nitrogen molecules deviate more due to their greater number of electrons and greater polarizability. Nitrogen molecules will form temporary dipoles more often than helium atoms making nitrogen's attractive forces greater, which makes them stick together more forming more massive particles.

16. A. The electronegativity values for O and Cl are 3.5 and 3.0, respectively. Oxygen has an effective nuclear charge of about 6+ because eight protons are screened by two inner-core electrons. Chlorine has an effective nuclear charge of about +7 because 17 protons are screened by 10 inner-core electrons. However, chlorine is larger than O so an electron pair cannot approach the Cl nucleus as closely as it can approach the O nucleus making the attractive force stronger for O.

17. B. Sulfur's greater electronegativity draws electrons away from the oxygen's in the sulfite ion making it more stable and allowing the proton to be more easily lost to water.

18. A. Because it is a gas, ammonia escapes the solution. However, ammonia is highly polar and can hydrogen bond with water and is very soluble in water. Therefore, ammonia does not nucleate into bubbles as does nonpolar carbon dioxide, which does not dissolve readily in water.

19. D. Hydrogen carbonate slowly reacts to form carbonate ion with the release of carbon dioxide according to the following equation:

$$2HCO_3^-(aq) \rightarrow H_2O(l) + CO_2(g) + CO_3^{2-}(aq).$$

While the other three statements are all true, CO_2 is acidic so the pH would go down with time and O_2 is neither basic nor acidic so it would not affect the pH. Evaporation of water would concentrate the hydrogen carbonate base but not enough to make the pH change by 2 pH units which represents a 100-fold increase in base concentration.

20. B. The balanced equation is: $2NO(g) + O_2(g) \rightarrow 2NO_2(g)$. The diagram shows eight NO molecules and five O_2 molecules available for reaction. Eight NO molecules require four molecules of O_2 to react whereas five O_2

molecules would require ten NO molecules. Therefore, NO is the limiting reactant so theoretically, eight NO molecules will produce eight NO_2 molecules. At 75% yield, there would be six NO_2 molecules formed.

21. B. Because F is smaller and more electronegative than O or N, it is closer to H and has a higher partial negative charge than O or N. Therefore, the coulombic attraction is greatest for H—F.

22. B. A linear plot of ln[A] versus time is characteristic of a simple first order process. A simple second-order process would yield a straight line for 1/[A] vs. time.

23. A. If just [Y] is halved, then the initial rate would decrease by a factor of $(1/2)^2 = 1/4$. To make the rate remain constant, [X] is quadrupled because $(4)^1 = 4$.

24. D . An "ICE" table would look like this:

	$H_2(g)$ +	$I_2(g)$ =	$2HI(g)$
I	1.0 M	1.0 M	0
C	$-x$	$-x$	$+2x$
E	$1.0 - x$	$1.0 - x$	$2x$

$K_c = 36 = (2x)^2/(1.0 - x)(1.0 - x)$

If we take the square root of both sides of the equation we obtain:

$6 = 2x/(1.0 - x)$ or $6 - 6x = 2x, x = 0.750$ $[H_2] = 1 - x = 0.250$

25. D. KOH is a strong base, which dissociates completely in aqueous solution. HCl is a strong acid, CH_3COOH is a weak acid and weak electrolyte, NH_4NO_3 is a weak acid and strong electrolyte, and CH_3OH is a neutral nonelectrolyte.

26. A. Fluoride ion is the conjugate base of the weak acid, HF. The solubility of calcium fluoride will increase as pH decreases because at low pH the available protons will react with the basic fluoride ion.

$H^+(aq) + F^-(aq) \rightleftharpoons HF(aq)$

Methanol is completely miscible in water and all the other choices are ionic compounds containing only neutral cations and anions.

27. D. The weakest acid has the strongest conjugate base ($K_w = K_a \times K_b$). At the equivalence point, all is left is weak base.

28. B. All are bases except NH_4^+. It is unlikely that the already positively charged ammonium ion will accept a proton.

29. D. K decreases with increasing temperature so the equilibrium is shifted to the left indicating an exothermic reaction. A negative value for the entropy change indicates a decrease in entropy.

30. B. Low temperature would drive the equilibrium to the right because it is an exothermic reaction. High pressure would also drive the equilibrium to the right because there are fewer number of moles of gas on the right.

31. C. At lower temperatures the reaction has a higher K, which would increase the amount of ammonia formed. However, at low temperature the rate of the reaction will decrease so a catalyst is of practical value because it will increase the rate of reaction even at low temperature.

32. A. $K_c = [NH_3]^2/[N_2][H_2]^3 = (2.0)^2/(2.0)(2.0)^3 = 0.25$

    (Remember that no calculators are allowed on the multiple choice section so the arithmetic required for complex quantitative problems is relatively simple.)

33. A. $AgCl(s) = Ag^+(aq) + Cl^-(aq)$

    $K_{sp} = 1.8 \times 10^{-10} = [Ag^+][Cl^-]$

    Let $x =$ molar solubility of AgCl.

    At equilibrium, $[Ag^+] = x, [Cl^-] = 0.050 + x \approx 0.050$ M

    $1.8 \times 10^{-10} = x(0.050)$

    $x = (1.8/0.050) \times 10^{-10}$

34. C. The concentrations of the ions are not sufficient to form calcium sulfate but are sufficient to form lead(II) sulfate.

    $[Pb^{2+}] = 0.0020$ M $(100/200) = 0.0010$ M,

    $[Ca^{2+}] = 0.0020$ M $(100/200) = 0.0010$ M,

    $[SO_4^{2-}] = 0.002$ M $(100/200) = 0.0010$ M

    $PbSO_4(s) = Pb^{2+}(aq) + SO_4^{2-}(aq)$

    $Q = [Pb^{2+}][SO_4^{2-}] = (0.0010)(0.0010) = 1 \times 10^{-6}$

    $K_{sp} < Q$ so $PbSO_4(s)$ will form.

    $CaSO_4(s) = Ca^{2+}(aq) + SO_4^{2-}(aq)$

    $Q = [Ca^{2+}][SO_4^{2-}] = (0.0010)(0.0010) = 1 \times 10^{-6}$

    $K_{sp} > Q$ so $CaSO_4(s)$ will not form.

35. B. The pH rises as titrant is added indicating that the titrant is a base. The high pH at 12 indicates that the base is strong.

36. D. $(20.0 \text{ mL})(M) = (50.0 \text{ M})(0.20 \text{ M})$. $M = 0.5$ M

37. B. At 25 mL of strong base, the pH of the solution equals the pK_a of the weak acid. This pH is approximately 5 so the pK_a is approximately 10^{-5}.

38. C. The equivalence point is approximately the midpoint of the steepest part of the curve where the pH changes the most.

39. B. A buffer is a solution mixture of a weak acid and its conjugate weak base, both in significant concentration so the solution resists a change in pH. At about pH $= 4$, significant quantities of the conjugate pair exist until about pH $= 6$.

40. C. The endpoint of a titration is the drop of titrant that causes the indicator, which is a colored weak acid, to change colors. The ideal titration is where the endpoint closely matches the equivalence point. That happens when the indicator has a pK_a that closely approximates the pH of the equivalence point.

41. A. The illustration shows sublimation an endothermic process with a positive enthalpy change. Gases are more random than solids so the entropy change is positive. The process happens spontaneously, which means that it is thermodynamically favorable, so the free energy change is negative.

42. C. Molecule i represents nitrate ion, NO_3^-. Molecule iii can represent sulfur trioxide, SO_3 or sulfite ion, SO_3^{2-}. The others, dichlorine and chloromethane, are neutral molecules.

43. C. In other words, the question asks which element has the highest first ionization energy. First ionization energy increases from left to right along a period because effective nuclear charge also increases. However, sulfur exhibits electron–electron repulsion in a p^4 configuration making it have a slightly lower ionization energy than phosphorus. This same dip in ionization energy is also seen in N to O and As to Se.

44. D. In other words, the question asks which element has the highest electron affinity. Generally, left to right along any period, electron affinity increases with increasing effective nuclear charge because of increased coulombic attractions. Note: Most elements have negative electron affinities. That is, they attract electrons exothermically, with the release of energy. However, nitrogen has a positive energy associated with its attracting an electron because of electron–electron repulsion when an electron enters nitrogen's p^3 configuration. The electron affinities of the other Group 5A elements, while negative, are also not as negative as the trend would indicate.

45. A. The atomic mass is the average mass of the natural isotopes of an element. The spectrum clearly shows two isotopes of mass 85 (about 70% abundance) and 87 (about 30% abundance). The average would be closer to 85 than 87. The atomic mass of rubidium is about 85.45 and that of strontium is 87.62.

46. A. Oxide ion has just eight protons in its nucleus, two of which are screened by its two $1s$ electrons. Its effective nuclear charge is the smallest of the species listed.

47. C. A valid octet structure can be written for N_2O.

48. B. As a reaction continues, its rate decreases as the concentrations of reactants decrease. The half-life remains the same for any first-order reaction.

49. C. Experiments 1 and 2 show that when [A] is constant and [B] doubles, the rate doubles meaning the exponent of [B] is 1. Experiments 2 and 3 show that when both [A] and [B] double, the rate increases by a factor of 8. Doubling [B] accounts for a factor of 2 so doubling [A] accounts for a factor of 4. Therefore the exponent of [A] is 2.

50. A. The spectrum shows decreasing energy along the x-axis with relative values of 2, 6, and 1 electrons. This could represent an electron configuration of $s^2p^6s^1$. These subshells correspond to three of the four subshells of the sodium atom: $2s^22p^63s^1$. The $1s^2$ subshell is apparently missing because the binding energy of its electrons is greater than the 12 kJ energy of the incident photons.

51. B. There is approximately 100 degrees between the melting points of each halogen.

52. C. With a melting point of 114 °C, iodine is a solid. The low melting points of fluorine and chlorine mean that their boiling points are low also. A melting point of about 0 °C indicates that bromine might still be a liquid at a temperature 20 °C higher.

53. C. Because both fluorine and chlorine are gases at common temperatures, their densities are proportional to their molar masses: 1.69 g/L × 35.5/19 ~ 3 g/L.

54. C. As the size of the atoms decreases up a group, the valence electrons are closer to the effective nuclear charge so coulombic attractions increase with decreasing distance from the nucleus.

55. D. The more elongated molecule provides a greater surface area, enhances intermolecular contact, and increases dispersion forces. Neopentane is more round so it has lower surface area and lower dispersion forces.

56. B. The chromium reaction is reversed because it has the lower voltage.
$E°_{cell} = E°_{ox} + E°_{red} = +0.41 + 1.69 = 2.10$ V.

57. D. To obtain the balanced equation, multiply by coefficients that make the number of electrons in the half-reactions cancel:

$$2[Cr(s) \rightarrow Cr^{3+}(aq) + 3\,e^-]$$

$$3[PbSO_4(s) + H^+(aq) + 2e^- \rightarrow Pb(s) + HSO_4^-(aq)]$$

$$\overline{2Cr(s) + 3PbSO_4(s) + 3H^+(aq) \rightarrow 2Cr^{3+}(aq) + 3Pb(s) + 3HSO_4^-(aq)}$$

58. A. Cr loses 3 electrons and is oxidized. $PbSO_4$ gains 2 electrons and is reduced.

59. C. Decreasing the pH will increase the $[H^+]$ and increase the voltage.

60. C. Round Faraday's constant to ~100,000 C/mol e^- and round the molar mass of lead to ~200 g/mol:

x g Pb = 100 s(10 C/s)(1 mol e^-/~100,000 C)(1 mol Pb/2 mol e^-)

(~200 g/1 mol) = ~1 g Pb

Free Response Answers for Practice Test 1

Answers to Question 1

a. i. $H_3PO_4(aq) + H_2O(l) \rightleftharpoons H_2PO_4^-(aq) + H_3O^+(aq)$

   $K_{a_1} = 7.5 \times 10^{-3}$

   $H_2PO_4^-(aq) + H_2O(l) \rightleftharpoons HPO_4^{2-}(aq) + H_3O^+(aq)$

   $K_{a_2} = 6.2 \times 10^{-8}$

   $HPO_4^{2-}(aq) + H_2O(l) \rightleftharpoons PO_4^{3-}(aq) + H_3O^+(aq)$

   $K_{a_3} = 4.2 \times 10^{-13}$

   ii. x g $NaH_2PO_4 \cdot 2H_2O = 1.00$ L $(0.250$ mol/L$)(156.0$ g/mol$) = 39.0$ g

   iii. $PO_4^{3-} + H_2O \rightleftharpoons HPO_4^{2-} + OH^-$

   $K_b = \dfrac{K_w}{K_{a_3}} = 1.0 \times 10^{-14}/4.2 \times 10^{-13} = 0.024$

b. i. $CH_3COO^- + H_2O \rightleftharpoons CH_3COOH + OH^-$

   The initial concentration of acetate ion is:

   $(41.00$ g$)(1$ mol$/84.0$ g$)/(1.00$ L$) = 0.500$ M

   Let $y = [OH^-]$

   $K_b = \dfrac{K_w}{K_{a_3}} = \dfrac{1.0 \times 10^{-14}}{1.8 \times 10^{-5}} = 5.6 \times 10^{-10} = \dfrac{y^2}{I} = \dfrac{y^2}{0.500}$

   $y = [OH^-] = 1.67 \times 10^{-5}$

   $pOH = -\log(1.67 \times 10^{-5}) = 4.78$

   $pH = 14 - 4.78 = 9.22$

   ii. Percent ionization $= 100 \times [OH^-]/I = 100 \times (1.67 \times 10^{-5})/(0.500) = 0.00334\%$

c. $H^+ + CH_3COO^- \rightleftharpoons CH_3COOH$

   mol $CH_3COO^- = 0.200$ L $\times 0.500$ M $= 0.100$ mol CH_3COO^-

   mol $H^+ = 0.200$ L $\times 0.200$ M $= 0.0400$ mol H^+

   All 0.0400 mol H^+ will react with 0.0400 mol of CH_3COO^-, leaving

   0.100 mol $-$ 0.0400 mol $= 0.060$ mol CH_3COO^- and 0.040 mol CH_3COOH.

   $pH = pK_a + \log[CH_3COO^-]/[CH_3COOH] = 4.74 + \log(0.0600/0.040) =$
   $4.74 + 0.18 = 4.92$

d. Hydrochloric acid as a limiting reactant needs to be added because sodium acetate is a base. The object is to convert some of the weak base to weak acid, leaving a solution containing both weak acid and base.

   $pH = pK_a + \log[CH_3COO^-]/[CH_3COOOH]$

   $4.44 = 4.74 + \log[CH_3COO^-]/[CH_3COOOH]$

   $\log[CH_3COO^-]/[CH_3COOH] = -0.30$

   $[CH_3COO^-]/[CH_3COOH] = 0.500$

   Two-thirds of the base needs to be converted to acetic acid leaving one-third of the acetate ion unreacted.

   82.00 g of sodium acetate is 1 mol.

   0.667 mol of HCl is 667 mL of a 1.00 M solution.

Answers to Question 2

a. rate$=k[HgCl_2]^a[C_2O_4^{2-}]^b$

Experiments 1 and 2 show that when $[C_2O_4^{2-}]$ is tripled, the rate goes up by a factor of 9: $5.10 \times 10^{-4}/5.63 \times 10^{-5} = 9.06$, so the value of the exponent $b = 2(3^2 = 9)$.

Experiments 1 and 4 show that when $[HgCl_2]$ is doubled, the rate increases by a factor of 2: $1.13 \times 10^{-4}/5.63 \times 10^{-5} = 2.01$, so the exponent $a=1(2^1 = 2)$.

rate$=k[HgCl_2]^1[C_2O_4^{2-}]^2$

b. rate$=k[HgCl_2]^1[C_2O_4^{2-}]^2$. Use the values of any experiment to obtain k.

$5.63 \times 10^{-5} \text{ M/s} = k(0.144 \text{ M})(0.132 \text{ M})^2$

$k = 0.0224 \text{ 1/M}^2 \text{ s}$

c. rate$=k[HgCl_2]^1[C_2O_4^{2-}]^2$

rate $= (0.0224 \text{ 1/M}^2 \text{ s})(0.150 \text{ M})(0.150 \text{ M})^2 = 7.56 \times 10^{-5} \text{ M/s}$

d. rate$=k[HgCl_2]^1[C_2O_4^{2-}]^2$

rate $= (0.0224 \text{ 1/M}^2 \text{ s})(0.20 \text{ M})(0.10 \text{ M})^2 = 4.5 \times 10^{-5} \text{ M/s}$

From the coefficients of the balanced equation, the rate of disappearance of oxalate is half the rate of appearance of chloride ion:

rate$=^1/_2(4.5 \times 10^{-5} \text{ M/s})=2.3 \times 10^{-5} \text{ M/s}$

e. The overall equation is not likely to be an elementary step because the rate law is third order. An elementary step would require a three-particle collision that is very rare. More likely, the reaction proceeds via a multistep mechanism that includes only second-order collisions.

f. Oxalate ion, $C_2O_4^{2-}$, is oxidized and mercury(II) chloride, $HgCl_2$, is reduced.

Answers to Question 3

The empirical and molecular formulas of a hydrocarbon are determined by combustion analysis.

a. i. x mol C $=$ mol $CO_2 = (4.059 \text{ g})/(44.0 \text{ g/mol}) = 0.0923$ mol C

   ii. x mol H $= 2 \times$ mol $H_2O = 2 \times (0.9494 \text{ g})/(18.00 \text{ g/mol}) = 0.1055$ mol H

   iii. $C_{0.0923}H_{0.1055} = C_{(0.0923)/(0.0932)}H_{(0.1055)/(0.0923)} = C_1H_{1.143} = C_7H_8$

b. i.   Molar mass $= 184 \text{ g/mol}$

   ii. $184.0 \text{ g/mol} = 2 \times 92 \text{ g/mol for } C_7H_8$

        $(C_7H_8) \times 2 = C_{14}H_{16}$

   iii. $C_{14}H_{16}(l) + 18O_2(g) \rightarrow 14CO_2(g) + 8H_2O(l)$

Answers to Question 4

a.

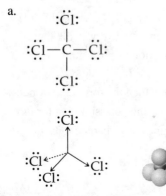

b. The molecular geometry is tetrahedral and the bond angles are all 109.5°.

c. All four C—Cl bonds are polar because of the large difference in electronegativity of carbon and chlorine. The molecule is nonpolar, because the four C—Cl dipoles are oriented in a way that they cancel each other, giving no net dipole.

d. Water is polar and effectively hydrogen bonds to other water molecules, excluding any carbon tetrachloride from strong intermolecular attractions to water. Also the nonpolar carbon tetrachloride molecules have dispersion forces that cause them to exclude the water molecules.

e. The principle forces acting in the carbon tetrachloride–hydrocarbon solution are London dispersions.

Answers to Question 5

$$NH_4Cl(s) \rightleftharpoons NH_3(g) + HCl(g) \quad \Delta H = +176 \text{ kJ/mol}$$

a. The solid will increase because an increased pressure of ammonia will increase the concentration of ammonia, the frequency of collisions, and the rate of the reverse reaction. The equilibrium will rebalance, forming more reactants.

b. The solid will decrease because increasing the temperature favors the endothermic reaction.

c. The solid will decrease because the gaseous products are both soluble in water, which will decrease their concentrations in the gas phase, shifting the equilibrium to the right.

d. The solid will increase because the partial pressures of both gases will increase, causing the reverse reaction to be faster than the forward reaction because of increased collisions.

Answers to Question 6

a. First ionization energy is the energy required to remove the most loosely held electron from the ground state of an isolated gaseous atom.
$$419 \text{ kJ} + K(g) \rightarrow K^+(g) + e^-$$

b. Electron affinity:
$$Cl(g) + e^- \rightarrow Cl^-(g) + 349 \text{ kJ}$$

c. $419 \text{ kJ} + K(g) + \rightarrow K^+(g) + e^- \qquad \Delta H = +419 \text{ kJ/mol}$

$\underline{Cl(g) + e^- \rightarrow Cl^-(g) + 349 \text{ kJ} \qquad \Delta H = -349 \text{ kJ/mol}}$

$K(g) + Cl(g) \rightarrow K^+(g) + Cl^-(g) \qquad \Delta H = +70 \text{ kJ/mol}$

d. i. $K(s) + \frac{1}{2}Cl_2(g) \rightarrow KCl(s) \qquad \Delta H = -435 \text{ kJ/mol}$

ii. The Cl — Cl bond must be broken in the formation of potassium chloride. Also the metallic bonds in solid potassium must be broken.

iii. The attractive force between the positive potassium ion and the negative chloride ion is very strong. The energy released in the formation of the very stable ionic bond is more than enough to compensate for the ionization of potassium and the dissociation of chlorine molecules.

e. The formation of calcium chloride will be more exothermic than the formation of potassium chloride because the calcium ion has a 2+ charge and the potassium ion forms only a 1+ charge. The force of attraction between two oppositely charged ions increases in direct proportion to the magnitude of the charges.

Answers to Question 7

a. Salt ΔG ΔS ΔH

NaCl $-$ $+$ undetermined

NH_4Cl $-$ $+$ $+$

$CaCl_2$ $-$ $+$ $-$

All three salts dissolved spontaneously, so ΔG is negative for all three processes. Dissolution of ionic solids will probably lead to more randomness or disorder, so ΔS is likely to be positive for all three processes.

Because no noticeable temperature change was observed for NaCl, it cannot be determined it dissolves endothermically or exothermically.

A decrease in temperature means that ammonium chloride dissolves endothermically. An increase in temperature means that calcium chloride dissolves exothermically.

b. i. $Heat + NH_4Cl(s) \rightarrow NH_4^+(aq) + Cl^-(aq)$

ii. Ammonium chloride contains ionic bonds that require heat to break them. Hydrogen bonds between water molecules also break. Upon dissolution, ion–dipole interactions form between water molecules and ammonium and chloride ions, with the release of energy. Because the process is endothermic, more heat is absorbed than released, so the ionic bonds and the broken intermolecular forces of the solvent must be stronger than the ion–dipole interactions.

iii. The driving force for the dissolution of ammonium chloride is the increase in entropy. ΔS for the process has a large positive value.

Considering $\Delta G = \Delta H - T\Delta S$, ΔG is negative because the process happens spontaneously and ΔH is positive because the system cools off. So, ΔS must have a relatively large positive value to offset the positive value of ΔH.

c. Yes, the dissolution of NH_4Cl will establish an equilibrium. The equilibrium condition is when $\Delta G = 0$. Consider $\Delta G = \Delta H - T\Delta S$. Both ΔH and ΔS are positive. As the temperature decreases, the $T\Delta S$ term will become less positive until a point is reached when $T\Delta S$ equals ΔH. At this point they cancel and ΔG equals 0.

TEST
2

CHEMISTRY PRACTICE TEST 2

Section I **Multiple Choice Questions**

90 minutes

Directions: For each of the following questions or incomplete statements, select the best answer or completion from the choices given.

1. The boiling points and molar masses of a series of similar polar compounds are shown in the table. Which molecule is likely to form hydrogen bonds?

Compound	A	B	C	D
Boiling point, °C	50°	100°	150°	0°
Molar mass	62	115	75	34

   A) A
   B) B
   C) C
   D) D

2. A reaction will always be thermodynamically favored at all temperatures if:

   A) it is exothermic with an increase in entropy
   B) it is exothermic with a decrease in entropy
   C) it is endothermic with an increase in entropy
   D) it is endothermic with a decrease in entropy

3. What is the specific heat capacity of an alloy if 100.0 g of the alloy warms from 20.0 °C to 30.0 °C when 100.0 J of heat are added to it?

   A) $10.0 \, \text{J/g K}$
   B) $1.00 \, \text{J/g K}$
   C) $0.100 \, \text{J/g K}$
   D) $0.0100 \, \text{J/g K}$

4. Which of the following ions will have the smallest ionic radius?

   A) Sc^{3+}
   B) Ca^{2+}
   C) K^+
   D) Cl^-

5. At a given temperature and pressure, hydrogen gas reacts with nitrogen gas to produce ammonia gas. How many liters of ammonia can be produced from 5.0 L of hydrogen and 2.0 L of nitrogen at the same temperature and pressure?

   A) 2.0 L
   B) 3.3 L
   C) 4.0 L
   D) 5.0 L

Questions 6–10 relate to the following information.

The plot shows the distributions of molecular speeds of a mixture of five different equal molar ideal gases at 1.00 atm and 25 °C.

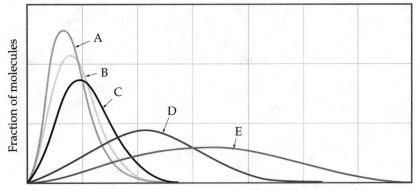

6. Which of these gases has the largest molar mass?

   A) A
   B) E
   C) C
   D) D

7. If the temperature is increased slowly, how will the data in the figure change?

   A) The line for gas E will begin to look more like the line for gas D at 25 °C.
   B) The line for gas A will begin to look more like the line for gas B at 25 °C.
   C) The lines for all the gases will shift to the left with higher peaks.
   D) The lines will not change significantly.

8. Which gas has the highest density?

   A) A
   B) E
   C) C
   D) All are the same.

9. Which gas exerts the highest partial pressure?

   A) A
   B) E
   C) All are the same.
   D) There is not enough information to make a prediction.

10. If the temperature changes so that all the gases begin to deviate from ideal behavior, how will the data in the figure change?

   A) The line for gas E will begin to look more like the line for gas D at 25 °C.

   B) The line for gas A will begin to look more like the line for gas B at 25 °C.

   C) The lines for all the gases will begin to have lower peaks.

   D) The lines will not change significantly.

Questions 11–15 relate to the following laboratory data.

One drop of each of the reagent solutions in the left column are mixed with one drop of each of the solutions in the top row and the observations are recorded in the table. All reagents are 0.2 M.

Reagent solutions	$NaHCO_3$	K_2CO_3
$CuSO_4$	Medium effervescence	Slight effervescence
$CaSO_4$	No visible reaction	No visible reaction
H_2SO_4	Strong effervescence	Strong effervescence

11. The effervescence displayed by all the reactions can be attributed to what chemical species?

   A) SO_2

   B) SO_3

   C) CO_2

   D) CO

12. How many reagents show evidence of acidic behavior?

   A) 1

   B) 2

   C) 3

   D) 4

13. What is the correct order of pH for the following solutions?

   A) $H_2SO_4 < CuSO_4 < K_2CO_3$

   B) $CaSO_4 > CuSO_4 > H_2SO_4$

   C) $H_2SO_4 < CaSO_4 < CuSO_4$

   D) $NaHCO_3 > K_2CO_3 > CuSO_4$

14. All the following statements are true. From the observations in the table we can conclude that:

   A) Potassium ion is larger than sodium ion.

   B) Copper(II) ion is smaller than calcium ion.

   C) Potassium carbonate is a stronger base than sodium hydrogen carbonate.

   D) Sulfuric acid is a strong acid.

15. The fact that potassium carbonate reacts less vigorously than sodium hydrogen carbonate with copper(II) sulfate is best explained by which statement?

   A) Carbonate ion is less basic than hydrogen carbonate ion.

   B) Sodium ion is a stronger base than potassium ion.

   C) There are more protons available to react in the $NaHCO_3$ solution.

   D) Sulfate ion is weakly acidic.

16. A sample of oxygen gas was collected over water at 29.0 °C and a barometric pressure of 725 torr. The sample of oxygen collected was 155 mL and the equilibrium vapor pressure of water at 29 °C is 30.0 torr. How many moles of oxygen were collected?

    A) $(695)(0.155)/(0.082)(302)(760)$

    B) $(725)(0.155)/(0.082)(302)(760)$

    C) $(755)(0.155)/(0.082)(302)$

    D) $(695)(0.155)(760)/0.082)(302)$

17. How many sigma and how many pi bonds are in
    $CH_2 = CHC = CCH_2CH = CH_2$?

    A) 6 sigma and 4 pi.

    B) 8 sigma and 7 pi.

    C) 11 sigma and 3 pi.

    D) 14 sigma and 4 pi.

18. The half-life of a certain radioactive isotope of mercury is four months. What mass of a 32-g sample of this isotope will remain after one year?

    A) 32 g

    B) 16 g

    C) 8 g

    D) 4 g

19. The rate law of the reaction, $2X + 2Y \rightarrow 2XY$, is rate $= k[X]^2[Y]$.

    If [X] is doubled and [Y] is halved, the rate of the reaction will

    A) increase by a factor of 4.

    B) remain the same.

    C) decrease by a factor of 4.

    D) increase by a factor of 2.

20. Corrosion of buried gasoline tanks can be minimized by attaching a "sacrificial plate" of zinc to the tank. This plate corrodes instead of the steel of the tank because

    A) the zinc behaves as a cathode, and is oxidized more readily than iron.

    B) the zinc behaves as an anode, and is oxidized more readily than iron.

    C) the steel hull behaves as a cathode, and is reduced more readily than zinc.

    D) the steel hull behaves as an anode, and is reduced more readily than zinc.

21. Which of the following is the most easily oxidized?

Half-reaction	$E°$, volts
$Al^{3+} + 3e^- \rightarrow Al$	-1.66
$Zn^{2+} + 2e^- \rightarrow Zn$	-0.763
$Hg^{2+} + 2e^- \rightarrow Hg$	$+0.854$
$F_2 + 2e^- \rightarrow 2F^-$	$+2.87$

    A) Al

    B) Zn

    C) Hg

    D) F^-

22. What is the voltage of a cell consisting of the following half-cells that are suitably connected?

$Ni^{2+}(aq) + 2e^- \rightarrow Ni(s)$	$E° = -0.25$ V
$Au^{3+}(aq) + 3e^- \rightarrow Au(s)$	$E° = 1.50$ V

A) 1.25 V

B) 1.75 V

C) 2.50 V

D) 3.00 V

23. The diagram represents a collection of carbon dioxide and water molecules which are the products of the complete combustion of a hydrocarbon. What is the most likely molecular formula for the hydrocarbon?

A) CH_4

B) C_2H_8

C) C_4H_8

D) C_4H_{16}

24. Nitrogen and hydrogen react to form ammonia. The diagram shows N represented as dark spheres and H as light spheres.

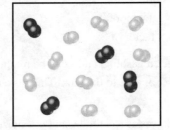

How many ammonia molecules would you draw if the reaction had a 50% yield?

A) 2

B) 3

C) 4

D) 6

25. Below is the mass spectrum of chlorine atoms. How many total peaks would the mass spectrum of naturally occurring chlorine molecules contain?

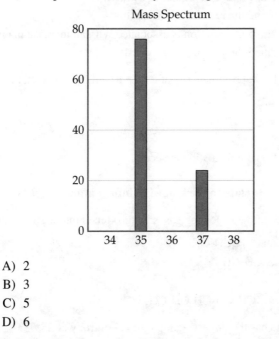

Mass Spectrum

A) 2

B) 3

C) 5

D) 6

Refer to the information in the graph showing the percent ionization in an acetic acid solution to answer Questions 26–28.

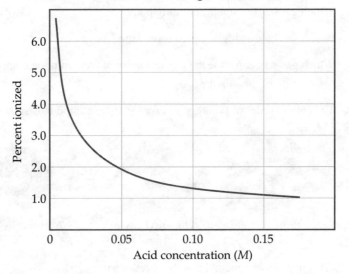

26. The general trend illustrated by the graph is also exhibited by all the following molecules EXCEPT

A) HF

B) HCl

C) NH_3

D) HCN

27. The phenomenon illustrated by the graph can be best explained by

    A) Reasoning using Le Châtelier's principle
    B) Reasoning the reaction is exothermic
    C) Reasoning the reaction is associated with an increase in entropy
    D) Reasoning the reaction is very fast

28. Estimate the approximate pH of a 0.15 M solution of acetic acid?

    A) 1
    B) 3
    C) 5
    D) Additional information is needed

Questions 29–33 relate to the following information.

One gram each of the following gases is introduced into a 10 L container at 25 °C.

    A) propane, $CH_3CH_2CH_3$
    B) ethane, CH_3CH_3
    C) methane, CH_4
    D) pentane, $CH_3CH_2CH_2CH_2CH_3$

29. Which gas has the largest standard molar entropy at 25 °C?

30. When liquefied, which substance will have the highest viscosity?

31. Which gas has the smallest boiling point?

32. Which gas has the highest partial pressure?

33. Which gas will consume the greatest mass of oxygen upon complete combustion of the mixture?

34. The correct order of boiling point for the three compounds shown below is

Propane   Dimethyl ether   Acetonitrile
$CH_3CH_2CH_3$ CH_3OCH_3 CH_3CN

    A) propane > dimethyl ether > acetonitrile
    B) acetonitrile > dimethyl ether > propane
    C) propane > acetonitrile > dimethyl ether
    D) dimethyl ether > acetonitrile > propane

35. A 0.10 molar solution of a weak monoprotic acid, HA, has a pH of 4. What is the value of K_a, the ionization constant of this acid?

    A) 1.0×10^{-3}
    B) 1.0×10^{-4}
    C) 1.0×10^{-7}
    D) 1.0×10^{-8}

36. Which salt will give an aqueous solution whose pH is significantly greater than 7?

    A) NH_4NO_3
    B) $Ca(C_2H_3O_2)_2$
    C) $Ca(NO_3)_2$
    D) NaCl

37. Which compound forms a basic aqueous solution?

    A) KBr
    B) $NaNO_3$
    C) BaI_2
    D) $NaHCO_3$

38. For the hypothetical reaction, A → B, the rate equation is, rate = $k[A][B]^2$. For each of the following systems representing reaction mixtures of A and B, rank the relative rates.

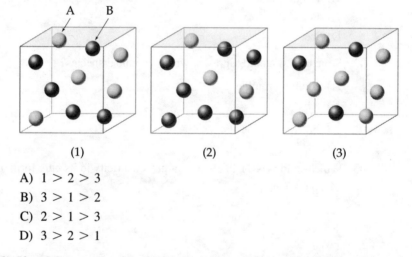

    A) 1 > 2 > 3
    B) 3 > 1 > 2
    C) 2 > 1 > 3
    D) 3 > 2 > 1

39. If a 10.0 g sample of each of four elements is heated to 100 °C and placed into 100 mL insulated containers of water at 25 °C, which element's container would show the greatest increase in temperature? The specific heat of each element in units of J/g K is listed.

Metal	Cu	Ni	Al	Pb
Specific heat	0.385	0.444	0.90	0.129

    A) Cu
    B) Ni
    C) Al
    D) Pb

40. From the given data, determine the heat of formation of carbon dioxide in kJ/mol.

$2C(s) + O_2(g) \rightarrow 2CO(g)$	$\Delta H = -220$ kJ
$2CO(g) + O_2(g) \rightarrow 2CO_2(g)$	$\Delta H = -560$ kJ

    A) $(-220) + (-560)$
    B) $[(-220) + (-560)]/2$
    C) $(-220) - (-560)$
    D) $[(-220) - (-560)]/2$

Use these atomic-molecular representations of solid materials to answer Questions 41–44.

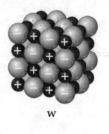

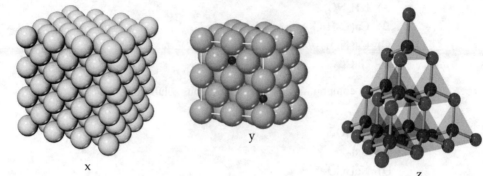

w   x   y   z

41. Structure "w" could represent which chemical species?

    A) zinc

    B) lithium fluoride

    C) brass

    D) ice

42. Structure "y" could represent which chemical species?

    A) sodium bromide

    B) silver

    C) diamond

    D) steel

43. Which solid is NOT likely to conduct electricity in its pure form or in aqueous solution?

    A) w

    B) x

    C) y

    D) z

44. Which solid(s) is(are) most likely to be high melting and brittle?

    A) x, y, and z

    B) x

    C) y

    D) z

45. According to Le Châtelier's principle, which effect will decrease the amount of CO(g) present at equilibrium in the following reaction?

    $$Heat + CO_2(g) + H_2(g) \rightleftharpoons CO(g) + H_2O(g)$$

    A) Decrease the concentration of $H_2O(g)$.

    B) Increase the concentration of $H_2(g)$.

    C) Increase the volume of the container.

    D) Decrease the concentration of $CO_2(g)$.

46. What is the partial pressure of $CO_2(g)$ at equilibrium if K_p for the reaction at a certain temperature is 0.50 atm^{-1}? $MgO(s) + CO_2(g) \rightleftharpoons MgCO_3(s) + \text{heat}$

    A) 2.0 atm

    B) 0.50 atm

    C) 0.25 atm

    D) 1.0 atm

47. K_c for the reaction $2A(g) + B(g) \rightleftharpoons 2C(g)$ is 10.0.

    The reaction will proceed to the right when:

    A) $[A] = 2.0 \text{ M}, [B] = 2.0 \text{ M}$, and $[C] = 1.0 \text{ M}$

    B) $[A] = 0.20 \text{ M}, [B] = 0.20 \text{ M}$, and $[C] = 1.0 \text{ M}$

    C) $[A] = 0.20 \text{ M}, [B] = 2.0 \text{ M}$, and $[C] = 5.0 \text{ M}$

    D) $[A] = 2.0 \text{ M}, [B] = 0.10 \text{ M}$, and $[C] = 10.0 \text{ M}$

48. Which statement describing a chemical system at equilibrium is NOT correct?

    A) The molar concentrations of reactants and products are constant.

    B) The rates of the forward and reverse reactions are equal.

    C) The concentrations of reactants and products are equal.

    D) Reactant and product concentrations change when the temperature is changed.

49. Consider the reaction at equilibrium: $2 SO_2(g) + O_2(g) \rightleftharpoons 2 SO_3(g)$ If increasing temperature decreases the amount of $SO_3(g)$, the reaction

    A) is exothermic

    B) is endothermic

    C) is catalyzed by heat

    D) has reactants whose enthalpies are lower than products

50. What is the molar solubility of lead(II) fluoride ($K_{sp} = 3.6 \times 10^{-8}$) in 0.10 M sodium fluoride?

    A) 3.6×10^{-8} M

    B) 3.6×10^{-7} M

    C) 3.6×10^{-6} M

    D) $(3.6 \times 10^{-6})^{1/2}$ M

Use the following information to answer Questions 51–53.

The atomic-molecular level pictures below represent, in no particular order, various stages of the titration of acetic acid with sodium hydroxide.

A

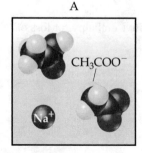

B

C

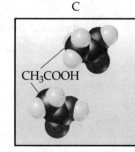

D

51. In the titration of acetic acid with sodium hydroxide, which picture is the best representation of the solution at the equivalence point?

    A) A
    B) B
    C) C
    D) D

52. If each particle shown represents 0.1 moles, which picture would best represent the solution if 0.2 moles of strong acid were added to Picture B? (Ignore the presence or absence of any spectator ions.)

    A) A
    B) B
    C) C
    D) D

53. Estimate the approximate pH of Picture D.

    A) 5
    B) 7
    C) 9
    D) 12

54. Which of these statements about atoms has been shown to be untrue using modern forms of spectroscopy?

    A) Each element is composed of extremely small particles called atoms.
    B) All atoms of a given element are identical.
    C) Atoms of one element cannot be changed into atoms of another element by chemical reactions.
    D) Compounds form when atoms of more than one element combine.

55. The table shows the mass ratios of four oxides of nitrogen.

Oxide	1	2	3	4
g N	7	7	7	7
g O	4	8	16	20

From left to right, the correct identity of the four oxides is:

    A) NO NO_2 N_2O N_2O_5
    B) NO_2 NO N_2O N_2O_5
    C) N_2O NO NO_2 N_2O_5
    D) NO NO_2 N_2O N_2O_3

56. Which element can be expected to have the least positive enthalpy for loss of an electron in the gas phase?

    A) Mg
    B) Al
    C) Si
    D) P

57. Which element can be expected to have the least negative enthalpy upon attracting an electron in the gas phase?

A) F

B) Cl

C) Br

D) I

58. The photoelectron spectra below show the binding energies of the $3p$ subshells of phosphorus, sulfur, and silicon. Which statement best accounts for their relative energies?

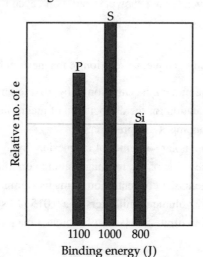

A) P has a higher binding energy than either S or Si, because P has a higher effective nuclear charge.

B) S has a lower binding energy than P because of electron–electron repulsion in a p^4 configuration.

C) The lower binding energy of Si is due to more effective screening by $3s$ electrons.

D) S has a higher binding energy than Si because it has more valence electrons.

59. Which species has the smallest bond angles?

A) CH_4

B) BrF_3

C) H_2O

D) BF_3

60. Which of the following molecules would be expected to hydrogen bond with each other AND with water?

I. CH_3CH_2CHO

II. CH_3CH_2COOH

III. $CH_3CH_2OCH_3$

IV. $CH_3CH_2CH_3OH$

A) I only

B) II and IV only

C) I and III only

D) I and II only

CHEMISTRY PRACTICE TEST 2

Section II

105 minutes

You may use a calculator for this section.

Directions: Answer each of the following questions, clearly showing the methods you use and the steps involved at arriving at the answers. Partial credit will be given for work shown and little or no credit will be given for not showing your work, even if the answers are correct.

Question 1

The pH of a saturated aqueous solution of magnesium hydroxide is 10.17.

a. Calculate the molar concentration of hydroxide ion in the solution.
b. Write the equation for the dissociation of magnesium hydroxide in water and the corresponding K_{sp} expression.
c. Calculate the molar solubility of magnesium hydroxide in water.
d. Calculate the value of K_{sp} for magnesium hydroxide.
e. Calculate the molar concentration of magnesium ion at pH $= 11.50$.
f. Calculate the volume in milliliters of a 0.0150 M solution of hydrochloric acid needed to titrate 500.0 mL of saturated magnesium hydroxide solution.

Question 2

The standard reduction potentials of some selected half-reactions are given below.

$$Cu^{2+}(aq) + 2e^- \rightarrow Cu(s) \qquad\qquad E° = +0.337 \text{ V}$$
$$2H^+(aq) + 2e^- \rightarrow H_2(g) \qquad\qquad E° = +0.000 \text{ V}$$
$$Cl_2(g) + 2e^- \rightarrow 2Cl^-(aq) \qquad\qquad E° = +0.1359 \text{ V}$$
$$NO_3^-(aq) + 4H^+(aq) + 3e^- \rightarrow NO(g) + 2H_2O(l) \qquad E° = +0.96 \text{ V}$$
$$Ni^{2+}(aq) + 2e^- \rightarrow Ni(s) \qquad\qquad E° = -0.28 \text{ V}$$

a. A piece of nickel and a piece of copper are placed into a hydrochloric acid solution.

   i. Predict whether nickel, copper, or both metals will react with hydrochloric acid.

   ii. Explain your answer(s) by writing the appropriate half-reactions and the overall net ionic equation(s) for the reaction(s) of the metal(s) with hydrochloric acid.

   iii. Calculate the cell voltage(s) for the overall reaction(s).

b. A piece of copper metal is placed into a solution of nitric acid.

   i. Write the net ionic equation.

   ii. Calculate the cell voltage.

   iii. Calculate the standard free energy change, $\Delta G°$, for the process.

   iv. Calculate the equilibrium constant for the process at 25 °C.

c. One product of the reaction of copper with nitric acid, nitrogen monoxide, reacts with oxygen in the air to produce nitrogen dioxide. The enthalpy of combustion of nitrogen monoxide is -56.53 kJ/mol. The standard enthalpy of formation, $\Delta H°_f$, for nitrogen dioxide is 33.84 kJ/mol. The standard free energy of formation, $\Delta G°_f$, for nitrogen dioxide is 51.84 kJ/mol.

   i. Write and balance an equation for the reaction of nitrogen monoxide with oxygen.

   ii. Calculate the standard heat of formation for nitrogen monoxide.

   iii. Calculate the standard entropy of formation for nitrogen dioxide at 25 °C. Be sure to specify the units.

d. In a separate experiment involving an electrolysis cell, how many grams of nickel metal can be plated onto an inert electrode in 30.0 min at 3.50 A?

Question 3

Using a pH meter, the titration of 50.0 mL of an unknown acid solution with 0.115 M NaOH was carried out in the laboratory. The following titration curve was constructed from the data obtained from the experiment.

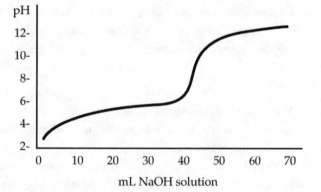

a. Does the graph represent the titration of a weak or strong acid? Explain.

b. Estimate the approximate pH at the equivalence point.

c. Estimate the approximate concentration of the acid. Show your calculations.

d. Estimate the approximate K_a of the acid. Mathematically justify your answer.

e. Clearly indicate the areas on the graph where the solution behaves as a buffer.

f. Which of the following indicators would be best suited to accurately determine the end point of the titration? What color change would signal the endpoint? Explain your reasoning.

Bromcresol green, $pK_a = 4.5$ (yellow to blue)

Thymol blue, $pK_{a_1} = 2$ (red to yellow), $pK_{a_2} = 8.5$ (yellow to blue)

Alizarin, $pK_a = 6.5$ (yellow to red)

Phenol red, $pK_a = 7.5$ (yellow to red)

Question 4

The formulas of four compounds are listed in the table along with the boiling points of two of the compounds.

Compound	Formula	Boiling Point
1	$CH_3CH_2CH_2CH_3$	
2	$CH_3CH_2CH_2OH$	97 °C
3	$CH_3CH_2OCH_3$	
4	$(CH_3)_2C=O$	57 °C

a. Which compounds are isomers? Justify your answer.

b. Consider Compound 4.

   i. Draw the Lewis structure and a space-filling model of Compound 4.

   ii. Predict the geometry around each carbon atom.

   iii. Identify the hybridization of each carbon atom in Compound 4.

   iv. Is Compound 4 polar or nonpolar? Explain.

   v. What kinds of intermolecular forces exist between molecules of Compound 4?

c. Explain why Compound 2 boils at a higher temperature than Compound 4.

d. Arrange the four compounds in order of increasing boiling point (lowest to highest). Justify your answer.

Question 5

a. Which element, potassium or chlorine, is more likely to have the higher first ionization energy? Explain using electron configurations, Coulomb's law, and effective nuclear charge.

b. Explain the following statements: The ionic radius of potassium is smaller than its atomic radius. The ionic radius of chlorine is larger than its atomic radius.

Question 6

Consider the following equilibrium systems:

a. $(NH_4)_2CO_3(s) \rightleftharpoons 2NH_3(g) + H_2O(g) + CO_2(g)$ $K_p = 0.250$ at 350 °C.

   i. Is the value of K_c at 350 °C greater than, less than, or equal to the value of K_p for this reaction? Explain your answer.

   ii. Predict the sign of ΔS for the reaction. Justify your answer with evidence.

   iii. Calculate the value of K_p for:
$$2NH_3(g) + H_2O(g) + CO_2(g) \leftrightharpoons (NH_4)_2CO_3(s)$$

   iv. Calculate the value of K_p for:
$$4NH_3(g) + 2H_2O(g) + 2CO_2(g) \leftrightharpoons 2(NH_4)_2CO_3(s)$$

b. $Cu^{2+}(aq) + CO_3^{2-}(aq) \rightleftharpoons CuCO_3(s)$ $K_c = 4.3 \times 10^{+9}$

State the effect on the solubility of solid copper(II) carbonate (increase, decrease, or stay the same) when the following changes are made. In each case, explain your reasoning using a balanced chemical equation when appropriate.

   i. Water is added to the container.

   ii. Gaseous hydrogen chloride is allowed to dissolve in the solution.

   iii. Solid sodium carbonate is added to the solution.

Question 7

In the laboratory, you are to determine the identity of a pure unknown white solid.

a. A 19.2 g sample of the volatile compound decomposes upon heating to yield 6.80 g of ammonia, 8.80 g of carbon dioxide, and the only other product is water. Calculate the empirical formula of the compound in the form: $C_wH_xN_yO_z$.

b. When a sample of the compound is dissolved in water and made basic with sodium hydroxide, wetted pH paper held above the solution indicates a pH of about 9 and the solution gives off a distinct smell of ammonia.
Write and balance a net ionic equation for the reaction of sodium hydroxide with the compound that explains this result.

c. When another sample is dissolved in water and made acidic with hydrochloric acid, the solution effervesces. Write and balance a net ionic equation that could explain this result.

d. Based on your answers to Parts b and c, rearrange the simplest formula you determined in Part a to identify the compound. Name the compound.

e. Use principles of intermolecular forces and polarity to explain why effervescence was observed in Part c but not in Part b.

Multiple Choice Answers and Explanations for Practice Test 2

1. C. Because of increased dispersion forces, the boiling points of a series of similar molecules will increase regularly with increasing molar mass. Molecule C is lighter than molecule D, yet it has a higher boiling point. This can be explained by especially strong dipole–dipole forces called hydrogen bonding in molecule C.

2. A. A thermodynamically favored reaction is one where ΔG is negative. Consider the equation, $\Delta G = \Delta H - T\Delta S$. ΔG is always negative when ΔH is negative and ΔS is positive no matter the temperature.

3. C. $x\,J/g\,K = (100\,J)/(100.0\,g)(10.0\,°C) = 0.100\,J/g\,°C = 0.100\,J/g\,K$

4. A. The choices are all isoelectronic: each has 18 electrons. In an isoelectronic series, the cation with the largest charge will be the smallest due to poor screening of the noble gas core. The anion with the largest negative charge will be the largest anion due to electron–electron repulsion.

5. B. The balanced equation is $3H_2(g) + N_2(g) \rightarrow 2NH_3(g)$. The limiting reactant is hydrogen. At constant temperature and pressure, the number of moles is directly proportional to the number of liters.
$x\,L\,NH_3 = 5.0\,L\,H_2(2\,L\,NH_3/3\,L\,H_2) = 10/3\,L = 3.3\,L$.

6. A. The higher the mass, the slower the average speed of the particles.

7. B. As temperature rises, the average speed of molecules increase and the distributions of molecular speed increase and the peaks will shift to the right.

8. A. Because the particles are in the same container, the most massive ones have the highest density.

9. C. Because each gas has the same number of moles at the same temperature, their partial pressures are equal. The area under each curve is proportional to the number of particles of each gas. If the number of particles are equal, the areas are also equal.

10. A. To deviate from ideality, the temperature must decrease making the distribution profiles move to the left as the gas particles slow down.

11. C. Carbonates react with acids to form carbon dioxide:
$$CO_3^{2-}(aq) + H^+(aq) \rightarrow CO_2(g) + H_2O(l)$$

12. B. Both copper(II) sulfate and sulfuric acid cause carbonates to bubble so they both show acidic properties.

13. A. Sulfuric acid is a strong acid, copper(II) sulfate is a weak acid, and potassium carbonate is a stronger base than sodium hydrogen carbonate.

14. B. The fact that copper(II) sulfate causes carbonates to effervesce and calcium sulfate does not indicates that copper(II) sulfate has acidic properties. The acidic property of copper(II) ion derives from the fact that a small charged cation can effectively attract a nonbonding electron pair of a water molecule. This polarizes the water molecule causing a H—O bond to polarize making the hydrogen ion more loosely held than in pure water. The effect is that small, highly charged cations in water solution make water molecules more acidic. The calcium ion is larger and has a smaller charge so its effect on the acidity of water is negligible.

15. C. Copper(II) sulfate is weakly acidic and does not provide enough protons to completely protonate the carbonate ion so the major product is hydrogen carbonate ion:
$$H^+(aq) + CO_3^{2-}(aq) \rightarrow HCO_3^-(aq)$$

16. A. The wet gas is contaminated with water vapor. The partial pressure of the oxygen is equal to the total barometric pressure minus the vapor pressure of water ($725 - 30 = 695$ torr). Once the pressure is converted to atmospheres, the number of moles of oxygen can be calculated from the ideal gas equation: $n = PV/RT = (695)(0.155)/(0.082)(302)(760)$

17. E. All single bonds are sigma bonds and all multiple bonds contain one sigma bond and one or two pi bonds. The molecule has eight C—H sigma bonds and six C—C sigma bonds. It also has four C—C multiple pi bonds.

18. D. One year is three half-lives. The sample will fall to half its value three times.
$$32\ g \times \frac{1}{2} \times \frac{1}{2} \times \frac{1}{2} = 4\ g.$$

19. D. Rate $= k[X]^2[Y]$. Substituting, rate $= k(2)^2(1/2) = 2$.

20. B. In such cases, zinc is called a "sacrificial anode." Zinc protects the iron from oxidation because zinc oxidizes more readily than iron.

21. A. An easily oxidized substance has a large positive oxidation potential or a large negative reduction potential. On a table of standard reduction potentials, find the product of the reduction with the most negative voltage.

22. B. Reduction of gold(III) ions is more favorable than the reduction of nickel ions because the voltage of the gold half-reaction is more positive. Therefore the nickel reaction will be the oxidation and the sign its voltage will change from – to +. The voltages are not multiplied by the coefficients that balance the equation.

$$Au^{3+}(aq) + 3e^- \rightarrow Au(s) \quad E^\circ_{red} = 1.50 \text{ V}$$

$$Ni(s) \rightarrow Ni^{2+}(aq) + 2e^- \quad E^\circ_{ox} = +0.25 \text{ V}$$

$$E^\circ_{cell} = E^\circ_{ox} + E^\circ_{red} = 1.50 + 0.25 = 1.75 \text{ V}$$

23. A. The diagram shows that four CO_2 and five H_2O molecules collectively contain four carbon atoms and sixteen hydrogen atoms. The formula for the hydrocarbon will be in this ratio: C_4H_{16}. However, having only four valence electrons, each carbon can form only four bonds and each hydrogen forms only one bond. Of the choices only CH_4 meets all the criteria.
$$4CH_4 + 8O_2 \rightarrow 4CO_2 + 8H_2O$$

24. B. The balanced equation is: $3H_2(g) + N_2(g) \rightarrow 2NH_3(g)$. The diagram shows nine H_2 molecules requiring three N_2 molecules for a complete reaction. It also shows four N_2 molecules that require twelve molecules of N_2 to react. Therefore, H_2 is the limiting reactant so theoretically nine H_2 molecules will produce six NH_3 molecules. At 50% yield, there would be three NH_3 molecules formed.

25. C. The possible diatomic molecules of Cl_2 that form from two isotopes of chlorine are $^{35}Cl-^{35}Cl$, $^{35}Cl-^{37}Cl$, and $^{37}Cl-^{37}Cl$. Because the mass spectrometer will break the $Cl-Cl$ bonds, peaks for both ^{35}Cl and ^{37}Cl will be present for a total of five peaks.

26. B. The percent ionization of all weak acids and weak bases decreases with increasing concentration. Strong acids ionize 100% at most concentrations.

27. A. Acetic acid is a weak acid where $K_a = [H^+][A^-]/[HA]$. As [HA] increases, the equilibrium shifts right increasing both $[H^+]$ and $[A^-]$. But the ions increase to a lesser extent than HA to keep K_a constant at constant temperature. So the percentage ionization decreases with increasing HA concentration.

28. B. At 0.15 M, the graph indicates that about 1% of the acid is ionized making the value of $[H^+] = 0.15/100 = 0.0015 \sim 0.001$. The pH is a little lower than 3. Because both the concentration and percent ionization are given, the K_a of acetic acid is not required. However, it can be estimated: $K_a = (0.0015)(0.0015)/0.15 = 0.000015$.

29. D. Entropy increases with increasing molecular complexity. Pentane having five carbon atoms and twelve hydrogen atoms is more complex than the others.

30. D. Viscosity of hydrocarbon chains increases with increasing length of chain because the longer the molecule, the more polarizable electrons it has and the greater the surface contact with other molecules. Increase in surface contact means higher dispersion forces.

31. C. Because it has fewer electrons, methane will have weaker induced dipoles (weaker dispersion forces) holding it together in a liquid. It will boil at a lower temperature.

32. C. Partial pressure is directly proportional to the number of moles in a mixture of gases. One gram of methane is 1/16 mole. The other gases will have smaller numbers of moles because of their larger molar masses.

33. D. One gram of pentane contains 60/72 of a gram of carbon. Methane has only 12/16 of a gram of carbon, ethane 24/30 g, and propane 36/44 g. Therefore one gram of pentane contains more moles of carbon than does methane. The number of moles of oxygen that will react is directly proportional to the number of moles of carbon present and therefore the number of grams of oxygen that will react is greatest for pentane.

34. B. For molecules of approximately equal molar mass and size, the strengths of intermolecular forces increase with increasing polarity. More polar molecules have higher boiling points. Although O is more electronegative than N, the fact that the acetonitrile molecule has an N on one end makes it more polar than dimethyl ether, which has an O in the middle of the molecule.

35. C. $K_a = x^2/I$ where $x = [H^+] = 10^{-pH} = 10^{-4.00}$ and $I = 0.10$.

$K_a = (10^{-4.00})^2/0.10 = 1.0 \times 10^{-7}$.

36. B. $Ca(C_2H_3O_2)_2$ contains the neutral calcium cation and the weak base acetate anion.

37. D. Although, without further information sodium hydrogen carbonate could be an acid, all the other choices are neutral because they are composed entirely of neutral ions, ions of strong acids and strong bases.

38. C. For 2, rate $= 3 \times 7^2 = 147$. For 1, rate $= 5 \times 5^2 = 125$. For 3, rate $= 7 \times 3^2 = 63$.

39. C. Its large specific heat means that, at the same temperature, aluminum can store more heat than the other metals. When the metals are placed into their containers of water, heat is transferred from the metals to the water making the temperature rise.

40. B. The heat of formation is the energy absorbed when one mole of a substance is formed from its elements. The heat of formation is the heat of a formation reaction. The formation reaction for CO_2 is:

$$C(s) + O_2(g) \rightarrow CO_2(g)$$

Applying Hess's law:

$2C(s) + O_2(g) \rightarrow 2CO(g) \quad \Delta H = -220\,kJ$

$+ \ 2CO(g) + O_2(g) \rightarrow 2CO_2(g) \quad \Delta H = -560\,kJ$

equals:

$$2C(s) + 2O_2(g) \rightarrow 2CO_2(g) \quad \Delta H = (-220) + (-560) \text{ kJ}$$

Dividing by two:

$$C(s) + O_2(g) \rightarrow CO_2(g) \quad \Delta H = [(-220) + (-560)]/2 \text{ kJ}$$

41. B. Structures w, x, y, and z represent the structures of an ionic solid, a metal, an alloy, and a covalent-network solid, respectively. Lithium fluoride is an ionic compound, zinc is a metal, brass is an alloy, and ice is a covalent solid.

42. D. Steel is in interstitial alloy with smaller carbon atoms occupying some of the spaces between larger iron atoms and forming covalent bonds with iron.

43. D. A covalent-network solid, such as diamond, typically does not conduct electricity.

44. A. Ionic solids are brittle and have relatively high melting points.

45. D. Removing $CO_2(g)$ will cause the forward reaction to slow making the reverse reaction faster than the forward reaction thus decreasing the amount of $CO(g)$. Because the number of moles of gas on both sides of the equation are equal, changing volume will not affect the equilibrium position. All the other changes listed will cause an increase in the amount of $CO(g)$.

46. A. $K_p = 1/P_{CO2} = 1/0.50 = 2.0$

47. A. For answer A:

$Q = [C]^2/[A]^2[B] = (1.0)^2/(2.0)^2(2.0) = 0.13 < 10, K_c > Q$, reaction goes right.

For answer B:

$Q = [C]^2/[A]^2[B] = (1.0)^2/(0.20)^2(0.20) = 125 > 10, K_c < Q.$

For answer C:

$Q = [C]^2/[A]^2[B] = (5.0)^2/(2.0)^2(0.20) = 31 > 10, K_c < Q.$

For answer D:

$Q = [C]^2/[A]^2[B] = (10)^2/(0.20)^2(0.10) = 25,000 > 10, K_c < Q.$

48. C. A common misconception is that the concentrations of reactants and products are equal at equilibrium. The fundamental equilibrium condition is that the forward and reverse reactions occur at the same rate. At equilibrium there are no observable macroscopic changes, including color, pressure, concentration, and temperature.

49. A. Increasing temperature always favors the endothermic reaction, which in this case must be the reverse reaction because the amount of SO_3 gas decreases. Therefore, the forward reaction is exothermic. (Notice that A and B are opposites and that B and D have the same meaning. This means that B and D are wrong because there is only one correct answer.)

50. C. $PbF_2(s) = Pb^{2+}(aq) + 2F^-(aq)$

$K_{sp} = 3.6 \times 10^{-8} = [Pb^{2+}][F^-]^2$

Let $x = $ molar solubility of $PbCl_2$

At equilibrium, $[Pb^{2+}] = x, [F^-] = 2x + 0.10 \approx 0.10 \text{ M}$

$3.6 \times 10^{-8} = x(0.10)^2$

$x = 3.6 \times 10^{-8}/0.01 = 3.6 \times 10^{-6} \text{ M}$

51. D. The equivalence point is when all the acid has been converted to its conjugate base.

52. A. A 0.2 mole sample of a strong acid would neutralize 0.1 mole of hydroxide ion and convert 0.1 mole of a weak base into its conjugate and leave the other 0.1 mole unreacted.

53. C. Picture D shows only weak base molecules and spectator ions. The solution of a weak base will normally have a pH greater than 7 but less than 12.

54. B. Isotopes are atoms of the same element that differ in the number of neutrons in their nuclei. Mass spectrometry separates isotopes of elements and measures their masses.

55. C. The mass of each element in one mole of oxide is:
    N_2O, 28:16;   NO, 14:16; NO_2, 14:32; N_2O_5, 28:80

56. B. In other words, the question asks which element has the smallest first ionization energy. Although the trend is first ionization energy increases left to right along a period because coulombic attractions increase with increasing effective nuclear charge. However, aluminum has a lower first ionization energy than magnesium because its 3s electrons partially screen the nucleus reducing its effective nuclear charge. This same dip in ionization energy is also seen between Be and B and between Zn and Ga.

57. D. In other words, the question asks which element has the lowest electron affinity. Generally, from bottom to top along any period, electron affinity increases with decreasing atomic size because of increased coulombic attractions. Note: Fluorine is contrary to the trend because it has a lower electron affinity (not as exothermic) than chlorine. This is because F is so small that electron–electron repulsion becomes important when that small atom attracts an electron.

58. B. Generally, binding energies increase with increasing effective nuclear charge. However, even though sulfur has higher effective nuclear charge than the other two elements, the electron–electron repulsion in sulfur's p^4 configuration make removing most loosely held 3p electron easier than a phosphorus $3p^3$ electron.

59. B. The t-shape molecular geometry of BrF_3 has roughly 90° bond angles.

60. B. The structural criteria for hydrogen bonding among like molecules is that a molecule have a hydrogen atom bonded directly to either a fluorine, nitrogen, or oxygen atom. Only compounds II and IV have a hydrogen bonded to oxygen. All the molecules will hydrogen bond to water because all have oxygen atoms with one pair of electrons available.

Free Response Answers for Practice Test 2

Answers to Question 1

a. $pOH = 14 - pH$, $14 - 10.17 = 3.83$
    $[OH^-] = 10^{-pOH} = 10^{-3.83} = 1.5 \times 10^{-4}$ M
b. $Mg(OH)_2(s) \rightleftharpoons Mg^{2+}(aq) + 2OH^-(aq)$
    $K_{sp} = [Mg^{2+}][OH^-]^2$

c. $Mg(OH)_2(s) \rightleftharpoons Mg^{2+}(aq) + 2OH^-(aq)$

I	0	0
C	+x	+2x
E	x	2x

$x = [Mg^{2+}]$ and $2x = [OH^-]$

$x = $ molar solubility $= 1/2\,[OH^-] = 1/2\,(1.5 \times 10^{-4}\,M) = 7.5 \times 10^{-5}\,M$

d. $K_{sp} = [Mg^{2+}][OH^-]^2 = (x)(2x)^2 = 4x^3$

$K_{sp} = 4(7.5 \times 10^{-5})^3 = 1.7 \times 10^{-12}$

e. $pOH = 14 - pH, \quad 14 - 11.50 = 2.50$

$[OH^-] = 10^{-pOH}, \quad 10^{-2.50} = 3.2 \times 10^{-3}\,M$

$K_{sp} = [Mg^{2+}][OH^-]^2$

$1.7 \times 10^{-12} = [Mg^{2+}](3.2 \times 10^{-3})^2$

$[Mg^{2+}] = 1.7 \times 10^{-7}\,M$

f. From Part a, $[OH^-] = 1.5 \times 10^{-4}\,M$ so $Mg(OH)_2$ is $7.5 \times 10^{-5}\,M$

x mL HCl $= 0.5000\,L\;Mg(OH)_2(7.5 \times 10^{-5}\,mol/L)\,(2\,mol\,HCl/1\,mol$

$Mg(OH)_2)(1\,L/0.0150\,mol)(1000\,mL/L) = 5.0\,mL$

Answers to Question 2

a. i. Only nickel will react with hydrochloric acid.

   ii. Only the reaction of nickel metal with aqueous hydrogen ion gives a positive voltage, indicating a spontaneous reaction:

   $2H^+(aq) + 2\,e^- \rightarrow H_2(g) \quad E° = +0.000\,V$

   $Ni(s) \rightarrow Ni^{2+}(aq) + 2\,e^- \quad E° = +0.28\,V$

   _____

   $2H^+(aq) + Ni(s) \rightarrow H_2(g) + Ni^{2+}(aq)$

   iii. $E°_{cell} = E°_{red} + E°_{ox} = 0.000\,V + 0.28\,V = 0.28\,V$

b. i. $3[Cu(s) + 2e^- \rightarrow Cu^{2+}(aq)] \quad E° = -0.337\,V$

   $2[NO_3^-(aq) + 4H^+(aq) + 3e^- \rightarrow NO(g) + 2H_2O(l)] \quad E° = +0.96\,V$

   $3Cu(s) + 2NO_3^-(aq) + 8H^+(aq) \rightarrow 3Cu^{2+}(aq) + 2NO(g) + 4H_2O(l)$

   ii. $E°_{cell} = E°_{red} + E°_{ox} = 0.96\,V - 0.337\,V = 0.62\,V$

   iii. $\Delta G° = -nFE° = -(6\,mol\,e^-)(96{,}500\,C/mol\,e^-)\,(0.62\,J/C)\,(1\,kJ/1000\,J)$

   $= -360\,kJ/mol$

   iv. $\Delta G° = -RT \ln K$

   $-360{,}000\,J = -(8.314\,J/mol\text{-}K)(298) \ln K$

   $\ln K = 145$

   $K = e^{145} = 9.4 \times 10^{62}$

c. i. $2NO(g) + O_2(g) \rightarrow 2NO_2(g)$

   ii. $\Delta H°_{rxn} = \Sigma\,\Delta H°_{f\,products} - \Sigma\,\Delta H°_{f\,reactants}$

   $2(-56.53\,kJ/mol) = 2(33.84\,kJ/mol) - 2\,\Delta H°_{f\,NO}$

   $\Delta H°_{f\,NO} = +90.37\,kJ/mol$

   iii. $\Delta G° = \Delta H° - T\Delta S°$

   $+51.84\,kJ/mol = 33.84\,kJ/mol - 298\,K(\Delta S°)$

   $\Delta S° = -0.0604\,kJ/mol\text{-}K = -60.4\,J/mol\text{-}K$

d. x g Ni $= 30.0$ min $(60$ s/min$)(3.50$ C/s$)(1$ mol e$^-/96{,}500$ C$)$

$(1$ mol Ni/2 mol e$^-)(58.7$ g Ni/mol$) = 1.92$ g Ni

Answers to Question 3

a. The graph represents the titration of a weak acid with a strong base. The pH begins at a relatively high value compared to a strong acid and the inflection is much less pronounced than that of a strong acid.

b. The pH of the equivalence point is approximately the midpoint of the inflection or about pH $= 9$.

c. mol acid $=$ mol base

$(\text{mol/L acid})(\text{L acid}) = (\text{mol/L base})(\text{L base})$

$(M_a)(50.0 \text{ mL}) = (0.115 \text{ M})(40.0 \text{ mL})$

or

$M_a = M_b V_b / V_a = (0.115 \text{ M})(40.0 \text{ mL})/(50.0 \text{ mL}) = 0.0920 \text{ M}.$

d. The pK_a is the pH at which half the moles of acid are neutralized. It is the pH corresponding to the point when 20 mL of NaOH are added. From the graph, p$K_a = 5$. $K_a = 10^{-5}$.

$HA(aq) + H_2O(l) \rightleftharpoons A^-(aq) + H_3O^+(aq)$

$K_a = [A^-][H_3O^+]/[HA]$

$[A^-] = [HA]$ when the volume of the NaOH is 20 mL.

Then,

$K_a = [H_3O^+]$ and p$K_a = $ pH

e. The solution behaves as a buffer between about pH $= 4$ to 6.

f. The most suitable indicator is the second color change, yellow to blue, of thymol blue. To determine the equivalence point accurately, the color change of the indicator at the endpoint must happen at or near the pH of the equivalence point.

Answers to Question 4

a. Compounds 2 and 3 are isomers because they have the same molecular formula but different structural formulas.

b. i.

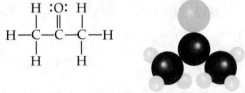

ii. The center carbon has a trigonal planar geometry. The geometry of each of the other carbons is tetrahedral.

iii. The center carbon is sp^2 hybridized and the other carbons are both sp^3 hybridized.

iv. Compound 4 is polar, owing to the very polar C$=$O bond, resulting in an asymmetrical distribution of charge around the central carbon atom.

v. Dipole–dipole forces and dispersion forces exist among molecules of Compound 4.

c. Compound 2 boils at a higher temperature than does Compound 4, because strong hydrogen bonding in Compound 2 holds the molecules together in a liquid with greater force than do the dipole–dipole interactions of Compound 4.

d. Order of boiling points: $1 < 3 < 4 < 2$. Generally, for molecules of similar molar mass, the stronger the intermolecular forces of attraction, the higher the boiling point. Butane has only weak dispersion forces holding its molecules together as a liquid. Ethyl methyl ether is slightly polar because of the polarity and orientation of the C—O bonds. Propanone is very polar because of the polarity of the C—O bond and its trigonal arrangement. Molecules of propanol are held together by strong hydrogen bonds.

Answers to Question 5

a. Electron configurations: $_{19}$K: $1s^2 2s^2 2p^6 3s^2 3p^6 4s^1$ $_{17}$Cl: $1s^2 2s^2 2p^6 3s^2 3p^5$. Chlorine has a higher first ionization energy than potassium because chlorine has a higher effective nuclear charge because of its poorly shielded valence electrons. Potassium's $4s$ electron is screened by 18 inner core electrons, whereas chlorine's 7 valence electrons are screened by only 10 inner core electrons. Coulomb's law states that the force of attraction between two charged particles is directly proportional to the magnitude of the charges. Chlorine's valence electrons effectively experience a larger charge than do those of potassium.

b. Cations are smaller than the atoms from which they are derived because the inner core electrons are poorly shielded from the nucleus and thus held closely and tightly.

Potassium's one valence electron is well screened from the nucleus by eighteen inner core electrons, making potassium a relatively large atom. Potassium ion has eight valence electrons that are poorly screened and held tight and close to the nucleus, making K^+ a relatively small cation.

Chlorine is a small atom because its seven valence electrons are poorly screened by only ten inner core electrons. Upon gaining an electron, the resulting chloride anion has an excess of electrons and experiences electron–electron repulsion in its valence shell. Anions are larger than their atoms because of electron–electron repulsion.

Answers to Question 6

Consider the following equilibrium systems:

a. $(NH_4)_2CO_3(s) \rightleftharpoons 2NH_3(g) + H_2O(g) + CO_2(g)$ $K_p = 0.250$ at 350 °C.

i. K_c is less than K_p for the reaction: $K_c = K_p(RT)^{-\Delta n}$, where Δn is the change in the number of moles of gas as the reaction proceeds left to right. In this case, $\Delta n = +4$.

ii. The sign of ΔS is positive as the reaction converts a solid of relatively low entropy to four moles of gas, which are much more random and disordered.

iii. $K_p = 1/0.250 = 4.00$. Whenever a reaction is reversed, its equilibrium constant becomes the reciprocal of the original equilibrium constant.

iv. $K_p = (4.00)^2 = 16.0$. Whenever a reaction is balanced with doubled coefficients, its equilibrium constant becomes the square of the equilibrium constant of the original reaction.

b. $Cu^{2+}(aq) + CO_3^{2-}(aq) \rightleftharpoons CuCO_3(s)$ $K_c = 4.3 \times 10^{+9}$.

i. The solubility will not change although more copper(II) carbonate will dissolve in the added water.

ii. The solubility of copper(II) carbonate will increase because the hydrochloric acid formed will react with the carbonate ions in solution, decreasing the carbonate ion concentration and shifting the equilibrium to the left.

$$2H^+(aq) + CO_3^{2-}(aq) \rightarrow H_2O(l) + CO_2(g)$$

iii. The solubility will decrease because the common ion, carbonate, will increase in concentration, shifting the equilibrium to the right.

Answers to Question 7

a. mol H_2O = (19.2 g − 8.80 g − 6.8 g)/(18.0 g/mol) = 0.20 mol H_2O

x mol C = mol CO_2 = (8.8 g CO_2)(1 mol/44.0 g) = 0.20 mol C

x mol N = mol NH_3 = (6.80 g)/(1 mol/17.0 g) = 0.40 mol N

x mol O = 2 × mol CO_2 + mol H_2O = (2 × 0.20) + 0.20 = 0.60 mol O

x mol H = (3 × mol NH_3) + (2 × mol H_2O) = (3 × 0.40) + (2 × 0.20) = 1.6 mol H

$C_{0.20}H_{1.6}N_{0.40}O_{0.60}$ = $C_{(0.20/0.20)}H_{(1.6/0.20)}N_{(0.40/0.20)}O_{(0.60/0.20)}$ = $CH_8N_2O_3$

b. $NH_4^+(aq) + OH^-(aq) \rightarrow NH_3(g) + H_2O(l)$.

c. $2H^+(aq) + CO_3^{2-}(aq) \rightarrow CO_2(g) + H_2O(l)$.

d. $(NH_4)_2CO_3$ ammonium carbonate.

e. Part c produced carbon dioxide, a nonpolar gas that is not very soluble in polar water. Polar water molecules can hydrogen bond with each other effectively and exclude the molecules of carbon dioxide, which nucleate and form distinct bubbles.

Part b produced ammonia, a very polar molecule that can hydrogen bond very effectively as it dissolves in water. Ammonia is a gas, however, and escapes the solution without forming bubbles.